Praise for *Creating Prehistory*

'Written in a sparkling, compelling and very accessible style, with a superb sense of pace, drama, fun and irony, *Creating Prehistory* is a wonderfully courageous and fluent questioning of the nature of archaeology, based on a tremendous amount of original research.'
Ronald Hutton, Bristol University

'In *Creating Prehistory* Adam Stout offers a compelling account of the visions, philosophies, rivalries and eccentricities shaping the British archaeological landscape.'
David Matless, University of Nottingham

'Adam Stout's book is a thrilling and innovative contribution to the history of archaeology. Stout makes the unprecedented move of placing the prehistoric archaeology of the inter-war years alongside druids, ley-hunters and hyper-diffusionists, investigating the social, political and historical conditions that affected each. The results are both surprising and enlightening.'
Julian Thomas, University of Manchester

'*Creating Prehistory* is an engagingly provocative contribution to current debates on how the past is produced, in writing and illustration and on the ground in excavation and preservation. It recovers the knowledge and imagination of lay, often local, enthusiasts in pre-war Britain from the condescension of a new archaeological establishment keen to enclose and police the boundaries of prehistoric expertise. Thoroughly researched, from many previously untapped sources, and accessibly and entertainingly written, *Creating Prehistory* will appeal to a wide readership, interested in sites of antiquity and how those places have been viewed and debated in the recent past.'
Stephen Daniels, University of Nottingham

'Prehistory is a contentious affair, and Adam Stout's story of just how competitive narratives can get is illuminating in its exposure of archaeology's dirty war against visionaries.'
John Billingsley, Editor, *Northern Earth*

'Adam Stout's new book gives the inside story of British archaeology in the first half of the twentieth century. He brings to light the various groups and individuals, especially the revived Order of Druids, who opposed the low-level, reductionist view of Stonehenge and prehistoric culture that the authorities were insisting upon. This is a new and well-told story about a controversy that is still going on.'
John Michell, author of *The View Over Atlantis*

For M
(By God, she's earned it)

CREATING PREHISTORY

Druids, Ley Hunters and Archaeologists
in Pre-war Britain

ADAM STOUT

© 2008 by Adam Stout

BLACKWELL PUBLISHING
350 Main Street, Malden, MA 02148-5020, USA
9600 Garsington Road, Oxford OX4 2DQ, UK

The right of Adam Stout to be identified as the author of this work has been asserted in accordance with the UK Copyright, Designs, and Patents Act 1988.

All rights reserved. No part of this publication may be reproduced, stored in a retrieval system, or transmitted, in any form or by any means, electronic, mechanical, photocopying, recording or otherwise, except as permitted by the UK Copyright, Designs, and Patents Act 1988, without the prior permission of the publisher.

Designations used by companies to distinguish their products are often claimed as trademarks. All brand names and product names used in this book are trade names, service marks, trademarks, or registered trademarks of their respective owners. The publisher is not associated with any product or vendor mentioned in this book.

This publication is designed to provide accurate and authoritative information in regard to the subject matter covered. It is sold on the understanding that the publisher is not engaged in rendering professional services. If professional advice or other expert assistance is required, the services of a competent professional should be sought.

First published 2008 by Blackwell Publishing Ltd

1   2008

Library of Congress Cataloging-in-Publication Data

Stout, Adam.
 Creating prehistory : Druids, ley hunters and archaeologists in pre-war Britain / Adam Stout.
   p. cm.
 Includes bibliographical references and index.
 ISBN 978-1-4051-5504-5 (hardcover : alk. paper)—ISBN 978-1-4051-5505-2 (pbk. : alk. paper) 1. Anthropology—Great Britain—History—20th century. 2. Archaeology—Great Britain—History—20th century. 3. Prehistoric peoples—Great Britain. 4. Antiquities, Prehistoric—Great Britain. 5. Great Britain—Antiquities. I. Title.

GN17.3.G7S86 2008
936.1—dc22
                                                   2007041746

A catalogue record for this title is available from the British Library.

Set in 10 on 12.5 pt Galliard
by SNP Best-set Typesetter Ltd., Hong Kong
Printed and bound in Singapore
by Markono Print Media Pte Ltd

The publisher's policy is to use permanent paper from mills that operate a sustainable forestry policy, and which has been manufactured from pulp processed using acid-free and elementary chlorine-free practices. Furthermore, the publisher ensures that the text paper and cover board used have met acceptable environmental accreditation standards.

For further information on
Blackwell Publishing, visit our website at
www.blackwellpublishing.com

Contents

List of Illustrations vii
Acknowledgements ix

Introduction: Power and the Past 1

Part I Disciplining the Past 7

1 Manufacturing the Past: The Victorian
  Background 9
2 Establishing the Discipline 17
3 Containing the Amateurs 36

Part II Contesting Utopia 49

4 Making Progress 51
5 The Politics of Socialism 62
6 The Diffusion Heresy: Nurture and the Primitive 74
7 Establishing Diffusion 90
8 A Clash of Narratives: Diffusion and the
  Archaeologists 102

Part III	**The Most Ancient Faith**	**113**
9	The Esoteric Revival	115
10	The Universal Bond	122
11	Stonehenge: A Mecca of Celtic Idealism	137
Part IV	**Order and Civilization**	**155**
12	The Aesthetics of Order	157
13	The Old Straight Track	173
14	The Straight Track Postal Club	190
15	Straight Track to Beyond	203
16	Visions of Civilization	215

Conclusion: Archaeology and Social Transformation	234
Notes	247
Bibliography	280
Index	305

List of Illustrations

1   O G S Crawford in 1936. 21
2   Grigson's 'flower of all periodicals'. 24
3   Mortimer Wheeler's autobiography, published in 1956. 28
4   Gordon Childe (right) and Stuart Piggott at Dorchester-on-Thames, 1946. 30
5   Grahame Clark in 1950. 34
6   The discovery of 'Piltdown Man' in 1912, lent credence to the racial theories of Arthur Keith. 76
7   W H R Rivers (left) and Grafton Elliot Smith at Maghull Military Hospital, 1915. 80
8   'Before the coming of civilisation there was a real "Golden Age" of peace and goodwill'. 86
9   Elliot Smith (left) and W J Perry, with Perry's wife and daughter. 88
10 *The Universal Bond at the Stonehenge Summer Solstice, 1913.* 'The Passing through the Gate', Macgregor Reid in the lead. 128
11 'Worshippers before the gnomen'. 129
12 Service in the circle. 129
13 'Before the Surrender Stone (Mahayoni). The Appeal unto The Great Mother is raised by the contrite heart'. 130
14 The Universalist cosmos: Stonehenge to the left, the religions of the book to the right, and a multi-faith trilithon in the centre. 132

List of Illustrations

15 The controversial Stonehenge turnstile, seen here in the 1920s. — 143
16 Sale of *The New Life and Druid Journal* at Stonehenge was banned. — 147
17 Hermetic interlude. *The Pendragon: Official Organ of the Ancient Order of Druid Hermetists*, Midsummer 1939. — 150
18 The Dream: Heywood Sumner's uncluttered vision. — 161
19 The Reality: caretakers' cottages at the crossroads, aerodrome in the background and – horror of horrors – a transport café. — 161
20 The Nightmare: 'Stonehenge in 1930? A dreadful vision of what might happen if the present appeal were to fail' — 162
21 Alfred Watkins. — 174
22 Frontispiece to *Early British Trackways*. 'A Glade on a Ley' links pictures of Castle Tomen, Radnor Forest, with the Four Stones near New Radnor. A composite of Watkins' own photographs. — 176
23 Ellis Martin's finely-designed map cover for the Ordnance Survey's ½″ series invokes the romance of the road. — 179
24 *The Ley Hunter's Manual*. Alfred Watkins woos the walkers. — 185
25 Members of the Straight Track Club gather around Alfred Watkins at Wellington, near Hereford, during their 1933 Annual Meeting. — 195
26 The Straight Track Club in action. Climbing Pont Hendre castle mound, Longtown, Herefordshire in 1933. — 197
27 'Proof by spade'. Alfred Watkins' photograph of a 'stoned trackway' found in a Hereford sewer cutting. — 208
28 *Eccentric Mirror Images*: 'Tracks to Badbury Camp'. — 209
29 'A Typical Roman Road: The Road from Chichester to Bitterne, near Southampton'. — 209
30 A ley hunter's vision: 'Midwinter Sunrise on Grey Hill', by Fred Hando. — 212
31 Mortimer Wheeler (left) welcoming O G S Crawford to Maiden Castle, 1934. — 219
32 Digging for Victory: part of the 'war cemetery' at Maiden Castle. — 222
33 The bronze bull with two human torsos, whose discovery at Maiden Castle unsettled John Cowper Powys. — 230

Acknowledgements

Most of the research for this book was undertaken for my doctorate, and I'd like to start by thanking the Arts and Humanities Research Council (it was a 'Board' then) for the three-year grant that made the project possible. Gratitude galore to pretty much everyone in the Department of Archaeology & Anthropology at the University of Wales, Lampeter, that hotbed of heretics, for instruction, inspiration and beer: in particular my three excellent supervisors, Mark Pluciennik, Paul Rainbird and Andrew Fleming, all of whom supplied wise counsel and encouragement which I sometimes took. Special thanks also to Jeremy Harte, Kitty Hauser, David Austin, Geoff Sawers, Adrian Blamires, Margaret-Mary Archer, Tim Hill, Julian Thomas, Cornelius Holtorf, David Matless, four anonymous reviewers and above all Ronald Hutton, all of whom have read large chunks of the manuscript and have given me really useful feedback. Their comments and encouragement have helped me to shape and improve the book, but I hereby exonerate them from any automatic taint of sympathy with my conclusions.

This project has been many years in the making and it would be daft to try to thank everyone who's ever played a part: I'd be bound to upset someone by leaving them out. In general terms, I'd like to thank the many librarians, curators and archivists who've had to deal with me; and all the people who live their lives out of bounds and dream of other ways of being.

Introduction: Power and the Past

Spinning the Past

Prehistory is a peculiar place. It's beyond history, beyond the tyranny and the constraints of the written record, and therefore it gets treated as a kind of empty space, a land that's ripe for colonization by pioneers and hucksters of every kind who use it as a testing-ground for ideas and views about human nature, society, destiny. There's plenty of conflict, for these ideas are often contradictory. Prehistory is a place where different visions for the future are passionately fought out in the present.

This was vividly brought home to me by the events of 2003. In February, I was one of two million to march on London to protest against the imminent invasion of Iraq. We achieved nothing. The invasion happened, and I was still reeling with the rest when in April, knowing my interest in unusual prehistory, a friend alerted me to an article that had just appeared in the Archaeological Institute of America's *Archaeology* magazine. This is an influential forum, with an estimated readership of 645,000, and claims to be 'the world's largest-circulation archaeology magazine'.[1] The article, by Garrett Fagan and entitled 'Seductions of Pseudoarchaeology', rehearsed all the usual reasons for dismissing it, and added a curious bit of sociological observation about the people who don't:

> They tend to be antiestablishment, suspicious of authority, suspicious of science. They like to strike this populist pose of the little man fighting

against the big university professors. Pseudoarchaeology fans get attracted to all sorts of odd notions. Their ancient civilizations, for instance, are better than ours, more peaceful, more spiritually attuned.

This phrase, significantly, was picked out by the Editor-in-Chief for quotation in the magazine's leader column. What really grabbed my attention, however, was another article altogether – the magazine's main feature, by Steven A LeBlanc on the 'Prehistory of Warfare', with the subtitle 'Humans have been at each others' throats since the dawn of the species'.[2]

Neither article said anything particularly new; both these positions are hoary with respectability. What was really significant is the context in which they appeared: their juxtaposition, the editorial spin, the cover design – and, above all, the timing. For that issue of *Archaeology* went on sale on news-stands across America in the middle of April 2003, with the words 'Prehistoric WAR' emblazoned in big letters across the front cover. On 3 April, the Americans seized control of Baghdad airport, on 9 April the statue of Saddam Hussein was toppled, and on 22 April the city formally surrendered. President Bush's approval ratings soared with the effect of the 'Baghdad bounce'[3] – and *Archaeology* magazine also cashed in on war-fever, using archaeology to make those feelings seem totally natural. Not only have humans always been 'at each others' throats', but those who think the opposite are akin to the 'pseudoarchaeologists' and therefore soft in the head. At a time when the Americans – and the British – were going into war in the face of global opposition, prehistory was being invoked to naturalize warfare. You couldn't really ask for a clearer example of how the ancient past gets used to underwrite modern agendas.

Issues of war and peace colour this book, and not only because it was researched and written with the Middle East invasions as a backdrop. The period I'm looking at was dominated by war: the horror of the Great War just past, and the second one looming. War and its aftermath influenced every aspect of life, including ideas about prehistory as people looked back to try to understand what was happening and what the future might bring. And yes, Garrett Fagan is right, 'pseudoarchaeologists' and the other sort do generally disagree about the nature of early humanity. Why that should be so is one of the big questions that underpin this book.

Making the Past

Why does the past matter? Why do people get so excited about what is, after all, finished? Probably because the past is the one thing that we all think we know something about. It's the place from whence we came: not for nothing is 'homesickness' the original meaning of the word 'nostalgia'. Knowledge of the past forms the bedrock of reality upon which the present is acted out. It gives form and shape and validity to actions of all kinds in the present. Historical precedent grants legitimacy, to kings and to laws, so it's not surprising that power to interpret the past has been closely linked to power to act in the present. 'History is past politics, and politics present history', as E A Freeman famously told his Oxford students in 1884.[4]

Deciding what matters about 'the past' is also politics. Making up the past is an open-ended debate, and the process works a bit like a democratic state. Everyone's free to take part, but some voices carry more weight than others. There are institutions that are authorized to produce authoritative statements, agencies that have custody of monuments and documents, and the media in all its forms, all of which collectively adds up to a tribunal of truth-production.

All engagements with the past are necessarily biased. Documents tell only partial truths, as archaeologists gleefully point out; they survive patchily and are used selectively. Documents are artefacts, made by people, and so they're part of the 'archaeological record' – but that, too, is an artefact, a framing device created by archaeologists, with parameters that are forever changing. Not just History, but Archaeology too, as its practitioners have somewhat belatedly come to realize,[5] has to be written; and writing is a guileful art. Describing the past means telling stories: imposing a narrative structure upon an inert range of incidents and moments which, from all the immensity of possible data, have been extrapolated by the historian – or the archaeologist – to shape or to colour the tale.

Relativism and Authority

Historians and, especially, archaeologists nonetheless like to believe that the 'facts' of the past act as constraints on the narrative. But these facts are also artefacts, human-made, since they're meaningless without interpretation, and interpretation is inevitably subjective. In short, there is no way of getting at the past except through a set of subjective tools and filters: all 'truth' about it must therefore be relative.

All this is the small change of what's been labelled 'post-processualism', the reaction to the deterministic, system-seeking 'processual' archaeology that preceded it. Post-processualist debate began in the 1980s, yet many people still endeavour to resist the disintegration of older certainties into the quicksands of 'relativism'. As professional keepers of the past, historians and archaeologists have much to fear from epistemic dissolution – and the fierce debate over relativism has demonstrated that what's at stake is power: the power of the professional to legitimize the past. Even Ian Hodder, who as a one-time 'post-processualist' guru might be thought to have much sympathy with the relativists, states quite frankly that

> A total commitment to relativism cannot be sustained by a discipline which seeks to retain a position of authority from which to speak and wield power. Disciplinary power and authority may come to be repression and must be open to critique, but they are also enabling. The archaeologist is enabled to act in the world from a position of disciplinary authority.[6]

In other words, don't saw off the branch you're sitting on.

Egemonia

This book examines the processes of professionalization that created that 'position of disciplinary authority', and also the nature of its relationship with authority in the wider world. What can the example of archaeology tell us about the workings of social 'hegemony', for instance, that hideous Gramscian term (it's better in Italian) much beloved of post-Marxian scholars since it apparently explains the failure of the masses to unite and throw off chains? Antonio Gramsci defined hegemony as ' "spontaneous" consent given by the great masses of the population to the general direction imposed on social life by the dominant fundamental group'.[7] Its cultural effects were glossed in terms highly relevant to my case by E P Thompson as

> a general 'common sense' as to what is possible and what is not, a limited horizon of moral norms and practical probabilities beyond which all must be blasphemous, seditious, insane or apocalyptic fantasy – a structure which serves to consolidate the existent social order, enforce its priorities, and which is itself enforced by rewards and penalties.[8]

Creating an academic discipline, ensuring that archaeology conformed to professional norms, meant establishing exactly what 'a general "common sense" ' might mean in archaeological terms, and enshrining it through processes of inclusion and exclusion. This book is an exploration of those processes from both sides of the fence. It's sociology, but also social history: an unusual look, from an unusual angle, at British society in a critical part of the twentieth century, through the prism of its beliefs about the prehistoric past. It is based on my doctoral thesis, and though it's been substantially rewritten this has been at the expense of some detail. Comprehensive literature surveys I've eschewed; also the detailed sociological analysis of (for instance) Crawford's contributors: I can only refer those who want more detail to my thesis.[9]

The book is arranged into four parts. Each part can more or less stand alone, and each will have a clear constituency who may be only peripherally interested in the other topics I've covered, but I hope this won't deter people from reading the rest of it. The whole is greater than the sum of its parts!

Part I, *Disciplining the Past*, looks at how the British archaeology became institutionalized. This is perhaps the less glamorous end of inter-war archaeology. You'll find few references to Tutenkhamun here, or to Knossos or Ur or the many British archaeologists who were excavating in other exotic places. Flinders Petrie, Arthur Evans and Leonard Woolley are bit players in this particular drama: my focus is on what O G S Crawford called 'the heroic band of the inter-war years', the folk who, Stuart Piggott claimed, made 'a conscious and concerted effort to professionalize prehistory for its own good'.[10] The second part, *Contesting Utopia*, begins by looking at the idea of progress and seeks to show how and why the archaeologists were steeped in it. Diffusionism is then examined in depth, since it was arguably British archaeology's greatest academic threat between the wars. I'm investigating the creed from a different and totally fresh angle – and wondering why this hasn't been done before.

The third part, *The Most Ancient Faith*, swaps academic groves for druidic ones, and investigates the revival of Stonehenge as a spiritual centre, and a place in which meaning and access were highly contested. Finally, *Order and Civilization* looks at a variety of 'prehistoric' responses to the inter-war world, contrasting clean-cut functionalism with the compelling vistas of the Old Straight Track, and how the narrative of the four-year excavation at Maiden Castle was spun into a metaphor of hope.

These were fertile times for the study of prehistory. A lot of the ideas floated then have been dismissed as wrong, as intellectual dead-ends, blind alleys and wishful thinking; and many of them were cooked up by the professionals. The discipline of archaeology was developed in response to the fever-stricken badlands of romantic amateurism. The pioneers were bold and brave as pioneers are, and also highly simplistic and reductionist. Archaeology today remains rooted in their assumptions: not just rooted, but stuck in them, enmired in a fixation with material culture. The strength of the disciplinary stockade that the pioneers built has been to create a well-defined, well-understood position, a set of shared epistemological values from which to argue its case. Its weakness is that, by trussing itself up in definition, the discipline has limited its own utility. However recondite and hifalutin the debates, the final appeal is always to the material record: 'archaeology' is about things. We need to get beyond the confines of a discipline defined for a different age.

However, I do want to make one thing clear at the outset. I am not claiming that the triumph of scientific archaeology was the result of some mass hoodwinking of the populace and/or the academy. Hegemony is a *recursive* business, as Gramsci insisted. The people in control are there with the consent of the people who are not. Ideas take root only in receptive soil; truths are made collectively. In other words, we got the archaeology we wanted.

The archaeology that we wanted and got was one that confirms our very high opinion of the human race. From *Time Team* to *Archaeological Dialogues*, archaeologists are prone to dwell on human achievement; and if there is a 'moral' to my tale then it's just that this human creature so triumphantly unearthed by twentieth-century archaeology has a lot of very twentieth-century ideas that are not necessarily going to be helpful for the future. The belief that we can invent ourselves out of the environmental mess we invented ourselves into, for instance. This may or may not be possible – let's hope that it is – but it's surely not unreasonable to try to take a more detached and less triumphalist view of the March of Progress that's brought us to the brink.

Part I
Disciplining the Past

Chapter 1

Manufacturing the Past: The Victorian Background

1848 and the Intellectual Evangelists

The early nineteenth-century English university was a fellowship of gentlemen, more precisely Anglican clergymen, who sought to imbue their pupils with their own values by the subtle process of social osmosis later dubbed 'liberal education'. As bastion and bulwark of the state, the university's role was not to pursue knowledge but to protect it; tuition, through the classical tripos, was about affirming established truths, not challenging them. This concept took on particular resonance in the wake of the French Revolution: as Samuel Parr said in a much-quoted phrase, the English university was a place in which 'young men can be so largely stored with principles that may enable them to detect the fallacy, and to escape the contamination of those metaphysical novelties, which are said to have gained a wide and dangerous ascendancy on the continent'.[1]

These 'metaphysical novelties' might be characterized as the 'enlightenment agenda': an approach, a set of values, that espoused the cause of Humanism, focusing on the achievements and potential of the human race. Constructed in opposition to what was perceived as the hidebound, static and oppressive doctrines of the Church and its political allies, the enlightenment agenda posed a continual challenge to those in positions of power, who saw it, with justification, as 'revolutionary'.[2]

Throughout the nineteenth century, British commentators both hostile and cautionary were quick to point out the relative superiority of the (state-funded, free-thinking) German universities and their academic achievements. Even the Prussian victory over France in 1870 was attributed to the effectiveness of the German university system, and the growing sense of competition with Germany in the run-up to the Great War helped promote the change in attitude which led to properly funded research within British universities.[3]

The German system fostered a sense of mission and intellectual zeal which even its opponents realized had political implications: already in 1820, the English conservative *Quarterly Review* had accused the free universities of Germany of producing students who 'are all puffed up . . . with their perfect fitness to introduce a new order of things and to become the regenerators of Europe'.[4]

Ron Eyerman believes that the advent of the intellectual-as-missionary was much boosted by the upheavals of 1848 in Europe: 'the idea began to take form that intellectuals were a social group with a distinct historical mission to perform . . . It was the intellectuals who claimed to perceive the laws of this motion, taking for themselves the role of leading blind social forces in the right direction . . . free from the domination of the state and the interests of private life, the idea of the intellectual is an inherently political idea.' The intellectual was an agent of change; merely to apply the knowledge that he possessed was a political act. In the words of Régis Debray, 'the diffusion of knowledge and the political crusade were one and the same thing. The savant was also a militant because he was a savant.'[5]

On the face of it, the situation was very different in England: conservative, reactionary (or at least anti-revolutionary), complacent. It is true that English university reform, when it came, was motivated primarily by a desire to expand the possibilities for the middle classes: the growth of 'professionalization' which, to some scholars at least, was driven by aspirations to gentility combined with the need for an income: 'Fundamentally, a profession was an occupation which a gentleman could follow without losing his claim to this coveted social position.'[6] This implied both a shake-up of the curriculum, to accommodate new subjects which had some potential professional application, and a revision in the status and prospects of tutors themselves that would recast them as 'professionals'. Tutors, like schoolmasters, had little status in their own right; as junior Fellows of their colleges, their only claim to gentlemanly status came from their position as clergymen, with the prospect of eventually receiving their own benefice.

In fact, the European 'intellectuals' had much in common with the English 'reformers' who succeeded in transforming most aspects of public life during the mid-nineteenth century – including the universities. The new University of London, opened in 1828, was conceived as 'a German university' according to contemporaries.[7] Forty-five years later, *The Times* declared that even within the older universities a 'restless educational fervour has taken possession of the most able residents and a propagandist spirit has been developed which desires to carry university teaching and university influence to every corner of the land':[8] these 'most able residents' were certainly 'intellectuals' on Eyerman's definition.

Professionalizing the Past

A widespread belief that English society was in some profound way 'different' has tended to occlude the fact that academic communities were engaged in very similar activities across Europe.

This was particularly true of the historians, creating seamless 'national' histories to legitimize polities whose foundations were often new and shaky. British historians propounded a similar mix of nationalism and progress as their counterparts in Europe, appropriately recast. Thus the events of 1848 prompted English historians to assert the enduring value of Anglo-Saxon institutions; and more generally, in Philippa Levine's words, 'to establish an organic continuity with the English past wherein present conditions could claim to be not just the only logical but the best outcome of a revered and celebrated past'.[9]

History was, quite literally, political. The niche which the discipline's professional advocates secured within academia was justified and underwritten by its vocation as training for the next generation of rulers. Thus E S Creasy, at his 1840 inaugural lecture to the University of London, spoke of the need to 'qualify ourselves by the study of the Past for our high prerogative of controlling the Present and moulding the destinies of the Future'.[10] Levine has shown how closely historical discourse was tangled up with national politics; many MPs had written works of history. Gladstone described it as 'a noble, invigorating manly study, essentially political and judicial, fitted for and indispensable to, a free country'.[11]

Historians and Antiquarians: Marginalizing the Amateur

Peter Slee argues convincingly that a profession of tutor-historians had emerged by the 1860s. But as an academic discipline, History had a sticky start. Opponents criticized it, amongst other reasons, for a perceived lack of rigour: 'In stark contrast to its ancient counterpart, modern history lacked concrete authorities', says Slee. 'Truth was a standard to be sought and discovered rather than inherited.'[12]

That standard was set by the new academics. Doris Goldstein believes that William Stubbs, J R Green and E A Freeman, the triumvirate of Oxford historian-reformers, regarded themselves as 'custodians of the new scholarly standard', and were keen to draw distinctions between 'workers at history', such as themselves, and 'impostors' such as J A Froude, Thomas Babington Macaulay and Charles Kingsley. In Slee's words, they stressed 'the importance of a university-based clerisy of historical scholars who would strive to maintain a conceptual hygiene and keep the professional study free from the grip of literary terrorists and editorial desperadoes'.[13]

These men were intellectual missionaries, in Eyerman's terms. Doris Goldstein observes that J R Seeley, Regius Professor of Modern History at Cambridge from 1870, had an 'almost messianic conception' of his role within the university. Professionalizing scholarship was to him a matter of national importance: 'in the warfare of thought we have hoped to resist regular troops by volunteers'.[14]

This statement highlights the fact that there was still virtually no professional historical research being carried out within the academy. What little financial support the universities did offer to research was channelled through the professoriat: a body of learned scholars who were funded (often nominally) to deliver a certain number of lectures each year, and (in theory) to bring lustre to the institution from their association with it. But attendance at their lectures was often very poor, since their work rarely bore any connection with the studies that undergraduates were expected to pursue; and in practice many appointments were political, and professors often unqualified.[15]

Even so, when the movement for Reform began to reach the ancient universities, there was much rivalry and bitterness between the college-based tutorial system and the university-funded professoriat, which was often seen as dangerously radical. A self-styled 'Sinecure Fellow' writing in *Macmillan's Magazine* in 1872 deplored the proliferation of 'extraordinary supplementary professors and private lecturers'; this 'industrious multitude ... have no genius in particular; they are simply meritorious hewers of wood and drawers of water in the temple of the Muses; they advance knowledge because it is their métier'.[16]

Others accepted the need for the 'Endowment of Research', although even reformers such as Benjamin Jowett expressed concern that such funding must 'have definite results in adding to knowledge' and not be used to subsidize 'mere unproductive study'.[17] In Oxford, the principle was accepted in 1877, but college obfuscation, coupled with a severe drop in university income owing to agricultural depression, meant that a career-path for in-house academic research stayed a dead-letter for a generation. It was not until Cecil Rhodes' famous bequest of 1902, providing funding for 300 post-graduate students, that a graduate school developed at Oxford; the first doctorates were introduced in 1917. London's first History PhDs were awarded in 1921.[18]

However, although formal remuneration for academic research may have been non-existent, a de facto corps of researchers had long existed in the form of university Fellows who, having done their time as university tutors, were rewarded with college benefices and thereafter devoted themselves to their researches; they account for the 'extraordinary preponderance' of clergymen that Levine has found amongst the membership of the many antiquarian, archaeological and historical societies that came into existence after the 1840s.[19] Confronted by the new breed of historians, they found themselves very much part of the 'old guard', often sympathetic to the Oxford Movement and its enthusiasm for the medieval past: as Francis Haverfield noted, 'the antiquary and the tractarian have much in common'.[20] Antiquarianism consequently became marginalized, as its practitioners were themselves marginalized within their own institutions, eclipsed by the new professionals who, by the 1870s, had decided what counted as history, how it should be researched and how presented: through their control of curriculae, the books that they wrote 'in their own time', and, later, the agendas of periodicals such as the *English Historical Review*.

The distinction between 'antiquarian' and 'historian', words that had once been more or less interchangeable, grew more and more loaded. As Levine has demonstrated, by the 1880s the word 'antiquarian' had 'acquired the sub-meaning amateur, and with it a definite depreciation in value'.[21]

Method was the touchstone. Antiquarians lacked the cohesion of a single methodology and set of standards, and antiquarianism was accordingly defined, or rather confined, by historians. In *Pass & Class*, a shrewd guide to undergraduate success in history examinations published in 1860, Montague Burrows advised candidates to concentrate on filling in the two-inch slots on their exam papers with facts and not opinions. In

1884 the same man, now Chichele Professor of History at Oxford, declared that 'Facts, naked, unadorned facts, are the objects of the love and reverence of the rigid antiquarian.'[22] Antiquarians were thus being steered into what was at best a supportive role. '[T]here is less and less room for the untrained, untaught and unscholarly amateur', declared Sir Henry Howorth in 1892. They were effectively marginalized, driven back to the fastnesses of local history: 'The triumph of the new professionals was in confining antiquarianism to the fringes of historical enterprise where their efforts posed no threat to the monopoly of expertise necessary to the standing of the new professions', in Levine's words.[23]

Archaeology: Academic Cinderella?

Archaeology had an even more equivocal status, even though some archaeologists were keen to distinguish their work from that of the antiquarians. 'Archaeology, by the use of strictly inductive methods, has grown from a mere antiquarian speculation into a science', declared William Boyd Dawkins in 1874;[24] in 1883 Flinders Petrie called for 'the mathematical and mechanical study of antiquities',[25] and General Pitt-Rivers obliged, with his thorough and pioneering excavation work at Cranborne Chase during the 1880s.

On the basis of such examples, although she acknowledges that archaeologists' poor purchase within the university 'did nothing to bolster their sense of a collective image', Philippa Levine suggests that the word 'archaeologist', like 'historian' (and unlike 'antiquarian'), had by the 1880s come 'to signify the trained and respected professional'. This optimistic assessment about the status of academic archaeology is at odds with her own evidence, since she demonstrates that the Cambridge Faculty Board tried to sever Archaeology from History three times during the 1880s by stressing its links with Classics. This was matched by Oxford, where attempts to include Classical Archaeology in the final exams were thrice foiled in the 90s.[26]

The historians tended to make little distinction between archaeologists and antiquarians. Between themselves, they were quite supercilious about the others' enthusiasm for minutiae and artefacts. In 1867, plans were mooted for 'a purely Historical Review . . . avoid[ing] the rock of mere archaeology', and when in 1886 the *English Historical Review* finally appeared, archaeology and antiquarianism were notable by their absence. '[T]he method of History is *extensive*, and that of Archaeology *intensive* cultivation', the historian Thomas Hodgkin declared in 1891: 'we may not improperly compare the instruments used by the Historians to the telescope, and those handled by the Archaeologists to the microscope ... the Archaeologist *collects* facts relating to the past and the Historian *arranges* them'.[27]

Anthropology and Archaeology

Post-Darwinian fascination with the origin of the species spurred the growth of interest in Palaeolithic archaeology, which crept into academia under the auspices of Geology. Boyd Dawkins, who made his reputation as an archaeologist with the publication of *Cave Hunting* (1874) and *Early Man in Britain* (1880), was Professor of Geology and Palaeontology at Owens College, later the University of Manchester. Geology provided a respectably academic basis for archaeological speculation well into the twentieth century: other well-known archaeo-geologists included the Oxford professor W J Sollas, whose influential *Ancient Hunters and their Modern Representatives* appeared in 1911, T McKenny Hughes and his successor J E Marr, Professors at Cambridge, and their pupil Miles Burkitt, who became the first lecturer in prehistoric archaeology.[28]

It was as an adjunct to the study of classical antiquity, however, that archaeologists and anthropologists managed to convince the academic authorities of their worth. The Disney Chair of Archaeology at Cambridge was established in 1851, its incumbent expected to deliver at least six lectures a year 'on the subject of Classical, Medieval and other Antiquities, the Fine Arts and all matters and things connected therewith'.[29] The Yates Chair of Classical Archaeology was established at London in 1880; a similar Chair was set up at Oxford in 1887, and the Edwardes Chair of Egyptology was established for Flinders Petrie at London in 1893.[30]

The emphasis on the classical world was a matter of some bitterness to would-be prehistoric scholars. Sir Arthur Evans turned down the Oxford Chair because, as he wrote to Freeman, 'to confine a Professor of Archaeology to classical times seems to me as reasonable as to create a Chair of "Insular Geography" or "Mesozoic Geology" '.[31]

Some professors of classical archaeology slyly sought to broaden their remits. Percy Gardner, who took the job that Evans had declined, sent his pupil J L Myres to work for the British School at Athens, where his brother Ernest was Director. Myres worked mostly on prehistoric sites, and went on to become a prominent anthropologist.[32] Reginald Poole,

Yates Professor from 1889 to 1894, turned his Chair 'into a centre for a wide range of archaeological studies'.[33] Ernest Gardner, Poole's successor, encouraged his pupil Mortimer Wheeler 'to embrace the more earthbound forms of archaeology'; in 1913 he and Evans contrived to award Wheeler the new Franks studentship.[34] The remit of the Disney Chair at Cambridge was likewise susceptible to broad interpretation, a freedom exploited to the full by Sir William Ridgeway, Disney Professor from 1892 to 1926, who played the leading role in setting up the Board of Anthropology Studies in 1904: early graduates included both Bronislaw Malinowski and A R Radcliffe-Brown.[35]

Yet the relevance of anthropology to the classical world remained the chief justification for its study. 'To have suggested that Greek art could ever have had an early stage comparable to that of modern savages had never entered the head of any student of classical archaeology and still less of any professor of fine art', thundered Ridgeway in his Presidential Address to the Royal Anthropological Institute in 1908.[36] That same year, Anthropology's Oxford champions, who had finally succeeded in introducing a postgraduate diploma in 1905,[37] published a series of lectures entitled 'Anthropology and the Classics', with the aim of 'inducing classical scholars to study the lower culture as it bears upon the higher'.[38] Prehistoric archaeology thus appeared in both institutions under the umbrella of anthropology, and in both cases its inclusion was justified by the light that it could throw on the origins of classical antiquity.

By 1918, 'archaeology' had come to mean two very different things: the residual antiquarianism of the mid-nineteenth century, and the thriving new 'scientific' study of ancient humankind which had grown out of geology and, later, anthropology. Between the wars, the 'scientific' school became professionalized, and thereby acquired almost complete ascendancy.

Chapter 2

Establishing the Discipline

When sociologists first began to look at the process of professionalization, they tended to treat their subject-matter with a good deal of reverence. Professionals, in Eliot Freidson's words, were seen as 'honoured servants of public need', their occupations distinguished from others 'by their orientation to serving the needs of the public through the schooled application of their unusually esoteric knowledge and complex skills'. Ideas of what constitutes a 'profession' have shifted substantially in recent years, generally in a more cynical direction, with the emphasis on power relations: thus Freidson, echoing Gramsci, sees the process of professionalization as the acquisition of organizational autonomy, granted 'by a dominant elite or by the state'.[1] Terence Johnson took the notion a stage further by emphasizing control: a 'profession' was no longer to be seen as simply an occupation, but rather as a method of institutionalizing the *control* of an occupation, a concept refined still further by Turner, who emphasizes the importance of internal hierarchy.[2]

Between the two wars British archaeology became professionalized. There is one problem with this definition, in that very few archaeologists were paid for their toil. Many had private incomes; of the few who found gainful employment, many worked for relatively low wages in jobs that were often insecure and/or part-time, or in full-time jobs whose archaeological component was often slight. Although they might look forward eagerly to a time when paid work would become more plentiful, archaeologists' primary motivation in seeking professional status was to ensure *epistemic* control of their subject matter: the power to pronounce with authority upon the past, to control all aspects of the archaeological record, from excavation to interpretation; and to marginalize those whose ideas were incompatible with their own. And like the historians of the previous century, many were driven by a sense of *mission*; a burning desire to bring some right thinking into the free-for-all of the prehistoric past.

The 'heroic band'

'Professionalization' was therefore about establishing a set of common ground-rules; setting standards (and epistemological values) in a process of deciding what counted as archaeology and what did not. This process was spearheaded by what O G S Crawford came to call 'the heroic band of the inter-war decades': a more-or-less self-conscious entity which bore a strong resemblance to the 'self-anointed "communities of the competent" ' that, to Goldstein, characterized the early stages of professionalization amongst historians.[3] Some found employment in work that was at least tenuously archaeological; around them gravitated a much larger number, whom Stuart Piggott described as 'those remarkable archaeologists who were amateurs only in that they did not hold professional appointments'. Mortimer Wheeler doubtless had the same group in mind when he wrote of 'professed archaeologists'.[4]

Such vague terms as these betray something of the problem confronting anyone looking for a statistical basis to define the size and sociology of the 'heroic band'. Membership records of national and local archaeological societies constitute no useful guide, as membership was rarely dependent on prowess or expertise; nor can much be adduced from the authorship of papers in archaeological periodicals. Although Joan Evans felt that the history of the Society of Antiquaries was synonymous with that of English archaeology, O G S Crawford was emphatic that it was not; to the 'scientific archaeologists' of Crawford's persuasion, the publications of the Society did not automatically constitute 'good archaeology'.[5] In pursuit of *some* kind of methodological rigour, I analysed 'the profession' in this formative phase in terms of published contributors to Crawford's journal *Antiquity* – a yardstick chosen because Doris Goldstein stressed the importance of journals to the creation of the 'invisible colleges' of academic history in the nineteenth century. Historical journals gave substance 'to the idea that all practicing historians were members of a peer group responsible for the cumulative growth of historical knowledge'.[6] Inter-war archaeology was just such an 'invisible college', and I hope to demonstrate that *Antiquity* fulfilled the same function.

I looked at the backgrounds of a total of 192 people who contributed more than once to the journal: repeat contributors presumably had both the confidence of the editor and sympathy with the journal's aims. I found that substantially less than half were working in what might now count as 'professional' archaeology; and although only about 5 per cent were clearly living on private incomes, or, in the case of married women, their spouses' income, it is certain that many others were living at least partially on their own means. The remaining half comprised academics from other disciplines, and those in unrelated employment, in almost equal proportions. Almost 90 per cent had themselves received university training; 67 per cent were Oxbridge alumni, with a marked bias in favour of Oxford; about 90 per cent were male.[7]

It is important to remember that the *Antiquity* contributor-base by no means included every 'professed archaeologist' in Britain. They constituted a distinct subset, but a subset with a strong commitment to the development of the discipline; and it is interesting that their total number equates well with the 'outer circle of professional acquaintance' which Tony Becher, in his now-famous study of 'academic tribes', finds to be a 'phenomenon . . . of virtually every discipline', ranging in size from 100 to 400 people and averaging around 200.[8]

There were many feuds and disagreements amongst them, but the 'heroic band' presumably had few problems with Crawford's definition of archaeology, as proclaimed in the first edition of *Antiquity* in 1927:

> Archaeology is a branch of science which achieves its results by means of excavation, fieldwork and comparative studies: it is founded upon the observation of facts.[9]

Their intention was to establish archaeology as a scientific and professional discipline, distinct from other disciplines yet able to hold its own with them. In spite (or perhaps because) of the emphasis on 'fact' and technique, they found themselves consciously upholding the humanist/scientific grand narratives of the previous century. *Antiquity*, claimed Crawford, belonged firmly 'to the school of Darwin, Tylor, Morgan and Pitt-Rivers'.[10] Radicals, believers in the promises and paradigms of Progress, they possessed a self-consciously missionary zeal that confirms their role as 'enlightenment activists' in the nineteenth-century mould. Edward Tylor, one of archaeology's mythic ancestors, concluded his *Primitive Culture* (1871) on a note that was as evangelical as anything emanating from his historian-contemporaries: 'To impress men's minds with a doctrine of development, will lead them ... to continue the progressive work of the past ages ... active at once in aiding progress and in removing hindrance, the science of culture is essentially a reformer's science.' Tylor's sense of mission and purpose was exactly matched by Crawford. *Antiquity* was conceived as a missionary tool: 'The main outlines of the evolution of human culture are now firmly established, and it was time that this knowledge should become diffused.'[11] Glyn Daniel has commented on Crawford's '[m]essianic desire to get archaeology and its message across to the people of the world', and biographers emphasize similar traits in Mortimer Wheeler and Grahame Clark.[12]

To what extent can the 'heroic band' be claimed to have had any objective existence? Becher contrasts the 'outer circle of professional acquaintance' with an 'inner circle', whose size 'is surprisingly small, ranging from half-a-dozen to a score, with a dozen as a fairly common average'. I think it can be demonstrated that an 'inner circle' of similar proportions existed amongst the radical reformers of the inter-war period: a handful of figures who, as Stuart Piggott remembered, made 'a conscious and concerted effort to professionalize prehistory for its own good'.[13]

Crawford and *Antiquity*

O G S Crawford was described by Charles Phillips as 'an outstanding figure among those responsible for the phenomenal rise in the status of archaeology in Britain'.[14] His success lay in bringing 'professed archaeologists' and their supporters together, and, through the journal *Antiquity*, providing a forum in which the *practice* of archaeology could be developed. Although Mark Bowden has recently described him as 'one of the most under-rated figures in the history of British archaeology',[15] Crawford is well known for his pioneering work in aerial archaeology, and also for the propagation of what might be called 'spatial awareness' in a discipline notoriously object-fixated and site-centred. Above all, his position as editor of *Antiquity* not only brought him into contact with archaeologists all over the world, but obliged him to try to get on with everyone. His position within the new discipline was thus pivotal. His reputation spanned three generations. His mentor, Sir John Myres, claimed that '[n]o single scholar has done more than O G S Crawford to place the study of the remoter past, and of Britain in particular, on the secure and sound basis

1   O G S Crawford in 1936. (*Bodleian Library, University of Oxford*).

upon which it now rests'. He was much respected by his peers: Ellis Minns once called him 'Gaffer Crawford', and Cyril Fox apparently described him as 'the Master'. Finally, he was an enthusiastic and encouraging mentor to younger colleagues: Piggott called him 'my Archaeological Godfather', and Clark described him as 'in very fact a kind of uncle to British Archaeology'.[16]

Born in 1886, Crawford went to Oxford, where he scraped a pass in Geography. He was introduced to archaeology by Harold Peake, curator of the museum at Newbury, and first made his mark in 1911 with a paper on early Bronze Age distributions. He was appointed Archaeological Officer to the Ordnance Survey in 1920, and the next year published *Man and his Past*. The book was a manifesto, a rallying-cry for a new generation of archaeologists who shared in the idealism and the faith in the potential of Progress. It set archaeology firmly in the anthropological tradition and at the same time spelled out a purpose for its study in the post-war world: 'The archaeologist has work to do for the good of the race; he is making bricks for the mansion that others after him shall build'; and it was widely read amongst his fellow radicals. To Piggott, it was 'one of the wisest books ever written on archaeology . . . a classic exposition of the philosophy of archaeology'; to Gordon Childe, 'a complete and accessible text book of archaeological method'.[17]

The idea for a new archaeological journal, according to notes drawn up on 19 December 1925 by a Crawford who already had one eye on posterity, had first been 'vaguely formed' a month earlier, in mid-November 1925. Originally to be called the *Archaeological Review* (a title inspired by Sir George Gomme's 1880s journal of the same name), he discussed it first with Harold Peake and with his friend Richard Clay (later to become a regular reviewer). After considering various options, Crawford decided to publish the journal himself, in collaboration with Roland Austin, the Honorary General Secretary and Editor of the Bristol & Gloucester Archaeological Society, and responsible for choosing the name *Antiquity*. At a meeting in the card-room at the Royal Societies Club, Crawford persuaded the marmalade millionaire and archaeologist Alexander Keiller, with whom he had collaborated on *Wessex from the Air*, to lend him £100, which he used to print and post 20,000 prospectuses to a list of names that included various national and international societies and 'as many local societies as the preliminary canvassing-funds will allow'. The response was immediate, and gratifying. Well over 500 advance subscriptions had been confirmed by 16 January 1927; and in the end over 1,270 copies of the first issue were duly sent out to subscribers by 15 March. No contemporary subscription-lists survive, but by 1936 Crawford claimed that this circulation figure 'has long been surpassed, and now looks small'.[18]

From the beginning, *Antiquity*'s influence was considerable. In 1927 alone, Crawford himself exposed the Glozel forgeries and wrote what Paul Ashbee considers to be the pioneer work on the field study of barrows, while Wheeler wrote a 'quite devastating' review of the Welsh Royal Commission's latest publication (the Secretary resigned, and the Commission was reorganized); in 1933 Clark and Piggott launched what Roger Mercer calls 'the first torpedo in British archaeology' with an attack on the Palaeolithic tendencies of the 'Old Guard'.[19]

As both editor and publisher, Crawford had a powerful position within the archaeological community. He had no systematic policy of peer-review, although he regularly asked colleagues such as Gordon Childe before publishing pieces about which he felt unsure;[20] but he established the journal's credentials by attracting contributions from writers whom he knew would command respect. This he did with considerable skill, finding a careful and diplomatic balance between articles and reviews by well-known heavyweights such as Flinders Petrie and R G Collingwood, and up-and-coming youngsters such as Stuart Piggott and Christopher Hawkes. The international flavour is another striking feature of *Antiquity* in the pre-war years – although, even allowing for problems in defining nationality, only 22 out of 192 contributors can unequivocally be counted as 'foreign' (12 per cent): this was essentially British archaeology 'looking out', rather than a major forum for archaeologists from all over the world. But Crawford did make a point of reviewing non-British work, and moreover almost all of his regular 'foreign' contributors held high academic posts in their own countries.[21] By bringing British archaeology into the international fold, *Antiquity* played an important part in introducing international standards of scholarship, thereby imposing a disciplinary yoke that had barely existed beforehand. This was in addition to the high proportion of contributions from academics in other disciplines. Establishing a high standard of scholarship, from whatever quarter and on whatever topic, was clearly a top priority.

Antiquity had two distinct roles of real importance. The first was the part that it played in the process of shaping and defining scientific archaeology. Crawford himself saw it as providing 'a sort of running commentary on current work'. It 'began as the organ of a small band of enlightened enthusiasts', and it rapidly became the trade journal for those who had 'the right ideas about archaeology'.[22]

The second was the part that it played in creating a wider audience amongst the intelligentsia for those 'right ideas'. Crawford's avowed intention was to 'found a journal which would raise the general status of archaeology and would popularize its achievements without vulgarizing them – in a word, which would take a place equivalent (both in form and content) to that already occupied by the monthlies and quarterlies in regard to public affairs generally'.[23]

He accepted that it might be a slow process. 'To look at the past in this way is difficult for many people and impossible, it seems, for some; it is to make it easier for them that *Antiquity* exists. You cannot teach a point of view, as you teach, say, Greek or motor-driving; you can only hope that it will gradually be acquired. There is often much to be unlearnt first.'[24]

In fact, *Antiquity* succeeded in propagating the Crawford gospel to a large swathe of the literate middle classes. Kitty Hauser has noticed that the *Times Literary Supplement* included *Antiquity* on the list of specialist journals whose contents it regularly monitored. The writer Geoffrey Grigson remembered it as 'the flower of all periodicals familiar to me in my day' and likened it to T S Eliot's *Criterion*, eulogizing Crawford as

2 Grigson's 'flower of all periodicals'. The logo was designed by Ellis Martin, the Ordnance Survey's resident artist and O G S Crawford's colleague. (*Antiquity Publications Ltd*).

'archaeology's Eliot'. It informed, shaped and influenced a generation of artists: John Piper, for instance, collected many articles from the journal and had them bound in two fat scrapbooks; David Mellor even claims that *Antiquity* had as much influence on British art as the avant-garde *Cahiers d'Art*.[25]

Other archaeologists were well aware of the educational importance of *Antiquity*. Mortimer Wheeler called Crawford 'our greatest archaeological publicist', which coming from him was praise indeed. To Childe, *Antiquity* had 'great value in democratizing archaeology as well as providing archaeologists with material and ideas'.[26]

It was a top-down sort of democracy, however. What Crawford and his colleagues sought to do was to broaden the constituency for a particular approach to the past, thereby legitimizing the concept of an archaeological profession, led by professionals; and the implications of this were profound.

Wheeler and the Antiquaries

Doris Goldstein ranks 'associations' with journals as 'the chief means' of giving substance to the notion of discipline amongst nineteenth-century would-be history professionals,[27] and a similar preoccupation is apparent amongst the 'heroic band'. In their case, however, the problem was not seen as one of starting up new societies, but in transforming existing ones, many of which remained rooted in the antiquarian tradition, in what Grahame Clark termed 'the "feudal stage" of archaeology – county societies ranged under the great London Society of Antiquaries, the whole draped with the cloak of snobbery'.[28]

The Society of Antiquaries was at the top of the hit-list. Established in 1717, it had all the hallmarks of an élite London club. In the meeting-room at Burlington House, Piggott recalled, the Fellows 'sat on the front benches, where they could chat, or look at *The Connoisseur* or *The Burlington Magazine* (or, alas, the evening papers) before and not infrequently during a lecture they found dull'. Members were elected, or rejected, on personal whim (Piggott himself was 'blackballed' because his employer, the upstart Alexander Keiller, was widely disliked). Aileen Fox, who worked there in the early 1930s, described it as 'still very much a man's preserve and youth was frowned on. Women had been specifically excluded from meetings until 1918 and had only been grudgingly admitted as Fellows after the passing of the Sex Disqualification Act of 1920.'[29]

To some, notably Crawford, 'during the growing years of archaeology between the wars the Society was completely out of touch and sympathy with all that was best in the growth. It was dominated by a clique of narrow-minded medievalists and collectors who had neither the wits to comprehend anything outside their own special interests, nor to conduct any worthwhile researches within them ... The contempt for prehistory shown, sometimes openly, at meetings was heartily reciprocated.'[30] *Antiquity* was conceived as direct competition to the *Antiquaries Journal*; and during the planning stage Crawford swore his printer to secrecy because he was aware that 'we shall be regarded as "deadly rivals", and I fear come wildly into collision with the Society of Antiquaries, over it'.[31] On the grounds that the Antiquaries 'had always appeared to be rather bored by prehistory', he chose to read his ground-breaking 1922 lecture on aerial photography to the Royal Geographical Society; and his proposal six years later for a map of the entire Roman Empire was likewise made, not to a body of archaeologists or even historians, but at the International Geographical Congress in Cambridge.[32]

Nonetheless, the Society of Antiquaries remained an important focus for archaeological endeavour. Members might have been bored by prehistory, but the Society was the chief source of funding for major domestic excavations such as Camulodonum and Maiden Castle, and Society meetings remained the major forum for 'breaking news' of the archaeological kind, which lent them a liveliness and vitality that belied the Society's stuffy reputation.[33] As the senior national institution, the Antiquaries had an important advisory role: the Office of Works turned to them for supervising restoration and excavation work at Stonehenge, for example,[34] and there was a cosy relationship between the higher echelons of the Antiquaries' hierarchy and relevant government departments. Successive British Museum Keepers of British & Medieval Antiquities and Chief Inspectors of Ancient Monuments became Directors and Presidents of the Antiquaries; Lord Crawford (no relation!), President from 1924–9, had been First Commissioner of the Office of Works in 1921–2.

Furthermore, after several decades in the doldrums, the Society was enjoying a steady increase in membership. The 1910 pre-war total of 750 had dropped during the war years to a low of 671 in 1918, but thereafter rose more or less continuously to an inter-war peak of 847 in 1939.[35] The increase in ordinary membership was in part a reflection of the growing numbers of 'dirt archaeologists' who may, like Piggott, have been 'not impressed' by the Society but nonetheless felt themselves obliged to join it (if they could).[36] Even Crawford allowed himself to be elected to the Council for 1928 and 1929, at a time when he had not only risen to prominence with the launching of *Antiquity* but was also involved in a high-profile campaign to acquire the Stonehenge hinterland for the National Trust (see Chapter 12). Whatever misgivings the 'heroic band' may have felt about the Antiquaries, their influence could not be ignored.

The slow modernization of the Antiquaries began after the War, when a combination of financial crisis and new legislation on sex discrimination forced the organization to allow the election of women as Fellows. In the words of the President, Sir Charles Hercules Read (a somewhat wispy-looking gentleman, despite the name), 'A Society that may be said to date from the time of Elizabeth is called upon to reform itself, and pursue its unaltered aims in the spirit and method of this period of reconstruction.'[37] This quote is from the 'Foreword' to the first volume of the new *Antiquaries Journal*, a (marginally) more user-friendly replacement for the Society's costly *Proceedings*. Some attempt was made to reach a mass audience. The first issue included the first report from Colonel Hawley, appointed by the Society to excavate Stonehenge, and a series of photographs of the re-erection of several of the stones.[38] There was even a somewhat unconvincing advertising campaign: 'This journal will, it is hoped, enlist the interest and support of the general public in touch with archaeological matters. An effort is made to furnish an adequate record of archaeological discovery...'[39]

Undoubtedly agitating behind the scenes was Charles Peers, Secretary of the Society since 1908, who took over as Director in 1921. Peers (1868–1952) was a shaker-and-mover of the previous generation, Her Majesty's Chief Inspector of Ancient Monuments and architect of the Ancient Monuments Act of 1913. He was a very influential figure, *éminence grise* and ally of the 'heroic band' – most notably in his patronage of the young Mortimer Wheeler.[40]

Wheeler (1890–1976) studied under Gardner at the University of London, and earned himself a place on the Royal Commission for Historical Monuments in England in 1913. In 1920, he became Keeper at the National Museum of Wales in Cardiff, and, in 1924, at the age of 33, Director. Wheeler was probably the best-known British archaeologist of the twentieth century, and his contribution to the institutionalization of the discipline was correspondingly huge. Like Crawford, he was a master of publicity: his achievements in using the popular media to build up a sizeable base of public interest and support for the new brand of archaeology will be examined in Chapter 16. Unlike Crawford, Wheeler was comfortable within 'the Establishment', and took pains to establish the network of connections that were necessary to inveigle the new archaeology into existing institutions.

Peers appears to have got on well with Wheeler from the start. He may have helped to secure Wheeler's election as a Fellow of the Society in 1922; in 1924, he wrote in support of Wheeler's application for the Cardiff Directorship, describing him as having 'a most attractive personality', and, Hawkes suggests, was probably the central figure in behind-the-scenes manipulations to ensure that Wheeler secured the job as Director of the London Museum two years later. It is probably due to Peers' influence that Wheeler was elected to the Antiquaries' Council in 1926; from 1928, he was on the influential Research and Executive Committees, became Vice President in 1935, Secretary in 1939, Director in 1940.[41]

Wheeler, in his autobiography, was quite blatant about the need to ingratiate himself with the Antiquaries: 'Contacts... had to be established or confirmed by lecturing or committee work.' He was equally aware that the Society was not naturally sympathetic to his brand of archaeology: 'To the great mass of professed antiquarian opinion the art of excavation was a hidden mystery',[42] claiming elsewhere[43] that 'the conventional centre of antiquarian studies was still dominated by the

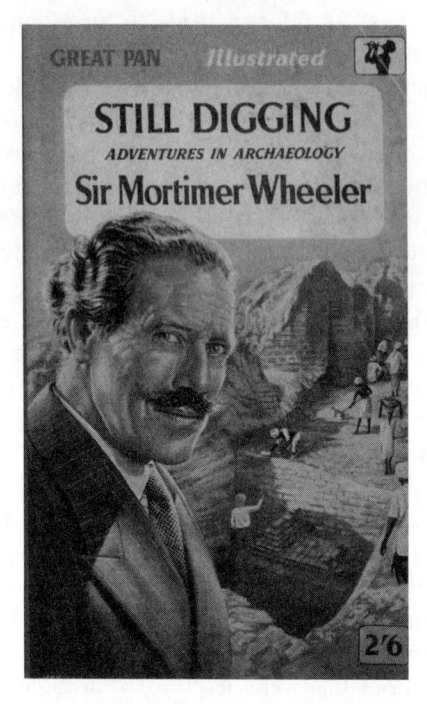

3 Mortimer Wheeler's autobiography, published in 1956. (*Macmillan Publishers Ltd*).

dilettante and the brass-rubber'. Jacquetta Hawkes claims that there was a growing divide 'between the old antiquarian Fellows ... devoted to medieval studies, including heraldry, and the rising party of the archaeologists, who had mud on their boots, potsherds in their pockets and "science" on their lips', and suggests that Wheeler, 'powered by a dangerous mixture of ability, ambition and missionary zeal ... appeared in a Mephistophelean light to the die-hards'. She contends that old and new, 'heralds' and 'diggers', reached an accommodation: 'overall peace maintained by an agreed balance in appointments and policies'.[44]

In fact, the Antiquaries' Council lists reveal a steady increase in the proportion of 'diggers'. In 1933, Wheeler's co-directors on the Maiden Castle dig (see Chapter 16), Colonel Drew and Tessa Wheeler, were both elected; the following year Christopher Hawkes joined the Research Committee. In 1935 Crawford swallowed his scruples and accepted election to the Executive Committee, and to the Research Committee the following year. Three more of the 'heroic band' were elected in 1936 (the Sussex excavator Eliot Cecil Curwen, Oxbridge lecturers J M de Navarro and Nowell Myres). In 1938, their numbers were swelled by the addition of *Antiquity* assistant editor Roland Austin, Kathleen Kenyon from Wheeler's Institute of Archaeology, Hawkes' colleague T D Kendrick from the British Museum, and Gordon Childe. Cyril Fox, Wheeler's successor at the National Museum, was elected Vice President, and the next year Childe joined him. This looks more like a steady takeover than 'an agreed balance', and it is significant that so many joined the Antiquaries' inner sanctum after 1935, the year in which Wheeler became Vice-President. It is also very significant that 1935 was the year of the 'coup' within the Prehistoric Society, of which more anon. 'Infiltration' – Wheeler's own word[45] – seemed to be working.

London Laboratory

Getting the right kind of archaeology into the universities was even more important. Academic archaeology in the 1920s – what little there was of it – had a definite whiff of the nineteenth-century professoriat about it. A handful of University Chairs provided status, and a (usually small) salary for scholars who had already made their mark, who in turn would cast lustre on the institution in return for giving a number of lectures and doing a minimal amount of teaching. Thus Liverpool's Institute of Archaeology functioned primarily as a place 'in which a group of colleagues might work together sharing materials and exchanging views'; according to W J Varley, it served as 'a postal address of the three professors, who were free to devote their time to the enrichment of learning'.[46] Gordon Childe, illustrious first incumbent of the Abercromby Chair at Edinburgh, gave many influential lectures and actually drew up a programme for a BSc degree in Archaeology, but only one candidate read Honours Archaeology during Childe's 19-year tenure.[47]

There was, however, a widespread and growing belief that archaeologists, especially excavators, required some sort of formal accreditation. In 1927, Reginald Smith, Keeper of British & Medieval Antiquities in the British Museum, made public the outline of a scheme to set up a London-based 'sort of school or institute for training young archaeologists, especially in fieldwork'. The scheme was Wheeler's: Smith was also a Vice-President of the Antiquaries, on whose Council Wheeler was that year serving, and he had been groomed specifically to give Wheeler's plan his blessing.[48]

4 Gordon Childe (right) and Stuart Piggott at Dorchester-on-Thames, 1946. (*Institute of Archaeology, Oxford*).

This was the beginning of the Institute of Archaeology, which, Wheeler grandiloquently claimed in his autobiography, 'represented the culmination of my efforts, begun almost *in vacuo* after the First World War, to convert archaeology into a discipline worthy of that name in all senses' (a claim that prompted Crawford to point out that he, too, had been involved in the early discussions!).[49]

Establishing an institute was not enough. It 'had to be insinuated into a university system', and to Wheeler this meant his own *alma mater*, University College London. Insinuation was a protracted process: the institution 'had to be led gently into the garden and up the right path', as Wheeler gleefully recalled.[50] He cultivated Ernest Gardner, his former tutor, Yates Professor of Archaeology, champion of Flinders Petrie, and a senior figure in the University administration. Wheeler, as Chairman of the Old Students Association, contrived to ensure that Gardner gave the speech at the annual dinner in January 1928, an event that he somehow succeeded in getting reported in no fewer than three national newspapers.[51] Later that year, University College assigned him an unpaid lectureship, the first step towards teaching a post-graduate diploma course. Wheeler also organized 'an ambitious exhibition', called *Recent Work in British Archaeology*, held at University College in 1929, which he ensured received a good deal of favourable press coverage.[52]

The break came in 1932, when Flinders Petrie, then planning to retire, handed Wheeler a donation of £10,000 he'd received, on condition that the Institute should house and use his extensive Palestine material. A proper Appeal Committee was thereafter launched, and Wheeler's long-suffering wife Tessa took on the work of wangling money out of the great-and-good, although, as Hawkes says, it arrived only 'in modest amounts'. In 1934, the Institute of Archaeology was formally constituted – although to the University Senate it was merely 'a comprehensive teaching collection of archaeological material', without full-time staff and without premises.[53]

Wheeler's prowess at top-level networking came to the fore in the quest for premises. In 1935, the Wheelers finally succeeded in finding a suitable building. St John's Lodge, a former wartime hospital in Regent's Park, was Crown-owned and derelict, and Wheeler persuaded the First Commissioner of Works, W G Ormsby-Gore, to give the building to the Institute for a peppercorn rent: Ormsby-Gore, by fortunate coincidence, was also the minister responsible for Ancient Monuments, and very proud to be so.[54]

In spite of the death of Tessa Wheeler in 1936, a skeleton staff was appointed. Kathleen Kenyon became Secretary, and with Wheeler gave lectures on Prehistoric and Roman Britain; appointments were made in Near Eastern and Biblical Archaeology, reflecting the interests of Flinders Petrie. The Institute was formally opened on 29 April 1937: its 'primary function', according to the University Chancellor who, according to Wheeler, 'had been at pains to study his brief', was to 'provide a laboratory which would fulfil in the study of civilization something of the function which the laboratory has long fulfilled in the study of chemical and physical science'.[55]

Cambridge Transformed?

Prehistoric archaeology finally made it onto the Cambridge undergraduate syllabus in 1927, with the introduction of a one-year Archaeology and Anthropology Tripos component. This followed the creation of the eponymous Faculty the previous year, and agitation from Sir William Ridgeway, the Disney professor, who unfortunately died before he could reap his reward. The Tripos consisted of a 'Section A', comprising Principles, including Physical Anthropology; Social Anthropology, Archaeology (restricted to European and Mediterranean prehistory) and Technology (or material culture). 'Section A' was augmented by a 'Section B', which was primarily concerned with the protohistory of the Celtic, Anglo-Saxon and Norse-speaking peoples of northern Europe. This course was taught by H M Chadwick, Professor of Anglo-Saxon, who transferred to Anthropology & Archaeology from Modern & Medieval Languages because, in Clark's words, 'he looked for a quieter atmosphere to develop his concerns than he might expect to find in the new Faculty of English'. Sections A & B, being 'substantially complementary', could be taken successively, thereby qualifying for an honours degree: a route taken by Glyn Daniel and John Brailsford.[56]

Although Glyn Daniel described Section B as 'a brilliant amalgam of prehistoric and protohistoric studies', it was very literary. Chadwick ignored the Palaeolithic, 'dismissing it as unhistoric . . . His main teaching was based extensively on non-archaeological sources: we read Tacitus and Bede, Procopius and St Germanus, the *Mabinogion* and the *Flateyjarbók*.'[57] Nor does a critical academic archaeology appear to have figured prominently in the teaching of Section A, for which Miles Burkitt was responsible. A graduate in Geology, Burkitt was first introduced to 'prehistory' in 1910 through an invitation to comment on the dating of some worked flints that apparently dated from the Tertiary, found by James Reid Moir, then *doyen* of the thriving Prehistoric Society of East Anglia. This brought him into contact with Henri Breuil, the French priest and Palaeolithic archaeologist known as the 'Pope of Prehistory', who told Burkitt that 'you cannot study this subject in England because nobody knows anything about it', and took him to Spain, where he spent several seasons in the cave-art site of Castillo.[58] In 1915–16, Burkitt began lecturing in Cambridge on 'Prehistoric Archaeology and Primitive Art'. These lectures formed the basis of Burkitt's book *Prehistory* (1921); both course and book are believed to have been the first of their kind in Britain. Burkitt, true to his mentor, taught a prehistory that was 'essentially French': the bibliography in *Prehistory* devotes $2\frac{1}{2}$ pages to the works of Breuil alone.[59]

Burkitt's *Our Forerunners* and *Our Early Ancestors* were on Childe's recommended reading list at Edinburgh,[60] but although he was highly rated as an undergraduate teacher, he was not generally perceived as being on the cutting edge of knowledge. The Faculty Board declined to nominate him for a Senior Doctorate in 1929, and even Breuil felt that Dorothy Garrod would be a better candidate for the Disney professorship when Ellis Minns retired in 1937: to him, Burkitt was '*un professeur en pantoufles*' (a professor in slippers).[61] Glyn Daniel's first published paper was 'written in anger', prompted by a lecture on megaliths that Burkitt had given. 'To my horror he propounded an old-fashioned doctrine based on the Montelian classification of dolmens, passage-graves and long stone cists. Even in 1936 it was ludicrously *vieux jeux*.' Burkitt had tried to dissuade Daniel from studying British megaliths as a PhD topic. 'It's all been said', he declared. 'There's nothing new to work on. Read the papers of Wilfred Hemp and you will see he has said the last word on the subject.'[62]

The transformation of Cambridge archaeology was to a large extent the work of one of Burkitt's pupils, Grahame Clark (1907–95), one of the century's most influential prehistorians, who had been told by Ellis Minns that he had no employment future as an archaeologist. In 1932, he threw himself with 'fanatical pertinacity' (Piggott's words) into coordinating the Fenland Research Committee: a major, scientific, Cambridge-led interdisciplinary environmental archaeology project, and the first of its kind.[63]

Miles Burkitt was supportive of his pupil's ventures. He wrote the foreword to Clark's first published book (Clark 1932), and was present at the inaugural meeting of the Research Committee. There are good grounds, however, for thinking that Burkitt was motivated less by professional enthusiasm for Clark than by institutional concern at the perceived threat from Wheeler. Burkitt did not actually get round to visiting Clark on site until the summer of 1934, and even then, according to Clark's colleague Charles Phillips, his visit was intended 'to enable him to judge how far the new people who were appearing at Cambridge such as Grahame Clark and myself could any longer be excluded from the official side of archaeology in the University'.[64]

This pointed reference to the overriding considerations of Faculty politics seems very apposite; for the University of London Senate had just (in May) formally agreed to accept Wheeler's Institute.[65] There was little love lost between Wheeler and the Cambridge archaeologists, who (according to Glyn Daniel) regarded him as 'a shit and a bounder'.[66] The bounder nonetheless had the active support of revered veterans such as Flinders Petrie and Leonard Woolley, as well as the Director of the British Museum and the President of the Society of Antiquaries; and as early as

5 Grahame Clark in 1950. (*Cambridgeshire Libraries*).

1932 there were signs that the Cambridge department was already getting jumpy. Indeed, as Burkitt wrote to Tessa Wheeler,

> there was nearly a letter sent to the *Times* a short while ago pointing out that there were enough facilities at 3 universities to supply the market with all the archaeologists which it can absorb . . . if it is merely that London feels left behind in the work done by the provincials, then . . . !!![67]

Seen in this context, Burkitt's overtures to the Cambridge scientists can be interpreted as a desire to compete with the 'bounder' on his own turf, namely, scientific archaeology, and to do it better: they were brought to the mark by the threat of competition from London just as much as from the achievements of Clark and Philips in the field. In October 1934, at Burkitt's behest, the Faculty Board agreed to appoint Clark as Assistant Lecturer; and thereafter undergraduate recruitment for 'Section A' began to increase noticeably.

Not until the Second World War was over, however, did the University really emerge as a serious player in the process of professionalization. As late as 1943, Burkitt pronounced himself hostile to the creation of the

Council for British Archaeology, maintaining that 'archaeology must remain a "hobby" subject', confirming an impression of elitism that aroused the indignation of W F Grimes.[68] Even within the University itself, academic recognition remained equivocal. In 1940, the University General Board tried to browbeat Dorothy Garrod, the new Disney Professor, into transferring 'Section B' to the new Faculty of English. Pamela Smith suggests that the Board was out to discredit Garrod personally,[69] but it was also a move calculated to weaken the new subject, since removal of Section B might have fatally undermined its prestige and its viability: it is clear that the subject still held a tenuous position within the Cambridge system.

Chapter 3

Containing the Amateurs

The County Societies

Academic training for archaeologists may have remained more of an aspiration than a reality, but by 1940 Crawford had little doubt that archaeology had become a discipline:

> Archaeology is no longer merely a hobby but a branch of science with techniques of its own ... the pursuit of archaeology requires study and training; it has become a skilled profession. (There is of course plenty of room still for the amateur; but he would be the first to admit that he now looks to the professional for guidance, and cannot profitably work alone).[1]

However, the vast majority of archaeologists between the wars were necessarily amateurs. It was just that there were different sorts of amateurs: those who might have been professionals had there been jobs for them – honorary members of the 'heroic band', so to speak; those who went to the professionals for guidance – and those who went their own sweet way.

After the Antiquaries, the chief villains, in the eyes of the radical generation, were the provincial archaeological societies. Some were very erudite and active: the Cambridge Antiquarian Society, for example, which had a direct influence on the early days of academic archaeology at

Cambridge, or the Wiltshire Archaeological & Natural History Society, 'one of the best in the country', in Crawford's estimation.[2] Others were less ruly: Alfred Watkins, whose *Old Straight Track* seemed to some to epitomize all that was wrong with amateur endeavour, retained a commanding position within the Herefordshire Woolhope Club until his death in 1935 (see Chapter 13).

It was this *unpredictability* that worried the radicals. There was no effective way to control the hobby-horses of influential or important members, no system of accountability. Crawford summed up the problem in a 1931 *Antiquity* editorial:

> A correspondent has asked us to express an opinion about the 'proper function of local societies', using the word 'local' in contrast to 'national'. As a matter of fact he gave one himself with which we are in complete agreement, namely, that it consists in the 'collection and publication of *facts* without attendant masses of verbiage which attempt the collation of all the various aspects of a given problem.' It is not, for instance, necessary to discuss the whole of the British Bronze Age when the discovery of a bronze axe is recorded in the Transactions of the Stilton and South Lincolnshire Natural History and Philosophical Association, to take an imaginary example. Such discussions do not arise on such occasions and should be firmly ruled out by the Editor. They make it more difficult for the reader to discover the facts, which is what he wants. Irrelevant theorizing has been the besetting sin of the local archaeologist from the earliest times, and it is time it stopped.[3]

This passage is revealing on many levels. The patronizing title of the mock-periodical is in keeping with the more general decline in respect for localism, which was already having an effect on local societies' membership and status in the late nineteenth century.[4] By extension, 'professionalism' equated with nationwide organizations that subscribed to the same, national (or international) values. True knowledge – epistemic authority – was concentrated in the hands of a body of scholars who conformed to these values. It was to their work, presumably, that 'the reader' would turn if s/he wanted more background information about the Bronze Age, which to Crawford was beyond the remit of the local archaeologist. The local societies' task was to record facts and not to venture opinions: clear echoes here of the distinctions that Seeley and Hodgkin were drawing between history and antiquarianism 40 years earlier, when their own discipline was still in the process of self-definition.

The Prehistoric Society: Us and Our Friends

Some radical archaeologists set up rival societies, for instance the small Devon Archaeological Exploration Society, founded in 1929 for the practice and publication of excavations in the county, which Aileen Fox called 'the "new archaeology" of its time'.[5] Others preferred to infiltrate and, eventually, to take over. The Prehistoric Society of East Anglia (PSEA) is the classic example. It had been established in 1908, at a time when the discovery of fossil remains in East Anglia was making national news. Dramatic claims were made for the antiquity of certain stone tools, known as 'eoliths' (from the Greek word *eos*, meaning 'dawn', as in 'the dawn of man'); and the PSEA consequently became the chief institution of accreditation for what might be called the 'Eolithic'. This was one of the shorter periods of prehistory, lasting approximately as long as the PSEA itself, and, in the eyes of Grahame Clark at least, only that long because of the astute institutional manipulations of its leading light, the Ipswich flint aficionado James Reid Moir.[6] Nonetheless, the PSEA retained a lustre which, coupled with its specifically prehistoric dedication, and its proximity to Cambridge, made it an attractive proposition for rising archaeologists.

The famous 'coup' of 1935 was engineered by a group of young archaeologists working on the Fenland Project based at Cambridge: Stuart Piggott, Charles Phillips, Christopher Hawkes and Clark himself, who had already served as editor of the PSEA's *Proceedings* for two years. The proposal was to drop the words 'of East Anglia' from the Society's title, a move which, Clark maintained, 'will be a contribution towards the much-desired rationalization of the subject in this country'.[7] Anticipating trouble, the key members of the radical tendency were summoned from all over the land, as both Phillips and Piggott gleefully recalled.[8] According to Piggott, they decided 'that it would be better to take control of a society that already existed than to start from scratch'.[9] Clark, perhaps anxious for his reputation, used the 50th anniversary of the reformed Prehistoric Society to deny this:

> My hands are not dripping with East Anglian blood nor have I just wiped them clean. The Prehistoric Society was not the outcome of a revolutionary putsch. It stemmed from nothing more dramatic than a recognition that the Prehistoric Society had long since ceased to be East Anglian.

He then went on to provide a comprehensive account of the Machiavellian machinations of his predecessor as PSEA *supremo*, Reid Moir, endeavouring to show how 'a man of such limited education and devoid of formal qualifications managed to impose himself and his ideas on the scientific establishment of his time'.[10] Pamela Smith supports Clark's version of events, claiming that the 'coup' took place more in the memories of its alleged perpetrators than in the deed itself, pointing out that the PSEA had functioned as a 'national' society for some time; and this interpretation has been accepted by Brian Fagan.[11] Closer scrutiny of the Society's activities over the next couple of years, however, suggests that the change of title was merely the first step. More substantial changes took place, aimed at breaking the East Anglians' hold by moving Society meetings to London: thus the 1936 February AGM, held as usual in Norwich, resolved that 'it was no longer desirable to restrict the Society's choice of a venue', and agreed to take 'the proper constitutional steps' to ensure that this happened.[12]

This was little to the liking of J E Sainty, who as Local Secretary for East Anglia was at the heart of the old guard. He chaired a 'Norwich Local Meeting' on 24 June,[13] and during the next few months 'wrote to all and sundry about various nefarious and unconstitutional machinations of our good society'. These words were written by Clark to Hawkes in a letter of 26 November, in which he suggested that the old guard were futilely attempting to turn the tide of history:

> Fundamentally we are faced with a reaction from the previous big-wigs of the Society as it used to be . . . there can be no question of capitulating to a parochial view . . . 'we' (us and our friends) believe there is room for a society – probably a trinity of societies – devoted to aspects of archaeology cutting clean across the local and feudal organization of a hundred years ago. . . . we must . . . face a struggle within as well as without our ranks. But it is a 'struggle' only in name because we cannot help winning. If possible let us win without offence – as we have with Armstrong and Maynard – but if necessary we must strike, and Sainty is calling loudly to be struck.

This important and indiscreet letter – 'several hundred thousand pounds worth of slander', as Clark admitted to Hawkes, suggests that a shrewd understanding of PSEA group psychology had allowed 'us and our friends' to take over the organization. Armstrong 'wants to be on the successful side'; Maynard 'has been bullied all his life – on a vote he would be with us every time – he savours the new situation thoroughly because it discomforts someone else'. Reid Moir 'is sulking . . . he will pull strings behind the scenes . . . but will not I think come into the open'. Sainty was described as 'the only open zealot . . . [he] fundamentally believes that the Society has "lost its soul" because it is successful'.[14]

The AGM in February following, described in the *PPS* as 'an occasion of the first importance in the history of the Society', voted overwhelmingly for the reformers' agenda; although, astute as ever, Clark as editor published a tidy tribute to Reid Moir, who had just been elected to the Royal Society.[15] Delocalized, the Prehistoric Society rapidly acquired an international reputation, 'the tangible expression of a new intellectual temper in British archaeology', as Piggott put it.[16] It also acquired a strongly Cambridge flavour: as Clark himself admitted, his dual role put Cambridge prehistorians 'in a strong position to influence the course of their subject'. University and society thus reciprocated and reinforced each others' professional status.

The Council for British Archaeology: Prehistory Nationalized

The process by which the Council for British Archaeology (CBA) came into being neatly encapsulates the gradual transfer of archaeological 'power' from the amateurs to the professionals. The CBA grew out of the Congress of Archaeological Societies, established in 1888 by the Society of Antiquaries as an early attempt to introduce national standards into archaeological endeavour: 'for the first time County Archaeological Societies were organized into a central consultative body,' in O'Neil's words.[17]

The CAS was made up of delegates from 'the leading local societies', and its aims were to promote 'the better organization of antiquarian research' and 'the preservation of ancient monuments and records'. In the words of one secretary, it saw its role as 'not so much the promotion of pure archaeology as the assistance of the work of local societies'. As well as providing general advice (for instance on transcription of archives and photography), the Congress produced an annual index of archaeological papers produced by local societies.[18]

Significantly, however, the annual index was abandoned after 1910 owing to lack of support from the very societies the CAS was meant to represent. This may suggest a tailing-off of energy amongst the local groups, at a time when national bodies such as the Royal Archaeological Institute and the Society of Antiquaries were registering an increase in membership; but it may also reflect a disinclination amongst local workers to follow research agendas imposed from above. The Congress began to take on a more independent role, dominated by its Earthworks Committee, which set out guidelines for recording earthworks and publishing an Annual Report on 'the preservation, destruction, and exploration of earthworks'. This report was extended to include other aspects of *The Year's Work in Archaeology* from 1921, and the remit of the Committee gradually extended to take in other artefacts, later periods – and an increasing number of archaeologists without affiliation to county societies. In 1931, the Earthworks Committee amalgamated with (and became known as) the Research Committee, of whom one of the leading lights was Christopher Hawkes,[19] soon to become the principal architect of the Council for British Archaeology.

Hawkes (1905–92) was Assistant Keeper of British & Medieval Antiquities at the British Museum. In 1931, in collaboration with his colleague T D Kendrick, he produced a book entitled *Archaeology in England & Wales, 1914–1931* which served, in Clark's words, to 'put a respectable front on British archaeology in time for the International Congress of Pre- and Proto-historic Sciences held in London in 1932'.[20] Hawkes played a major part in organizing that conference;[21] like Wheeler and Clark, he was skilful in the arts of committee organization. According to Phillips, he took an active part in convincing 'the rank and file' of the PSEA of the need to change it to 'the wider foundation' of the Prehistoric Society;[22] and since 1928 had been playing a key role in Wheeler's transformation of the Royal Archaeological Institute. This was yet another institution that was taken over by those who 'had the right ideas'. Wheeler became editor of the Institute's *Archaeological Journal* in 1929, and in 1931 gave the ailing organization a new home in his London Museum. The secretary was eased out and replaced by Hawkes, who eventually (in 1943) replaced Wheeler as editor too. A product of the antiquarian zeal of the 1840s, the RAI focused on more local concerns than the Antiquaries, and made a natural complement to the CAS. From 1932 to 1935 (from 1933, jointly with his wife Jacquetta), Hawkes produced an annual review of research into 'Prehistoric Britain' for the *AJ*, as published largely in the journals of the local societies – work which supplemented the summaries which appeared in the CAS annual *The Year's Work in Archaeology*.[23]

Hawkes thus coupled a thorough-going knowledge of contemporary excavation work-in-progress with a close understanding of the workings of county archaeological societies. 'It is easy to laugh at them', he and Jacquetta wrote in 1944, but these societies have given and continue to give invaluable service to learning. Let anyone who encounters one of their excursions and watches the party . . . toil with limbs no longer young to the tops of hills, pause and think with some pride of the English tradition which, with all its absurdity, it worthily represents.[24]

Absurd and worthy, but hardly the force of the future. In 1938, the CAS asked Hawkes to draw up a strategic document, entitled *A Policy for Research*.[25] This document was never published; neither was the paper on 'What To Do With Our Old County Societies' that in December 1940 he recommended to Crawford for *Antiquity*,[26] but it was clear which way his thoughts were turning. Many years later, Hawkes claimed that the idea of 'a strong National body, covering the whole of British archaeology, to replace the existing annual Congress of Archaeological Societies' was first discussed with Nowell Myres and the Romanist Margerie Venables Taylor at Easter 1943.[27] In fact, he and Taylor had been toying with the idea for several months before 21 November 1942, when he drafted a letter to Sir Alfred Clapham, President of the Society of Antiquaries, which was apparently sent under Miss Taylor's name,[28] asking him to call a Joint Committee of archaeological societies, together with certain key individuals. The Committee was duly convened by Clapham (whose 'wisdom and robustness made him ideal for promoting the plan', according to Hawkes) on 4 May 1943 as the Conference of Archaeological Societies, which in turn created the CBA on 6 August.[29]

Not all participants at the May 1943 meeting were enthusiastic about the new organization. Miles Burkitt saw 'great danger' in many of the proposals, particularly that of government control. It was on this occasion that he insisted that 'archaeology must remain a "hobby" subject', a 'remarkable statement', as Grimes wrote to Crawford soon afterwards, wondering whether 'the Cambridge contingent are going to maintain their preference for an archaeological-free-for-all in the future'.[30]

Burkitt also ridiculed the proposed panel of excavators, 'asking who was to judge their qualifications';[31] and the issue of authority also exercised the minds of several radicals. The first version of the CBA was to comprise 'a small body of persons of acknowledged standing in the archaeological world'. These were the words of Sir Alfred Clapham, as relayed to Crawford by Grimes in May 1943. 'This seems to be the only way of forestalling criticism of dictatorship', Grimes continued. 'Already Clark and Piggott have been unburdening themselves with talk of hole-in-corner work and the like . . . My own fear is for the identity of the persons of "acknowledged eminence" or "authority", whatever it is. [Cyril] Fox for instance would have to be one; but his idea of developing archaeology and culture seems to be from his own statements to wait patiently while authority decides what it will do, without telling it what it ought to do.'[32]

Crawford himself was lukewarm about the new organization. Although he had been assiduously wooed by Hawkes since 1940, and appears to have drafted a 'Plan for Post-War Archaeology',[33] he took little part in the new organization. He was present at the May 1943 meeting, but he declined to serve on the first Council[34] and, though later co-opted, told Kenyon that he 'cannot give time to Council business'.[35]

Clark, although he took his seat on the new Council, appears to have had fairly ambivalent views about whether the new organization could triumph over establishment inertia, even whether there was any need for it at all. '[O]ur cause can be well served by a virile independent society with strong finances and a really large membership', he wrote to Hawkes in January 1944, and it's no surprise to find that he had one in mind: 'I believe we may achieve what we desire through the Prehistoric Society.'[36]

Most of the younger radicals, however, were very enthusiastic. Some promptly began agitating for an extended role for the new organization. 'I do feel that there should be some body to which suggestions could be referred and which could give authoritative views on archaeological matters', wrote Kathleen Kenyon to Crawford. 'I feel that the Joint Archaeological Committee should be this body and we are trying to bring it to life in connection with the general supervision of archaeological work overseas.'[37]

Kenyon, acting Director of the Institute of Archaeology during Wheeler's absence on active service, was responsible for convening an influential 'Conference on the Future of Archaeology', which was held at the Institute on 6–8 August 1943. It was timed to provide disciplinary support for the CBA, whose role was being determined by CAS delegates at the Antiquaries over the same period of time.[38]

A wide range of topics were discussed, ranging from the need for total excavation, better and more thorough recording (through photography and a nationwide card-index), more laboratory analysis, to better training and more posts for professional archaeologists. The Conference was, however, inevitably dominated by the prospect of the new CBA. Many speakers spoke to issues that had been raised at the May meeting, either directly or obliquely. There was much discussion about the pros and cons of greater state intervention. 'Uppermost in the minds of those who attended', wrote Hencken, 'was the question of State-supported archaeology, with the problems of how to muster public opinion behind such a scheme.' Myres warned against too much of it: 'In this country archaeology can only be built up on the tradition of voluntary effort which has made the subject what it is... we must never confuse planning with progress or to mistake the creation of machinery for the advancement of knowledge'; and in this he was warmly supported by Clark.[39] In summing up, however, Sir Cyril Fox declared that '[c]lear approval was given to that very national compromise; State control exercised by means of an authoritative body, constituted for ourselves and by ourselves, the Council for British Archaeology, now in process of formation', and proposed 'that the views of so authoritative a body of experts as has been present on these two days' should be forwarded to the CBA: a proposal which, needless to say, was carried unanimously.[40]

An impressive number of delegates attended: 282 in all, and, as the organizers acknowledged, there were many others who would have liked to have been there but who were abroad on active service. Those present included representatives from 63 different organizations, including seven regional museums, 21 local archaeological societies, three British Schools, two exploration societies, 18 national bodies (including, for instance, the Association for Planning and Regional Reconstruction and the Royal Asiatic Society), and no fewer than 12 universities and colleges.[41] It was a somewhat eclectic mix, but the list does serve as an interesting guide to those organizations that considered themselves concerned with archaeology.

The conference was generally deemed to be a success, and a follow-up conference on the future of European archaeology was planned (and held) the following year.[42] Its success was taken as a sign that archaeology had reached the age of discretion: 'Only when sciences are established in technique and achievement do they begin to study themselves: introspection is a mark of maturity', declared Fox.[43] His wife Aileen, who attended the first Conference as the representative of University College Cardiff, was very impressed by the event: 'the atmosphere was exhilarating. I left inspired by a sense of missionary zeal and a feeling that there were good times ahead. After the conference, there was a new mood and sense of purpose; everyone realized there was need for a central body representative of all branches and aspects of British Archaeology which could speak with authority when the time came for planning the rebuilding of the bombed cities...'[44]

A Coming of Age?

Although the Institute of Archaeology, through Kathleen Kenyon and the Conference, played an important role in bringing the CBA into being, it is probably significant that Mortimer Wheeler was abroad on active service, since he had envisaged a similar role for the Institute itself. In a 'Memorandum' to a funding application made 10 years earlier, Wheeler had claimed that British archaeology urgently needed a 'central focus, to which effort and material may be directed . . .'[45] Sir George Hill, Director of the British Museum, writing in support of the same bid, suggested that the Institute might serve as a 'sister institution' to his own, charged with carrying out similar work 'on modern lines'.[46] These comments suggest that the remit of Wheeler's dream Institute would not be confined to education alone. This hunch seems to be confirmed by the unguarded letter which Sir Leonard Woolley, one of Wheeler's first lecturers, sent to the *Sunday Times* in August 1937, in which he described the newly opened Institute as a potential 'competent central authority' for administering excavation funding.[47] The ideal Institute would make archaeology as well as archaeologists.

Thus, although Kenyon's activities might be seen as a partial realization of the Wheeler project, it is unlikely that he would have seen it that way. It is interesting, too, that neither '*Antiquity*' Crawford nor 'Prehistoric Society' Clark were overly enthusiastic about the appearance of a new body that could claim to speak with authority on matters archaeological. The advent of the CBA marks the end of what might be called the 'Big Man' stage of disciplinary evolution; in its place, a democratic organization appears. It is true that the CBA never quite lived up to the aspirations of its founders, largely because of government unwillingness to delegate its own powers; but in the disciplinary history of British archaeology, the creation of the CBA marks a coming of age.

Closed Shop

The CBA held its first formal meeting on 8 March 1944. Sir Alfred Clapham was confirmed as its president; two vice-presidents were appointed, one from each of the two 'factions' within the Antiquaries: Gordon Childe for the 'Diggers', and the medievalist J G Mann for the

'Heralds'. It was agreed that the national council would concern itself with 'national' issues: lobbying for larger state grants, better protection for sites and monuments, and better archaeological education at all levels. 'Most of the work' would be left to 'regional groups', and the country was soon divided into numbered districts[48] – a rationalization that could have been designed to undermine the local societies. On 30 November 1945, the Congress of Archaeological Societies obligingly wound itself up, but it was a close call: '14 votes to 12 in an assembly of 28 . . . the Council is the child of the Congress', said O'Neil,[49] but many local societies were clearly unhappy with the nature of their offspring.

Insult was added to injury when a provocative paper written by Stuart Piggott appeared in the first issue of the *Archaeological News Letter* in 1948. Piggott (1910–96) had been working for Alexander Keiller at Avebury in the 1930s, and soon after his war service was appointed Abercromby Professor at Edinburgh in succession to Gordon Childe. In 'Archaeology and the Amateur', Piggott argued that archaeology had grown too complex for the amateur: 'the days when the Bronze Age of Blankshire could be discussed chattily by the dear Vicar are gone never to return'. He suggested that the role of the amateur was to subscribe to journals, to keep an eye out for sites in peril and to help out on excavation 'under expert guidance'.[50]

His article provoked some indignant replies. Some urged the importance of county societies; others were unimpressed by attempts to relegate amateurs to 'the tame dog role'. T Dayrell Reed, an experienced 'amateur', refused to limit his activities 'to those of a milch cow, an unpaid navvy, and a special constable'; and was not the only one to warn of the danger of the Closed Shop:

> If archaeology is to retain and increase its vitality, the amateur has, in my view, got another function to fulfil.
>
> He has to see to it that archaeology and prehistory do not become Closed Shops; to preclude the creation of a complacent academic hierarchy, the only authoritative source of the true archaeological faith . . . professionals . . . are beset by temptations which do not threaten the amateur . . . [t]here are, of course, many who, at least in great measure, escape these perils but that does not detract from the danger: a danger which a Closed Shop containing none but 'experts' and 'authorities' would enormously increase.
>
> To meet it I would encourage the amateur to interfere boldly in discussion, to ask 'why' and insist on obtaining a satisfactory answer. 'Expert' opinion unsupported by sufficient evidence should cut no ice.[51]

Although Piggott's piece appeared in a rival publication, Crawford weighed in belatedly to what he himself described as 'an unnecessary war':

> Some of those who are most vocal seem to imagine that professionals want to suppress amateurs or monopolize opinions; the truth is that whole-time students are much too deeply immersed in masses of fact to bother too much about mere opinions, which too often take the form of vague theorizing unsupported by evidence.[52]

This was probably intended as a reply to Reed's concerns, but it is striking that Crawford shows no desire to engage in any kind of debate: the thrust of his case is that professional scholars are far too busy to do so. Indeed, in the next issue of *Antiquity*, Crawford published a lengthy review of the CBA's *Survey and Policy of Field Research in the Archaeology of Great Britain* (editors: Hawkes and Piggott). It was written by the philologist F T Wainwright, who responded to the 'bitter retorts' that Piggott's piece had provoked by declaring that

> Archaeologists, historians and place-name scholars are all plagued by amateur frivolities until they wish they were nuclear physicists, a class honoured by the State, favoured by the Exchequer and apparently untormented by the cranks ... If there is a quarrel it is against the blunderingly incompetent and the presumptuously ignorant.[53]

It seems unlikely that Reed felt reassured by these words. Wainwright set up the dichotomy between 'scholars' and 'cranks' in brutal fashion; although the mechanisms for establishing competence were barely in place, his conviction demonstrates the extent to which a distinct and confident profession had emerged, certain not only of its right to exclude undesirables, but also to recognize and define them.

Conclusion: Claiming Authority

Although the 'heroic band' had invaded the fastnesses of antiquarianism, they did not set out to destroy them. Reformers sought to take over and 'inject new life' into existing organizations, to promote at least the appearance of continuity. Thus the CBA was born of the Congress, with the Society of Antiquaries as midwife; in East Anglia the Young Turks sought to legitimize their brand of archaeology by taking over the framework of an established society; Wheeler's Institute was grafted onto the University of London, and, even at Cambridge, Clark was careful to work within the hierarchy. Crawford railed against the Antiquaries but served on its Research Council – and *Antiquity*, although a new publication, derived much of its authority from the fact that so many of its contributors had formal academic accreditation of one kind or another. Legitimacy lay with institutions which, by virtue of being well established, had the right to pronounce with authority; and to bestow their own qualities onto daughter-organizations, or to reformers whose agendas were rendered acceptable because they took place 'from within'.

Grahame Clark once claimed that in Britain 'we feel that new things prove more acceptable if they are termed old'.[54] Just how 'new' were these 'new things', however? The transformation of inter-war archaeology was only possible because the epistemic ground-rules conformed to established expectations: if, as Clark maintained, the archaeologists' 'struggle' was 'a "struggle" we cannot help winning', their victory lay not in mounting some profound challenge to hegemonic values but by bringing archaeology firmly into line with them. 'If the "new" intellectuals put themselves forward as the direct continuation of the previous "intelligentsia", they are not new at all', wrote Gramsci scathingly.[55] Establishing the discipline as an academic force capable of speaking with authority meant that the radicals had to work very closely with the authority that empowered them. Ultimately, radical archaeology aimed at becoming orthodox archaeology, and in this they succeeded all too well.

Part II
Contesting Utopia

Chapter 4

Making Progress

Progress and the Nineteenth Century

The work of the inter-war pioneers was cast, consciously and proudly, in the context of a deeply teleological belief in human progress. 'Archaeology is concerned with the development of the human race and of the various forms of civilization which it has evolved', as Crawford put it.[1]

The idea of progress has had profound implications on the way that prehistoric culture has been perceived. It seems hard not to agree with Clifford Geertz that 'there is no such thing as a human nature independent of culture',[2] but since classical antiquity notions about the condition of 'primitive' humanity have been closely interlinked with notions about the nature of human nature. Primitives ancient and modern are treated as idealized archetypes, untrammelled by civilization and its distortions, and they get routinely attributed with failings or qualities that serve to bolster rhetorical positions. Archaeologists were not immune to such things, and this chapter seeks to show that the logic of social evolution locked the inter-war prehistorians into a series of *a priori* assumptions about the nature of prehistory.

Crawford's wholehearted social evolutionism was inherent in the structures of knowledge in which scientific archaeology evolved: the nineteenth-century faith in progress, humanist, evolutionist, above all nationalist, which served to naturalize British dominance and British aspiration. In this discourse, history was simply the detailed continuation of a prehistory in which the same ineluctable evolutionary forces were at work: as Boyd Dawkins put it, '[t]he continuity between geology, prehistoric archaeology and history is so direct that it is impossible to picture early man in this country without using the results of all these three sciences'.[3]

Change could be accommodated and even supported by adopting 'progress' as a peculiarly national attribute. Henry Buckle's influential *History of Civilization in England* (1857, 1861), attempting to apply the laws of science to historical development, suggested that the English experience could be considered to be normative, since, more than any other race, the English 'had worked out their civilization entirely by themselves'. English history accordingly demonstrated 'the laws of progress acting in a state of isolation'.[4] Man is self-made: an understandably popular doctrine in a *laissez-faire* society that lauded self-made men.

A doctrine of progress that placed Victorian England at its pinnacle required another sort of society at its base. The peaceable Noble Savage of eighteenth-century authors such as Rousseau and Herder was accordingly re-cast as a grim and warlike creature: 'In perfectly barbarous countries, there are no intellectual acquisitions, and the mind being a blank and dreary waste, the only resource is external activity', wrote Buckle: 'the purely savage state is the state in which military glory is most esteemed, and military men most respected'. This change of status was apparently justified by new knowledge: the older opinion 'has been decisively refuted by the immense additions which, since the time of Herder, have been made to our knowledge of the feelings and habits of savages'.[5] As the British Empire expanded, so a world of brutal primitives was being discovered, all conveniently in need of British civilization.

The appearance of Charles Darwin's *The Origin of Species* in 1859 had little impact on the 'progress agenda'. Peter Bowler has shown how Victorian scholars, unable to accept or to understand the lack of unilinear purpose inherent in Darwinism, simply integrated the new paradigm into the existing doctrine of 'progressionism', the belief in universal progress:

> As understood by modern biologists, Darwin's theory threatens the whole foundation of progressionism . . . he was successful in promoting the idea of evolution precisely because he adapted his published accounts of natural selection to the prevailing faith in progress . . . Instead of falling into Darwinian materialism, Victorian evolutionists used the idea of progress to retain the traditional belief that the universe is a purposeful system. Teleology was modernized, not abandoned.[6]

Paul Crook suggests that Darwin himself abetted the process by couching his case within a framework of 'natural theology' in order to 'cushion his work from criticism'.[7] A similar motivation might explain why he anticipated a time when

> the civilized races of man will almost certainly exterminate and replace throughout the world the savage races. At the same time the anthropomorphous apes . . . will no doubt be exterminated. The break will then be rendered wider, for it will intervene between man in a more civilized state, as we may hope, than the Caucasian, and some ape as low as a baboon, instead of as at present between the Negro or Australian and the gorilla.[8]

This was no doubt intended to be reassuring to mid-Victorian Christian sensibilities, but it did little for the standing of the primitive. To archaeological notions of stadial development (Stone Age–Bronze Age–Iron Age), Darwin added 'the possibility that our savage ancestors might have been biologically as well as culturally primitive', as Bowler points out. 'From the image of our distant ancestors as brutal savages, it was a short step toward seeing them as "ape-men".'[9]

Some anthropologists, notably Edward Tylor, were content to integrate Darwin's findings into the pattern of unilinear development; others, such as Sir John Lubbock, took the argument a step further by integrating the concept of an ascent of mankind from an animal ancestry – and therefore 'spared no effort to paint a depressing picture of savage – and hence of prehistoric – life'.[10] To Lubbock, 'the primitive condition of man was one of utter barbarism', and he explicitly justified his views in terms of 'the cheering prospects which they hold out for the future . . . if the past has been one of progress, we may fairly hope that the future will be so also'.[11]

Tylor's 'doctrine of survivals', which maintained that remnants of an earlier evolutionary stage might survive alongside later ones, was evoked by John McLennan to explain practices such as infanticide and 'bridal capture', which he found to be widespread amongst 'primitive' peoples. These he took to demonstrate that famine was endemic in prehistory, and consequently people lived in a 'State of Hostility':

> Whoever is not with you is against you. All who are not of your immediate group are your enemies. It is not so much that there are frequent and sanguinary encounters as that at any moment there may be an encounter. There is a total absence of security. Men search for food stealthily, warily, ever on

the watch for enemies – armed; they cultivate their fields – armed; and actual combats are just frequent enough to sustain perpetual distrust and fear.[12]

In the 1860s, the new science of phrenology appeared to confirm that anatomically different races succeeded each other in prehistory. These population replacements were widely understood to be the result of invasion, which cranked the hate-and-horror factor up a further notch. When lower civilizations were driven out by higher ones, according to Boyd Dawkins, their feelings of 'terror and defenceless hatred' were 'met by ruthless extermination'.[13] Entire races of invaders could be phrenologically characterized as hideous: thus Abercromby invoked a Dickens villain to describe his newly identified 'Beaker Folk', who presented 'the appearance of great ferocity and brutality, in a degree which far surpasses our modern conventional appearance of the criminal of the type of Bill Sikes'.[14]

By the early twentieth century it was taken for granted that pre-civilized peoples lived in truly Hobbesian gloom: a state of perpetual warfare, 'continuall feare, and danger of violent death. And the life of man, solitary, poore, nasty, brutish and short.'[15] This concept was fuelled, paradoxically, by growing uncertainty about the nature of progress. Peter Bowler suggests that the doubts promoted by imperialism, by growing economic competition and by the rise of socialism all conspired to help British scholars grasp the non-progressive thrust of Darwinism: 'Natural selection left the organism at the mercy of both the environment and its own biological inheritance. Precisely because variation was not directed towards a goal, evolution could be seen as a branching, open-ended process in which even the appearance of a human level of intelligence was unpredictable.' Writers such as T H Huxley and H G Wells began to acknowledge that Nature would one day overcome, and Huxley accordingly evolved 'a philosophy of "cosmic pessimism" in which human moral values were seen as standing in violation of all natural trends'.[16]

Progress was becoming a conscious defiance of nature, rather than its inevitable outcome. Mid-Victorians were convinced that evolution had reached its climax with the mid-Victorians; by 1900 there was a growing sense that evolutionary supremacy might have to be fought for. Social Darwinism was rife. Newly formulated Mendelian ideas on heredity bolstered notions of racial traits and characteristics, while the new science of eugenics fostered concerns about racial fitness in the struggle for survival that the world now appeared to have become. Writers such as Peter Kropotkin tried vainly to argue that humanity was essentially cooperative by nature, traits to be seen in 'a wide series of social institutions developed already in the lower savage stage, in the clan and the tribe';[17] against such a backdrop the Noble Savage stood little chance. Some archaeologists were willing to concede him a primeval place in the human family tree, but only as a loser in the struggle for existence. W J Sollas' *Ancient Hunters* (1911) conceded that Palaeolithic peoples had been 'peaceful hunters' until dispossessed, as the Tasmanians had recently been, by a stronger and better strain of agriculturalists, which is when warfare began. This was as it should be: 'It is not priority of occupation, but the power to utilize, which establishes a claim to the land.' Might was literally right: 'Justice belongs to the strong', he maintained, and for the good of the species as well as the race it was the duty of every race to increase its own strength, or otherwise to incur 'a penalty which Natural Selection, the stern but beneficent tyrant of the organic world, will assuredly exact'.[18] J L Myres, *doyen* of Oxford anthropology and one of Crawford's mentors, concluded a 1909 historical survey of the literature of the Noble Savage with a stern tut-tut: 'In the struggle with Nature, as in the struggle with other men, it is the weakest who go to the wall: it is the fittest who survive.'[19] Flinders Petrie likewise characterized warfare as essential to the advance of civilizations: 'Man must strive with Nature or with man, if he is not to fall back and degenerate.'[20]

Environment, culture, nurture lost their explanatory power: as the eugenicist Karl Pearson put it, 'We have placed our money on Environment, when Heredity wins in a canter.'[21] Hereditarian discourses flourished, usually of a pessimistic nature: 'There was evoked a fatalistic language of innate human criminality, bellicosity and atavism', in Crook's words.[22] McLennan argued that man was 'not only a creature with natural jealousy, but a conspiring creature'; not only capable of gang-rape, but naturally inclined to it. 'Now, unless we assume that the nature of man has much changed, we may see in our own time and towns what their conduct has always been. The men in that situation, or very many of them, just do as they can, and are neither over-nice nor over-scrupulous as to the manner'; and he cited the inclination of the ancient Greeks to '*paiderastia*' as evidence that humanity had been even less 'nice' or 'scrupulous' in the past.[23]

Naming the Primitive

To British writers of the nineteenth century, the Primitive had a name, and the name was 'Celt'. As local exemplar of a prehistoric people, the 'Celt' acquired characteristics defined in opposition to the 'Anglo-Saxon'; these, with the rise of imperialism, were in turn attributed to 'savages of the non-Western world, in which the Celtic character was painted with a darker brush', in George Stocking's words.[24] The whole discourse of Victorian social evolution was thus ultimately dependent on the redefinition of the Celt as the archetypal primitive; and it was a pretty unflattering one.

The concept of 'Celticism' is a highly problematic one these days. Malcolm Chapman's devastating deconstruction demonstrates, amongst much else, that the word *Celt* was itself first used in Classical times to define peoples of uncertain nationality but whose main characteristic was 'otherness': they were of a different kind to the writer's own people.[25] A similar usage is apparent amongst 'Anglo-Saxonist' English writers of the first half of the nineteenth century such as Knox (1862) and Thomas Arnold (1841), in that 'Celts' were understood to include not just the Welsh, Irish and Scots but also the French. 'Celt' thus served as an identifier for all of England's neighbours: a category against which the English could define themselves.

Sam Smiles demonstrates convincingly that the Ancient Briton of the eighteenth century was often seen as quite a noble fellow, regularly championed as the defender of Liberty against foreign aggression. Even contemporary 'Celts', however backward and brutish they might be, were not inherently immune to the possibility of 'progress': 'There was nothing intrinsic to the Celts that doomed them to an "inevitable" character or condition.'[26] The stock of the Ancient Briton – and his modern counterpart – fell sharply once the concept of 'Liberty', in the eyes of English historians, had acquired unpleasantly revolutionary connotations in the light of Continental events. Ancient Britons became excluded from paeans to the origins of British genius; instead, the Celts were stigmatized as slave-nations, their claims to culture ridiculed. Thomas Wright, founder of the Royal Archaeological Institute, maintained that the 'mass of the Celtic population, as we learn from Caesar, were serfs, without civil influence or even civil rights; the mere slaves of their superior orders.'[27]

The Anglo-Saxons were conquerors; and it is no coincidence that the same, Germanophile, reforming historians who were establishing History as an academic discipline were now proclaiming that the Celts had been wiped out by the English. 'Our history clearly begins with the coming of the Saxons; the Britons and Romans had lived in our country, but they were not our fathers', declared Thomas Arnold. Stubbs agreed: 'The English are not aboriginal', while E A Freeman was apparently 'in the habit of referring to Schleswig as "Old England" '.[28] The roots of English democracy were now to be found amongst the primitive Teutons, reconstructed for the purpose in direct opposition to the Celts. Reforming historians praised a Teutonic 'primitive democracy' which provided useful antecedents both for those who sought to broaden the electoral franchise and to stress the differences between the 'English way' and the ways of foreigners who were prone to unnecessary and violent revolution; Freeman, indeed, promoted the concept of the 'free village "mark" community' 'with all the vigor and aggressiveness of an academic crusader', in Curtis' words.[29]

As the French threat receded, the Celts were increasingly identified with the non-English peoples of the British Isles, and the triumph of the Anglo-Saxon over the Celt was understood to apply to Celts both ancient and modern. New racial narratives served to 'fix' the Celt in time as well as space: in effect, the modern Celt became a prehistoric survival, with attributes that attested to a lowly place in the hierarchy of progress. This tied in conveniently with English notions about the Irish. Robert Knox, in his *The Races of Men* (1862), summed up the Celtic 'character' as 'Furious fanaticism; a love of war and disorder, a hatred for order and patient industry; no accumulative habits; restless, treacherous, uncertain: look at Ireland.' Political dissent, often violent, supported by the 'evidence' of large numbers of dissolute and impoverished Irish migrant workers, served to create an image of the Celt as the living primitive, the savage survival to be found polluting English cities and undermining the conditions of decent Teutonic workmen. 'Crowds of miserable Irish darken all our towns ... [are] the sorest evil this country has to strive with', wrote Thomas Carlyle in 1839; he even suggested that the Irish might need to be 'exterminated'.[30]

Irish refusal to conform to English norms, as Smiles points out,

> could be employed as the 'proof' of Celtic failure to accept the finer tenets of civilization ... contemporary Irish 'brutality' could thus support a judgement on the Celtic peoples as a whole, contemporary and aboriginal, and such a judgement tended towards the conclusion that the Celts had been and in some quarters still were prone to the worst excesses of savagery.[31]

Belief in Celtic backwardness was bolstered by Edward Tylor's 'doctrine of survivals'. Tylor himself, having recently come across a modern set of crockery from Stornoway that 'might pass in a museum as indifferent specimens of savage manufacture', was disposed to suggest that 'cases of exceptionally low civilization ... the relics of ancient unchanged barbarism' were still to be found on the Celtic fringe, despite the fact that '[t]he Irish and the Hebrideans have been for ages under the influence of comparatively high civilization'.[32] The invasion hypothesis lent support to this analysis, since it was assumed that people on the geographic margins had been driven there. The West of Ireland was rife with survivals, including, according to some, living Neanderthals.[33]

Nor were field-archaeologists immune. Boyd Dawkins, writing of the endlessly warring tribes of the Neolithic, believed that the medieval English view of the Welsh would serve as a good illustration: 'The social state of Britain at this time is fairly represented in the well-known nursery rhyme of the marauding "Taffy".'[34] General Pitt-Rivers, renowned for his extreme form of social evolution, after an unhappy experience trying to quell the Fenian uprisings of the 1860s concluded that the problems of Ireland were racial rather than political or social. Recent scholars suggest that his idea of the 'primitive' was accordingly modelled on the Irish. Mark Bowden cites Pitt-Rivers' explanation of the disc-barrow as a grave-monument begun in a frenzy of grief but then wilfully abandoned as 'laziness' set in: 'The habit of all primitive people, including the modern Irish as a familiar instance, of lashing themselves up into a frenzy on the occasion of a death, and general excitability upon any common occurrence, followed by a speedy relapse, favours this hypothesis.'[35]

The Proletarian Primitive

During the later nineteenth century, class began to conjoin with race as a measure of evolutionary advancement – and threat. In *The Races of Britain*, published in 1885, John Beddoe, using 'Indices of Nigrescence' of his own devising, stressed the 'undoubted fact that the Gaellic and Iberian races of the west, mostly dark-haired, are tending to swamp the blood Teutons of England'. He qualified his observation, however, by acknowledging 'the relative increase of the darker types through the more rapid multiplication of the artizan class, who are in England generally darker than the upper classes'.[36]

Here, then, was the ancestral proletariat, racially distinct from its rulers. The working classes in George Gissing's *Demos* (1886) were depicted as lower evolutionary types, and Sam Smiles suggests that the new science of phrenology supported 'the general idea that the lower classes of civilized nations correspond physiognomically to savages'.[37] Smiles' fascinating analysis of mid-nineteenth-century historical painting demonstrates the 'proletarianization' of the Ancient Briton. Thus William Bell Scott's *Building a Roman Wall* (1855–6) 'shows subdued Britons put to use as labourers under the control of Roman officers': no longer the 'idealized patriots' whose resistance to Rome had once been seen as laudable, but 'navvies, with coarse features and sun-burnt limbs'. In Ford Maddox Brown's *Building a Roman Fort at Mancenion* (1879–80), a Celtic navvy, tattooed and long-haired, shovels while Roman architects study plans.[38] Similarly, Richard Hingley demonstrates that Celtic races which had refused the Roman yoke could be seen as evolutionary failures: 'To persist in a native form was a failure of progress, a refusal by uncivilized ancient people to accept the logic of Victorian and twentieth-century ideas of social evolution.'[39]

Such ideas reflect growing middle-class unease at the rise of organized labour and social unrest – and an enduring belief that, beneath the veneer, the proletarian 'race' was still steeped in prehistoric savagery. As Sir James Frazer put it, in his inaugural speech as Professor of Anthropology at the University of Liverpool in 1908, 'though they are drilled by their betters into an appearance of civilization, [they] remain barbarians and savages at heart'.[40]

Ancient Friendliness

Amongst the proletariat, however, different views prevailed; and also less conviction in the blessings of progress – indeed, there was a fairly general belief that things had been better in the past than they were now. There was nothing new in this: in the seventeenth century, when Thomas Hobbes was inventing his bleak 'naturall condition of mankind' to explain the English Civil War and the need for strong governance, 'nostalgic yearnings for a vanished past' were commonplace amongst the poor, according to David Underdown; and E P Thompson has demonstrated how ancient customary rights were regularly invoked by the eighteenth-century poor in their struggle against a progress that often left them worse off than before.[41]

Thompson has revealed the existence of a whole galaxy of 'obscure intellectual currents' in the eighteenth century.[42] Largely 'artizan' in social profile, their claims were characteristically couched in terms of challenges to the religious values of their social betters. These trends continued: Logie Barrow (1986) has discussed at length the prevalence of 'democratic epistemologies' amongst late-nineteenth-century 'plebeian' spiritualists and socialists, in which the common thread was a sense of oppression or antipathy to the values of mainstream society.

Theirs was a world of fiery politics and radical historiography, in which the idea of a benevolent 'prehistory' played a prominent part. It is, I think, apparent in the very names of the many working-class 'Ancient Order' Friendly Societies that sprang up during this period. Although the Friendly Society movement grew to be very influential (1,282,275 members in 1872 and that's just counting societies with over 1,000 members[43]), the fascination of the ancient past for such organizations has been little investigated. P H J H Gosden suggests that the impression of longevity may have been designed to imbue a sense of permanence and stability to an organization in which people were expected to invest,[44] but it is surely significant that so many of these early societies chose names with Edenic or Arcadian overtones: the Ancient Order of Foresters (who claimed Adam for the 'First Forester'), The Ancient Fraternity of Gardeners, The Loyal Ancient Shepherds. 'Ancient' times were times when people looked after each other. In direct contrast to contemporary doctrines of *laissez-faire*, Friendly Societies were evoking a state of antique friendliness and mutual aid, which modern working-men could seek to emulate.

Most famous of these Ancient Orders were the Druids. Despite the fact that the few written references had demonized the original druids by linking them to human sacrifice, the Ancient Order of Druids in 1850 maintained that their forebears 'were regarded with the highest veneration by every People over whom their influence extended', and strove to attain 'the great aim of Druidism – namely, "*Universal Friendship, Philanthropy and Brotherly Love*" '.[45]

Edward Williams was another who believed in 'the restoration of the primeval state of *Innocence, Peace* and *Benevolence*'.[46] Williams, better known as Iolo Morganwg, was responsible for giving the idea of a peaceable and highly cultured 'druidic' prehistory its fullest and most public expression. He was a Glamorgan stonemason, part of what Gwyn Williams has characterized as 'a freemasonry of organic intellectuals from the excluded classes': artisans, dissenters and radicals.[47] Perhaps inspired by the example of William Stukeley, Iolo convinced himself and the world that he and his friend Edward Evans had inherited the mantle of the Druids, and held the first recorded 'Druidic' ceremony on Primrose Hill in 1792.

Returning to Wales, he set up a network of 'Gorseddau' – bardic cells – around the country, and proceeded to create 'a druidic corpus of lore for them'. This canon, composed of ancient works both ancient and, um, modern, served the nascent Welsh sense of nationality very well indeed. His concept of the 'Gorsedd of Bards' was grafted onto the newly revived Welsh cultural festivals (*Eisteddfodau*), which from 1819 were held concurrently, with associated neo-Druidic ceremonial and the building of stone circles at each place in which the Eisteddfod was held; further 'druidic' ceremony of Ioloan inspiration was added in the late nineteenth century once the Welsh National Eisteddfod had become formally constituted in 1860.[48] All of which served to fix a view of Welsh prehistory that – like the high antiquity of the Friendly Societies – was exactly the opposite to the permanent 'State of Hostility' then being concocted in anthropological fantasy.

Chapter 5

The Politics of Socialism

Utopia or Destiny?

To Sir James Frazer and his peers, society without civilization was innately aggressive: the bonds of civilization were necessary to keep evil human instincts in check. To many socialists, however, 'civilization' itself was the problem. Edward Carpenter's influential *Civilisation: Its Cause and Cure*, first published in 1889, saw civilization simply as a phase, 'a definite stage through which the various nations pass', and detected a 'tendency... towards a return to nature and community of human life. This is the way back to the lost Eden, or rather forward to the new Eden, of which the old was only a figure'.[1] His antipathy was shared by both William Morris and Friedrich Engels. To Morris, '[M]y *special* leading motive as a Socialist is hatred of civilization: my ideal of the new Society would not be satisfied unless that Society destroyed civilization.'[2] Engels similarly maintained that, '[s]ince civilization is founded on the exploitation of one class by another class, its whole development proceeds in a constant contradiction. Every step forward in production is at the same time a step backward in the position of the oppressed class, that is, of the great majority...'[3]

Both Morris and Engels believed in the inherent decency of humanity. People would live harmoniously together if the conditions were right. Their approach to civilization, however, was profoundly different, and very different schools of socialism developed from their ideas.

Both sought some kind of exemplar in the past. Engels' famous investigation into 'primitive communism' in *The Origin of the Family* (1884) closely followed that of Lewis Morgan's *Ancient Society* (1877). This classic statement of the case for social evolution nonetheless contained a whiff of wistfulness: 'the next higher plane of society ... *will be a revival, in a higher form, of the liberty, equality and fraternity of the ancient gentes*'. This phrase, italicized by Engels, was used to conclude his own account,[4] and on the face of it suggests that Engels was taking a distinctly benign view of antiquity. However, we are reminded, 'we must not forget that this organization was doomed'. Furthermore, these qualities managed to co-exist within a world of constant warfare. People were only nice to each other within their own tribe. 'Outside the tribe was outside the law. Wherever there was not an explicit treaty of peace, tribe was at war with tribe, and wars were waged with the cruelty which distinguishes man from other animals and which was only mitigated later by self-interest.'[5]

Even so, there was a fall from grace. 'The power of this primitive community had to be broken, and it was broken. But it was broken by influences which from the very start appear as a degradation, a fall from the simple moral greatness of the old gentile society. The lowest interests – base greed, brutal appetites, sordid avarice, selfish robbery of the common wealth – inaugurate the new, civilized, class society. It is by the vilest means – theft, violence, fraud, treason – that the old classless gentile society is undermined and overthrown...'[6]

Civilization would be succeeded by a new form of 'barbarism', vigorous, democratic, with full sexual equality, analogous to that of the Teutons which had replaced the 'slime' of the Roman world: 'All the vigorous and creative life which the Germans infused into the Roman world was barbarism. Only barbarians are able to rejuvenate a world in the throes of collapsing civilization. And precisely the highest stage of barbarism, to which and in which the Germans worked their way upward before the migrations, was the most favourable for this process. That explains everything.'[7]

Morris would have agreed with most of Engels' analysis, including his enthusiasm for Teutonic vigour, but he added an important new dimension by suggesting that the prevalence of prehistoric art demonstrated that these societies enjoyed 'a sense of pleasure and dignity even in the process of the acquisition of food'. Evoking that sense of pleasure and dignity was vital, since the *desire* for change was an essential ingredient in the creation of socialism: people had to feel 'a longing to bring about the complete change which will supplant civilization by communism'.[8] The beauty of the past could fuel this longing, particularly the beauty and the workmanship that Morris found in old buildings (and one of his many ventures was the creation of the Society for the Preservation of Ancient Buildings). This interest, he agreed, was 'romantic' –

> but what romance means is that capacity for a true conception of history, a power of making the past part of the present.[9]

It was his concern with such superstructural fripperies that led Engels to dismiss Morris as 'utopian'. This concept had been criticized by Marx in the *Communist Manifesto*, and the critique was developed by Engels. In *Socialism: Utopian and Scientific* (1880), Engels claimed that Utopia was too subjective. Utopian socialists saw their creed as 'the expression of absolute truth, reason and justice, and has only to be discovered to conquer all the world by virtue of its own power. And as absolute truth is independent of time, space, and of the historical development of man, it is a mere accident when and where it is discovered.' But each school of socialism had a different set of 'absolute truths', which therefore cancelled each other out. 'To make a science of Socialism, it had first to be placed upon a real basis.' This involved collecting the 'facts' that

> more and more strenuously gave the lie to the teachings of bourgeois economy as to the identity of the interests of capital and labour . . . the new facts made imperative a new examination of all past history. Then it was seen that *all* past history, with the exception of its primitive stages, was the history of class struggles. . . . From that time forward Socialism was no longer an accidental discovery of this or that ingenious brain, but the necessary outcome of the struggle between two historically developed classes . . .[10]

The ingenious brain of Karl Marx had simply revealed the scientific process that was Communism. The forces of modern civilization – nationalism, urbanization, industrialization, the proletarianization of the workforce – just had to be accepted as steps along a road that would lead inevitably to civilization's own extinction. The 'progress agenda' was accepted wholeheartedly, because it would *inevitably* lead to something better. 'Desire' didn't come into it, and there was therefore no need to distract the proletariat with hypothetical role-models from the ancient past, or indeed any evocative ideas about how life might be in the future.

Aspiring to Socialism

This is the cardinal difference between Marxist Socialism and that of its competitors. People such as Morris believed that socialism had to be *aspired to*. There was nothing inevitable about it. People had to want it and to work for it, and to know what they wanted (and didn't want) they had to look back. Nor was this just rhetoric. William Morris' utopianism was of considerable importance in kick-starting mass socialism in Britain, especially through the activities of his disciple Robert Blatchford, whose *Merrie England*, published in 1893, sold two million copies: making it one of the most successful socialist publications of all time.[11] *Merrie England* – as the very title suggests – is no paean to progress; Blatchford firmly believed that the working classes were better off before the agricultural enclosures that forced them from the countryside, and the 'Merrie England' of his Utopia would consist of state farms supporting 'communal towns'.[12]

This is an allusion to the medieval 'craft guild', the idealized cooperative society that influenced much 'utopian' socialism at this date. Morris's conviction that mercantile capitalism was not progress but aberration provided the political underpinnings for the Arts and Crafts movement's medievalism, designed to restore dignity to the worker and beauty to the world: like his mentor Ruskin, Morris believed that the craft guilds of the Middle Ages had done both. In 1906, the architect Arthur Penty published his influential *Restoration of the Gild System*, in which he set out explicitly to marry the aspirations of Ruskin, Morris and Edward Carpenter with a practical programme for implementation: 'society by a reverence for the past may renew its lease of life. We live the life of the past to-day in our thoughts, to-morrow we may live it in reality.'[13]

Penty's ideas were taken up enthusiastically by his friend and fellow-socialist A R Orage, editor of *The New Age*, a journal which inspired thinkers on the 'romantic' left for several decades. Orage's form of socialism was a development of Morris'. In Martin's words, the 'idea of "progress" in the writings of most Liberals was entirely materialistic, and the Socialists, he felt, had uncritically accepted this usage. As a result, "progress", having no realistic object, became a continuous search for novelty.'[14] Orage accurately predicted the totalitarian tendencies latent in 'State Socialism', and espoused Guild Socialism as a decentralized alternative. It was a view that brought him into direct conflict with George Bernard Shaw and the grandees of the Fabian Society, the intellectual wing of the

Independent Labour Party, who set up their own journal (the *New Statesman*) to compete with the *New Age*.[15] The Fabians prevailed, of course. Guild Socialism foundered in the early 1920s. Morris lost out to Marx and Methodism, and people were beginning to forget that socialism before the Great War had been, in Orage's words, 'a cult, with affiliations in directions now quite disowned'.[16]

Predicting Progress

'Progress', already in disgrace once Britain lost its monopoly, took a major tumble with the Great War; and with it, the Victorian reverence for the past that the reformist historians had used to demonstrate its existence. To many on the Left, this veneration was a feature of the social system that had made the war possible: a deferential, hierarchical, repressive world whose leaders had used history to maintain their own position and stifle opposition. As an object of academic study, 'The Past' was consequently under suspicion; and those who worked with it were generally suspect themselves.[17] History teaching was hopelessly nationalistic. To Crawford history textbooks 'are as a rule completely out of touch with current ideas, and are "survivals", as functionless as the vermiform appendix'; like the appendix, they were 'dangerous anachronisms', tales of nationalism 'well calculated to jeopardize the fortunes of a project like the League of Nations'.[18]

The 'dirt archaeology' of the radicals was intended to cut through all this. Ownership of the past had become way too important to be left to antiquarian whimsy if its lessons were to be absorbed, and the new breed of archaeologists hoped to reclaim history of and for 'the common man', by using the techniques and methodologies of science. The spade was pitched against historical sophistry and the lies of the written word: 'the nameless Common Man, of all ages and places, was beginning to displace kings and quarterings as a primary object of study', as Mortimer Wheeler put it.[19]

Such caricatures tended to obscure more profound differences between the lessons that historians and archaeologists were drawing from the past. 'We naturally expect the Historian to travel over a wide extent of time, and probably of space likewise', said Thomas Hodgkin in 1891, urging archaeologists to collect 'facts which are worth collecting, facts which have some bearing . . . on the great historic interests of our country or our race'.[20] Three decades later, archaeologists sought to reverse these disciplinary attributes. E H Carr claims that there was a loss of nerve to be found amongst British historians, who were now steeped in a pessimistic 'fear of the future' that was typified by H A L Fisher, who rejected the idea that there was any pattern in history: 'progress is not a law of nature'.[21] The archaeologists, by contrast, were optimistic, gleefully annexing the grand vision abandoned by the historians to justify their faith in progress. The *longue durée* ('long term') became central to archaeology's *raison d'être*:

> We deal wholesale in time; and having strengthened our vision by scanning the vistas of the past, we find that we can also view the future with less uncertainty. We may not be able yet, perhaps, to see far into it, but we have acquired the time-habit of mind, and that is what matters. We no longer live from day to day; we take long views.[22]

Crawford's stirring definition allowed archaeologists to put the Great War into context. It was just one event in half a million years of events, and social evolution could demonstrate that the underlying trend was always up.

The doubts of the historians, however, were widely shared by the public at large. To many people, the carnage of 1914–18 simply confirmed the reality of human 'degeneration'. Oswald Spengler's influential *Decline of the West* (1922) took the war as demonstrating not just humanity's innate violence, but that civilization was no longer capable of containing it. Western civilization had reached the end of its cycle. It was a view that had to be confronted if the public was to be reassured about the reality of progress, and in the first year of *Antiquity*, Crawford persuaded R G Collingwood, Oxford University Lecturer in Philosophy and Roman History, to write a closely reasoned two-part article rebutting Spengler's belief in a cyclical view of history that gave prophetic status to his views. Collingwood concluded that the historical cycle was a social construction, 'incidental to a point of view. The cycle is the historian's field of vision in a given moment.' History, he said, could not predict the future, thereby refuting not only Spengler but 'the crowd of sociological writers, led by Marx, who have made just that claim'.[23] The *possibility* of progress was thus reinstated, but Collingwood's paper hardly supported Crawford's contention that archaeologists could 'view the future with less uncertainty'.

Undaunted, Crawford invoked the *longue durée* to propose a role for the archaeologist as expert adviser on current affairs. Flinders Petrie, interviewed in 1930, maintained that

> The value of archaeology is to discover the histories of other nations, to bring to light the reasons why they became powerful and why they fell. Our work is to provide the world with data to avoid the mistakes of those who have gone before us. We have revealed the fall of the Romans and the causes for that fall, and we present the results of our investigations to the Governments of today. They must act upon them.

This passage was quoted by Crawford in an *Antiquity* editorial, endorsed as 'the ultimate aims of archaeology, concisely'.[24] He could not, however, abandon the idea of predetermination. Petrie, back in 1911, had written a short work entitled *The Revolutions of Civilisation*, in which he had essentially reiterated the 'decline and fall' trope. It was roundly slated by Collingwood in his *Antiquity* article, prompting a tart rejoinder from Petrie.[25] In 1931, Crawford published a remarkable piece on *Historical Cycles*, written by himself, in which he took Petrie's work as a starting-point (he had 'proved his case quite conclusively'), claiming that he had no space to 'anticipate objections' or 'to deal with criticisms'. New work in the biological sciences appeared to place cultural evolution in the context of biological evolution. 'What the cell is to the human body, the human body is to the world-state', which was to be 'the ultimate achievement . . . in which the whole human race shall be organized as a single social organism'. The whole process tended to suggest

> that life evolves in a spiral. It begins with a single cell. After countless ages of complex development an organism is evolved which becomes in its turn the unit of another cycle. We are back where we started but on a higher plane.[26]

The concept of the spiral of progress was taken up by other archaeologists, notably Stanley Casson, one of *Antiquity*'s most prolific contributors, in his *Progress and Catastrophe* (1937), Stuart Piggott in *The Progress of Early Man* (1935), and above all Gordon Childe, who concluded his *What Happened in History*, written in 1942 when the world was once more at war, with a reiteration of Crawford's premise: 'Progress is real if discontinuous . . . no trough ever declines to the low level of the preceding one; each crest out-tops its last precursor'.[27]

Socialist Evolution

Crawford's article was coy about analysing the signs of cyclicality to be read in the contemporary world, but elsewhere he was more forthright. The year after 'Historical Cycles' appeared, Crawford visited the Soviet Union and was impressed by the 'practical Marxian anthropology' he found in its museums. On his return, he wrote an article entitled 'Putting *The Past* in Its *Place*', for *Russia To-day*, in which the Russian Revolution was described as 'by universal consent, an epoch-making event; and archaeologicals [*sic*] (who make museums) are chiefly concerned with epochs'.[28] His views were spelt out in further detail in a lengthy letter to his friend Neil Hunter, written in 1933:

> The Cycle theory needs to be restated by a Marxist, but even in its present form it undoubtedly reflects a good bit of historical truth... There are many objective correspondences (1) between the present epoch of the break-up of Capitalism and the break-up of the Roman Empire and (2) between the emergence of Christianity and the emergence of Communism.[29]

Crawford's belief in the Marxist version of social evolution was the source of his archaeological optimism, and he took the idea very literally: no doubt inspired by his trip to the Soviet Union, he daydreamed about creating a 'Museum of Human Evolution' that would be 'a link in a chain extending backwards into the geological and astronomical past, and forwards into the future of planned Socialist economy'.[30] Socialism *à la* Marx had a central role to play in the development of inter-war archaeology – to Crawford, it was 'the natural corollary of science in human affairs'.[31] His views were shared by his friend and fellow-archaeologist Gordon Childe (1892–1957), who suggested, in *Man Makes Himself*, published in 1936 soon after his own visit to the Soviet Union, that the common people were largely responsible for the technical innovations of prehistory, which they achieved *in spite of* the élite classes who maintained their authority by a mixture of military might and superstition.[32]

Demonstrating the reality of progress was an important theme of Childe's work. The prospectus for his first course at Edinburgh, in 1927, promised students that 'archaeological remains [are] always treated as concrete embodiments of Man's progress in culture'.[33] Reaffirming faith in progress, in the face of economic depression, was an explicit intention of *Man Makes Himself*, which begins by acknowledging the 'rude shock' that Victorian progress had received: 'The World War and subsequent crises, producing even in the midst of horrible poverty an apparent surplus of goods, have undermined its economic foundations.' He admits that '[d]oubts as to the reality of "progress" have been widely entertained'; and like Crawford invokes the *longue durée* as a reason for crediting the archaeologists' optimism:

> from an impersonal scientific standpoint, history may still justify a belief in progress in days of depression as well as in the heyday of last century's prosperity... by the inclusion of prehistory the purview of history is extended a hundredfold. We survey a period of over 500,000 years, instead of a beggarly 5000.[34]

Crawford used his *Antiquity* review of *Man Makes Himself* to reaffirm his view of the archaeologist as seer:

> what social changes should we expect to result from the Third (Industrial) Revolution? The answer is being written today on the map of the world in letters of blood. But it becomes intelligible only to those who have a sure grasp of the main, essential facts of human history as a whole. Then the forces arrayed against each other can be seen in their true historical relationship... and against their economic background, unobscured by nationalist, political or religious facades.[35]

Archaeology was *progressive*. It had a major part to play in shaping the future; indeed, that was its primary justification. As Wheeler wrote to Crawford, 'The Future is on our side, but it ain't no good unless it is also the present. The present and the future are all that matters to us *real* archaeologists. The past is merely an impediment.'[36]

Naturalizing Progress

It is hard to quantify the extent of 'active socialism' amongst inter-war archaeologists. Bill Wedlake, site foreman on the Maiden Castle excavation in the mid-Thirties, was surprised to find 'strong Marxist tendencies' amongst the Cambridge graduate students he was working with: 'they were rebels against their family background and had a genuine dislike of the "set-up" as they found it in Britain and seemed determined to do something about it'.[37] Socialist sympathies were by no means universal, however; and Crawford learnt from 'rather bitter experience', as he told

H G Wells in 1940, to avoid being too overt about his own views in *Antiquity*.[38]

As far as the 'spiral of progress' was concerned, he did not need to; for in practice, the premise of progress inherent in Marxian socialism dovetailed with the now-traditional discourse of social evolution, in which both nationalism and Eurocentrism played a major part.

Nationalist archaeology between the wars received a significant theoretical boost from the concept of geographically bounded 'archaeological cultures'. The idea was conceived independently by Gustaf Kossinna in Germany, who applied himself to developing an Aryan prehistory; and, ironically enough, by that great internationalist Gordon Childe, who just as energetically dedicated himself to refuting Kossinna. Archaeological historians such as Bruce Trigger and Glyn Daniel are at pains to stress the novelty of Childe's 'cultural-historical' approach; Daniel, indeed, called Childe's *Dawn of European Civilisation* (1926) 'a new starting-point for archaeology'.[39] It could equally be argued that the new approach served to confirm archaeology's role as the handmaid of history, since it provided 'deep time' corroboration to the now-traditional genre of nationalist histories. Nationally bounded archaeological textbooks now appeared, such as Cyril Fox's influential *The Personality of Britain* (1932), which eulogized 'the essential Britain, wherein Man ensconced himself so snugly'.[40] At Cambridge, undergraduates who wanted to study archaeology full-time combined Miles Burkitt's 'Section A' with Hector Chadwick's 'Section B', in which this professor of Anglo-Saxon inculcated them with a largely book-based proto-history of northern Europe.[41] Taken together, the student could pursue the history of 'humanity' from the Palaeolithic to the Norman Conquest . . .

This is not to say that British archaeology was consciously nationalist. Crawford himself believed that archaeology, as the history of the whole species, could play an important role in breaking down nationalism: '[the] idea of the unity of man has been steadily growing all over the world amongst thinkers and amongst the "working classes" '.[42] But in practice, this tended to translate into the pursuit for the origins of European civilization. This was implicit in the classical tradition that gave both anthropology and archaeology their first tenuous academic credentials. '[T]he track of advance that leads past Athens and Rome', declared Marett in 1908, 'remains the central and decisive path of social evolution',[43] and it was followed wholeheartedly by Grahame Clark, who felt that archaeology could demonstrate that European civilization was 'a peculiar and individual manifestation of the human spirit'.[44] European civilization, of course, was well 'in advance' of less fortunate parts of the world. As late as 1961, in his *World Prehistory: An Outline*, Clark maintained that Africa 'had already during Late Pleistocene times slipped far behind in the race of progress'.[45]

Naturalizing Nastiness

The functionalism of inter-war archaeology tended to confirm the inferior status of ancient peoples. Bowden has noticed that Crawford was 'entirely environmentally deterministic ... He believed that people in traditional societies invested all their time and effort in the struggle for survival.'[46] Food came first. He praised Childe for having 'taught us that ... the rise of civilization was dependent upon *bread*'.[47] The acquisition of 'civilization' was to be interpreted in terms of a steadily-increasing autonomy from natural constraints, the 'struggle against nature'.[48] Primitive man was strictly *homo faber*, 'Man the Maker'. It was a convenient conclusion for a discipline that relied upon analysing artefacts for its existence.

It was also a reaffirmation of nineteenth-century ideas on social evolution. Human progress, whether conceived in Marxist, racist, nationalist or any other terms, remained a concept which required an upward trajectory from a very low starting-point; and the inter-war archaeologists continued to paint a truly bleak picture of early humanity. To Childe, life in the Palaeolithic was a 'constant struggle to snatch a bare livelihood';[49] to Stuart Piggott 'Life was insecure – a constant battle for the essentials of food, shelter, warmth, existence itself.' Mocking the notion of the 'Simple Life or the Noble Savage' as a luxury of people 'living in a high state of society', Piggott claimed that 'if we look at the facts we are bound to conclude that the life of the most primitive men were, in Hobbes' classic phrase, "nasty, brutish and shorte" '.[50] Flinders Petrie agreed: 'This Rousseauism is nonsense', he wrote in his *Antiquity* review of H J Massingham's *The Golden Age*. 'It is no use to bleat for paradise ... the candle of civilization is worth the tallow.'[51] To Clark, prehistoric unpleasantness was self-evident: 'it was by their hands that the early Europeans dragged themselves out of the primeval mire of savagery, struggled up the long and undulating slopes of barbarism and ultimately attained to some kind of civilization'.[52]

In conclusion, although the reformers hoped that the new science of archaeology would retrieve the history of the 'common man', there was a marked gulf between intention and result. By lending renewed respectability to notions of 'progress', they brought the time-depth of the *longue durée* to the aid of the status quo. They placed all humanity's hopes in a progress whose course they felt able to predict with almost astrological certainty; and in the process they showed little empathy for the peoples they were studying, of inherent interest only in their display of evolutionary strategies. The result was that the infant discipline found itself tangled up in some fundamental, a priori assumptions about its subject-matter – prehistoric people – that were inherited, with only minor modifications, from the hard primitivism of the nineteenth century.

Chapter 6

The Diffusion Heresy: Nurture and the Primitive

Scientific archaeology had no monopoly on ideas about the ancient past. There were plenty of other contenders, many of whom drew upon the older tradition espoused by socialists of the William Morris ilk. One particular set of ideas managed to set the academy ablaze. This was the Diffusionist revival (often called 'hyperdiffusion'), a product of the backlash to evolutionism. After Darwin, most anthropologists looked to racial differences to explain social change or lack of it. The Diffusionists, however, posited a unique source of civilization: Egypt, from whence it was subsequently 'diffused' around the world, but that is the least interesting aspect of their argument. To them, civilization was very much a mixed blessing, driven by warfare and imposed by a warrior élite on a humanity that was otherwise peaceful.

The Diffusion Project

Diffusionism's main proponent was Grafton Elliot Smith (1871–1937), an Australian-born, Cambridge-trained anatomist who in 1900 became the first Professor of Anatomy in the new government medical school in Cairo. There he met William Halse Rivers, also from Cambridge and considered by some to be both the foremost British anthropologist and psychologist of his day. Rivers invited Smith to examine predynastic mummies: an encounter which, he later claimed, was responsible for 'drawing me into anthropology'.[1] Smith was soon involved in studying the mummification process, both in the field and in the laboratory, and through his massive labours on the salvage archaeology project at the Aswan Dam in 1907 ('supervising the study of six thousand skeletons and mummies in the first season alone') became established as one of the world's leading palaeoanatomists.[2] Smith was much preoccupied with trying to understand *why* the Egyptians had gone to such trouble to embalm their leaders, and slowly developed the idea that they travelled far and wide in search of 'givers of life' that would restore life to the dead: expeditions that eventually resulted in the colonization of the world by an élite warrior caste. In 1909, Elliot Smith became Professor of Anatomy at the Victoria University of Manchester, and used his new position to promote the theory, first publicly expounded in *The Ancient Egyptians and Their Influence upon the Civilization of Europe*, published in 1911.

Nature or Nurture?

Elliot Smith's ideas were firmly grounded in his palaeoanatomy. He argued, against the *doyen* Arthur Keith, that humankind had been recognizably human for a relatively short period of time, and certainly not long enough for existing 'higher' races to have evolved from 'lower' ones. Differences between races had therefore to be explained in terms of culture change, not genetic change, and to him these were 'unquestionably the direct effects of migration and the intermingling of races and culture'.[3]

To Smith, the evolutionary catalyst for *homo sapiens*' large brain was not the result of struggle, whether against other species or members of its own, but the long gestation that he claimed for proto-humanity in the relative safety of the trees. Emergence from the trees was thus a choice: freed from the over-specialization that condemned other species to evolve in highly specific ways, humanity's intelligent forebears chose to come out 'from their original forest home, and in troops invaded the open country, led no doubt by the search for a more plentiful supply or a more appetizing variety of food'.[4]

Peter Bowler suggests that Smith's hypothesis was a response to the uncomfortable early-century realization that Darwinian evolution ruled out teleological predictability. Smith restored teleology by defining a 'main stem' of primate evolution, from which non-humans were but lesser offshoots, evolutionary experiments on the high road to humanity.[5] Henrika Kuklick takes a rather different view, suggesting that it was precisely the need to make sense of Darwinian unpredictability that dictated the 'absurdity' of Smith's Diffusionist vision: 'the origin of a new civilization was an unpredictable, chance variation, just as the origin of a new species was. Originating in a single place, a new species of culture became dispersed through migration to various locations, there to undergo adaptation to local conditions.'[6] Civilization, in Smith's words, was 'a wholly artificial and unnatural outgrowth of human thought and activity':[7] a cultural product in today's parlance, whose development was largely determined by cultural factors and not natural ones.

Arthur Keith, by contrast, drew upon the work of Sollas and Pearson to formulate an influential form of social Darwinism. In order to extend human chronology sufficiently to allow enough time for 'higher' races to have evolved from 'lower' ones, Keith seized with alacrity on hominid fossil evidence such as the finds at Galley Hill and, later, Piltdown to demonstrate that humanity had been on the planet for a great deal longer than had been thought.[8] Competition was the mechanism by which the different species of 'fossil man' had competed for survival, and the same

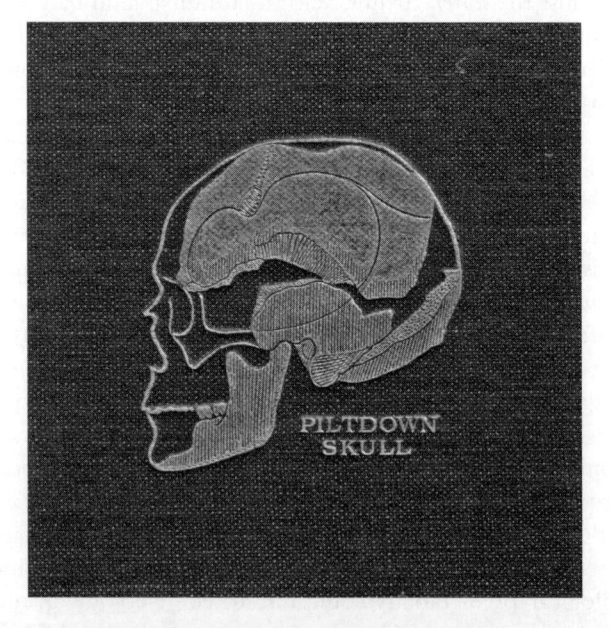

6 The discovery of 'Piltdown Man' in 1912, lent credence to the racial theories of Arthur Keith. This embossed impression of the skull adorned the cover of his 1915 book, *The Antiquity of Man*. Piltdown Man was exposed as a hoax in 1953, although the hoaxer has never been identified.

process was to be seen at work today: 'certain races are becoming dominant; others are disappearing. The competition is world-wide and lies between varieties of the same species of man.'[9]

The outbreak of war seemed to confirm Keith's position. In August 1914, large numbers of men from all over Europe volunteered to fight for their 'tribal territories', and Keith began to disseminate his ideas with growing confidence. In an 'Additional Note to Preface' to his *The Antiquity of Man*, dated July 1915, Keith claimed that the book had been completed before the war had begun – since when 'we have burst suddenly into a critical phase in the evolutionary progress of mankind'. This, he believed, gave the book a new topicality: 'The author hopes there may be some who will wish to survey the issues of the present fateful period from the distant standpoint of a student of man's early evolution.'[10]

The Antiquity of Man was published in October 1915.[11] In the same month, Keith gave a lecture to the students of St Thomas's Hospital in which he argued that racial competition functioned as the chief agent of human evolution, and that war was its tool: 'To my way of thinking this war is not an isolated event; it is part of the real biological processes which shape the future of living races.' Nationalism, the clash and the forging of nations, was evolution in action. Germany, France, America, all 'are race builders in a true Darwinian sense'; and he repeated his claims in his Presidential Address to the Royal Anthropological Institute in January 1916, drawing upon eugenicist notions such as Francis Galton's 'law of tribes', and William McDougall's theories of primal pugnacity, to substantiate his claim that 'the tribe was nature's evolutionary unit'.[12]

Shell-Shock and the Nature of War

Elliot Smith's views could not have been more different, but he also found them confirmed by the war: as a result of the war-work which he and Rivers undertook on shell-shock victims. His interest in brain structure had already led him to investigate psychology, a discipline which, although elsewhere seen as decidedly suspect, had established a firm base at his own University of Manchester. Smith had given lectures to psychology students on the brain and the sense organs, and greatly encouraged the young psychologist Thomas Hatherley Pear, who in turn had become a valuable ally in diffusing Diffusion, 'teaching our stuff on his course on social psychology', in Smith's words, 'and asked questions on it in the examination – to the great surprise of his external examiner'.[13]

Even before the war Elliot Smith had taken an interest in mental health reform, advocating the need for research in psychiatry;[14] in July 1915, he became a voluntary 'physician' at the Maghull War Hospital near Liverpool, where he and Pear joined a team of distinguished psychologists and anthropologists who were investigating the causes of shell-shock and endeavouring to treat it.[15] During the first half of the war, the military authorities had been reluctant to concede that such a thing as 'shell-shock' existed. In accordance with prevalent thinking, mental disorders among soldiers were attributed to hereditary mental feebleness, if not simple cowardice, to be punished accordingly. However, the sheer weight of numbers – 200,000 men were eventually discharged from active service for being 'mentally incapable'[16] – forced a change of attitude.

At Maghull, the discrepancy between the theory and the reality of war psychology was daily made manifest. The Diffusionist experience of the war was not one of races clashing for evolutionary destinies, but of individuals suffering massive trauma. Their 600 patients, in Pear's words, 'did not fit' into the 'new pattern of so-called civilization':

> Thousands of civilized Britons had failed to adapt themselves to the sudden unexpected change from peace to a life of hatred (which often had to be instilled), violence, atrocities and counter-atrocities, the possibility of burial alive, the fear and boredom of the trenches, the feeling that they had been let down, the tragic 'accidents' inside our own lines – such facts contradicted complacent early reports from the front (before trench warfare had become common) that men who cracked up were poor types who would eventually have broken down even in peace-time.[17]

Elliot Smith played a pivotal role in forcing the change in attitude to shell-shock victims. He threw himself into his new task with enthusiasm; two days after he was appointed he claimed to be already 'doing *real* psychology',[18] and he and Pear took it upon themselves to act as informal press officers for the project. He submitted a provocative paper to the *Eugenics Review* in which he claimed that the war was demonstrating 'the importance of early experience and education upon the mental and moral characteristics of each and every unit of the nation'.[19] By November 1915, Smith had produced a first draft of a paper on the work at Maghull, supplemented by research into 'the foreign medical journals', which was published in next April's *Lancet* under the title of 'Shock and the Soldier'. A 'stream of requests for fuller information' led him and Pear to revise and expand their work, which was published in book form as *Shell Shock and its Lessons* in April 1917.[20]

Shell Shock proved to be a turning point in the understanding and acceptance of psychological disorders. The authors claimed that

> The war has shown us one indisputable fact, that a psychoneurosis may be produced in almost anyone if only his environment be made 'difficult' enough for him. It has warned us that the pessimistic, helpless appeal to heredity, so common in the case of insanity must [be abandoned]... In the causation of the psychoneuroses, heredity undoubtedly counts, but social and material environment count infinitely more.[21]

Their case was greatly bolstered by the fact that, prior to the introduction of conscription in 1916, the victims of shell-shock were volunteers: 'men who before the war were the strongest, bravest, most daring, yet level-headed, members of the community', as they triumphantly replied to a hostile reviewer in *Nature*, critical of 'the great stress laid upon nurture rather than nature, which shows the authors to be out-and-out environmentalists'.[22] Shell-shock was a perfectly 'natural' reaction to an unnatural situation: there was nothing 'natural' about the First World War.

Rivers and Freud

According to Shephard, the pamphlet had an 'enormous' influence on an increasingly anxious and disillusioned public.[23] It certainly did much to enhance the reputation of Maghull, where, Shephard claims, Elliot Smith became the 'dominant personality'.[24] He himself claimed to have merely played 'some small part' in the process; and that in this, as in matters anthropological, he was content to follow the intellectual lead of Rivers, whom he had convinced to join the Maghull team within weeks of his own arrival.[25] Rivers' belief in the supremacy of cultural factors over racial ones, and his consequent suspicion of social evolution, was based upon his experience as part of the Cambridge Anthropological Expedition to the Torres Straits in 1898–9, during which the researchers conducted psychological tests upon islanders and Europeans, and found little difference: 'whatever variations obtained between the sensory skills of primitives and Europeans had to be products of cultural conditioning rather than biological propensities', in the words of Henrika Kuklick.[26]

Rivers, by now a renowned experimental psychologist, saw the war as 'a vast crucible in which all our preconceived views concerning human nature have been tested'. Sigmund Freud's controversial views on

7 W H R Rivers (left) and Grafton Elliot Smith at Maghull Military Hospital, 1915. (*Clay Dillingham*).

subconscious motivations were particularly relevant; in Rivers' words, 'It is a wonderful turn of fate that just as Freud's theory of the unconscious and the method of psycho-analysis founded upon it should be so hotly discussed, there should have occurred events which have produced on an enormous scale just those conditions of paralysis and contraction, phobia and obsession, which they were especially designed to explain.'[27]

At Maghull, Pear gave Rivers a crash-course in Freudian theory at his own behest, and the Viennese scholar's work helped shape all their activities.[28] Yet Rivers' enthusiastic endorsement of Freud's methodology led him almost immediately to a rather different conclusion about basic human instinct:

> The first result of the dispassionate study of the psycho-neuroses of warfare, in relation to Freud's scheme, was to show that in the vast majority of cases there is no reason to suppose that factors derived from the sexual life played any essential part in causation, but that these disorders became explicable

as the result of disturbance of another instinct, one even more fundamental than that of sex – the instinct of self-preservation, especially those forms of it which are adapted to protect the animal from danger.[29]

Overcoming the 'instinct for self-preservation' took a great deal of training; the preparation 'which long ages have shown to be the means by which man is adapted to warfare'.[30] The results of inadequate preparation, as hundreds of thousands of soldiers were shipped to the Front after the briefest of training periods, were made manifest in the war-neuroses that could no longer be denied. Warriors are made, not born. Pugnacity had to be inculcated: *homo pugnax* was a product of nurture, and not nature.

Psychology and Archaeology

In this manner, the nature–nurture argument between Evolutionists and Diffusionists spilled over into psychology. Freud, like Rivers, was deeply interested in the relationship between psychology and early human society. Freud's interest in archaeology both as practice and as metaphor is well attested; words such as 'archaic' and 'prehistoric' were commonplace in his works to describe early phases of human development; childhood he described as 'the prehistoric epoch'.[31] By 1916, he felt sufficiently confident to match his new discipline against that of archaeology as a more promising source of information about the ancient past: 'It is in the psychology of neuroses, and not archaeology, that one finds more of the antiquities of human development than any other source.'[32] With this the Diffusionists agreed: to Smith, 'the interpretation of ethnological material is essentially a problem in psychology, an analysis of the motives that propelled men to act in certain ways, and the reconstruction of the history of events'.[33]

Freud's 'archaeology', however, was firmly rooted in the bleak anthropology of his peers. The Oedipus complex implied a primeval parricide that Freud believed had happened; primitive man 'was, in truth, a very violent being, more cruel and more malign than other animals. He liked to kill, and killed as a matter of course.' Modern humanity springs 'from an endless ancestry of murderers'; war – including the Great War that prompted his musings – 'strips us of the later accretions of civilization, and lays bare the primal man in each of us'. Civilization was thus a construct, paralleled by an individual process of 'censorship', designed to hold humanity's aggressive impulse in check, 'to keep watch over it, like a garrison in a conquered city'.[34]

The Diffusionists took the opposite view. Working daily with servicemen who lacked the inner 'primal man' lusting for the fight, they found that war neurosis was bringing up traumas from the childhood of the individual and not the childhood of the species. Individual experience could not be generalized, and Elliot Smith took Freud's followers to task for trying to force the dreams and experiences of individual patients into 'the same uniform mould' in order to fit their evolutionary expectations.[35]

There were significant political implications. Freud's analysis, like the social evolution in which it was grounded, served to justify the *status quo*: as Philip Rieff says, the lesson of *Totem and Taboo*, his 1913 essay which introduced the Oedipus complex to the world, is 'the necessity of authority'.[36] Rivers suggested that Freud's concept of an inner 'censorship', far from keeping violent instincts in check, had all the hallmarks of an *external*, socially constructed concept that served a very similar process to 'censorship' in its usual sense, and constituted 'a very small part of the total mass of inhibiting forces by which more recently developed social groups control tendencies belonging to an older social order'. Freud's 'censorship' was lifted only in sleep, when the subconscious was allowed free reign in dreams. Rivers suggested that the 'nightmare' of revolution was the direct result of social repression: 'the processes of suppression and distortion point to some fault in the social order, to some interference with the harmony and unity which should characterize the acts of a perfectly organized society'.[37]

Perry and the Peaceful Primitive

Maghull led the Diffusionists to re-evaluate the foundations of social evolution. In 'Thoughts for the Times on War and Death', written in 1915, Freud dismissed out of hand the notion that people were born innocent.[38] The Diffusionists' work, however, was revealing *individual* traumas, not universal ones. People were essentially innocent until warped by experience. If the growth of 'civilization', and not natural instinct, was to blame for violence, it followed that societies with little 'civilization' were also free from warfare.

The idea, it seems, first came to William James Perry (1887–1949), the third and perhaps the most interesting of the Diffusionist trio. Perry and Rivers first met in 1910, when Perry was a Mathematics undergraduate

The Diffusion Heresy: Nurture and the Primitive 83

at Cambridge. He became keenly interested in anthropology, attending lectures by both Rivers and A C Haddon.[39] After graduation, he taught maths and 'physiography' (physical geography) at Pocklington School in Yorkshire; but he stayed in close contact with Rivers, who in 1913 invited him to investigate the relationship between megalithic monuments and sun-cults in Indonesia. Perry was soon convinced that there was a clear correlation between the geographical siting of megalithic structures and the presence of metals, particularly gold. His findings appeared to provide a motive for Elliot Smith's Egyptian explorers, and before the end of 1914 Rivers had introduced him to Smith, who gave him a prominent platform for his ideas at the 1915 meeting of the British Association for the Advancement of Science, which that year was fortuitously held in Manchester.[40]

Perry took an active part in the various clubs and societies at the school where he taught, and the school magazine throws some valuable light on the development of his ideas. It seems that the popular maths teacher took a distinctly 'advanced' stand on issues of the day, from Women's Suffrage to the 'Yellow Peril'. His anti-conscription stance in 1912, in which he claimed that Germany could not afford to go to war, was clearly derived from the ideas of the pacifist Norman Angell, whose book *The Great Illusion* (1909) had aroused much interest, and later ridicule (though in 1922, when the costs of the war were being counted, Perry felt that Angell had been vindicated).[41] In 1913 he argued that 'civilization does not conduce to the benefit of mankind', pointing out 'the evil effects of civilization on the savage races with which it had come into contact'.[42] This oblique critique of colonial policy was later developed by Rivers;[43] Perry's great contribution was to extend the analogy into prehistory.

Early in 1916, Perry wrote to Smith suggesting that warfare had been diffused in antiquity by 'military aristocracies' which, from an account of a talk he gave at his school in March, he was already calling 'the Children of the Sun'. They were 'the first teachers of warfare and head-hunting', innovations which they introduced to tribal peoples 'to whom warfare was unknown'.[44] Smith was very impressed. He considered Perry's idea to be 'simply splendid', and promptly suggested that he should 'publish it in stiff covers as a book. The Univ. Press here would probably jump at it.' Rivers too was enthusiastic: 'It is a splendid idea and it will be most exciting to see how it catches on.'[45]

Perry's preliminary paper was duly sent to two national reviews, but was rejected by both. Elliot Smith offered to try to get it published himself, but Perry by now was unsure: in October, Smith told Rivers that

Perry considered it 'so crude that I am not to get it published', even though, as he added, James Bryce, the veteran Liberal historian and one of Manchester University's founding fathers, had just sent Smith a paper of his own which Smith claimed was 'feeling towards Perry's point of view'.[46] Bryce's paper, 'War and Human Progress', rhetorically re-branded Keithian notions of racial struggles as an unpleasantly Germanic quality: the aggression of Germany had forced better races into a war they didn't want. Bryce duly dissected the 'biological-drive-to-warfare' trope, under the guise of analysing German motives, and concluded that survival-of-the-fittest arguments were worthless. Warfare was not a necessary constituent of progress; war had 'causes' that could be removed by the 'friendly cooperation' of nations.[47]

Bryce, as President of the British Academy, issued a personal invitation to Elliot Smith to deliver his paper on 'Primitive Man' to the Academy in November 1916.[48] In it, Smith echoes Bryce's dismissal of inherent racial pugnacity, and refers to the Maghull work on shell-shock as evidence for the 'enormous' role that social conditioning plays in determining human behaviour. Smith maintained that 'the human spirit has ever remained the same ... human nature is based upon the same primitive instincts and emotions ... There is no innate tendency in man to be progressive.' Only the 'definite and explicit circumstances' of the Near East could explain how the process of civilization began. Citing Perry's still-unpublished paper, he argued that prior to the introduction of agriculture

> the world really enjoyed some such Golden Age of peace as Hesiod has described. Man was not driven into warfare by his instinct for pugnacity, but by the greed for wealth and power which the development of civilization itself was responsible for creating.[49]

'Primitive Man' was delivered as the Battle of the Somme was petering out. Well over a million men had been killed – and with them, in A J P Taylor's words, 'the zest and idealism with which nearly three million Englishmen had marched forth to war'.[50] The paper went down well. 'The [Manchester University] Press tells me that there has been a run on all my stuff since my visit to London', Smith told Perry a month later.[51] Thus comforted, Perry accepted an invitation from the Manchester Literary & Philosophical Society to deliver a lecture the following April (1917), which was duly published under the title of 'An Ethnological Study of Warfare'.

The Diffusion Heresy: Nurture and the Primitive

This paper was framed as a response to William McDougall, whose doctrines on human belligerence had inspired Arthur Keith. Perry denied 'the natural pugnacity of mankind' and suggested instead that warfare was a by-product of a sun-worshipping aristocracy which had 'enslaved' peaceful populations around the world so that they might live a 'parasitic' existence: 'Does not their need of labour and wealth explain the utility of warfare to a governing class? It is a means of ensuring their own luxury and ease.' They, in turn, were not driven to 'the enslavement of humanity... from any innately cruel motive, but from that powerful stimulant which, once at work, will drive men to extremes – greed'. Not even the warrior caste was instinctively belligerent: it took a 'powerful stimulant', in the form of greed, to make them so.[52]

Perry next turned his attention to the Golden Age, with a contribution to a theological review, the *Hibbert Journal*, in October 1917. 'The Peaceable Habits of Primitive Communities: an Anthropological Study of the Golden Age' tested Hesiod's claim that a Golden Age had once existed with a rapid tour of primitive societies past and present. His conclusion was that Hesiod had been right, and there had been a Golden Age – a fact 'of supreme importance to mankind; for it shows that man is capable, in certain circumstances of moral behaviour'; and he suggested 'that our civilization is pathological in condition, a vast social organism suffering from a cancer that must be removed before amelioration can be hoped for'.[53]

Elliot Smith then arranged for Perry to lecture at his own university. It seems that Perry had wanted to wander from the theme a touch, but Smith kept him to the mark, insisting that 'War and Civilization' was to be the topic: ' "Priesthood" will do for times of peace the following year.'[54] 'War and Civilization' was duly delivered in the Rylands Library at Manchester in February 1918. The talk was a highly charged polemic:

> Warfare... appears to owe its origin to migrant military aristocracies... *Warfare is the means whereby the members of a parasitic ruling class of alien origin endeavour, while exploiting their own subjects, to dominate those surrounding peoples who produce wealth*... This process of exploitation and domination of the many by the few will last until the common people of the earth recognize their condition and become aware of their power... the very patience with which the peoples of this earth have submitted to domination, and their resignation under the most unjust and cruel treatment, constitute powerful evidence of the innate peacefulness of mankind.[55]

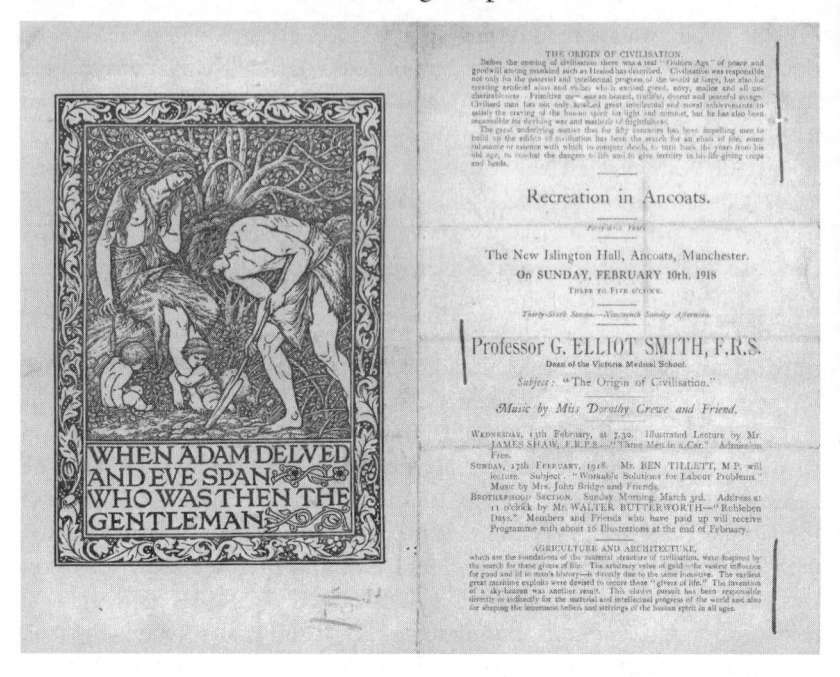

8 'Before the coming of civilisation there was a real "Golden Age" of peace and goodwill'. On 10 February 1918, Elliot Smith gave a talk on *The Origins of Civilisation* to the Ancoats Brotherhood in Manchester, who were much imbued with William Morris socialism. According to Smith, the talk was intended to 'prepare the way' for Perry's *War and Civilisation* broadside at the John Rylands library a week later. (*University College London, Library Services Special Collections*).

This was rousing stuff to deliver to a respectable audience just five months after the Russian Revolution; testimony not just to the strength of Perry's convictions but to a widespread sense that major political upheaval would follow in the wake of the war. It certainly did Perry no harm with the University of Manchester, for the following year (1919) he was appointed Reader in Comparative Religion.

The Children of the Sun

This surprising career-move, certainly engineered by Smith, was designed to allow Perry to develop the Diffusionist claim that dream symbolism

The Diffusion Heresy: Nurture and the Primitive 87

was akin to religion, and that both provided evidence, not only of the primeval diffusion of culture, but of the motivations behind it. Diffusionist interest in dreams began at Maghull, which constituted, in Rivers' words, 'a society in which the interpretation of dreams and the discussion of mental conflicts formed the staple subjects of conversation'.[56] In the evenings, Pear recalled, Elliot Smith and Rivers 'would talk, like priests, of mysteries', as Rivers began to consider the scope for integrating 'the processes of psychology and ethnology into one discipline'.[57]

In October 1916, Rivers was transferred to Craiglockhart Hospital near Edinburgh, where his empathy and insight won him the lifelong admiration of two young and disillusioned patients, Siegfried Sassoon and Robert Graves (a relationship explored in Pat Barker's *Regeneration* trilogy[58]). His closeness with Elliot Smith endured, however, and Sassoon recalled an evening not unlike Pear's, during which Smith and Rivers

> ... floated
> Through desiccated forests; mangled myths;
> And argued easily round megaliths.[59]

Under Smith's influence, Rivers finally 'went all the way' on Egyptian hyperdiffusion in 1918:[60] under Rivers' influence, Smith began to look more closely at the role of symbolism in the transmission of ideas. In 'Primitive Man', Elliot Smith had described the motives of the 'children of the sun' in terms of 'greed'.[61] Yet even 'acquisitiveness', as Rivers was to show, could be seen as a cultural construct.[62] The Maghull experience led Smith to probe more deeply:

> If we seek for the deep motives which have prompted men in all ages so persistently to search for the elixir of life, for some means of averting the dangers to which their existence is exposed, it will be found in the instinct of self-preservation, which is the fundamental factor in the behaviour of all living beings, the means of preservation of the life which is their distinctive attribute and the very essence of their being.[63]

The quotation is from Smith's *Evolution of the Dragon*, published in 1919. Maghull psychology is, as Smith acknowledged, 'manifest upon every page of this volume'.[64] Rivers' work into the significance of dreams convinced Smith that 'myth' and 'dream' had much in common: '[t]he myth resembles the dream because it has developed without any consistent and effective censorship'.[65] This allowed him to construct a hypothetical mythology, in which he set out his stall against James Frazer's *Golden Bough* whilst at the same time contriving to sound very much like his opponent. Symbols from cultures all around the world were claimed to represent deeper, underlying concepts whose universality, Smith claimed (unlike Frazer), was due to their diffusion from a single source. The ultimate 'giver-of-life' was the Great Mother Goddess, whose worldwide presence Smith detected in the cowrie shell, taken to represent the divine vagina (a singularly 'Freudian' interpretation, for a scholar loud in his plaints against the Viennese 'pornological' school[66]).

Elliot Smith in 1918 claimed to be writing a book on 'The Story of the Flood', which would tell 'the real story of mankind's age-long search for the elixir of life'; but in fact all future Diffusionist forays into the meaning of symbolism were to be undertaken by Perry, whose work, Smith claimed, was 'shedding a brilliant light upon the early history of civilization'.[67] A surviving list of Perry's Manchester lectures suggests that he saw his teaching role as an attempt to reconcile the ideas set out in *Evolution of the Dragon* with the work of Frazer, which – despite Smith – he admired.[68]

His main task, however, was to provide a history of the process by which the belief in immortality had developed in Egypt, and a detailed account of the Egyptians' global pursuit of the 'givers of life'. The fruits of his labours was a series of books, of which *Children of the Sun* (1923) and *The Growth of Civilization* (1924) became the best-known titles in the Diffusionist canon.

9 Elliot Smith (left) and W J Perry, with Perry's wife and daughter. (*Veryan Scott-Hayward*).

The Diffusion Heresy: Nurture and the Primitive

Children of the Sun purported to chronicle in depth the process by which the Egyptian explorer-caste and their descendants spread the 'Archaic Civilization' of sun-worshipping warriors around the world. Social evolution was turned upside-down. A new culture sequence was imposed upon the ancient history of the world, and Perry charted a widespread pattern of 'loss of culture' and the decline of civilizations to bolster his case. A warlike caste had imposed civilization upon a peaceful population, and the modern class-system was its direct descendant. Civilization was an aberration of the human mind, with minimal restraints from geography or nature, and this is where hope lay: 'when warfare is studied scientifically like any other social institution, it can be shown that mankind has undergone an education in organized violent behaviour'.[69] Armed with the knowledge that humanity was inherently peaceful and decent, the institution of warfare could be abolished.

Diffusionism caught the popular imagination in those post-war years. *Children of the Sun* and *The Growth of Civilisation* were both reprinted during the 1920s, and so was Massingham's *Downland Man*, acclaimed by the left-leaning *Manchester Guardian* as 'one of the most exciting books of history ever written'. Elliot Smith's *Human History* (1930) was on the *Observer*'s best-seller list, and sold out in three weeks.[70]

Their ideas were taken up with alacrity by organizations such as the British Federation of Youth. 'Those engaged in Peace work are constantly assailed with the assertion that war is inevitable, "Human Nature being what it is",' wrote the Chairman, Wilfred Pohl. Now, thanks to the work of the Diffusionists, 'we can re-educate ourselves back to a more peaceful mode of life'.[71] As Perry told Workers' Education Association members in 1931, 'the social scientist can set out on his task with the assurance that the golden age lies before us as well as behind us. That is the contribution of anthropology to the social sciences.'[72]

Chapter 7

Establishing Diffusion

Other anthropologists demurred. Anthropology was already a reputable and recognized academic discipline, if as yet only precariously institutionalized. Establishing the Diffusionist creed called out for little short of epistemic revolution, but that is what Elliot Smith and his colleagues set out to achieve. For a while, a combination of factors made it seem as though this might even be possible; but by the mid-1920s the whole edifice was crumbling. This chapter seeks to explain how the Diffusionists got as far as they did – and why they got no further. The intellectual reception of the Diffusionist project by the wider anthropological community has been painstakingly and convincingly reconstructed by Ian Langham (1981), who also throws some valuable light on the institutional context. I am attempting to tease out the importance of the institutionalization process itself both in establishing Diffusionism as a credible academic concept, and in its subsequent demolition.

The Manchester School

The Victoria University of Manchester, chartered in 1880, was Britain's first civic university. By 1909, when Elliot Smith became Professor of Anatomy, it had already acquired an enviable reputation for innovation: 'scientifically far and away ahead of all the newer English universities', as the zoologist John Graham Kerr told Smith upon his inauguration.[1] The University was adventurous, and willing to take risks. The suspect science of psychology acquired an early toehold at Manchester, and the School of History, under T F Tout, was one of the most innovative in the land.[2]

Manchester's newness made it an institution in which a scholar with an outstanding international reputation was sure to make a mark. Elliot Smith, as Dean of the Medical School, which had over a third of the total student population during the war years, was a prominent member of the University Senate and, according to a later Vice-Chancellor, did 'much to mould the destiny of the University at a time made unusually difficult by the War'.[3]

Smith was quick to exploit his institutional vantage-point. He joined the Manchester Egyptian Association as soon as he arrived, becoming President in 1910, and was influential, in both planning and detail, in the extension of the Manchester Museum to include Egyptian Antiquities. Warren Dawson astutely noticed that the 'literary resources of Manchester' played a major role in establishing Diffusionism at this critical stage in its development.[4] As Treasurer of the Manchester Oriental Society, Elliot Smith helped to publish its first *Journal* (1911), and was probably influential in the merger of the Egyptian and Oriental Societies in 1912. The *Journal* then became one of Elliot Smith's platforms.[5] Many of Smith's regular lectures in the John Rylands Library were collected and published by the Librarian, Henry Guppy. Others were reprinted in book form by Manchester University Press – a route also followed by the school of history, which Goldstein suggests was partially responsible for its growing reputation.[6]

Smith was not confined to University publications, however. Many of the Diffusionists' papers were first read to the revered Manchester Literary and Philosophical Society and subsequently published in their *Memoirs and Proceedings*. The 'Lit & Phil' was flattered by such attentions; as the *Manchester Guardian* recorded, in a full-column 'Appreciation' published when he left for the metropolis in 1919, 'the Society has on many occasions been honoured by receiving the first account of his important contributions to science'.[7]

Manchester Mythology

Elliot Smith soon attracted a group of scholars from many disciplines who were willing to assist in propagating, researching, publishing and generally diffusing what Smith was fond of calling 'the Diffusion heresy'. Sympathizers included Dr Guppy of the Rylands, Professor Maurice

Canney (head of the Oriental Department);[8] Dr J Wilfrid Jackson (Geology), Rendell Harris (Theology),[9] the psychologists Pear and Gleaves[10] and, briefly, the Egyptologists Alan Gardiner[11] and T Eric Peet.[12] Early converts outside Manchester included Professor Armitage of Leeds, who in 1916 was said to be 'preaching our gospel vigorously' using lantern-slides supplied by Smith; and the Scottish folklorist Donald Mackenzie.[13] In contrast to the speculation of the 'evolutionists', the Diffusionists considered their approach to be 'historical';[14] and in this they were succoured by Manchester historians such as George Unwin, who shared Perry's anti-militarism, socialism and antipathy to 'the State'. Unwin, Professor of Economic History, was credited by Perry with advice and help in preparing both *Children of the Sun* and *The Growth of Civilisation*; in the case of the former, indeed, Perry claimed that Unwin had suggested 'the scheme of the book'.[15]

Taken together, they constituted what the Cambridge anthropologist Jane Ellen Harrison described as 'a new school of mythology' with a thoroughly scientific and interdisciplinary approach to their subject:

> The Manchester School have their special characteristics. Mythology used to be the special province, almost the preserve, of classical scholars seeking to elucidate mythological allusions. Mythology is now seen for what it is, a form of primitive thinking, and its study is attended by Orientalists and men of science, psychologists and doctors; and naturally the new outlook is revolutionary.[16]

UCL: the Anatomy of Diffusion

Smith's institutional position was unassailable at Manchester, which until 1923 functioned as Diffusion's stronghold, an academic lair from which Smith and his colleagues would sally forth on raiding parties into other domains. In that year, the seat of Diffusionist operations transferred to the capital, where Perry, now Reader in Cultural Anthropology, presided over a Rockefeller-funded division of a prestigious and lavish new department.

The Rockefeller Foundation had been set up in 1913 by the oil tycoon John D Rockefeller to help him spend some of his money. Its mission was 'to promote the well-being of mankind throughout the world', and in its early years the Foundation's philanthropy was directed particularly at medicine. It was almost certainly Smith's reputation as an innovative anatomist that brought him to their attention. In *Shell Shock and its Lessons*, Smith and Pear had argued for the integration of research and clinical practice, as recommended by Abraham Flexner, the Foundation's medical adviser. In 1919, Elliot Smith left Manchester to take up the Chair of Anatomy at University College London, which had just begun to put a Flexner-style system in operation, and Smith was instrumental in persuading the Rockefeller Foundation to award UCL a massive grant, much of which was spent on the Department of Anatomy.[17]

At some point, Smith managed to persuade the Foundation to fund a Readership in Anthropology as well. He went to America in early 1920, and it is highly probable that he first mooted the possibility to Foundation officials then,[18] but the first explicit reference to establishing an 'Institute of Ethnology' at UCL seems to have appeared in an internal memorandum of 1921, which argued for the integration of ethnology and physical anthropology at UCL. Smith claimed that this decision had been taken because 'physical anthropology . . . cannot be separated from the study of culture without serious interference with its efficiency'. The new Reader was expected to work with the anatomists on 'integrating teaching and research in the study of man', but from the outset it was clear that his prime function was to foster the Diffusionist cause, since, as Smith told a colleague in 1926, '[w]e soon discovered that it was hopeless to solve any of the more difficult problems of physical anthropology unless one took into consideration the facts which led to the movements of people about the earth'.[19]

The new department made its mark. Raymond Dart, one of the first students, called it 'the fountain-head of information about human structure, prehistory, and an understanding of human bodily and mental activity'. H A Harris, one of Smith's anatomical protégés, described it affectionately as a 'bedlam' in which missionaries, miners and millionaires jostled for attention, and '[r]esident magistrates and anthropologists from all parts of the Empire came in and stayed for months on study leave'.[20] Gordon Childe may have been amongst the latter. Credited for 'help in preparation' of the second edition of Perry's *Growth of Civilisation* in 1926, Childe was then new to London and scratching around for work.[21] It seems possible that he was briefly on the UCL payroll; certainly, Smith supplied his fellow-Australian with a reference when he applied for the Abercromby Chair in 1927.[22] Other employees included the journalist H J Massingham, an enthusiastic supporter of the Diffusionist project, who was given 'a kind of roving commission to prospect the upland homes of prehistoric man in England and to act as their assistant both in research work and in preparing and editing their books for publication'.[23] His work culminated in the publication of *Downland Man* in 1926; explicitly written as a continuation of Perry's work on the Pacific and the Far East,[24] this book was an evocative blend of ruralism and Diffusionist archaeology that proved to be one of the Diffusionists' most successful texts.

Anthropological Terrorism

Perry's appointment was controversial. Smith published two descriptions of the new Department, in May and July 1923,[25] but although Perry was in post by October neither account makes any allusion to anthropology. The most economical explanation of this secrecy, particularly in view of Malinowski's later tactics, is that Smith did not want other anthropologists to know that the Rockefeller Foundation had agreed to fund a Readership until it was too late for them to try to stop it.

Even so, according to Harris, the new post 'raised a protest in many quarters'.[26] This was largely because the Diffusionists refused to enter into normal academic debate with their peers. Relations had been deteriorating steadily since the Diffusionists used the four successive annual British Association meetings between 1912 and 1915 to promote their work to an increasingly unsympathetic Anthropology Section. At every meeting, they were met with heated debate and marked hostility from other anthropologists that led to their virtual ostracism.[27] The Manchester Lit & Phil paid a price for opening their pages so freely to Diffusionism: in June 1916 the Society of Antiquaries decided to cease exchanging publications, a move which Smith saw as aimed at the Diffusionists (the Antiquaries' President, Sir Arthur Evans, was an outspoken critic).[28]

Academic recalcitrance was epitomized (to Smith at least) by the unwillingness of the Royal Anthropological Institute to publish the Diffusionist case in the pages of its periodicals, the *Journal of the RAI* and *Man*.[29] Indeed, he claimed, 'the refusal of important scientific work, and the elimination of frank and free discussion' in their pages had led Rivers to consider starting a journal of his own, to be called *The British Journal of Ethnology*, plans for which had begun as early as 1914 but dropped due to 'the war-conditions in November 1916'. This claim, made in a letter to J L Myres written in 1922, needs to be taken with a pinch of salt. A letter from Smith to Rivers, written in November 1916, makes it clear that Smith, not Rivers, had wanted to initiate the journal. Rivers, concerned that a rival journal could do irreparable damage to the RAI, had refused to support him, and Smith therefore dropped the idea.[30] Whether or not Rivers did at some point advocate the creation of a new journal, it is clear enough that Smith very much wanted one. He was talking about it again the following June; and as late as 1925 he was rumoured to be considering launching one – which last event, as will be seen, was one of the catalysts for Crawford's *Antiquity*.[31]

Ostracism was a two-way process. With the exception of a single year, 1921–2, in which Rivers was President of the Royal Anthropological Institute, Smith refused to have anything to do with the RAI until the late 1920s, actively undermining its attempts to become the 'clearing-house' for anthropological research and training that the British Association had hoped it might become.[32] The schism reached its lowest point in 1922, when it became apparent that Elliot Smith had contributed the article on 'Anthropology' to the 12th edition of the *Encyclopaedia Britannica* without any reference to his opponents' views. The previous edition (1911) had been written by Edward Tylor; Smith used his authoritative platform to demolish his predecessor's paradigm, which, he claimed, had been 'paralysing the study of ethnology and removing it farther and farther from the stimulating influence of serious discussion and honest observation'.[33] Anthropology was re-defined as Diffusionist – a fact which 'gave the greatest offence to the "orthodox" school of anthropologists', as Dawson recalled.[34]

By the time that Perry was appointed to UCL, the rest of the discipline had become thoroughly suspicious of Smith and all his works. When, in January 1925, a letter from Smith appeared in *The Times*, in which he called for better funding for academic anthropology and a central institution to coordinate it,[35] the RAI immediately interpreted this as a 'covert attack'. Prominent members were persuaded to send a series of individual letters to the newspaper, urging the suitability of the RAI to fulfil the coordinating role: 'We must prevent a job on the part of Elliot Smith and push the Institute's claim at all costs', as one told the Institute's secretary.[36]

By now, the intellectual content of the Diffusionist programme had become a side-issue. As Buxton wrote to Haddon of Perry, 'His appalling ignorance combined with his entire lack of critical sense are such that no attacks appear to be worthwhile.'[37] However, Smith's policy of antagonism and non-cooperation – T D Kendrick called it 'anthropological terrorism'[38] – had transformed the concept of Diffusionism, in the eyes of his peers, into an insidious toxin that had to be kept away from other institutions. Ian Langham has shown how A C Haddon had ensured that his successor as Reader in Ethnology at Cambridge was selected in order to deny the Diffusionists a foothold in 'Cambridge anthropology'.[39] Bronislaw Malinowski, Perry's rival at the LSE, went one step further: it seems that he approached the Rockefeller Foundation, and succeeded in pulling the plug on their funding.

Torpedoed

The Diffusionist toehold at UCL, as the RAI suspected, was merely the beginning for Smith. He dreamed of a far grander scheme: an institution 'whose centre of interest would be definitely the study of Man, his history, behaviour and beliefs. It would eventually involve the study of the humanities in a much more rational and fruitful way than is done at present', and would serve as 'an instrument for establishing these associations between the different departments of the study of Mankind, so as to build up a rational and serious interpretation of the nature of Man and the fundamental principles of human behaviour'.[40]

This ambitious project was a logical development of the work Smith and Rivers had begun at Maghull, where, according to Smith, Rivers had first dreamt of integrating 'the processes of psychology and ethnology into one discipline'.[41] All three leading Diffusionists considered that their work had major implications for the study of 'social psychology',[42] and Rivers' Presidential Address to the RAI in 1922, entitled 'The Unity of Anthropology', called for more coordination between psychology and the different branches of anthropology.[43] The new scheme was tailored to fit the new priorities of the Rockefeller Foundation's Division of Studies, set up in 1924. According to Stocking, the Director, Edwin Embree, 'played a key role in organizing a program of research in "Human Biology"',[44] a term which Smith understood as 'only a euphemism for Anthropology, a discredited word which they do not wish to make use of'. A submission was duly made, and Embree sent Smith 'several men . . . to prepare the field, and informally discuss projects for building up the subject of a Department of Human Biology in London'[45] but in February 1927 Embree wrote to Smith telling him not to count on funding for anthropology projects at UCL.[46]

The project had been 'torpedoed': Smith's word,[47] and he took it very personally. During the early 1920s, the Foundation had treated Smith as their 'expert anthropological adviser', in George Stocking's phrase, and he had made recommendations on funding for projects all over the world.[48] The decision to withdraw funding, he told Embree, implied a lack of confidence in him. Embree denied this, stressing rather a 'lack of agreement' with him on spending such a large proportion of the Anatomy grant on Anthropology;[49] but Smith's Rockefeller star had definitely begun to wane. In 1925 Joseph Oldham, an active and effective champion of educational reform within British Africa, had convinced the Rockefeller Foundation to support a programme of practical anthropology. Although in February 1925 Oldham had been assured by the Foundation's Dr Flexner that Smith was 'a first-rate man', within months Oldham had become convinced that Smith, like other prominent anthropologists, was too theoretical. Flexner then recommended that he should meet Malinowski, which he did, describing him as 'the most creative and original mind in the field and in his own way a great man'.[50] Malinowski's functionalist anthropology promised to offer practical solutions to contemporary 'anthropological' problems in a way that Diffusionism could not, and he gradually came to replace Smith as the Foundation's anthropological adviser, and – eventually – as its chief anthropological beneficiary.[51]

There's little doubt that the 'torpedo' that sank the Diffusionist ship was launched by Malinowski. Smith himself believed as much,[52] and from the outset, Malinowski knew that he and Perry were engaged on 'a sort of race', in which he represented the 'strong movement' that sought to supply an 'antidote to Elliot Smithism', as he told Frazer in March 1923.[53] A year later, in his surprisingly measured *Nature* review of *Children of the Sun*, Malinowski praised the increasing Diffusionist interest in 'psychological interpretations and sociological analysis', which he thought was bound to lead to 'some common ground for collaboration' between their 'new' approach and his 'old' one: 'there is some hope that the war of extinction may end in a peace treaty'.[54] In practice, however, he had little desire for a 'peace treaty'. Malinowski's problem, in Stocking's words, was 'to define a theoretical position' that would distinguish his brand of anthropology from that of the Diffusionists, 'the chief rival claimants to leadership in British anthropology'.[55] A well-funded Institute at UCL was not on his agenda.

Rapprochement (Too Late?)

The Rockefeller snub led Smith, as the cultural historian he saw himself to be, to investigate both the philosophical roots of what he saw as his opponents' blind evolutionism and the pathology of conceptual advance. 'I thought I might change the attitude of scholars and those who do not rely on puerile subterfuges to bolster unsound arguments if I turned to the discussion of the philosophical issues involved', he explained afterwards.[56] Already in September 1926 he was lamenting, in the Letters pages of *The Times*, the 'Cartesian scholasticism' into which British anthropology had lapsed,[57] and over the next five years endeavoured to demonstrate that the position of the 'evolutionists' was underpinned by what he saw as Descartes' attempts to reduce epistemology to a handful of innate ideas, into which all experience was subsumed. It was hard for scholars, in fact harder for scholars than for other people, to accept major new ideas, as he told the audience for a 1928 Huxley Memorial Lecture that was nothing if not audacious. *Conversion in Science* is an attempt to look at the sociology of scientific change, three decades before Thomas Kuhn: 'The psychological process of conversion in science, the nature of the factors that convince a man of the validity of a theory as an adequate expression of the results of observation and experiments, have, so far as I am aware, never been the direct aim of any enquiry.' Scientists from Copernicus to Lister had faced major problems in getting their ideas accepted; 'Darwin's difficulty in converting his fellows . . . was due precisely to the fact that most of his colleagues were living in a world of delusion in respect of the vital natural phenomenon'.[58]

In spite of his disgust at the mental shortcomings of his fellow-anthropologists, there are clear signs of a real rapprochement, both institutional and intellectual, between Smith and the anthropological community in his last decade. It is intriguing, for instance, that the 'cultural' (i.e. Diffusionist) section of *The Evolution of Man*, first published in 1924, was removed for the second edition in 1927. This was, he claimed, because the book 'deals with the evolution of Man himself', and may have been in response to colleagues who had used the first edition to suggest that Smith was 'opposed to the idea of evolution, solely because for ten years I have been repeatedly calling attention to the misuse of the term by many ethnologists'.[59] This suggests that Smith was aware that his anthropological leanings were beginning to undermine his primary reputation as an anatomist, and sought to redeem it even at the cost of a platform from which to argue the Cause.

The second indication is Smith's decision to rejoin the Royal Anthropological Institute and to play an important part in its proceedings, albeit firmly wearing the hat of a Physical Anthropologist. Langham suggests that the RAI's approach was prompted primarily by a desire to create an impression of unity amongst British anthropologists in order to once more draw down Rockefeller funding.[60] The surprising point is that Smith was quite amenable, at the end of 1928 penning an appeal for funds on behalf of the RAI in which, in Langham's words, 'he unequivocally referred to the Royal Anthropological Institute as "the central clearing house for anthropological knowledge" ', with which all British universities should cooperate.[61] He took part in a series of public lectures organized by the RAI in 1929–30, which were published as *Early Man* in 1931; and in December 1931 he agreed to chair its Human Biology Research Committee.[62] The term 'Human Biology' was clearly chosen to impress the Rockefeller Foundation; and in June 1932 C G Seligman, Professor of Ethnology at the LSE, wrote to Smith thinking that the Foundation might be intending to help Perry, presumably by funding some assistance for him at UCL. Smith's reply was remarkable. Marked 'confidential', he implied that Perry might soon have to retire owing to ill-health: 'When he does give up I intend to recommend the College to make the Readership one of Human Biology (not necessarily altering the title), and leave the strictly cultural things to you.'[63]

This letter may provide the clue to Smith's new spirit of cooperation. Perry had been suffering from increasingly severe bouts of Parkinson's disease since 1922;[64] and it seems probable that by 1929 Smith realized that his friend would not be able to front or to further the Diffusionist cause for much longer. Rapprochement with the anthropological community was essential if Diffusionism had any hope of regaining institutional credibility. Both Smith and Perry now showed themselves willing to modify their intransigent intellectual positions, as Smith's extraordinary offer to the LSE indicates. In spite of his illness, Perry managed to produce another book, *The Primordial Ocean*, published in 1935, in which he acknowledged that the last ten years had seen 'the deepening of our knowledge of social processes'. Although he admitted that the book did not try to 'bridge the gap' between the Functionalists and the Diffusionists, he nonetheless felt 'confident . . . that the candid reader will agree with me that the gap between the two Schools is not nearly as wide as might appear', thereby – much too belatedly – echoing Malinowski's own published view of 11 years previously.[65]

Even Smith began to unbend a little. In 1934, presiding over Section A (Anatomy and Physical Anthropology) of the International Congress of Anthropological and Ethnological Sciences, he prefaced a well-publicized refutation of Hitler's 'Nordic Race Claims' by finally admitting that cultural diffusion had not necessarily begun in Egypt:

There is still some diversity of opinion as to the places where civilization first originated, but we now have evidence to show that whether it happened in Egypt, Sumer, India or elsewhere, in any case it was the work of the Mediterranean race of Sergi.[66]

An Egyptian origin had been central to Smith's creed for over 20 years; for him to now be suggesting that there were other possibilities was an extraordinary climb-down. The context is important: for a statement so critical of Nazi anthropology to have any influence, it was necessary that it should have the support of all shades of anthropologist. Smith himself admitted as much in a letter to Seligman, deploring an article in *The Times* published during the conference by Arthur Keith (in which he reiterated his claims that nations were incipient races, from which, incidentally, the Jews 'held apart'): 'It is a pity he barged in to the correspondence in the Times to create the appearance of a lack of unanimity.'[67]

It does seem, however, that Smith was genuinely trying to rebuild some intellectual bridges as well as institutional ones. In his valediction to Smith (Perry outlived his mentor, who died in 1937), published in 1938, Perry claimed that he had 'imbued the evolutionary history of human culture with a sense of proportion and continuity'.[68] This was a long way from any published statement made by Elliot Smith during his lifetime, but these words might have been written about Rivers. In the end, Smith and Perry returned to Rivers' ground, but by that time Diffusion had become a dirty word.

Conclusion

Why did the Diffusion project fail? It is true that the whole venture was floated on a highly ramshackle raft of conjectural history. But the 'functionalist' credo of Malinowski which succeeded it has stood the test of time no better, while the 'heroic band' of inter-war archaeologists were also trapped in another form of conjectural history – a Eurocentric, teleological brand of social evolution.

There was much that now sounds very modern about Diffusionism. The emphasis on nurture over nature, for instance: the good horse Heredity, which Karl Pearson declared to win against 'Environment ... in a canter' (p. 55, above), has turned out to be as lame a mare as ever fouled a nest. By insisting that social institutions were cultural and not natural, the Diffusionists sought to remove the determinism implicit in

Establishing Diffusion

social evolution, and permit the fundamental overhaul of such artificial social constructs as class and warfare. There's nothing 'natural' about warfare, except to those few who want wars to be waged. In its avowed emphasis on understanding war and peace, Smith's proposed interdisciplinary School of Human Biology foreshadowed institutions such as Bradford's School of Social and International Studies by three generations.

Perhaps the single biggest reason for Diffusionism's failure was the refusal of its proponents to engage in normal academic discourse. To Radcliffe-Brown, their lack of interest in 'attempting to seek out points in which agreement can be reached with others' smacked of 'disciples of a cult rather than that of students of a science'.[69] Rivers' untimely death in 1922 greatly exacerbated that situation; it was, as Elliot Smith himself realized, 'a real catastrophe' for the cause.[70] Rivers' kudos, his caution and his highly insightful academic work had served both to give weight to the Diffusion project, and to restrain Elliot Smith's *ex cathedra* blusterings and Perry's more reckless forays into conjectural history. Without him, the academic Diffusion project began to fall apart. Elliot Smith and Perry became increasingly dogmatic and often belligerent, and although they invoked what Langham calls 'the ghost of Rivers'[71] in their intellectual disputes, the academic community viewed their works and their tactics with mounting distaste. They were completely isolated. When Malinowski's Rockefeller manipulations left them high and dry, no other academic anthropologist felt inclined to protest on their behalf.

All of which was in striking contrast to the parallel experience of Mortimer Wheeler, who also found a platform for his credo within the University of London. Like Smith, Wheeler hoped to win Rockefeller funding[72] but when his application failed the Institute of Archaeology did not then peter out, for Wheeler was making friends and keeping them. His institutional success was based on developing a complex network of connections and supporters which insinuated itself convincingly into the mechanisms of hegemony. Elliot Smith's 'anthropological terrorism', on the other hand, simply succeeded in alienating everyone. In the final analysis, perhaps Smith was just a stroppy Ocker who tried to hijack his discipline when he should have been infiltrating it. The Diffusionists simply didn't play the game.

Chapter 8

A Clash of Narratives: Diffusion and the Archaeologists

The Rift with Anthropology

The Diffusion project had far-reaching implications on the development of Anthropology and Archaeology as separate disciplines. With some justification, Chris Gosden accuses Malinowski of 'using strategies of institutionalization which deliberately emphasized and exacerbated the differences between the two'.[1] For the 1926 edition of *Encyclopaedia Britannica*, Malinowski not only wrested the right to speak for Anthropology from Elliot Smith, but used his article to banish the Diffusionists to the other discipline. He dismissed their arguments as 'belonging to archaeology', and soon afterwards was telling Seligman that Anthropology needed to discard 'the purely Antiquarian associations with Archaeology and even pre-history'.[2] That disciplinary separation was confirmed in 1931 by Radcliffe-Brown, who had inherited the Presidency of the British Association's Anthopology Section that Elliot Smith had once held. In his Presidential Address, Radcliffe-Brown sought to re-categorize the whole discipline into three distinct areas: Human Biology, Prehistoric Archaeology and Ethnology, and Comparative Sociology. 'Prehistoric Archaeology is now an independent subject with its own special techniques and carried on by specialists. The archaeologist, of course, requires to have a knowledge of Human Palaeontology, but equally he needs a knowledge of general prehistory and geology. The natural affinity of Archaeology, however, is with History.' To which he generously added Ethnology, at least 'in as far as it attempts not merely to classify races,

A Clash of Narratives: Diffusion and the Archaeologists

languages and cultures, but to reconstruct their history'; and at the same time urged the Comparative Sociologists to 'avoid being entangled in the conjectural reconstructions of history which I have described above as belonging to Ethnology'.[3]

Such categorization could have been designed to alienate the new archaeologists of Crawford's ilk. Crawford himself had had a great deal of respect for anthropology. He studied it with R R Marett at Oxford and in *Man and his Past* had lamented the 'fairly wide gulf fixed between archaeology and anthropology'.[4] Ten years later, Radcliffe-Brown was attempting to widen the gulf by packing the archaeologists off to sit with the distinctively unfashionable historians, and to take the discredited Diffusionists with them.

He could do this because archaeologists were stuck in an old-fashioned form of anthropology. As editor of *Antiquity*, Crawford displayed a marked lack of interest in current anthropological issues: Malinowski is listed only once in the index between 1927 and 1949, Radcliffe-Brown not at all. His teachers' generation was better represented, and the veterans Myres and Haddon were amongst the journal's contributors. The anthropology that Crawford respected and understood was that of his youth, in which anthropology's main function was to cast light on the processes of social evolution: 'It is the business of the anthropologist . . . to throw light on the past by studying its existing survivals', Crawford declared in *Man and his Past*.[5]

It was a view that was widely shared by his peers. Although social anthropology was being taught alongside archaeology at Cambridge, Glyn Daniel was 'intensely suspicious' of it, and at the end of his life was still claiming to 'hanker after the wide anthropological vision of E B Tylor'.[6] His fellow-student Grahame Clark claimed to have been inspired by Malinowski and Radcliffe-Brown, but it was not until 1944 that Clark first credited 'the new trend' in print. Even so, Clark's brush with anthropological functionalism merely confirmed his view 'that what prehistorians were concerned with was in the final resort the processes of social evolution'.[7]

Functionalist anthropologists, on the other hand, urged their followers to study societies on their own terms. They had little interest in the premises of social evolution, and both Stocking (1996) and Kuklick (1991) are at pains to point out that the Functionalists were unimpressed with the idea of 'progress'. In the aftermath of the Great War, Tylor's evolutionary ladder, from savagery to civilization, no longer held: 'Malinowski pushed the ladder aside, virtually collapsing the distance between the two states', in Stocking's words.[8] In 1922, Malinowski claimed that modern anthropology had finally brought 'the savage races' into the discourse of civilization, a process which 'may well be called, without too much pretension, the New Humanism . . . a broad philosophical view of the laws of human society and human nature'. Like the Diffusionists, he believed that contemporary primitive peoples might have much to offer: 'it is not too far-fetched an idea as might at first seem, to appeal to the savages for some light to be shed on our own nature'.[9]

Archaeologists, however, continued to see such societies as survivals. Their material culture could illustrate earlier steps on the evolutionary path – and off it. Thus, although the tool-making processes of the Australian Arunta people might serve as 'an illuminating and probably reliable guide to the techniques and skills of our remote ancestors', Gordon Childe felt that their archaeological relevance was diminished because they had followed 'what we regard as blind-alleys of superstition', rather than the high road that led to civilization.[10] In short, inter-war archaeology became archaeology with the anthropology taken out.

The Prospectors

Crawford was just as keen as Malinowski and Radcliffe-Brown to steer his own discipline away from the Diffusionist reefs. In his 1924 survey of Diffusionist literature for the *Edinburgh Review*, Crawford had described them as 'a band of scientific adventurers . . . skirmishing over the regions of the past'.[11] Putting an end to piracy of this nature was one of *Antiquity's* earliest objectives. In a letter marked 'very confidential' of January 1926, Crawford asked John Bellows, *Antiquity's* putative printer, to be very discreet about the proposed journal, as 'I have heard rumours that a similar scheme *might* be set on foot by the leader of a very unscrupulous school of archaeologists (save the mark!) though I doubt whether it will see light.' A later annotation in Crawford's hand identifies this as 'The Elliot Smith and Perry school now defunct'.[12]

Crawford thus defined his brand of archaeology quite explicitly as the antithesis of the 'Elliot Smith and Perry school'. He needed to, for initially, some archaeologists had been quite excited by the promise of Diffusionism. T D Kendrick, if unimpressed with Diffusionist attitudes to academic discourse, nonetheless found much to praise in Perry's *Children of the Sun*, which he described as 'a patient and illuminating survey of the

A Clash of Narratives: Diffusion and the Archaeologists

primitive world that deserves the earnest gratitude of every anthropologist'.[13] Harold Peake, impressed by Perry's correlation between the distribution of megaliths and precious metals, transformed the 'Children of the Sun' into 'Prospectors'. In his *The Bronze Age and the Celtic World* (1922), Peake suggested not only that they had left megalithic traces from Ireland to India, but that they constituted a distinctive 'race' of merchants and overseas commodity-dealers, whose descendants could be traced from Sumeria (rather than Egypt), via the Etruscans and the merchants of the Renaissance, to modern financial centres such as the City of London, where their descendants, still racially recognizable, were still engaged in similar employment. Unlike Perry's 'Children', however, the ancestors of the warlike upper classes, Peake's Prospectors were 'not the kind of men to lead warlike expeditions', and their political supremacy had been lost.[14]

Gordon Childe believed that Peake's version of Perry's ideas was 'in some form . . . the right one'.[15] Childe, who had helped Perry in preparing the second edition of *The Growth of Civilisation*, was happy to acknowledge the Diffusionists' influence in his own *Dawn of European Civilization*. Samuel Hooke, briefly Perry's protégé at UCL, even suggested that the *Dawn* was essentially a more detailed version of Perry's *Children of the Sun*, whose shortcomings Hooke ascribed to Perry's ambitiously global remit.[16] In private, however, Childe was much more critical; as early as 1924 he was making sardonic allusions to the Diffusionists in his correspondence with his patron J L Myres; by June 1926, he was describing Myres' 'demolition of Perryligion' as 'glorious'.[17] Elliot Smith wrote him a reference when he applied for the Abercromby professorship the next year, but by 1930 the rift was out in the open.[18]

The Clash of Arms

Gordon Childe twice chose to grapple with his former colleagues' central claim that 'war is a perversion of human nature due to by-products of civilization'.[19] In *Man Makes Himself*, he admitted that 'it is not easy to prove warfare by archaeological evidence': weapons could have been used for hunting, ramparts might be stock-fences; but '[m]ost probably these were defences against human foes', and when a village was succeeded by another of different morphology 'that must mean the arrival of a new people to replace or dominate the former settlers. But such replacement or domination can hardly have taken place peacefully. It must surely have been achieved by force, *i.e.* by war . . . In a word, warfare has to be admitted though only on a small scale and of a spasmodic kind.'[20]

He returned to the fray in 1941. Claiming that archaeological evidence was 'direct and free from the ambiguities inherent in ethnographers' inferential data', he then proceeded to get bogged down in the same ambiguities inherent in archaeologists' material data (the purpose of weapons, for instance). Concluding, Childe succeeded in demonstrating the limits of archaeological interpretation, while nonetheless making his own position clear. 'As far as the archaeologist can tell . . . warfare may have been waged throughout Palaeolithic times', he claimed: a perfectly plausible statement, but no more so than its opposite. Palaeolithic population densities were very low, however; and therefore 'opportunities, still less economic motives, for war can hardly have arisen often'.[21] Lack of opportunity, not lack of inclination, kept Palaeolithic peoples from each other's throats.

Other archaeologists made similar claims. Grahame Clark's *From Savagery to Civilisation* (1946) explicitly accepts Elliot Smith's contention that humanity's ancestors had evolved peacefully in the trees. Aggression began soon after the species touched the ground, in the form of the primeval patriarch: 'Against a background of women and children engrossed, like their simian forebears, in the collection of vegetable food, there emerged the resplendent figure of man the hunter, prototype of man the warrior.' Clark, like Freud and Frazer, believed that the *bête humaine* still lay stratigraphically embedded in the human psyche. 'As we of this generation have every reason to appreciate, beneath the veneer of civilization there lurks the barbarian, and beneath the barbarian the savage, and beneath the lowest trace of culture there lies exposed a solid core of animal appetite.' He agreed with Smith that civilization and warfare had developed together, but saw it as inevitable, 'the price of civilization. The most advanced communities are ultimately those which survive . . . The noble savage, the proud and vigorous barbarian, the cultured citizen, all have bowed the neck to the lethal onslaught of enemies superior in the means for taking life.'[22]

There was more than a touch of Arthur Keith's racial determinism here, and indeed elsewhere in Clark's work. Neither felt disposed to lament the disappearance of indigenous peoples, for instance, which they accepted as an evolutionary necessity. 'The inevitable must happen', wrote Keith; to Clark, 'Regrets are vain. One cannot stay the hand of history. One can only mitigate the brutality of the process.'[23]

A Clash of Narratives: Diffusion and the Archaeologists 107

The influence of Keith is apparent in much of the inter-war archaeological narrative. To Crawford's friend Richard Clay, '[i]t is common knowledge that the weapons of the chase were the weapons of war'. This 'common knowledge' underpinned Keith's theories of tribal warfare, as Landau points out.[24] Crawford himself was a convert. Once a keen supporter of Elliot Smith's brain-led theory of human origins, in 1921 he suggested that the early struggle of humanity was primarily with his environment: warfare 'has up to now had far too prominent a place in historical text-books'.[25] During the 1920s, however, he underwent a change of heart. In 1931, impressed by Keith's ideas on socio-biological evolution, Crawford maintained that 'in primitive civilizations external action is generally synonymous with warfare. Primitive tribal warfare, like the still earlier encounters of individual hunters, is the blind instinctive clash of conflicting interests, acting usually under the stimulus of hunger or sex.'[26]

Crawford's paper was published just three months before Keith's notorious claim that 'Nature keeps her human orchard healthy by pruning; war is her pruning-hook.'[27] This was pure Social Darwinism, and its sentiments were echoed by Glyn Daniel (1914–86), a rising star at Cambridge, destined eventually to succeed Crawford as editor of *Antiquity*, scourge of the archaeological fringe in the 1960s and 1970s. During the War he was on active service in India:

> I am afraid I cannot see how the problem of the teeming millions of the East can be dealt with without letting them plunge themselves in war . . . War is without doubt unaesthetic and tragic to the persons involved, but it is a natural function and has a biological purpose. The principle disease of the East is the cancer of peaceful breeding . . . I have never noticed that sheer goodwill was a very obvious and persistent characteristic of mankind . . . let us get away from this doctrine of an anthropocentric world with its sentimental assumptions of the 'brotherhood of man . . .'[28]

Mortimer Wheeler was an enthusiastic warrior, and during his Second World War service earned himself the reputation of being 'a bristling disciplinarian', in Jacquetta Hawkes' words, with the unfortunate nickname of 'Flash Alf'.[29] 'War is a natural condition of man', he wrote to Cyril Fox from the North Africa front. '[T]o regard war as a temporary lapse from a normal condition of peace is to invert nature and to falsify history. What major moment in the course of human culture has not had war for its background or its stimulus, is not rooted in contention?'[30] He was not alone in thus 'naturalizing' warfare to explain culture change. The Egyptologist T Eric Peet used a similar argument in his review of Perry's *Origin of Magic and Religion* in 1924. 'I believe . . . that the early world had its Alexanders and its Napoleons, men urged on by little more than a blind personal or patriotic ambition, and that they helped to mould its history and spread its culture.'[31] It would be wrong to suggest that all archaeologists were closet warriors, of course, but there is clearly something in H J Massingham's claim that, in the eyes of the orthodox, 'early history and the growth of civilization are a record of the survival of the fittest by the clash of arms'.[32]

Conclusion

The second edition of Elliot Smith's *Human History* (1934) opened with a very forthright statement:

> The fundamental aim of this book is to throw light upon the truth concerning human nature and in particular to call attention to the fact that . . . man is by nature peaceful and truthful . . . the maintenance of peace is a matter of allowing man's innate qualities unimpeded expression.[33]

The central argument of Diffusion is not the detailed process of culture change outlined in their vulnerable conjectural history, but the notion that civilization was imposed by force of arms upon a species that was essentially peaceful by nature. They made no secret of it: for upwards of 20 years they said the same thing in every forum they could find. Yet today this *raison d'être* for the creed is barely recognized. Peter Bowler acknowledges the pacific implications of Smith's arborealism but does not consider its connection with cultural diffusion.[34] Henrika Kuklick, despite a lengthy and thoughtful analysis of the Diffusionists' work on shell-shock victims, dismisses the 'peaceful' trope in a single throwaway line, and erroneously attributes it to the post-war period;[35] A P Elkin also believes that it was a 'pet' topic of Smith's later years.[36] George Stocking accords Perry's peaceful primitivism a mere paragraph, and ignores Smith's entirely;[37] Misia Landau[38] is little better. Tim Champion concedes that Perry's vision held out the 'hope that a future world could recreate the lost utopia of the past', but he prefers to see it as a 'lament' for the post-war decline of Europe. Diffusionism was a product of imperialism, he suggests, providing 'a mythical charter and a validation for the project of empire'. The Children of the Sun were consequently 'prototypes for Britain's imperialists', but he crucially ignores the biting critique of imperialism that this implied.[39]

This blindness to Diffusionist intentions may in part be due to the deliberate obfuscation of Gordon Childe, who in his *Social Evolution* of 1951 sought to put as much distance as possible between his own position and that of his erstwhile colleagues. To take one example, that of 'independent invention'. It was widely accepted, amongst 'civilized' anthropologists of the early twentieth century, that 'primitive' peoples were immune to evolution. Thus J L Myres, Childe's mentor and Perry's tormentor, in *The Dawn of History* (1911), claimed that in 'savage society all is fixed ... Such people as these can hardly be said to have any history, except in the wider one of "Natural History" ... for that involves the doings of all animals alike.'[40] Elliot Smith accepted the same premise, with the important difference that his primitives, unassailed by civilization, were otherwise endowed with a capacity 'nearly if not quite as high as our own ... except for the fact that they lacked the advantages which we enjoy of the knowledge and experience accumulated during many millennia by them and their successors, they were quite as competent and as well-endowed by nature as we are'.[41]

This view was reiterated throughout Smith's career,[42] and he was equally ready to explain how the beginnings of civilization had brought enforced social inequality in its wake. It was in the development of 'extensive irrigation works' on the Nile and the Euphrates that some individuals first learnt how to organize labour. This 'prompted the idea of exploiting his fellow-man in vast works of personal aggrandizement such as pyramids ... The exploits of this military aristocracy, the "children of the sun", during the past forty centuries makes up the greater part of what usually passes for "history".'[43]

Childe, however, summarized Smith's case thus:

> Savages are represented by Diffusionists as totally without initiative, without the desire or the capacity for inventing a device, a myth, or an institution. All the major inventions were made but once by some chosen people. From the latter they were diffused through the outer darkness of savagery.[44]

This interpretation is not merely economical with the truth, but smears Diffusion with a taint of both racial and social superiority that has been eagerly embellished by later archaeological historians. Glyn Daniel attempted to liken Smith to Arthur de Gobineau as a theorist of racism, claiming that 'the cultural hyperdiffusionists demanded a master people'.[45] Even more remarkable is Bruce Trigger's assertion that, to the Diffusionists, 'most human beings are naturally primitive and will always revert to a state of savagery if not stopped from doing so by the ruling classes'.[46] By ignoring the inversion of emphasis which the Diffusionists placed on the concepts of 'primitive' and 'civilization', their critics have succeeded in inverting their entire argument.

Why the travesty? Why do they do it? The personality of the Diffusionist ringleader has much to do with it. There is, as Graham Richards rightly observes, 'an intangible whiff of scandal' around the name of Elliot Smith, who 'apparently left an impression among British colleagues of tendencies towards sharp practice and rule bending'.[47] There is some truth in this, even beyond the Diffusionist aversion to normal academic debate. Richards points out that there was some controversy over Smith's posthumous control of Rivers' papers, which were allegedly doctored to suit the Diffusionist agenda, and certainly Smith was not above invoking Rivers' name for causes to which he was actually opposed (for instance the creation of a new anthropological journal (above, pp. 94–5). He was capable of manipulating his own lieutenant, setting Perry up to talk on 'War and Civilization' when he had had other plans (above, p. 85). He was even capable of doctoring his own work: when his 1912 Presidential Address to the Anthropology Section of the British Association, which had already posited an unusually favourable background for humanity's arboreal ancestors, was incorporated into his *The Evolution of Man* (1924), any lingering suggestion of primitive pugnacity was systematically expunged (a fact noted by both Landau and Bowler who, however, do not appear to appreciate its significance[48]). Furthermore, Diffusionist writing could get very confusing sometimes, and to a casual reader it is not always apparent that the 'archaic civilization' was a bad thing.

Elliot Smith was no saint, in short, and his academic peers – and heirs – have good reason to dislike him. Yet the fact remains that his Diffusionism was no mental aberration, but a logical development from his research into palaeoanatomy. To recapitulate: a 'short' evolution for *homo sapiens* implied a minimum of racial and inherent differences between groups of people, which then had to be explained by culture, by nurture and not nature. In the laboratory of the Great War, claims of innate human belligerence were disproven. Soldiers are made, not born: and it is on this central point that the work of the three great Diffusionists met, and their project began in earnest.

A Clash of Narratives: Diffusion and the Archaeologists 111

Diffusionism failed because it didn't fit either the expectations or the aspirations of those who believed that human progress was a force of nature. The Diffusionists posed a major challenge to the 'hegemonic' grand narrative of social evolution, and therefore were not to be taken seriously. A shame, for the creed had the seed of something truly revolutionary. Childe and Crawford, for instance, sought to reconcile Europe to the enormity of the Great War by invoking the *longue durée*, and thereby putting it into a much longer time-frame. Yet by stressing the *innateness* of belligerence, they rather disastrously undermined their own didactic purpose. The insistence upon a prehistory that was 'nasty, brutish and shorte' dovetailed all too neatly with the dark fantasies of the Social Darwinists. The Great War was not some isolated catastrophe, but the expression of a natural human tendency, nature's pruning-hook at work. 'War is a natural condition of man', said Mortimer Wheeler.[49] It would be hard to think of a better example of how scientific archaeology came to serve the *status quo* than that.

Part III
The Most Ancient Faith

Chapter 9

The Esoteric Revival

What is Stonehenge? That must be one of archaeology's most hackneyed questions, and with any luck no one will ever come up with an answer that convinces everybody. Orthodox interpretations in the 1920s varied widely, but despite their increasing sophistication, and a seven-year dig conducted on behalf of the Society of Antiquaries, their conclusions were overshadowed and their thunder stolen by a remarkable band of Druids who came to Stonehenge to celebrate the summer solstice. The three-way tussle between Druids, State and Archaeologists which ensued reveals much about how the struggle for control of the prehistoric past was played out in practice.

Religion and Superstition

Religion, so closely interwoven with political power in the *anciens régimes* of Europe, was anathema to the reforming intellectuals of the nineteenth century.[1] In England, the universities were slowly transformed from bastions of conservative piety into centres of rational enquiry, and post-Darwinian social scientists were in the vanguard of the process. Anthropologists in particular had an epistemological antipathy to anything that smacked of religion: Sir Edward Tylor saw it as his duty 'theologians all to expose' by demonstrating the parallels between religion and savage superstition, a process greatly furthered by his follower, Sir James Frazer, who scoured the world for 'savage' analogies to the Christian myth.[2]

Many inter-war scientific archaeologists were similarly imbued with a pronounced scepticism about matters religious. Piggott, following Frazer, attributed the beginnings of religion to 'the primitive misinterpretation of dreams'.[3] Daniel, Casson, Hemp, Wheeler,[4] Childe (see below) were all discretely agnostic or atheist. To Crawford, being anti-religious was an article of faith. A note in his own handwriting, written probably in 1932, reveals the strength of his feelings:

> There are signs that religion, crippled and knocked senseless by the hammer-blows of the Huxley-Darwin period, is trying to enter the ring again . . . Had the issue been a straight one, religion would now be extinct in Great Britain. Scientific knowledge would be taught in the schools, two generations so educated would have grown up and passed away. This would have happened, had not religion been useful to the governing classes as a mere invention to keep the vulgar in obedience . . . there can be NO reconciliation between religion and science; it is war to the end – of religion; a fight between the forces of light and those of obscurantism harnessed to class exploitation.[5]

As late as 1954, he was writing to the *Listener* in protest at an attack on Frazer, proposing a talk to balance it, to be entitled 'The Mass as a Fertility Rite'.[6]

By no means all inter-war archaeologists were hostile to religion, however. Eliot Curwen, a prominent Sussex archaeologist whose excavation-work was lauded by Crawford, was a Creationist and a firm believer in the chronology of Archbishop Ussher (who had calculated that the world began in 4004 BC). Curwen's *Prehistoric Sussex* attempted to reconcile archaeological time-scales with the 'Familiar Contemporary Events' of the Old Testament; the Neolithic thus '[e]nded about the time of the patriarchs Isaac and Jacob', while the Palaeolithic was simply termed 'Immense antiquity'.[7] Grahame Clark, if no Ussherian, was a committed Christian; so too were Cyril Fox and Christopher Hawkes.[8] As a discipline, therefore, orthodox archaeology could present no united front on Christian matters, but discretely fudged the issue by targeting pre-Christian faiths instead. Thus Gordon Childe, unequivocal in his conviction that religion was an unfortunate and reactionary by-product of progress that served the interests of established elites,[9] was nonetheless able to emphasize the evolutionary superiority of Christianity over primitive religion: 'Christianity as a religion of love surpassed all others in stimulating positive virtue.'[10]

The Esoteric Revival 117

In much the same way that a common faith in progress helped to unite both socialist and traditionalist archaeologists, the unpleasant nature of pre-Christian religion became a concept on which both atheist and Christian archaeologists could agree. Cyril Fox, interpreting the evidence from the Iron Age site at Llyn Cerrig Bach on Anglesey, suggested that the 'slave-chains' they found were evidence of Druid involvement on the site, citing Tacitus as evidence that Druids were not only 'cruel' but provoked 'passionate hatred'; the Llyn Cerrig chains were thus to be seen as 'the means of keeping safely and transporting the wretches doomed to ceremonial slaughter'.[11] Early religious practice generally was made to conform to the prehistorians' bleak view of prehistoric life. People took part in religious rituals out of desperation, since the forces of Nature, as Childe explained, 'act capriciously and terribly. At all costs they must be compelled, cajoled, or conciliated. Now, once you can make yourself believe that you have found a system of magic to achieve that compulsion, or a ritual to ensure that conciliation, the belief becomes a solace in the terrors of life that one dare not surrender.'[12]

The belief that primitive religion was based on fear and manipulation was used to inform public interpretation of ancient monuments. The official guide to Stonehenge, written by Frank Stevens, curator of the Salisbury Museum and later to be a regular contributor to *Antiquity*, assumed the existence of a manipulative priesthood: a 'body of "wise men" ' able to intercede with the spirits – good or bad. The ' "wise man" . . . realized the importance of his knowledge, and doubtless used it to his own advantage, thus winning support and respect from his simple followers'.[13] Doris Chapman, author of the official guide-book to Avebury, was determined to crush any romantic speculation about the purpose of the site: 'You may have heard all kinds of stories about sun worship, serpent worship and so on, but there is absolutely no foundation for any of these tales, which have been put about by people with more imagination than knowledge. I am afraid we cannot tell you anything as exciting but, on the other hand, all that we do so we have proved to be true.' This included the suggestion (the only suggestion proposed) that the ditch at Avebury may have been dug

> to keep the spirit or spirits of the Circle from getting out. For primitive people are terrified of spirits although they depend so largely on them for help, and believe them incapable of passing such barriers as high banks, deep ditches, fire and water. It is in all probability for some such reason as

this that the really tremendous work of digging a ditch and bank of such vast size was undertaken.[14]

A Universal Religion

All in all, the mind-set of the 'heroic band' was hardly conducive to respect for esoterica, whether prehistoric or modern. Archaeology's revered ancestor Edward Tylor had been scathing about the revival of interest in matters occult that occurred during his own lifetime: 'The modern educated world, rejecting occult science as a contemptible superstition, has practically committed itself to the opinion that magic belongs to a lower level of civilization', he wrote; and yet 'a great philosophic-religious doctrine, flourishing in the lower culture but dwindling in the higher, has re-established itself in full vigour'.[15]

What is truly remarkable is the extent to which Tylor's own work, like that of Sir James Frazer, not only became engulfed by the esoteric revival but served as foundation texts for its premises. Tylor's 'doctrine of survivals' was intended to provide illustration of the workings of social evolution by allusion to surviving 'superstitious' practice in the present, which could then be stigmatized as belonging to a discredited past; but as Hutton has shown, the work of Tylor and Frazer was soon adopted by a public disposed to find opposite readings in it.[16]

One of the earliest results of Tylor's work was the creation of the Folk-Lore Society in 1878: an organization whose aim, in the words of Richard Dorson, 'was to establish a science devoted to reconstructing the world view of prehistoric savages from the contemporary lore of peasants'.[17] The leading light of what Dorson calls 'The Great Team of Folklorists' was Andrew Lang, an early disciple of Tylor. George Stocking devotes 13 pages of his magisterial *After Tylor* to the conversion of Lang 'From Tylorian Folklore to Primitive Monotheism', as the chapter section is neatly entitled.[18] Lang, an active member of the Society for Psychical Research, came to believe that what Tylor saw as the 'animistic' religions of primitive peoples might actually reflect real experience: 'man may have faculties which savages recognize, and which physical science does not'. In Stocking's words, 'Purely materialistic theories of the world must be reconsidered; and the doctrines of theism and of the soul might not after all be false.' By 1898, armed with information from 'modern psychology and physiology', Lang was wondering whether telepathy and clairvoyance might have been a feature of early humanity: 'one might expect that

The Esoteric Revival

faculties so useful would be developed in the struggle for existence'; and, most significantly, that 'they may still exist in savage as in civilized races'.[19]

Lang concluded by positing a universal primitive religion, from which all surviving manifestations were degradations, a concept that sat well with the claims of fellow-folklorists such as Sir George Gomme that the British peasantry were effectively pagan until the Reformation.[20] The survival of universal paganism remained an influential concept for several generations, and was found at its most audacious in the work of Margaret Murray, Assistant Professor under Flinders Petrie in the Department of Egyptology at UCL until 1935. Her claim, that an 'old religion' of perhaps Neolithic origins had survived as a more or less underground 'witch cult' into the twentieth century, still commanded respect amongst academics well into the 1960s.[21] Others made less ambitious but equally influential claims: anthropologists such as H J Fleure and Jessie Weston, amongst others, discovered a sense of 'spiritual continuity', from paganism to Christianity, immanent in the English countryside, and Ronald Hutton has shown how prominent archaeologists, including 'such giants as Sir Flinders Petrie, Stuart Piggott and O G S Crawford' were guilty of subscribing to a belief in pagan survivals.[22] To this list can be added Mortimer Wheeler, and also the keen young members (male) of the Cambridge Antiquarian Society who spent May's Eve 1931 concealed 'in a small clump of gorse bushes' beside the Cerne Abbas Giant, that reputed fertility symbol, 'with a view of learning whether any pagan practices were still carried out'. None were spotted, but the party resolved to return the following year.[23]

If Andrew Lang had subverted the master's intention by suggesting that 'savage' religion may have been 'true', Frazer's intentions were all but lost amid alternative readings of his work. In Gellner's words, Frazer 'was read as the Columbus of a world of life-giving, indispensable symbols. Their role in our psyche was held somehow to vindicate religion.'[24] The influence of Frazer's *Golden Bough* was colossal: 36,000 copies of the twelve-volume edition were published between 1911 and 1921; 33,000 copies of the one-volume abridgement were sold in the following decade; there were 51 editions between 1922 and 1955. As Hutton says, 'Its images became part of the Western popular consciousness.'[25] But perhaps Frazer's greatest inadvertent contribution to twentieth-century paganism was the credibility that his notorious global eclecticism gave to the concept of a universal ancient culture. In attempting to undermine Christianity by combing the planet to find roots, routes and parallels, he provided intellectual authority for the 'universalism' that underpins modern paganism.

The Celtic Renascence

Andrew Lang played an important role in the rehabilitation of the Celts, who, in spite – or rather, because of – mid-nineteenth century English disapprobation, had once more become the focus of romantic opposition to orthodox prehistory. Celtic cultural nationalism, indeed, came to function as a sort of intellectual 'liberation theology' for those who sought cultural or political autonomy from the values of English hegemony.

The survival of a Celtic substratum within the English race, acknowledged, despite the Anglo-Saxonist historians, by a steadily increasing number of authorities as the nineteenth century wore on, proved to be of some importance to those who looked for leaven to counter what they saw as the stodgy boorish values of bourgeois Teutonism.[26] The pioneer English Celticist was Matthew Arnold, who considered England to consist of 'a vast obscure Cymric basis with a visible Teutonic superstructure'. This submerged Celticity was responsible for the good bits in English art, notably literature.[27] Arnold's Oxford lectures *On the Study of Celtic Literature* were published in 1867. '[W]e are emperilled by what I call the "Philistinism" of our middle class', he wrote. 'On the side of beauty and taste, vulgarity; on the side of morals and feeling, coarseness; on the side of mind and spirit, unintelligence, – this is Philistinism.'[28] The English needed to get in touch with their Celtic roots in order that these qualities could be restored to English life.

Malcolm Chapman credits Arnold with re-creating the Celts as sentimental, spiritual, artistic, natural and, above all, magical: in touch with 'the magic of nature', as Arnold put it, 'the intimate life of nature, her weird power and fairy charm'.[29] His interpretation, according to Chapman, 'became an established fact, a security with which an argument could be begun rather than a conclusion to be reached'.[30] At least some of these 'attributes' were already current, however: Robert Knox's highly unsympathetic 1850 account described the Celts as '[c]hildren of the mist'. In spite of the enlightenment radiating from their English neighbour, 'they dream of the past: nature's antiquaries'.[31] Arnold's contribution was simply to re-categorize these vices as virtues. He, too, believed that the Celts were ill-adapted to the modern world. His idealized, ethereal Celt was a creature of the past: and since Celticity was an inherent racial resource, a cultural attribute available to all Britons, modern Celtic languages and cultures were not in need of preservation.[32]

Arnold had been instrumental in establishing a Chair of Celtic Studies at Oxford in 1877, of which John Rhys was the first incumbent. In his *Celtic Britain* (1882), Rhys contrived to add to Celtic magic by invoking the unfortunate Edward Tylor's work on 'the well-known tendency of higher races to ascribe magical powers to lower ones' to explain the survival of druidism.[33] Rhys, who, as we shall see, was to have a considerable influence on Welsh archaeology, to the consternation of Mortimer Wheeler, was the Folk-Lore Society's 'most eminent spokesman' in the cause of Welsh folklore;[34] but there was a decidedly pro-Celtic bias amongst many of the FLS' founding members. Alfred Nutt, publisher of the Society's journal *Folk-Lore*, built on Tylor's evolutionism to champion 'Celticism' against diffusionary Aryanism of the Max Müller school. His project culminated in the Cambrianization of King Arthur, which at last gave Celticists a significant cultural icon to offer the dominant culture, since in order for the English to share in the Arthurian connection it was first necessary for them to acknowledge their kinship with the Celts. 'However much it may be regretted in certain quarters, the Celt is an abiding element in the imperial life of the British race', wrote Nutt.[35]

To Arnold's heirs and followers, the romantic rehabilitation of the Celt brought with it a corresponding improvement in the fortunes of all prehistoric primitives, for the two categories were, once again, blurred. Andrew Lang brought the weight of his anthropological reputation to the 'Celtic Renascence movement' of the *fin de siècle*, of which, with W B Yeats, he was a leading light. Malcolm Chapman points out that both Lang and Yeats 'argued that what had appeared Celtic to Arnold was in fact primitive'.[36] Yeats, indeed, suggested that Arnold had only been so specific about the Celts because comparative folk-lore was then undeveloped: 'I do not think he understood that our "natural magic" is but the ancient religion of the world, the ancient worship of nature and that troubled ecstasy before her.' It was purely the accident of proximity to 'the main river of European literature' that was responsible for its Celtic flavour.[37]

By the end of the Edwardian era, the Celt had been transformed. Poetic and mystical, in touch with nature and the ancient world, Celtica was beginning to take on a decidedly modern appearance, and the 'prehistoric' world which the Celts exemplified was beginning to emerge as a major site of intellectual resistance to mainstream values. Socialism and Celtic natural magic were not so far apart.

Chapter 10

The Universal Bond

Spiritualism and Socialism

Marxian antipathy to matters esoteric was just one thread among the many threads of socialism. Logie Barrow's pioneering work on 'Spiritualism and English Plebeians' suggests that many aspects of the esoteric revival can be seen as a sort of democratization of religious expression and authority, as much 'post-atheist' as 'post-Christian'. He finds strong links between secularism and socialism in the 'democratic epistemologies' of nineteenth-century organic intellectuals, to whom spiritualism provided access to the 'supernatural' unmediated by an oppressive Christianity.[1] 'Spiritual regeneration' was likewise central to Guild Socialism. 'It is obvious that by spiritual regeneration something very different is meant from the morbid and sickly sentimentality which very often passes for spirituality today', wrote Penty; 'rather must we be understood to mean the recovery by society of that "sense of the large proportion of things" ... which in all ages of spiritual activity was in a greater or lesser degree the common possession of the whole people ... There can be no Socialism without it.'[2]

Barrow demonstrates the spiritualist movement's close connections with vegetarianism, teetotalism, 'food reform', homeopathy and the cluster of alternative medicines he collectively dubs 'medical botany'.[3] This was the same social milieu which, according to Harvey Taylor,[4] produced the nascent outdoor movement, in which healthy outdoor leisure pursuits were encouraged 'to reinforce a challenge to the *status quo*', and distinct from the middle-class 'moral reformers', who were motivated by 'a primarily pessimistic Hobbesian analysis of human nature'. Robert Blatchford's *Merrie England* ranked access to the countryside with access to culture as a basic human need. Over 70 'Clarion Cycle Clubs' had been set up by 1897, their purpose to combine exercise and country air with the dissemination of socialism in the form of Blatchford's journal *The Clarion*; in the words of the CCC's founding member, Tom Groom, 'the frequent contrasts a cyclist gets between the beauties of nature and the dirty squalor of towns make him more anxious than ever to abolish the present system'.[5]

Alternative religion, Socialism, healthy living and the 'call of nature' were thus ingredients in the heady mix of working-class politics at the start of the twentieth century, with Edward Carpenter's *Civilisation: Its Cause and Cure* for its Bible:

> when the Civilisation-period has passed away, the old Nature-religion – perhaps greatly grown – will come back ... Man will once more *feel* his unity with his fellows, he will feel his unity with the animals, with the mountains and streams, with the earth itself...'[6]

These various traditions – universal paganism, socialism and ruralism – all came together in the fiery epistemology of George Watson Macgregor Reid, leader of the Universal Bond and the founding father of modern Druidry. He was probably born in Skye (or India, or America) in 1850, but this fascinating individual was such a fantastic fabricator of facts that it is hard to be certain.[7] One version of his biography claimed that he had formerly been a ship's doctor, a Buddhist who 'tramped as a beggar through Tibet', medical officer to Chilean revolutionaries, a trade union activist in the USA and the first Socialist candidate to stand for the US Congress.[8] R. Bruce Aubry's painstaking researches suggest a more pedestrian trajectory, starting life as a fisherman, followed by a stint in the Navy and then a spell as a docker in Glasgow, where he tried to launch a Labour Federation. In 1888 and 1889 he is found addressing open-air meetings of the Social Democratic Federation in Glasgow, and was recruited as an activist for the National Amalgamated Union of Sailors and Firemen, who sent him to Hull to undermine a local union. He was forced to stand down after being fined for assaulting a blackleg and was sent to New York to organize a local branch there, but by this time had fallen out with the British leadership. He was accused of having decamped with the Hull branch funds, and was once more forced to resign.[9]

One version of the Reid story has it that he stayed in New York for several years. Alan Seaburg has verified Reid's claim to have run for Congress in 1892 (he won approximately 1 per cent of the vote); and in order to stand he must have become a naturalized American citizen.[10] His pamphlet, entitled *The Natural Basis of Civilization*, however, was published the following year in London and bristles with British statistics, which suggests (though not conclusively) that he was back in Britain by 1893.

It was probably during his sojourn in New York that Reid first came across Universalism, the creed that was to shape his life. Universalism must rank as one of the most optimistic and upbeat varieties of Nonconformism. The concept is simple: the universe, being divinely ordered, is therefore ultimately sane and beneficent. Good will triumph over evil; there is accordingly no room for hell; all will ultimately be saved; and furthermore, this is the basic Truth that underlies all religions. Universalism was first formalized in the mid-eighteenth century by a Pembrokeshire Dissenter called James Relly, but this pleasingly comprehensive and tolerant creed thereafter found itself squeezed between hellfire orthodoxies and scientific materialisms. By the late nineteenth century, Universalism had all but died out in Britain, although it retained a strong following in New England.

The Natural Basis of Civilization, a pamphlet produced by the Proletarian Publishing Company of Clerkenwell, is a curious blend of millenarian socialism and universalism: 'the Socialist and Anarchist looks forward to his ideal state – his free state – his millennium – the exact counterpart of the Christian or Mohammedan or Indian ideal'. His opposition to 'Government' and to civilization as currently constituted owed much to Morris and to Carpenter: 'Nature having given us the right to live, we must live in a natural manner', he claimed. 'All we look upon is good until tampered with by selfishness and greed. Then Nature is good; and man to be good must be natural, and strive to find for himself "The Natural Basis of Civilization".'[11]

The Path that is Light

I've yet to find any firm evidence of Reid's activities between 1893 and 1906. One of his hagiographies claims that he came back to England around 1901; another, that he began to take an active interest in 'Nature

Cure' at around that time; and he also claimed to have met most major Socialist figures during this period. All of this is quite possible, but Reidian facts are such slippery creatures that without the banalities of external corroboration there is little hope of convincing the unconvinced.

During this period, Reid acquired a son (Robert, who was eventually to succeed him as Chief Druid), enough money to free him from the need to work (a later Chief Druid was under the impression that he invented and patented the health-drink Sanatogen, but Seaburg's investigations have demonstrated otherwise), and an impressive extra name, 'Macgregor', which may suggest a connection with the occult Order of the Golden Dawn.[12]

Reid re-emerges in 1906 as the editor and co-publisher of the *Nature Cure Journal*, produced by the British Nature Cure Association (BNCA), of which he himself was President. The magazine was pitched at 'all Food Reformers, Vegetarians, Temperance Enthusiasts, Anti-Vivisectionists, Anti-Vaccinists and believers in Simple Life ideals', this last an allusion to the work of Edward Carpenter. Its Universalism was revealed by its avowal to 'search for good in all, believing that what is sought for will ever be found, and its ideals are based upon the good teachings of the whole world', with a range of inspirations from Confucius via Ruskin to Walt Whitman.[13] At first the magazine was prosaic enough, carrying articles on medical topics, Nature Cure institutions and subjects likely to interest readers, such as the newly founded Letchworth Garden City. As time went on, it grew steadily more eccentric, its prosaic health-care articles larded or replaced with flights of literary imagination and, increasingly, esoterica. Most of which seems to have come from the pen of the Editor, who believed that he had become 'a peculiar mixture of clergyman, philosophic teacher, health advisor and dietetic guide',[14] and in truth the BNCA was something of a cult.

Between 1908 and 1912, Macgregor Reid went through a process of profound mystical transformation which he eventually codified into a creed of which he was the focus. In 1910, under the *nom-de-plume* of 'Ayu Subhadra', Reid published a lavish esoteric text called *The Path that is Light*, which revealed him to be 'the Chosen Servant of the Holy Brotherhood of the Elect', required to transmit 'the ideals of Universalist Theosophical Belief, as compiled and taught by Kapilya, the Holy Messenger'. Universalism 'guides away from all sorrow and hunger, preaches against idolatry, and builds up the power and the joy of Islam in the leading of human thought towards Simple Life Ideals of Universal

Brotherhood. All of its fruits are grown upon trees that are known. It has nothing new. It loves and venerates the Old, because Truth is old, and Truth is God.'[15]

During this period the BNCA seems to have disappeared as a formal entity. The last issue of *The Nature Cure* was dated Midsummer 1909 – a victim, probably, of editorial whim. In its place emerged another organization: the South London Temple of the Universal Bond, installed at 57 Cavendish Road, Clapham Park, a large South London house. Here were held three weekly services (two on Sundays), and an assortment of weekly classes in topics that ranged from politics to economics, psychology, world religions, the occult, mysticism, yoga and medicine. The temple was furnished with an altar that had apparently been made in 1643 and, according to one account, had been presented to them by Gerard Winstanley, the Digger leader. This date – 1643 – is one of few fixed reference points in the shifting sands of Reid's Druidic Universalism: it was mentioned regularly (according to some accounts, it was actually carved into the altar), and was variously deemed to be the date at which this congregation had been established, or record-keeping had begun.

The Ancient Druid Faith

Reidian Universalism borrowed widely from a range of other religions, including elements from the Buddhist, Hindu, Zoroastrian, Jewish, Islamic and Babi traditions, but one creed alone won Macgregor Reid's wholehearted approval, perhaps because it had no living exponents; and that was Druidism.

Widely understood to be the Celtic *credo*, as a 'Celtic' Scotsman, Macgregor Reid may have considered Druidical wisdom to be his birthright. It certainly dovetailed perfectly with his feisty form of Universalism, since it was seen as the ancient universal religion. These first Universalists, 'the Ancient Druids, the Buddhists of another age', had left their mark upon the land in the form of their ancient monuments; and thus it was that 'the Round Towers of Ireland and of Scotland, the cromlechs and burrows [*sic*], and silent stones of the Ancient Faith in many parts are again brought to our attention'.[16]

Of these silent stones, Stonehenge was the greatest. Its links with Druidism had been convincingly reaffirmed in the public mind by the major ceremony which the Ancient Order of Druids had held there in August 1905. Between 650 and 700 Brothers turned up, complete with white robes, sickles and 'Father Christmas' beards ('a Druid without his beard is like a peacock without his tail', as one observer put it).[17]

The Universalists at Stonehenge

The Ancient Order's visit inspired emulation. One observer of the Stonehenge solstice in 1907 commented on a current trend amongst solstice visitors 'to greet the rising sun in garments of daring design, and of a pattern which would, in all likelihood strike terror into the shades of the original Druidic worthies they are supposed to personate'.[18] However, when Macgregor Reid first took the Universal Bond to Stonehenge, for the solstice of 1912, they did not go dressed as Druids. A series of photographs of the Stonehenge ritual reveal a distinctly Oriental feel to Universalist *couture* at this point, particularly in the matter of turbans, with nary a false beard or a sickle to be seen.

An account of that first Universalist solstice was 'communicated' to the *Salisbury Journal* by an unknown though well-informed source. Two services were held on the Sunday after the solstice by 'the Universal Bond of the Sons of Men'. Participants included Ayu Subhadra (i.e. Reid), 'the messenger from Tibet, with his little flock', and one J. Turnbull BA, 'a Persian gentleman'. A verbatim account of the 'Confession of Faith' was included:

> I believe in the existence of Divine Purpose within all that is. That there is no order or wrong within Nature; That Nature is the reflected Majesty of The Powers, and of The Almighty Power that lies beyond the All . . . I believe . . . [i]n the purposed evolution of all things towards the better and the best, I believe in the Ultimate Growth of All Things into good . . .[19]

Evidently pleased with the way things went, Macgregor Reid returned the following year, although this time with just one follower; but it seems that the 1912 service had angered Sir Edmund Antrobus, the landlord. Antrobus was notoriously irascible. When he inherited Stonehenge from his father in 1901, he promptly tried to blackmail the government into buying it for a huge sum. The government refused, so Antrobus enclosed the monument and began to charge for admission. A consortium of local and national amenity groups tried to challenge his right to do so in the High Court, but lost: a landlord was perfectly entitled to decide who could and could not come on to his land.[20] Antrobus thereafter expected total control over everything that went on behind his fence. The AOD event of 1905 was one thing, especially since it was held partly in his honour: he had that day been initiated into the Order;[21] but he was not about to tolerate the right of just anyone to turn up and hold a service at the Stones.

On the day before the 1913 solstice, Macgregor Reid (now in the guise of the Dastur Tuatha de Dinaan: *Dastur*, 'High Priest', from the Parsi Zoroastrians, *Tuatha de Danaan*, the Irish gods) was informed that no political or religious meetings would be tolerated by 'the state-recognized possessor' (i.e. Antrobus). Speaking 'as the direct successor of the Chief Druids who have been', Macgregor Reid announced his intention to return the next day and hold the service anyway. He did so, and the caretaker, backed by several policemen, refused to let him in unless he promised to abide by Antrobus' rule. 'This he absolutely refused to do', but he bought his tickets and more or less forced his way through.

The service was duly held, and afterwards he addressed a sympathetic audience, a gathering 'of a composite character, and it was pleasing to see

10   The Universal Bond at the Stonehenge Summer Solstice, 1913 'The Passing through the Gate', Macgregor Reid in the lead. (*Wiltshire Local Studies Library*).

11 'Worshippers before the gnomen'. (*Wiltshire Local Studies Library*).

12 Service in the circle. (*Wiltshire Local Studies Library*).

13 'Before the Surrender Stone (Mahayoni). The Appeal unto The Great Mother is raised by the contrite heart'. (*Wiltshire Local Studies Library*).

the military element predominating. The soldiers lay upon the mossy embankment looking towards the Dastur Tuatha as he told the story of our Druid sires... Truly it was an inspiring meeting, and the spirit guardians of the Sacred Circle rejoiced as the words of the message were wafted outwards from the gathering.' But back at the wicket gate, he brought down 'the Kara' on the landlord's head: 'In grief and sorrow I call down the curse of Almighty God, and of his Spirit Messengers, that the weak may be liberated from the molestation of the tyrannical... Response is sure.'[22]

Ten Universalists made the solstice pilgrimage in 1914, when Zoroastrianism was the flavour of the day: the *Wiltshire Gazette* correspondent was told that some of Macgregor Reid's party 'claimed descent from ancient fire worshippers in India, followers of Zoroastrianism', and Zoroastrianism was the topic upon which Macgregor Reid lectured the multitudes after the solstice ceremony.[23]

But Antrobus this time was determined that his will was not to be flouted. When Macgregor Reid began to recite 'the prayers of the sun worshippers', all 10 Universalists, including Reid himself, George Catchlove and two un-named women, were forcibly removed by the police. Once outside, Macgregor Reid reopened old wounds by declaring to the crowd that Antrobus had had no right to enclose the site, and demanded his money back. The accounts vary somewhat between newspapers, but one version has it that a crowd of 'about 400 men and youths' either urged the Universalists to rush the gate or endeavoured to do so themselves, 'and threatened to pull down the fence' until restrained by the police.[24]

Macgregor Reid apparently made no attempt to hold a service at the 1915 solstice, contenting himself with advising people on the best place to stand to see the sunrise. Another Universalist, however, was marched out from the circle for standing in the wrong place, which was enough to trigger Macgregor Reid into 'a series of emphatic protests' concerning access to the site. Sir Edmund Antrobus had died the previous February; the 'Kara' had been fulfilled. Thus emboldened, Macgregor Reid declared that 'no man had a right to stand between God and man. The promise of their Order shall be carried out, and "the remnant shall be saved" . . . I am called the Last of the Druids', he continued, 'but I shall not be the last, for you cannot destroy truth and justice.'[25]

This trivial incident was well reported, particularly in the local papers, which by now were becoming aware that Macgregor Reid provided good copy. Not everyone was amused, however; and this year's episode made 'The Londoner' in the London *Evening News* 'intolerably angry'. This 'brawling party of cranks', these 'suburban dervishes' were unacceptable in time of war. Their 'silliness touches sacrilege': 'at the back of my mind I have a fancy that the grey and ancient stones are the heart of the England for which we are offering such sacrifice in battle'. Stonehenge was coming up for auction, and the columnist concluded by hoping that the new owner would find a way of keeping out 'the whole tribe of squabbling cranks'.[26]

The new owner proved to be one Cecil Chubb, who bought Stonehenge at auction in October; and despite the *Evening News* he allowed the Universal Bond to hold their services. Indeed, his three-year ownership of the site proved to be the Bond's Golden Age. In 1916, four services were held, including 'the Ritual of the Golden Dawn' at sunrise and an evening service attended by 'fully a thousand people', at which Macgregor Reid preached on the subject of 'The Unity of Truth'. The previous evening, Macgregor Reid preached to an audience which the *Salisbury Times* put at between five and six hundred, in which he explained that all religions had grown from Druidism, 'this one root of religious life' that 'seeks to call man back to Nature, so that he can look through Nature, to Nature's God.' Druidism did not require people to leave their existing

14 The Universalist cosmos: Stonehenge to the left, the religions of the book to the right, and a multi-faith trilithon in the centre. (ADUB letterhead, 1918).

faiths: all 'right service', of whatever faith, would lead through 'a knowledge of God to the Brotherhood of Man'.[27]

I have found no record of a Druid presence in 1917, but in 1918 Macgregor Reid told a 'large congregation' that although 'as children of God all are part of one great faith', Druidism was nonetheless more wholesome than the religions of 'Canterbury and Rome'. 'Faith in the Druid God will make homes sacred, make houses replace barracks, and make wars cease. The present churches were powerless to stop the war.'[28]

People

It was in this year that the order began styling itself *An Druidh Uileach Braithreachas*, hereinafter ADUB, which in Scots Gaelic means literally 'The Universal Druid Brotherhood'. A somewhat garish and portentous letterhead was devised, prominently featuring a Stonehenge trilithon as a gateway to greater things. The organization was very much dominated by Reid, but a few scanty details about other Universalists can be gleaned. Reid's son Robert, a civil servant, was an active member; and one Arthur Thomas Ap Llywellyn of Kingston-on-Thames, described as 'a Councillor within the life and light of ADUB', wrote a lengthy letter to the *Salisbury Journal* during the burials dispute of August 1924.[29] In the early days, the hierarchy included a 'Chief Arch' of indeterminate function. Walter Rodway was one, a Hammersmith grocer, allegedly initiated in 1918, although he died not long afterwards: it was his ashes, together with those of George Catchlove, that were at the centre of the 1924 burial dispute.[30]

Rodway's successor was Valentine Haig, after 1925 no longer 'Chief Arch' but 'Secretary'.[31] Catchlove was a Clapham schoolmaster, a vegetarian, 'food reformer' and 'a regular enthusiast regarding camp-open-air-life', who died before 1919.[32] He was described as a 'Corresponding Councillor' (press officer); others included one 'Thomas Ireland', a shadowy figure about whom nothing else is known. His outbursts were so like those of Reid that I am inclined to see him as a pseudonym for Reid himself. Arthur Peacock, another 'Corresponding Councillor', had a more definite existence. Reid's most devoted follower, Peacock first heard Reid's fiery socialist oratory on Clapham Common in 1917, when he was a teenage shop assistant, and gradually became the mainstay of the Clapham temple. A one-time Guild Socialist, closely connected with the New Britain movement of the 1930s, Peacock became editor of the once-famous Socialist journal, *The Clarion*, finding time to edit the *Druid Journal* on the side. From 1931 to 1946 he was Secretary-Manager of the National Trade Union Club, and latterly became a part-time Unitarian minister, which he remained until his death in 1968.[33]

There were female Druids too, notably the Leamington hairdresser Julia Steer. Two women were recorded as present at the 1914 solstice, a woman was involved in the scrap at the Stonehenge turnstile in 1925, and another is found selling the *Druid Journal* in 1930; but their names were not recorded. Perhaps the most eccentric of the ADUB Druids, apart from Reid himself, was John Soul, Amesbury grocer and a bitter opponent both of the Stonehenge fence and of its custodian, whose job he felt he could do better. Soul 'became a member of Macgregor Reid's party' around 1920, and acted as *agent provocateur* throughout ADUB's various confrontations with authority. Soul published two short guides to Amesbury (1923, 1926), and in 1927 produced a 42-page compilation entitled *Stonehenge and the Ancient Mysteries*, whose 'philosophy of Joy' has a distinctly Universalist flavour.[34] In the recollection of Amesbury councillor and peace activist Austin Underwood, Soul's presence was an important feature of the Solstice atmosphere: 'John Soul in his topi, his white twill trousers tucked into puttees, a haversack slung over his shoulder and his shepherd's crook and oak twig with leaves in his hand, was certainly a central figure.'[35]

It seems pretty clear, however, that the core membership of the ADUB was the Clapham congregation; indeed, the two were probably synonymous. Some American Universalists who tried to visit the Clapham church around the 1930 solstice found the doors locked: they were told that the congregation was away 'to a summer Assembly down Stonehenge way'.

In the late 1940s, after the Church had been bombed, the 'basic membership' of the Universalist congregation was put at 37, with an extra 100 on a mailing list.[36] These figures tally with the Stonehenge custodians' headcounts: 34 Druids took part in the solstice ceremony in 1928, and 52 the following year, when the Druids were reported as arriving in 'two motor coaches'.[37] An average 'Druid population' of around 50 seems about right during the 1920s, but there were many other sympathizers.

These scant biographical details suggest that ADUB members, like their leader, came from the same artisanal/lower middle class substrata that produced the 'organic intellectuals' of earlier centuries, but there is simply not enough data for categorical statements to be made. They had some well-placed supporters, notably Pamela Tennant, who married two prominent members of the Liberal Party in succession (making her Lady Glenconner from 1911 to 1922, thereafter Lady Grey until her death in 1928). She lived close to Stonehenge at Wilsford Manor, and was an admirer of 'the noble teaching of the Universal Church', which she saw as an authentic source of 'lofty' Druidism.[38] She was present at the 1915 solstice service[39] and helped the Druids in a practical fashion not only by allowing them to camp on her land from 1913 onwards, but by giving them the right to hold their services at the 'Double Circle' at Normanton Gorse during their various tussles with temporal authority.[40]

Furthermore, since Druid Universalism did not require its adherents to formally subscribe to anything, it was not necessary to be conscious of being a Druid Universalist in order to be one. In Macgregor Reid's words, 'Where the old ideas are taught it is sufficient for us to say, "Here lies the ancient message in another guise".'[41] This convenient arrangement not only allowed Reid to augment the Universalist population at will when importuned for statistics by journalists, but also to invoke all the great names of the socialist canon as founding fathers. The Druid order, which he brazenly claimed to have been meeting at the Stones since 'the days of the Digger movement', was at different times said to have included Gerard Winstanley, John Lilburne, John Ruskin, Charles Dickens, Robert Owen, Tom Paine, Dante Gabriel Rossetti, Walter Crane, William Morris, Pierre-Joseph Proudhon, Eliphas Levi, Gerald Massey, the Buddhist Edwin Arnold, the Theosophist Colonel Henry Olcott and a host of lesser luminaries, as well as writers on Druidry such as John Aubrey, William Stukeley, William Blake, John Toland and Godfrey Higgins. James Relly, generally known as the first formal Universalist, was described by Reid as 'the Druid who restored the movement, and gave to it the name of Universalism'.[42]

The Labour Druid

From this catalogue of radical idealists, a list of 'Chosen Chiefs' was eventually elaborated by Macgregor Reid's son Robert; but the only one to achieve that distinction during Reid senior's own lifetime was his immediate 'predecessor' John Barry O'Callaghan (described as 'the late Chosen Chief' in 1929[43]). O'Callaghan was a civil engineer, an Irishman fervently loyal to the former Home Rule leader Charles Stuart Parnell, and a close personal friend of Macgregor Reid; on his death in 1909, Reid published a four-page black-bordered obituary in *The Nature Cure*. He was a Simplicitarian, an anti-vivisectionist, a one-time Roman Catholic who ended his days as an 'unabridged Universalist'; but what seemed to have impressed Macgregor Reid the most about his friend's career was his role as social reformer. He was 'The Founder of the Ideal of an Equitably Governed State', President of the Rational Reform League and 'the originator of the most equitable system of taxation yet evolved'.[44] At first sight, this might seem to be a somewhat curious credential for a latter-day Druid chieftain, but to Macgregor Reid fiscal reform was inseparable from more esoteric matters. 'Political economy ... is the application of morals to business. Eliminate the moral element, and political economy becomes the science of dust and ashes; all the heart of affairs scorched out of them.'[45] In Reid's journal, *The New Life*, space was found to print lengthy book reviews and articles about the nature of 'the Body Economic' and its relationship to higher things. 'Religious advancement must go hand in hand with economic advancement. The one cannot be separated from the other.'[46]

Considerations such as these led Reid to join the British Labour Party. Towards the end of the Great War, Macgregor Reid began regularly preaching Socialism on Clapham Common, apparently under the banner of the 'Commonwealth and Free State League'. 'Huge crowds' came to hear him, summoned from a bright red Daimler in which he toured the streets, banging 'a huge dinner gong'.[47] When the Labour Party was formally constituted in 1918, the CFSL morphed into Clapham Labour Party, with Reid as Chairman. His tenure was, not surprisingly, controversial: his autocratic and outspoken manner alienated many people. After the collapse of the General Strike in May 1926, Reid rounded on some of his fellow-socialists, branding them as '[t]hieves, swindlers and scoundrels'. The national Labour Party was called in to 'make a close inquiry into the conduct and management of the Clapham Labour Party', and headquarters insisted on imposing a constitution on the local party. Macgregor Reid resigned, taking half the Clapham party with him.[48]

His Stonehenge solstice platform remained, however. Six hundred people walked across Salisbury Plain to the 'Double Circle' to take part in the 1926 druid solstice, and he told them that the miners, who alone were still on strike, 'were lied against by the press', and railed against 'progress' that he claimed was increasing poverty: 'the great struggle for what they called progress threw more men and women into the army of the unemployed, made hunger abound more than ever – and still they talk of progress'.[49]

The Universalists' evening services at the 'Double Circle' continued to attract people in surprising numbers: 1,000 in 1928, 2,000 in 1929 and 1930.[50] Macgregor Reid's utterances were covered in detail in the local papers; several times in the 1920s druidic activities made national headlines, and once they caused a stir in the government. Reid's peculiar blend of radical politics and esoteric wisdom was becoming a thorn in the side of authority both archaeological and political.

Chapter 11

Stonehenge: A Mecca of Celtic Idealism

The Office of Works

Stonehenge was Alpha and Omega to the Universal Bond. 'Here the offices now performed by Canterbury, Westminster, Greenwich and Eton were unified. Some day it may become a new Jerusalem and the temple of peace among the nations', explained Macgregor Reid in 1932.[1] It was to them a living temple, and they were profoundly – and volubly – indignant at all attempts to interfere with their right to celebrate their faith without toll or interference.

In 1918, when Cecil Chubb gave Stonehenge to the nation, the Office of Works resolved to retain both the admission charge and Antrobus' former caretaker, both of which were anathema to the Druids. The following June, someone (possibly George Engleheart, of the Wiltshire Archaeological & Natural History Society, and later a contributor to *Antiquity*), was writing to the local papers urging that the Druids' rights to celebrate the solstice should be curtailed. ADUB promptly lobbied the Prime Minister, Lloyd George, urging him to extend his influence 'to the maintenance of peace within our little Mecca of Celtic idealism at Stonehenge'.[2] The Inspector of Ancient Monuments, Charles Peers, agreed to let 'these curious persons' carry on as before, 'as they do no harm to the stones, nor outrage conventional public decency'. Not, however, as of right: the power to include or to exclude now rested firmly with the civil servants; and that summer (1919), the caretaker prevented the Druids from holding an extra service on another day. In this he was supported by Peers: 'They have no claim to be treated as other than ordinary members of the public.'[3]

Although Peers and his staff were scrupulously correct in their dealings with the Bond, they were not prepared to exempt them from payment on religious grounds, even though – as they were regularly reminded – places of worship were freely open to the public. It may not be coincidental that Peers was implementing a policy which, as principal architect of the 1913 Ancient Monuments Act, he had largely devised; a policy that specifically differentiated between 'buildings' (classed as 'living') and 'ruins' (classed as 'dead'): 'Buildings which are in use are still adding to their history; they are alive. Buildings which are in ruin are dead; their history is ended.'[4] Keith Emerick has explored some of the repercussions of this classification on inter-war heritage management; for present purposes, it is clear that Peers could have few sympathies with any contemporary religious use of a site whose 'history has ended'.

Next year, when the Druids asked for permission to hold services not just on the Solstice but on two further days as well, Peers instructed his staff to refuse: 'Some limit must be set to this absurd and degrading nonsense.' ADUB complained; Peers endorsed their letter with a memo to his subordinate: 'it might be as well to inform these people that if attempts to take more than is granted are made, we may have to reconsider the concessions already given'.[5]

In the event, they were eventually given permission for the extra days, but were still required to pay the entrance fee. The Bond responded by refusing to hold their service at Stonehenge at all, transferring their activities to the 'Double Circle' instead. Here, in the rain, Reid 'made some strong remarks on the action of the Government in refusing to allow them inside Stonehenge', and gave a lecture which, according to the *Salisbury Times*, was 'listened to very attentively by a good number'.[6]

In 1921, a tirade of letters from ADUB to the government prompted a flurry of correspondence between the Office of Works and Downing Street. Once again, the government agreed to let the Druids use the Stones but insisted on payment. Once again, the Druids made a point of refusing to pay for access to what they considered to be a place of worship: 'You persist in regarding Cathoir Ghall [i.e. Stonehenge] as a Circus or Museum', the First Commissioner was told. Things had not changed for the better since the government had taken control of Stonehenge: 'Tyranny, greater than that of the private citizen, is a great factor of State Control.'[7] Insult was added to injury at the 1922 solstice, when a group of soldiers from the nearby Larkhill base performed a mock-ceremony in white sheets and false beards, allegedly with the connivance of the caretaker. The Druids were ferociously indignant at this 'burlesque', and refused to hold their solstice service there the following year. 'Pass this word along to the People', said the handbill they produced, 'and demand that all Ancient Rights of the People shall be respected. Judge between the Druids and all who stand within the Coward's Castle.'[8]

Rakings and Diggings

Meanwhile, the Office of Works was sanctioning the removal of half the site in the name of archaeology. When Stonehenge was enclosed by Sir Edmund Antrobus in 1901, the countryside access campaigner Lord Eversley lamented that the effect was 'to rob it of its peculiar character – a strange relic of the twilight of the world, standing untouched through countless centuries – and to convert it into an antiquarian's specimen'.[9] This is precisely what Stonehenge became in the early 1920s. In 1919–20, the Office of Works financed a programme of selective restoration to their new acquisition, and called in the Society of Antiquaries to appoint an 'expert antiquary' to supervise the operation. The Antiquaries, however, had more ambitious plans. The President, Sir Arthur Evans (the excavator of Knossos), was nearing the end of his five-year term of office, which had coincided with the Great War. Chris Chippindale suggests that he'd found it 'frustrating ... The Stonehenge restoration gave him a chance to make his mark with "a new outlet for the Society's energies"; the small excavations required by the Office of Works would only be preliminaries to a grander scheme, "an eventual exploration of the whole monument within and including the circular bank and ditch" '. In 1920, the Office of Works decided that the urgent work had been done, and suspended their operations. The Antiquaries' chosen excavator, however, Colonel Hawley, was 'empowered' to continue excavating the site, which he did, usually alone, for the next six years. Chippindale says frankly that the Hawley years were 'a disaster'. By 1926, half the site had been dug away, and yet the monument remained as mysterious as ever.[10]

Hawley, although he kept a watchful eye on the Druids and once suggested privately to the Office of Works that all ceremonies should be stopped,[11] seems to have maintained good personal relations with them;[12] but they were upset by the wholesale destruction his excavations were causing, which Reid described as 'desecration'.[13] As he told Lord Crawford, President of the Society of Antiquaries:

> all the rakings and diggings of the Archaeologists have taught us nothing about Stonehenge, and all the promises of today will but lead us to the carefully planned assumptions and suppositions with which the Archaeologists have tried to make a position for themselves. Archaeologists cannot explain Stonehenge. They do not know its message. The Druid Universalists are established in the life and light of its message. There is nothing to be discovered, and it is time that the disfigurement of Stonehenge ceased. The pleasure of a few Archaeologists should not be permitted to disfigure that which is so sacred to others as well as to the Druids. The prolonged excavations of Colonel Hawley have led to what? . . . Archaeologists having discovered nothing definite regarding Stonehenge, now seek to establish an authority based upon assumption – this we Druids object to . . .[14]

In the context of Hawley's work, they could see little reason why they should not bury the ashes of their dead at the monument. They claimed to have been doing so for years,[15] but in the summer of 1924 they formally requested permission. The first Labour Government had just been elected, 'after every Druid vote had been cast for Labour', as Reid proudly announced. It is conceivable that he knew that the new First Commissioner, Fred Jowett, a veteran of the Morris, Carpenter and Blatchford school of socialism, might be sympathetic; at any rate, permission was granted, 'provided that no danger is done to the monument'.[16]

The reaction was immediate. The 'burials issue' became a minor *cause célèbre*, entangled in anti-government politics, and fanned by the fact that it happened during August, at the height of the newspapers' 'silly season'. It was a storm in a teacup, or maybe, an urn: what damage could the burial of two sets of ashes make, compared with the wholesale activities of Colonel Hawley?; but the furore provides an important insight into the relationship between orthodox archaeology, authority and the Druids.

The protest seems to have been orchestrated by the Wiltshire Archaeological & Natural History Society. The WANHS was a particularly vigorous and vigilant organization, well aware of the exceptional splendour of their county's archaeology. It was dominated by the Cunnington family, descendants of Colt Hoare's famous colleague, who considered that Wiltshire was the home, not just of the finest monuments, but to the first and best archaeologists. They were a force to be reckoned with, as Alexander Keiller was to discover two years later when he wanted to dig at Windmill Hill. In the words of his biographer, 'Wiltshire was the Cunningtons' domain.'[17]

The WANHS Annual Meeting, fortuitously held the same month, resolved to send 'an emphatic protest' to the Minister. G H Engleheart, a scathing critic of the 'orientation' theory of Stonehenge, declared that the Druids' request was 'an almost unbelievable outrage on a national monument that ought to be absolutely sacrosanct'. He was seconded by Frank Stevens, Curator of the Salisbury Museum, and author of the official guide to Stonehenge: 'the prestige of British archaeology was at stake in this matter. What would their friends on the Continent say if they allowed this monument, absolutely unrivalled in the world, to become the scratching-ground or burial-place of a rather obscure sect of which they knew nothing?'[18]

But Jowett decided to stick by his decision. The WANHS immediately got on to the local MPs. Jowett dismissed the concerns of Major Fletcher Moulton (Salisbury, Lib), prompting his colleague A J Bonwick (Chippenham, Lib) to invoke the expert authority of the WANHS, who, he told the Minister, 'are very much troubled about the answer you gave ... The people of Wiltshire are very much concerned ... '[19]

The Society of Antiquaries was particularly worried about the impact on Hawley's excavations. 'The very idea of burials, even on a modest scale, taking place within the area seemed to militate against the whole scheme of research', Lord Crawford told the Fellows a year later. If the government had acquiesced, 'what I look upon as the most important archaeological work in Europe, with the possible exception of Knossos, would have been brought to an abrupt conclusion'.[20] On 26 August, he wrote to Jowett saying that 'my society is much exercised on the subject', and offered to deal diplomatically with the Druids rather than put Jowett on the spot – while at the same time urging him to 'take action' if they failed to cooperate.[21] His letter in *The Times* (28 August) was indeed a model of diplomacy: 'The Druid movement cannot fail to affront public opinion by exercising the rights just conferred on them. They will earn gratitude by waiving this privilege ... '[22] The same issue carried a similar letter from the veteran Boyd Dawkins, as president of the Royal Archaeological Institute; and a long leading article, in which the 'Thunderer' clearly indicated where authority ought to lie:

> archaeological opinion clearly looks upon the Druids' projected action as an intrusion and a trespass ... No wonder the Wiltshire archaeologists are up in arms. They know the stones better than Whitehall; their county may be said to be the birthplace of English field archaeology, and it is their voice, rather than that of an extraneous sect, which ought to carry the day.[23]

There was more sympathy for the Druids down-market, or, more accurately, less sympathy for the archaeologists, tellingly caricatured by D

Wyndham-Lewis in the *Daily Mail* (then the foremost tabloid): 'Nobody with an ear for music can have failed to be aware within the last few days of the grunts of rage issuing from archaeologists all over the country . . . At the thought of handing over a national monument for such purposes archaeologists are up on their hind legs as one; and (like very aged sheep) they are terrible in their anger and greatly to be feared . . .'[24]

Most papers were as incensed as the Wiltshire archaeologists, however. The *Daily News* (29 August 1924) said that it was 'the sort of silly thing one would expect this sort of society to want to do'. 'The Londoner' in the *Evening News*, who had castigated the Druids nine years earlier, was particularly scathing, declaring Stonehenge to be 'a temple and a holy place for us English who are not Druids of the Clapham sect, whose souls are offended by the thought of this ancient circle of stones being made a chapel for the rites of nonsense, its earth a common grave-yard for the feeble-witted'.[25]

On 5 September, Jowett capitulated. He wrote to Reid withdrawing his permission, explaining frankly that he was doing so 'in view of the protests of the archaeologists and the strong public feeling on the matter'.[26] The *Manchester Guardian* declared itself satisfied. 'In the ordinary run of things it is easier to get a camel through the eye of a needle than to induce a public department to own to a mistake . . . It is to be supposed that when permission was sought Mr Jowett took the Latter-Day Druids at their own pretentious valuation; but having done so with more amiability than research, he was quickly corrected by people of authority.'[27]

Meanwhile, of course, Colonel Hawley at the site itself was pursuing his one-man excavation, with the approval of 'people of authority'. '[Y]ou are in favour of *Government by Clamour*', ADUB told Jowett bitterly. 'Druids have done more for Stonehenge than all the archaeologists put together. They talk and accomplish nothing.'[28] Reid wrote to Ramsey MacDonald, the Prime Minister, offering to meet the archaeologists in public debate, 'so that the people may have an opportunity of deciding between the religious claims of the Druids and their astronomic teachings, and the arbitrary conclusions and assertions of the archaeologists . . . are Druids to be classed as inferior, and Archaeologists as superior? Or, are both sections of the community to be regarded as possessing equal rights?'[29]

The following solstice (1925), the Druids were in militant mood. There was a record crowd at the Stones (the police estimate was 3,000), and according to the caretaker's report, Reid went round the perimeter fence inciting people to tear it down, while his son Robert picked a squabble

15 The controversial Stonehenge turnstile, seen here in the 1920s. (*Wiltshire Local Studies Library*).

with the man on the turnstile, and called out ' "Come on People". The crowd then rushed the Big Gate, and burst it open, and also tore down the wire above the Sunstone.' About a thousand people got in without paying.[30]

For the next two years the Druids stayed away from the Stones. There were rumours that they'd been banned after the troubles of 1925,[31] and it's true enough that civil servants toyed with the idea of raising the cost of admission on solstice night, 'in view of the disorderly conduct of the Druids', but decided against it. In August 1925 they did resolve to 'bear in mind their attitude next year', but next year the Druids stayed away. When in June 1928 Robert Macgregor Reid wrote asking for permission to hold a service, he specifically states that 'we did not seek this permission for the last two years'.[32] Perhaps their exile was self-imposed, and the Druids chose not to risk another confrontation with the authorities. At any event, they celebrated the 1926 and 1927 solstices at the 'Double Circle', in 1926 declaring that 'the Druids had been driven from Stonehenge not because they had done wrong, but because monetary considerations were deemed to be of greater significance than all else'.[33]

Prehistoric Wisdom

Although the Universal Bond's first venture to Stonehenge was probably inspired by the Ancient Order of Druids' grand gathering in 1905, there was little love lost between the two orders. The AOD, in the words of Imperial Grand Arch Buckland, was 'a firmly established and properly organized society', and took great pains to distance itself from the Universal Bond when the latter's activities generated bad publicity.[34] However, on one subject at least, they were both agreed: the wisdom and the virtue of their prehistoric antecedents. The AOD were proud of the connection, mediated through the monument: as Buckland told his members, the link the Stones made between their order and the original Druids was 'wonderful to contemplate'.[35]

The theme of prehistoric wisdom recurred regularly in Reid's public utterances. A week after the AOD gathering in 1925, Reid preached ancient wisdom to 'the biggest crowd within living memory' at the summer solstice: 'Men told them that their forefathers were savages. When they said that they lied. The men who raised these stones possessed information greater than the majority of our people possessed to-day. He asked them not to believe that we were descended from mere barbarians.'[36] Although the Druids were defeated over the burial issue, and Stonehenge was accordingly 'won' for orthodoxy, the public was clearly listening to the Druids. Some academic reaction was inevitable.

Contemporary archaeological interest in 'the meaning of Stonehenge' centred around the issue of 'orientation'. During the nineteenth century, there had been a widely held but vague belief that Stonehenge had been used for sun-worship; in 1906, this was refined by the astronomer Sir Norman Lockyer into an influential theory that the monument had had an astronomical function.[37] Lockyer's ideas were firmly resisted by many archaeologists, and none more so than George Engleheart, of the WANHS. Engleheart believed that Hawley's excavations 'went far to banish for good and all the solar theory of the origin and purpose of Stonehenge . . . nowhere could anyone point to a stone ring in any part of the world that had been proved to have any connection with sun worship.' Like Sir Arthur Evans, he believed that Stonehenge had been built as a tomb; indeed, as readers learned from his *Antiquity* article 'Concerning

Orientation', '[t]he sepulchral origin of Stonehenge can no longer be questioned'.[38] Mortimer Wheeler likewise deplored the fact that Lockyer-style speculation had 'led a generation of antiquaries to waste much time and ink upon the supposed astronomical properties of these circles', and his comments were cited by Kendrick in 1927, who assured his readers that 'there is no ethnographical warrant that primitive man of the culture-level represented by the circles was capable of elaborate astronomical measurements of this kind'.[39] Not only was the contemporary Stonehenge solstice thus deprived of all legitimacy, but the intellectual capacities of its builders were dismissed according to the best social evolutionary preconceptions.

Other archaeologists sought to dismantle the perceived connection between Stonehenge and the Druids. O G S Crawford's brief letter to *The Times* during the burials controversy attacked ADUB's two 'incorrect' assumptions: 'that their Order is descended from the real Druids, and that the real Druids were connected with Stonehenge'.[40] Boyd Dawkins similarly tried to discredit the Druids' claims to represent 'the most ancient faith' by stressing the time-gap between the building of Stonehenge and the date of the 'Celtic' Druid cult.[41]

The theme was developed in 1927 by Thomas Kendrick, Christopher Hawkes' colleague in the Department of British & Medieval Antiquities at the British Museum, in his *The Druids: A Study in Keltic Prehistory*. The book began by acknowledging the extent of public interest in his subject: 'There is little need to remark upon the inextinguishable affection with which the Druids are still regarded in the popular imagination.' To the 'unlettered public ... the Druids are rapidly becoming synonymous with the Ancient Britons, that is to say, the pre-Roman population of this country'.[42] The timing of *The Druids* is testimony to the strength of public feeling and the need for orthodoxy to reply effectively to the much-publicized claims of the Druids. But although Kendrick's credentials were certainly pukka, it's a surprising book.

Clearly and conscientiously written, Kendrick sought to demonstrate the lack of continuity between the original builders of Stonehenge, the 'Celtic' Druids of the Iron Age, and the present day; but then provided startling and unexpected succour for the Druid cause by suggesting that the *present* structure may indeed have been built by the Druids. He based this claim on what he took to be 'the indirect influence of classical architecture', a recorded La Tène burial, and the 'surprising amount of British and Romano-British pottery' that Hawley's diggings had uncovered, an ironic twist:

> My view, then, is that the Kelticized population of Wessex took advantage of the ancient *national* sanctity of the old circle-site on Salisbury Plain to construct thereupon a temple for their faith that should serve as a rallying-point, and more than that – a stimulus, for Druidism after the beginning of the failure of the order in Gaul, that is to say, in the 1st century BC. And in the final effort to assert the national faith in the face of the distant rumours of Roman aggression, the Britains [*sic*] tried to build for themselves, though preserving the ancient circle- and grove-tradition, as grand a temple as those the refugee Druids from Gaul had seen erected by the Greeks and the Romans.[43]

He even suggested that Druid re-use of the monument might have survived the fall of Rome (even if not by very long). Kendrick was well aware that 'even this much will be challenged by most archaeologists of to-day', but criticism was surprisingly muted. The Cunningtons, for instance, were suitably impressed by the man from the British Museum, and revised their histories accordingly. 'The inception may after all have been due to that romantic order, the Druids', wrote R H Cunnington in 1935.[44]

Kendrick's case was picked up promptly by the author and occultist Lewis Spence, whose book, *The Mysteries of Britain; or, the Secret Rites and Traditions of Ancient Britain restored*, was published the following year (1928). Kendrick, said Spence, 'has succeeded in placing the entire question on a much more tolerable basis than formerly'; he had supplied 'a treatment of the subject so convincing, yet so free from dogmatism as to provide a most suitable starting-point' for the thesis of Spence's own book.[45] He then went on to refute Kendrick's claims for lack of continuity and to set out the beliefs of the Druids as Spence perceived them, based upon a panoply of Celtic literature whose authenticity Kendrick would certainly have questioned. Orthodoxy was becoming disoriented.

Information Control

Although the newspapers reported no more trouble, in 1930 a retired army major informed the Office of Works that Macgregor Reid was still inciting visitors to tear down the fences, amongst other things: 'he spoke against the Church and religion and upheld the Soviet Government . . . His general speaking was communistic and anti-Government . . . Although one or two present argued with him there were others who shook him by the hand as evidence of their appreciation of what he said.'[46]

Stonehenge: A Mecca of Celtic Idealism

The New Life and
DRUID JOURNAL
Official Organ of
AN DRUIDH UILEACH BRAITHREACHAS
Special Summer Solstice Number, 1931

Back to the past we all must go! There is
One way for all within the great abyss,
In which to-morrow, like to-day, must fall;
Thus Druids turn in faith to Cathoir Ghall.

16 Sale of *The New Life and Druid Journal* at Stonehenge was banned.

The Office of Works did not take any action over this part of the Major's allegations, but they were concerned over his claim that '[c]ertain pamphlets were being sold within Stonehenge by a girl and a man who were evidently his associates'. The pamphlet in question was *The New Life*, now revamped as *The New Life & Druid Journal* and sporting a rather stylish, arts-and-craftsy trilithon on the front cover. Inquiries were duly made of the (new) custodian, who reported that 'there was nothing to take exception to in it'.[47] Further complaints were received the next year from 'local residents', however, perhaps involved in a protest Christian service that was held at this solstice. Sensing trouble, Arthur Peacock, editor of the *Journal*, sent a courteous letter to the Office of Works asking for formal permission to sell the *Journal* as they had been doing. He was refused: 'none but official publications can be sold at ancient monuments in their custody'. It does not seem that any slight was intended – nine years earlier, Peers had turned down a similar request from the WANHS – but the Druids felt strongly that the official guide-book was biased against them. 'It is only just and fair that if Mr Stevens' book which gives the anti-Druid view is on sale at the turnstile, then on the day of our Service, at least, copies of the *Druid Journal* might be placed with the caretaker, and then made available to enquirers who might wish to have them', wrote Peacock.[48]

The ban, Reid claimed, was the last straw. Not only had they had been 'forced to beg from an authority of the Earth to worship in their own temple', but '[t]he ideas contained in the guide book to Stonehenge issued by the Government brought shame to every man and woman who understood aught about this great question'.[49] This was the last solstice they'd hold at Stonehenge, he declared, and announced plans to build a new temple at the 'Double Circle': a scheme for which, he claimed, he had already raised £4,000. This utterance was designed to upset everyone, particularly in view of the contemporary National Trust campaign to have all visible buildings in the Stonehenge landscape removed. '[T]o erect it within sight of genuine Stonehenge is a proposition of atrociously bad taste', opined the *Wiltshire Gazette* (30 June 1932).

No more was heard of the scheme, but the Universal Bond duly stayed away from the Stones for the rest of the decade. As if to compensate, the AOD and other Druidical groups held ceremonies regularly at other times of the summer, but to many, the Druids had become synonymous with the Stonehenge solstice. Numbers of participants dwindled steadily during the 1930s, and at least one observer attributed some of this decline to Druidic abstinence.[50]

The Druid Hermeticists

By 1932 Reid was by any reckoning getting on a bit, ample excuse for being a tad less confrontational; but it was his old calling of Nature Cure that lured him away from the Stones. Nature Cure had been enjoying quite a revival during the 1920s, and Reid somehow found the money to open his own 'Nature Camp' in Sussex, 'a communal settlement . . . where men and women in the vanguard movement of politics and religion might come for rest and recuperation'. He died in 1946.[51]

After Reid's *de facto* retirement, his spiritual empire divided naturally into two. Arthur Peacock, who succeeded Reid as Minister of the Clapham church in 1937, endeavoured to bring it into line with more orthodox forms of Universalism by making contact with the wider (essentially American) Universalist community; but in August 1944, the building was bombed and subsequently demolished. The Church then met in various buildings in central London, until Peacock eventually took himself, and presumably whatever was left of the Universalist congregation, into the Unitarian church.[52]

Macgregor Reid's Druidic mantle was inherited by George W Smith, also from Clapham, who was as proud as Peacock to proclaim his debt to Reid: 'He was the most remarkable man I have ever met. He was very learned and I am only too proud to say he taught me all I know, both of the Druid movement and of the Socialist movement.'[53] Smith first came across Macgregor Reid when he came out of the Army in 1919; he promptly joined the Clapham Labour Party, and served on the Executive as Secretary for South Ward until 1930.[54] At some point before June 1938, Smith became the General Secretary of the 'Ancient Order of Druid Hermetists'. In 1938, Smith wrote to the Office of Works requesting permission to celebrate at Stonehenge, and also played a major part in producing the Order's journal, called *The Pendragon*, the first issue of which appeared at Midsummer 1938. The timing suggests that it was designed for distribution at Stonehenge, like the *Druid Journal* before it; and the following year, when he applied for permission on behalf of the AODH's Grand Council, the letterhead bore the same winged-sun symbol that Macgregor Reid had used for *The New Life* 25 years earlier.[55] Here, however, the similarities begin to fade; for the simple reason that Smith, perhaps faced with the indifference or disinterest of George Reid, had found another elderly, eccentric guru for the cause.

This was William George Hooper, who at one time had been considered a physicist of note: his *Aether and Gravitation*, published in 1903, won him a Fellowship of the Royal Astronomical Society. Hooper had been a practising Christian, a volunteer worker for the YMCA and an active member of the Brotherhood Movement, a sort-of working-class equivalent to the Rotary Club. Shocked by what he saw in France during the Great War, he vowed thereafter to 'work, teach and live for peace and fellowship, based on eternal and cosmic principles of Divine Wisdom and Divine Love'. In 1920 he joined the Brotherhood of Healers, a Christian-based faith-healing network founded by the eccentric Brother James Macbeth Bain, hymn-writer and barefoot advocate; and established a 'New Age' centre at Highcliffe on Sea near Bournemouth, a well-heeled strip of Southern England that became something of a centre for occult and mystical activity between the wars.[56]

Smith's Stonehenge speeches, reported in the local press as reliably as Reid's had been, are an interesting fusion of Hooper and Reid.

17 Hermetic interlude. *The Pendragon: Official Organ of the Ancient Order of Druid Hermetists,* Midsummer 1939.

Celebrating the 'Rites of Caevron' at the 'Double Circle' in 1943, to an audience of over 200, he claimed that

> The Druids' inspiration, passing from out of the deepest antiquity, causes the Druid to dedicate his power to the unseen, to the spirit of beauty, of wisdom and of universal love. Thus inspired, the Druid sees the coming of a New Age ... when men will have lost that terrible prerogative we have so long used for cruelty and wrong towards those who are weaker than himself.[57]

The 1943 service was not held at the Stones themselves because Smith's party had apparently once more declined to pay the Office of Works entry fee. In 1946, he requested – and was granted – permission to use the Stones for what was described as the Festival of the Summer Solstice, and the following year arranged to hold a memorial service to Reid on the afternoon of 22 June, at which the BBC was present.[58] Smith was making changes, seeking to open the organization up, endeavouring to underpin the Druids' cause with the symptoms of a more conventional organization. New lodge names appeared, and at the 1948 solstice, he announced that 'the combined Order intends to embark on widespread teaching of pure Druid science and philosophy throughout the British Isles'.[59]

George Smith clearly had the blessings of George Macgregor Reid in his endeavours: he had both the letterhead and the seal, as he told the Office of Works.[60] He and Peacock between them had inherited Macgregor Reid's mission. Reid's son, Robert, however, was none too impressed with the way things had turned out. His father's faithful and devoted follower for much of his life, at some point they fell out, and Robert was cut out of his father's Will completely. He didn't even have the right to call himself Chosen Chief. Although Smith himself was careful to call himself 'Secretary', the title of Chief was bestowed on him by Macgregor Reid senior because he considered his son 'to lack both philosophic depth and leadership'.[61] It seems that some of his father's former Druids considered that he'd been hard done by. Robert had obviously taken part in AODH activities, since in 1947 he resigned from it; and he took several members with him.[62] Someone close to Robert later said that he had been given 'a Mandate to carry on the Druid order' by one Harry Chadwick, 'the last extant member' of Macgregor Reid's Universal Bond Council, and a meeting was duly held at Leamington in November 1949, which confirmed Robert Macgregor Reid as Chosen Chief.[63]

Smith and his party refused to acknowledge the 'coup', and for several years thereafter two groups of Druids, both claiming the legitimacy bestowed by George Watson Reid's precedent, were petitioning the Office of Works for the right to hold the dawn service at the Stonehenge solstice. In 1953, officials of the Office of Works debated the issue, and in the end they found for 'the older group', by which they meant the one led by the well-known name of Macgregor Reid.[64] Having to accept the 'authority of the earth' to arbitrate in matters of Druidic legitimacy was a humiliating moment. When the solstices became riotous during the 1950s the Druids, formerly the scourge of authority, became dependent on such earthy authorities as policemen in order to hold their services at all.[65]

The Power to Pronounce

Stonehenge, one of the world's most famous archaeological sites, is also one of the most contested.[66] The history of its management is perhaps the defining example of the way in which archaeological authority has been exercised in the world beyond the academics' grove; and it demonstrates the very close links between disciplinary authority and legal authority, between intellectual property and property of other kinds.

Chris Chippindale's account of Stonehenge in the nineteenth century reveals that the landowner, Sir Edmund Antrobus (the third baronet), had a marked antipathy to officialdom of all kinds, and would tolerate neither police, nor ancient monuments inspectors, nor archaeologists on his land. The public were free to come and go; and if there were no restrictions on their activities – souvenir-hunting, for instance – there were also no restrictions on the availability of information about the site: Henry Browne and his children published nine editions of his antediluvian speculations between 1823 and 1871, on sale at the Stones, where they acted as informal caretakers.[67]

When the fourth baronet (another Edmund) failed to blackmail the government into buying the site, he enclosed it and charged for admission. His right to do so was upheld in the High Court, on the grounds that a landowner had every right to exclude the public from his private property.[68] In 1918, the government inherited not only the site, but the fence; and the right to control and charge for access, which they have, controversially but lucratively, retained ever since. The Office of Works empowered the Society of Antiquaries to excavate the site and heeded their counsel over the burials issue: a relationship facilitated by the prominent role of Charles Peers and, formerly, Lord Crawford in both organizations. It was not, however, willing to acknowledge any religious vocation for the site as claimed by the Druids, whose 'absurd and degrading nonsense' was tolerated with bad grace.

The government also maintained the right to official interpretation: the only guide-book on sale at the site was that produced by Frank Stevens, the Curator of Salisbury Museum, and also a prominent member of the WANHS known for his lack of sympathy for the latter-day Druids. Evenhandedly, the Office of Works refused to sell either WANHS publications or the *Druid Journal*, but it is easy to see why the Druids were unconvinced. Henry Browne's days were long gone; there was now an 'official line' on the meaning and interpretation of Stonehenge.

The Druids were not alone in their dislike of this closing down of meaning. The artist John Piper contrasted the terse reductionism of the official guide-book with the exuberance of earlier visitors such as the eighteenth-century antiquarian William Stukeley, who according to Piper had 'tumbled over himself with imagery and delightful assertions'.

He declared himself disgruntled with the way the site had been commodified:

> Today we are permitted to call Stonehenge beautiful and ugly at will, but we are warned that it is not the point about it; we refer to its atmosphere of worship at our own risk, on the same terms as we leave our car in the car-park; but if we make a guess about its date and about who built it and why, and if these guesses do not add up to an arid, 'Megalithic, for an unknown purpose,' then we are drunk and disorderly.[69]

The Druid Takeover

To enclosure both physical and epistemic, the Druids mounted a serious challenge. Although Wheeler, Kendrick and Engleheart strove to deprive the solstice of legitimacy, the public attended in steadily increasing numbers throughout the 1920s, and (literally) went out of their way to attend the Druid services. By the 1930s, the Druids had become synonymous with the solstice; and yet the Druid presence at Stonehenge barely antedated the Great War. A tradition had been established, whose origins were wilfully lost in the mists of time, not only by the protagonists themselves, but by the wistfully uncritical journalists who reported their goings-on: indeed, the scorn with which the London papers treated the 'burial issue' is in marked contrast to the annual reports on the solstice in the local press, whose journalists were presumably privy to local informants who could have demolished the Druids' claims, and yet chose to endorse them instead. George Long included the solstice celebration in his *Folklore Calendar*, even though he was sceptical about the Druid's historical claims: 'they deserve a place in this work by reason of so picturesque a ceremony on so historic a site'.[70] Perhaps the local press was similarly motivated.

The popularity of the solstice doubtless owed much to a widespread desire for colour, for mystery and for diversion at a time of growing social unease; and for the same reason the Druids' claims to the antiquity of their religion may have been reassuring. The desire for some sort of encounter with ancient religion, however, did not translate into a massive membership increase for the ADUB; nor did they expect it to. 'Druidism is not likely to become strong in a numerical sense, since few now care to devote themselves to a course of study that has nothing in common with Jazz, Talkies or Cocktails', railed the *Druid Journal* in 1929 (Reid was prone to damning imprecations upon the propensity of visitors to get drunk, or to listen to 'jazz'[71]). For all his populism, it is clear that Reid had strong ideas about what 'the people' ought to want, and the whole 20-year span can even be seen in terms of a 'Druidic takeover' of an anarchically uncontrolled event, in which the role of the temporal powers who controlled the Stones was crucial. Thrown out in 1914 for trying to hold a service, a supporter ejected in 1915 for standing in the wrong place, Chubb's willingness to allow the Druids to hold their service vested Reid with the necessary authority to assume control of the solstice; by 1918, he was already turning visitors into participants by rearranging them around the stone circle. Refusal to pay the modest entrance fees imposed by the Office of Works allowed the Druids to portray themselves as martyrs, and to entice away large proportions of the crowd to a space of their own, where their rights to the monument were rehearsed to sympathetic audiences. The oppressed underdogs, victims of state intolerance and religious persecution, thereby enhanced their status considerably, to the point at which their right to preside over the Solstice rituals was questioned neither by journalists nor, eventually, by the Office of Works itself.

Part IV
Order and Civilization

Chapter 12

The Aesthetics of Order

Finding order in the past is an intrinsic part of any approach to it: including mine, of course. Julian Thomas sees this as archaeology's contribution to 'the modern "war against chaos" ', whilst astutely pointing out that '[t]his may be an order that would be entirely unfamiliar to past people'.[1]

To Macgregor Reid and his followers, ill at ease with the values and the limitations of contemporary civilization, the ancient past contained evidence of values or of knowledge that might defy or even undermine it. Modern 'civilization' represents not only a 'loss of innocence' but a 'loss of knowledge': the knowledge of the Golden Age, when people truly understood the universe, and lived in harmony with its laws. 'Stonehenge proves that its builders were not savages, but men of great attainments, to whom both Celestial and terrestrial laws were known even more clearly than they are at present', declared the Druids in 1921. 'Knowledge is not a monopoly of our present age. Humanity cannot be classed as a product of that which we have called civilization.'[2] Druidic universalism made real the 'primitive religion' that so many were striving for, the faith of a world in harmony.

To those who were happy with the social order, on the other hand, or who believed, like the Marxian socialists, that the social order was destined to change in the correct direction, it made sense to find laws that underpinned and justified the current epistemology. The search for 'laws' of culture change and human behaviour, later to blossom into 'processualism', had barely begun – but in creating a discipline based upon the nineteenth-century faith in social evolution, archaeologists were systematically seeking to bring the ancient past into modern comprehension by imposing modern notions of order upon the chaos of the past. The archaeology they created is as recognizably a construction of the 1920s and 1930s as the architecture of the time, and stands in a similar relationship to what they saw as the rambling deviousness of romanticism as the Senate House Library does to St Pancras Station Hotel.

Tidying Up the Past

'Simple', 'clean' and 'orderly' are concepts that can be applied to all aspects of the nascent discipline. From the emphasis on practical skills and techniques in excavation and recording; from the preservation and display of monuments and other artefacts, to the new emphasis on economy and ecology as constraining and defining influences on prehistoric society, inter-war scientific archaeology was unequivocally 'functionalist'. George Stocking perceptively notes that the concept of functionalism 'had a resonantly innovative, clarifying quality, at once liberating and reassuring, in the intellectual and ideological context of the 1920s'; the term 'had a cultural resonance far outside of anthropology, from biology and psychology to architecture and furniture design'.[3] It could be argued that 'functionalism' was an aesthetic of science: a 'streamlined' style of knowledge acquisition, reflecting the values of the society within which it was constructed. Accretions of theory and speculation were ruthlessly discarded in favour of the true, bare lines of honest fact.

Archaeology's factiness was certainly part of its appeal. 'We speak from facts, not theory', Richard Colt Hoare's famous adage, was regularly quoted with approval by Crawford. Aileen Fox, writing in 1944, suggested that Hoare's words 'might well serve for the body of archaeologists at the present day', contrasting the 'laborious collection of facts' with 'superficial generalizations, the easy product of the amateur'.[4]

Others chose to contrast the honesty of archaeological evidence with the trickery of words. Clark's *Archaeology and Society* began by emphasizing how archaeology, with its flints and potsherds, is free 'from all those defects of fallible humanity which impair the value of documentary evidence'.[5]

The unadorned, vibrant quality of cave paintings similarly mocked the florid formalism of what was widely understood as 'art'. It is no coincidence that 'modern' art began with the rediscovery of Palaeolithic art.

The Aesthetics of Order

Jonathan Jones sees this as 'a liberation from a history that had become stale and burdensome... This art is not only prehistoric; it is anti-historic'. In similar vein, Gordon Childe felt that 'it is permissible to doubt whether the "Highland Cattle" on the sitting-room wall or the diamond necklace on the dowager's throat be an advance on the bison on the limestone cave or the shell necklace on the Crô-Magnon savage.' Crawford, too, hoped that the 'World Museum' of which he dreamed in 1921 would contain devices 'to beautifying necessary objects, not by secondary and often hideous "ornament" (as now) but by closer adaptation of design to ends'.[6] Stuart Piggott in 1937 explicitly contrasted the content of the Blackmore Museum in Salisbury with the 'exuberant Gothicism' of its architecture:

> In this scene of Puginesque splendour the Fisherton paleoliths or the Danish flint axes look oddly out of place – the scientific typological series struggling amidst the Romantic fog in which the science had its origins.[7]

The prevalence of such ideas is crucial to understanding the inter-war generations' 'no-nonsense' approach to archaeology, and the desire to strip away romantic clutter from all aspects of the craft. 'The primary purpose of my appointment', wrote Crawford of his job as Archaeological Officer to the Ordnance Survey, 'was to reduce to order the chaotic mixture of antiquarianism and speculation that disfigured the Ordnance maps, and to bring it into conformity with existing knowledge', removing 'such blemishes as "druidical altars"'.[8]

Nowhere was the modernist aesthetic more apparent than in the display of ancient monuments. A *Times* leader of 1936 summed up the situation succinctly, claiming that 'our modern pride in the past' was driven by

> a desire for accurate knowledge, not of Roman England only, but also of the earlier England which excavation is turning from prehistoric into historic... indeed sentimental regard for the picturesque has little encouragement these days anywhere with reach of the wholesome matter-of-factness of the Office of Works and the National Trust.[9]

The reference to the Office of Works is not fortuitous. Keith Emerick's interesting discussion on the heritage management philosophy of Charles Peers, Chief Inspector of Ancient Monuments from 1913 to 1933, reveals an emphasis on simplicity, both of interpretation – 'the presumption was for the presentation of the single-period monument' – and of presentation: Peers himself felt that ruins were best 'set reverently in a simple setting of grass lawns'.[10]

Peers' policy was renowned. To Mortimer Wheeler, '[t]he stern puritanism with which Peers stripped abbeys and castles of their "romantic" but destructive weeds found compensation in the smooth lawns and clean masonry which became a sort of sign-manual of our national monuments under his direction'.[11] It is significant, however, that the remodelling of the country's two most famous prehistoric sites was not the work of the Office of Works. Peers' preoccupations were widely shared.

Streamlining the Neolithic 1: Stonehenge

Stonehenge became an icon during the Great War, 'the heart of the England for which we are offering such sacrifice in battle', in the words of the *Evening News* columnist angered by Macgregor Reid's 'suburban dervishes' in 1915.[12] The following year saw the first edition of Frank Stevens' guide-book, *Stonehenge Today and Yesterday*. His text was unadventurous, but it was supplemented by a series of superb line-drawings by the arts and crafts veteran Heywood Sumner, a friend of Crawford and himself an archaeologist. Wistful and evocative, full of space, they depict a monument wide open to the skies; supplemented with maps that stressed geometry and drawings of artefacts that stressed simplicity. Sumner's Stonehenge became official once the Stones came into public ownership in 1918, for Stevens' book (much to druidic disgust) was adopted by the Office of Works, reprinted by Her Majesty's Stationery Office in 1919 and then went through six further editions before the Second World War. His vision was thus shared with many thousands of visitors, and may perhaps be seen both as defining and creating the modernists' ideal of antiquity, uncluttered and clear.

Stonehenge itself, however, was far from being uncluttered and clear. During the war, an aerodrome had been built a few hundred yards to the west, replacing a pair of caretakers' cottages that Antrobus had built, which were then rebuilt close to the crossroads. Then, in 1926, Miss Margaret Billett opened 'The Stonehenge Café' just across the road. She offered 'Light Refreshments, Teas, Minerals, Tobaccos, Cigarettes, Curios & Postcards ... Bathroom and Every Convenience',[13] but it hardly fitted with the Sumner image. It was 'a cheap, flashy little building like the worst

Stonehenge, Today – Looking West.

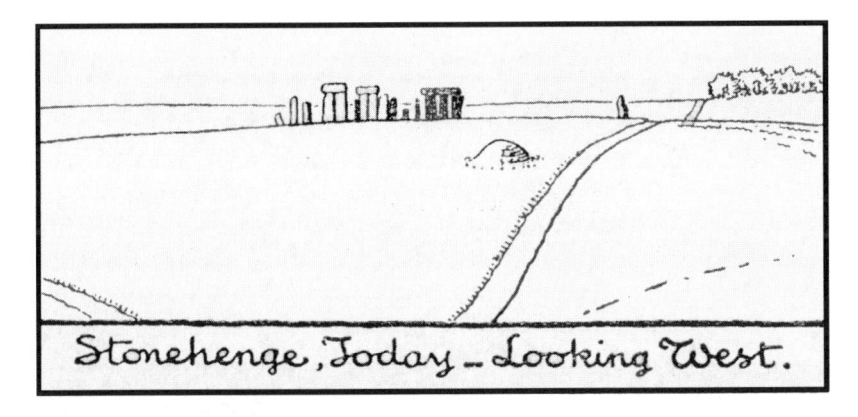

18 The Dream: Heywood Sumner's uncluttered vision.

19 The Reality: caretakers' cottages at the crossroads, aerodrome in the background and – horror of horrors – a transport café. (*English Heritage*).

20 The Nightmare: 'Stonehenge in 1930? A dreadful vision of what might happen if the present appeal were to fail.'

type of bungaloid growth', esteemed the Office of Works; it 'spoils the whole scene and vulgarizes [the vista] unspeakably'.[14] Crawford called it 'odious'.[15] It was rapidly becoming apparent that there was nothing to prevent the monument from being engulfed by development. Crawford, Keiller and Sir John Squire discussed the issue over lunch in a London club, and, with the active support of the Wiltshire Archaeological & Natural History Society, an Appeal was launched in August 1927 to buy the adjacent land and donate it to the National Trust.[16] Under the telling heading of 'The Heart of England', the Appeal, signed by the Prime Minister (Stanley Baldwin) and other political leaders, declared that 'The solitude of Stonehenge should be restored, and precautions taken to ensure that our posterity will see it against the sky in the lonely majesty before which our ancestors have stood in awe throughout all our recorded history.'[17]

The Appeal succeeded in raising sufficient money to buy the land to the west and east of the Stones, but only enough to buy an option on the land to the north. In March 1929, with less than a month to go, a further appeal was launched, signed by the same luminaries as before; and this time they pulled out all the stops. 'This tract, which includes the southward-facing road frontage immediately opposite the stones, is in obvious and immediate danger of building. Unless it is saved, the whole work of the committee and the subscribers will have been in vain, and Stonehenge will have a solitude to the south and a street to the north. Our generation will be vilified by all posterity if we allow the surroundings of this monument, the frontispiece to English history, to be ruined beyond repair.'[18]

A letter was sent to *The Times*, signed by a number of prominent writers and artists, including Arnold Bennett, Sybil Thorndike, Rebecca West and A P Herbert. They expressed their 'consternation that Stonehenge should be threatened by submergence under the rising tide of bungalows . . . Failure to preserve Stonehenge would, surely, be a blow delivered at the roots of culture.'[19] The same theme was developed in the *Illustrated London News*: 'Stonehenge stands in peril of desecration by the imminent sale of adjoining land as "a desirable building plot", with all it involves of villadom and vandalism, of teashops, charabancs and petrol pumps.' A map showed the precise bounds of the plot 'now menaced by the builder', and two illustrations contrasted 'Stonehenge in 1830 . . . seen in its solitary grandeur against the sky' with 'Stonehenge in 1930? A dreadful vision of what might happen if the present appeal were to fail': charabancs and smoking chimneys, industrial units, advertising hoardings and telegraph poles evoked the nightmare image of ribbon-development along an arterial road, so evocative to the preservationists in that era of large-scale and unrestrained building development.[20]

The appeal succeeded. The land was bought, and the offending buildings were demolished.[21] The setting of Stonehenge was thus preserved, or rather, restored; but in the process it was transformed into a new sort of monument. 'Every age has the Stonehenge it deserves – or desires': Jacquetta Hawkes' famous observation.[22] The Stonehenge of the 1930s was set apart, removed from the forces of commercial vulgarization: the modernist anticipation – indeed, epitome – of the Town & Country Planning Act.

Streamlining the Neolithic 2: Avebury

Stonehenge was not the first time that Crawford and Keiller worked together in the pursuit of archaeological conservation. In 1923, Crawford launched a campaign to prevent the Marconi Company from erecting a radio mast on Windmill Hill, near Avebury. At his prompting, Alexander

Keiller wrote a duly indignant letter to the *Scotsman*, in which he revealingly described associated plans to build a large number of houses just outside the village as 'perhaps an even more horrible side of the proposal' than the actual mast. The project was duly cancelled, but Crawford wrote to Keiller suggesting that the survival of sites such as this depended upon their acquisition by well-heeled, well-intentioned private owners such as Keiller.[23] The millionaire heeded the Marxist's counsel; not only did Keiller buy the Windmill Hill site, but he later acquired the West Kennet Avenue, and ultimately, the Avebury circle itself.

The Windmill Hill site was, memorably, excavated; but on the Avenue, and in the circle itself, Keiller indulged in a programme of what a disillusioned Stuart Piggott, his archaeological assistant, was later to call 'megalithic landscape gardening'.[24] When Keiller acquired Avebury, it was, in his words, 'the national archaeological disgrace of Britain'. He removed 'unsightly' accretions, such as barns, sheds and cottages, and blew up extraneous tree stumps. Twenty-seven megaliths were re-erected in the Avenue, firmly re-embedded in concrete, and a further eight within the north-western sector of the circle. Keiller told a friend 'that the sound of the concrete mixer pounding was the most beautiful sound in the world, knowing that each newly unearthed stone would be fixed in her hole and in three thousand years she would still be standing'. Where no stone remained to be unearthed, neat concrete plinths like Ordnance Survey trig-point markers were erected in their stead.[25]

Brian Edwards considers it 'quite incredible' that Keiller could get away with it, in view of the 'increasingly potent legislation' that then existed; he cites the Ancient Monuments Act of 1931, which required local authorities to protect areas around monuments as well as the monuments themselves.[26] Although Peers himself retired in 1933, the Office of Works continued to pursue a policy of minimal intervention on its own monuments. 'New work is only introduced, and then very rarely, for the sole purpose of ensuring the stability of ancient structures', First Commissioner Ormsby-Gore told the Congress of Archaeological Societies in 1935. He lamented that 'the most important [stone circle] of all, Avebury, is not in our guardianship', but praised 'the great progress made this year in the excavation and re-erection of the West Kennet Avenue'. This apparent contradiction was probably due to the delicate negotiations his department was then involved in with Keiller, which ultimately led to the donation of the site;[27] for Keiller's work was clearly 'restoration' and not 'preservation', on a par with the nineteenth-century cathedral rebuilds of

Viollet-le-Duc and Gilbert Scott. The net result was an 'impeccably modern preservationist restoration'. Avebury was returned to archaeological grace, 'landscaped into a modern monument to prehistory', as David Matless has memorably put it.[28]

Neat and orderly, the no-nonsense prehistoric monuments of the 1930s became museum pieces, interpreted by authority, neutral places of education and instruction, outside time. Ruins, in Peers' words, 'are dead; their history is ended'; this, as we've seen, underpinned his department's whole philosophy. Decay was abolished; gone was the Romantic notion of ruins as *memento mori*. 'We regard the conservation of structures as our first task', declared Ormsby-Gore, 'first and foremost by the removal of ivy and other growths so dear to our romantic-minded forefathers and so harmful and dangerous to masonry.'[29] The past was thoroughly modernized, its monuments refashioned to look as clean-cut, streamlined and civilized as the future.

Conquest and Colonization

Romantic interpretations were somehow just as harmful to epistemological structure as romantic ivy was to brick, stone and mortar; and distinguishing the scientific approach from the romantic was an absolute necessity for those who sought to establish archaeology as a profession. It was their mission to take the torch of enlightenment science through the romantic 'mist' and 'fog' they so regularly alluded to[30] into the dark places of wild antiquarianism.

Time was to be colonized much as space had been in the previous century. Prehistory, hitherto barely charted, was to be systematically explored, the frontier rolled back: 'in six progressive stages', Wheeler wrote of his work on Cassivelaunus' earthworks, 'developing gradually and logically from known to unknown, the vista of a formative phase of protohistoric Britain began to unroll itself'.[31] In an archaeological variant of the White Man's Burden, the techniques and the prejudices of modern civilization were used to make sense of prehistory, ordering its inhabitants according to their level of material culture, and bringing the sanitary blessings of modern academia to bear upon the epistemic jungle. For prehistory before the scientists came was an unhealthy place, plagued with 'lush but fever-stricken valleys of amateurish guessing' in Piggott's words, but now 'finding its true haven in the bright cold air of at least the foothills of the scientific mountain range'.[32]

The Frontier

Of all the unhealthy antiquarian accretions, the inter-war archaeologists had particular problems with the Celts. Rehabilitated as the antithesis of mainstream English 'Victorian values', they appealed to a similar audience; and the 'heroic band' needed to define a position from which to dismiss them.

Literally and metaphorically, the frontier between civilized Romans and barbarian Celts was a *locus* of much intellectual activity amongst orthodox archaeologists. Richard Hingley has demonstrated its importance in the work of Francis Haverfield, Professor of Ancient History at Oxford before the Great War, and the most prominent pre-war Romanist of his day. He maintained that '[t]he greatest work of the imperial age must be sought in its imperial administration – in the organization of its frontier defences which repulsed the barbarian, and in the development of the provinces within those defences . . . In the lands that [Rome] had sheltered, Roman civilization had taken firm root.' It was a boundary that Rome had to maintain: thus Haverfield described Roman Cumbria as 'a tangled chaos of hills in which wild hill-men defied Rome and Roman ways. Rome could not leave them alone.'[33]

Hingley acknowledges that inter-war Romanists such as Collingwood and Birley continued to focus their efforts on the Roman frontier, but for some reason overlooks the work of Mortimer Wheeler. Although he claimed to suffer from occasional 'satiety of Roman things' and 'the pretentious Roman machine', Wheeler was emphatically a Romanist: indeed, at the end of his life, a BBC producer described him as 'the greatest Roman of them all'.[34] Collingwood and Birley concentrated their energies on the physical boundary between Roman and Celt; Wheeler was particularly interested in the temporal boundary: the transition from 'native' to Roman represented by the Conquest. Last stands were his speciality. During his career, Wheeler claimed to have found the last stands of the Catuvellauni (at Wheathampstead), the Durotriges (Maiden Castle) and the Brigantes (Stanwick). This last site, as Jacquetta Hawkes says, was 'ideally suited' to him, since it gave him the chance 'to reveal the last figures of our British Iron Age retreating before the historic forces of Rome'.[35] Native resistance was useless. The Brigantian general was 'pitting an embattled mob in unwonted conditions against an army engaged upon a normal manoeuvre. Stanwick is at the same time a very notable memo-

The Romanization of Wales

In 1920, Wheeler became Keeper of the National Museum of Wales, at a time when renascent Welsh nationalism had fostered a tendency to downplay the Roman conquest and seek the roots of Welshness in a pre-Roman past. To Haverfield, 'the revival of Welsh national sentiment has inspired a hope, which has become a belief, that the Roman conquest was an episode, after which an unaltered Celticism resumed its uninterrupted supremacy'.[37] His lengthy survey, *Military Aspects of Roman Wales* (1908/9), attributed much of the problem to the lack of excavation. 'On every side the same need faces us. We must dig. Careful excavation, systematically planned, patiently and scientifically supervised, recorded and illustrated . . . will solve most of the problems in those four centuries of Welsh history which form the Roman period.'[38]

Wheeler took up the challenge. All three of his major Welsh excavations were Roman forts. Segontium, near Caernarvon, which he described as 'pivotal in the Roman occupation of Wales', was followed by Y Gaer, near Brecon. Caerleon was 'the inevitable next step: the examination of the great legionary fortress from which the Gaer and its fellows had depended, as it were the prehensile fingers of a strong hand'.[39]

This choice of sites, he claimed, was quite deliberate, part of a preconceived campaign 'to integrate a given portion of Roman Britain by selective excavation'.[40] That word 'integrate' is intriguing. It implies not merely 'integration' into a contemporary programme of investigating Roman Britain, but also an investigation into how that 'given portion of Roman Britain' was integrated in the first place. The integration of Wales involved a process of subjugation. Wheeler considered the Antonine and Hadrian's Walls as 'symbols of defeat': 'the reserve of unpacified territory was sufficiently large and amorphous to necessitate some palpable line of delimitation'. In the case of Wales, the Romans 'realized from the outset that to set up a boundary was to dare the enemy to cross it, and that the only safe frontier was a subjugated Wales'.[41]

Subjugation did not automatically bring about Romanization. The native population was allowed to continue with its customs so long as control lay firmly within the grasp of that 'strong hand', prompting

Wheeler to draw a parallel with the contemporary zone of 'influence' north of British India: 'In this zone our policy is one of non-interference with native affairs so long as our military outpost-forts, such as Chitral, remain unmolested.'[42]

Roman hegemony had to be periodically reasserted. The second-century reparation of military installations was not a response to external threat, but because 'a generation had grown up in Wales which knew little of the majesty of Rome. It had therefore become necessary to "show the flag".'[43.] When invasions did happen, in the fourth century, the Welsh demonstrated their *romanitas* by defending themselves:

> Not that these hillmen were necessarily fired by any particular flame of imperial patriotism – though the magic of the Roman name had a curious power of insinuation; but in fighting, as they must have done, for the safety of their herds and their huts they were incidentally fighting for the safety of Rome. In this sense the interests of native Wales were at one with those of the Empire, and our social or political 'progress' – from the isolated cave-community to an entity in a great imperial system – may be brought to a convenient term.[44]

These words end his *Prehistoric and Roman Wales*: a native population, ultimately Romanized through their own self-interest, 'integrated' into the great imperial system. Celticism came afterwards: '[we] may regard Celtic Wales, like Celtic Ireland, as pre-eminently a phenomenon of the historic age'.[45]

Tuning the Archaeological Engine

Having defined the nature of Welsh prehistory, Wheeler turned his attention to the means of producing it. Wales was unusually well endowed with archaeological institutions, as Wheeler himself noted. In addition to the National Museum, and such 'flourishing' organizations as the Cambrian Archaeological Society, Wales also possessed its own Royal Commission on Ancient and Historical Monuments, and its own University, with a newly constituted Board of Celtic Studies that provided 'practical assistance' to archaeological field-work. H J Fleure, teaching Geography at Aberystwyth, and J E Lloyd, teaching History at Bangor, were both much interested in archaeology; and Wheeler himself held an *ex officio* lectureship in Archaeology at University College, Cardiff. '[W]orking as they are in close co-ordination, they form a more formidable engine of archaeological research than has ever been possessed by any other region in the world.'[46]

Ironically, the existence of this 'engine' owed much to what Theodore Watts-Dunton called the 'vigorous renascence of the Cymric idea' that between 1894 and 1922 had resulted in the creation of a host of national cultural institutions. It was an appropriate display of cultural vitality for 'the land of the Druids', as Watts-Dunton termed it, 'very specially beloved by the Spirit of Antiquity'.[47]

It was this sort of sentiment that Haverfield and Wheeler saw it as their duty to exterminate. As Lecturer at University College, Cardiff, Wheeler's aim was 'to secure for archaeology a recognized place in the curriculum of the Welsh university'.[48] His 'introductory public lectures' formed the basis of *Prehistoric and Roman Wales*: 'It was not a good book', he reminisced, 'but it was better than anything that had gone before.' This was a coded allusion to the 'vision of Druids and mistletoe and mighty bards and barbaric rites' that the *Observer* reviewer had expected to find. 'Firmly, but authoritatively, the author puts them in their place, and long may they remain there.'[49]

In 1929, Wheeler was asked to give the Sir John Rhys Memorial Lecture at the British Academy, and used the occasion to delicately dismiss the work of Rhys himself. Answering the question posed by Haverfield, 'Can a good patriot be a good historian?',[50] Wheeler attributed the Welsh lack of scholarship to a romantic temperament and nationalist tendencies:

> Welshmen have always been famed for their intense love of their country – a love accentuated by that touch of jealousy which has on occasion been a cause of wonderment to the more phlegmatic Saxon. Intense love of one's country can do many things. It can produce oratory, a popular heroic poetry, a popular choral music, a popular education. It cannot produce, nor does it foster the production of, that minute, critical, unwearying, undeviating evaluation of evidence and inference which is essential to enduring and constructive science. That there have been great Welsh scholars is undisputed; that there has in the past arisen no great corpus of Welsh scholarship in equally beyond question.[51]

Nineteenth-century Welsh archaeology was 'miscellaneous, haphazard, unequal . . . essentially invertebrate'.[52] '[S]tructural unity' for the Celtic jellyfish came with the appearance of Rhys's *Celtic Britain*, first published in 1882, which maintained that a first wave of 'Goidelic' Celts had swept through Wales and Ireland, to be replaced (with Tylorian survivals) by a second wave of 'Brythonic' Celts. 'He was avowedly a philologist,' wrote Wheeler of Rhys, 'but there was nothing of the Teuton word-monger in his composition. He saw words as living entities, jostling each other as the full-blooded denizens of a three-dimensional world. Gaelic and Welsh sprang Minerva-like from his head as living Goidel and Brython and hurried across his Olympic stage. It follows that the scene was one which archaeology alone could give him; and so – and thus far – Rhys became the acclaimed archaeologist of Wales.'[53]

Rhys, however, like all typical Celts, was renowned for changing his mind: Wheeler cites an anonymous critic, frustrated at failing to find 'firm ground in the track of the Celtic Will-o'-the-Wisp'. His contribution to Welsh archaeology was essentially primeval, legendary: 'Romulus is none the less the founder of Rome for that he was not the architect of St Peter's.'[54]

Wheeler suspected Rhys 'of a special liking for the guise of archaeologist, and I am told that his duties as the first Chairman of the Royal Commission on Ancient Monuments (Wales) were nearer to his heart than most others of his multitudinous interests'.[55] But Wheeler had no such special liking for the Commission, whose reputation he had torpedoed the previous year, claiming that '[f]rom the outset' the Commission had 'failed completely to realize its responsibilities'. Rhys died in harness in 1915, but the antiquarian tenor he had set was pursued by his successors, whom Wheeler accused of 'a consistent ignorance of prehistoric and Roman material'.[56] Rhys' immediate legacy to archaeology, therefore, had been to sabotage the archaeological engine, and it had to be fixed if the Welsh were ever to progress. Wheeler accordingly wrote a devastating (and anonymous) review of the Commission's *Pembrokeshire* survey for the first volume of *Antiquity*, in which he concluded that 'with all restraint it may be urged that the Commission as at present constituted is a laughing-stock amongst professed archaeologists and is financially an unjust charge upon the State'. As a result of the review, the Commission's Secretary resigned, to be replaced by W J Hemp, a prehistorian whom Wheeler held in high esteem.[57] Celtic antiquarianism had been rooted out; the engine was fixed.

Romans and Romantics

To the champions of Celtica, however, *romantitas* remained unredeemed. To the Druids of the Universal Bond, 'Pict, Caledon, Goidel and Brython

The Aesthetics of Order

are one against Rome, and they are still united against all that plays the part of the Roman invader', as Macgregor Reid told the President of the Society of Antiquaries in 1924, with the clear implication that his organization was sliding Romewards. 'We Druids deny that our forebears were ignorant and benighted savages, and claim that the one really bad setback of the greatest of the Roman generals was from brave and wise Celts who valued freedom more than all of the flesh pots and allurements of Roman Imperialism.'[58]

Ancient Rome came to serve as a metaphor for a scientific materialism that oppressed an older and more natural world. Humanity's drive to harmonize with nature, according to D H Lawrence, was by them twisted into 'a desire to resist nature, to produce a mental cunning and a mechanical force that would outwit nature and chain her down completely'.[59] 'They were sceptic, those Romans, like to-day's science', wrote the Diffusionist H J Massingham, not in tune, as their predecessors were, 'with the deeper rhythms of nature'.[60]

Massingham was a forthright opponent of conventional archaeology, dangerous because of his popularity; and when he came to visit the Avebury reconstruction project Stuart Piggott made a point of cultivating his acquaintance, even, apparently, reading the proofs of Massingham's *Through the Wilderness*, for which he was effusively thanked. Piggott's efforts to steer him away from Egyptian hyperdiffusion, however, merely led him to substitute Crete for Egypt as the ultimate source of civilization;[61] and by 1941 Piggott was toying with the idea of tackling Massingham head-on by producing a book on British field archaeology that would entice 'a new public – the non-scientific literary and artistic world – into the domains of sound archaeology with nothing of the Massingham touch about it'.[62]

He was hoping to involve his friend John Piper in this project, but it is significant that the book was never produced. Sam Smiles suggests that Piper was less than impressed with the totalizing claims of modern archaeology: 'while the "sound archaeology" Piggott promotes is concerned to distinguish fact from fancy, a work of art can still take on the emotional charge of a monument'.[63] Another artist, Paul Nash, visited Piggott and Keiller at work at Avebury, and mourned the 'wild state' of the stones prior to their restoration, 'wonderful and disquieting . . . [a] primal magic' now lost:

> Avebury may rise again under the tireless hand of Mr Keiller, but it will be an archaeological monument, as dead as a mammoth skeleton in the Natural History Museum. When I stumbled over the sarsens in the shaggy autumn

grass and saw the unexpected megaliths reared up among the corn stooks, Avebury was still alive.[64]

Smiles suggests that 'Nash's insistence on the vitality of the past is, ultimately, a plea for another sort of knowing, an alternative, even a resistance, to empirical data and orthodox methodology . . . Rational enquiry might help explain a long-standing puzzle, but it ran the risk of emptying the monuments of all but the most literal meanings.'[65] Resistance to orthodox methodology was a major ingredient in the popularity of the Old Straight Track, whose fortunes will be chronicled in the next few chapters.

Chapter 13

The Old Straight Track

Alfred Watkins

Alfred Watkins' *The Old Straight Track* (1925) introduced the world to the concept of the 'ley' (now more often 'ley-line'), and consequently had an enormous influence on perceptions of high antiquity. Loathed by archaeologists, the book was one of the twentieth century's most popular books on British prehistory and also, in the view of O G S Crawford, 'one of the craziest'.[1]

Watkins was born in Hereford in 1855, the son of a successful brewer and miller. The brewery was sold in 1898, but Watkins kept an interest in the mill throughout his life and was thereafter freed from the need to earn an income. He was a renowned photographer, patenting and then manufacturing an award-winning light-meter; a Fellow of the Royal Photographic Society, his *Photography: its principles and applications* became, according to his biographer, 'the standard reference book'.[2] He had a passion for matters archaeological, and in 1888 joined the Herefordshire county society, the Woolhope Naturalists' Field Club (which, in spite of its title, had by now become, like many county societies, primarily archaeological in focus). He became a member of the Woolhope's Central Committee in 1893, and, from 1917 until his death in 1935, was Archaeological Editor, a task that involved preparing concise 'Annual Reports on Archaeology', which his peers deemed to be 'models of what such reports should be'.[3] He was Club President in 1918–20, and played an increasingly important part both in the Club's administration

21 Alfred Watkins. (*Rev. Felix Watkins*).

and in editing their *Transactions*. Over 90 per cent of its photographs were taken by Watkins, and the *Transactions*, in the words of Woolhope Secretary, George Marshall, 'became known as the best illustrated publications of any local Archaeological Society'.[4] In short, Watkins was at the heart of the Herefordshire archaeological 'establishment', his contribution to the county society indispensable. His death in 1935 (at the age of 80) was described by the President as 'a tremendous blow from which it will take long to recover': the members stood in silence as a tribute to his memory.[5]

On 30 June 1921, at the age of 66, Watkins made his sensational discovery. Following a visit to Blackwardine (near Leominster), he noticed a straight line on the map from Croft Ambury to Stretton Grandison:

> I followed up the clue of sighting from hill top, unhampered by other theories, found it yielding astounding results in all districts, the straight lines to my amazement passing over and over again through the same class of objects, which I soon found to be (or to have been) practical sighting points.[6]

He unveiled his ideas to the Woolhope Central Committee on 25 July, and, on 9 August, took George Marshall to see the Blackwardine alignment for himself.[7] On 29 September, the Woolhope Club convened an Autumn Meeting specifically to consider Watkins' discovery. An afternoon field trip was followed by an evening lecture, attended by 43 members, which was published the following year under the title *Early British Trackways: Moats, Mounds, Camps and Sites*.[8]

Early British Trackways was, as Watkins himself admitted, 'a somewhat breathless production';[9] the result of a 'vivid ... rush of revelations ... Once started, I found no halt in the sequence of new facts revealed by active search on the tracks.'[10] He acknowledges his own astonishment and anticipates that his readers will feel the same, while inviting them to verify his results both in the field and 'on an inch to the mile ordnance map with aid of a straight edge'. He then explains the method, which, as the first set of rules for ley-hunting, are worth quoting at length:

> Taking all the earthworks mentioned [tump, tumulus, mound, twt, castle, bury, cairn, garn, tomen, low, barrow, knoll, knap, moat and camp], add to them all ancient churches, all moats and ponds, all castles (even castle farms), all wayside crosses, all cross roads or junction which bear a place name, all traditional trees (such as gospel oaks), marked on maps, and all legendary wells. Make a small ring round each on a map. Stick a steel pin on the site of an undoubted sighting point, place a straight edge against it, and move it round until several (not less than four) of the objects named and marked come exactly into line.
>
> You will then find on that line fragments here and there of ancient roads and footpaths, also small bits of modern roads conforming to it. Extend the line into adjoining maps, and it will usually terminate at both ends in a natural hill or mountain peak, or sometimes (in the later examples) in a legendary well or other objective.[11]

'Mark stones' and 'sighting stones' were also added to this not inconsiderable list of features.[12]

The purpose of what Watkins was already calling 'the ley or lay' was for trade. 'Presume a primitive people, with few or no enclosures, wanting a few necessities (as salt, flint flakes, and, later on, metals) only to be had from a distance. The shortest way to such a distant point was a straight line ...' The existence of the ley presupposed a class of 'skilled men, carefully trained' to sight them: 'Men of knowledge they would be, and therefore men of power over the common people.' He wondered whether

22 Frontispiece to *Early British Trackways*. 'A Glade on a Ley' links pictures of Castle Tomen, Radnor Forest, with the Four Stones near New Radnor. A composite of Watkins' own photographs.

they might have made their craft a mystery, like the Druids, and suggested that they might have degenerated into the witches of the Middle Ages: 'It may be that the ancient siting methods were condemned as sorcery by the early Christian missionaries.' He even suggested that they may have been called 'cole-men', after an obsolete word 'cole' meaning 'false magician' or 'juggler', a surmise apparently supported by the considerable number of place-names with a 'col-' or 'cold-' component.[13]

Early British Trackways was distributed through the London firm of Simpkin, Marshall & Co., and seems to have been quite widely read. Watkins' 'ley-bitten' correspondents spanned the land from Devon to the Midlands and East Anglia, where the Suffolk antiquarian W A Dutt led a school of alignment researchers that lasted into the early 1930s.[14] Local informants came forward with new sightings, and, in April 1923, Watkins proudly told the Woolhope Club of 'Two Hereford Trackways' – metalled surfaces on leys that had been discovered during new sewer trenching.[15]

Watkins' work did not go uncriticized. The objections to the ley theory that Watkins received were the same that have been levied ever since: that people would not climb over hills if they could go round them; that people would not have chosen to walk through ponds; that many 'sighting-mounds' were in fact burial-mounds; that the land was too thickly wooded; that many sites were more recent; that the whole ley system was coincidental.[16]

The Old Straight Track, published by Methuen in October 1925, was in part designed to answer these criticisms, and to invite more informed debate on the basis of the mass of new evidence which he had accumulated: 'What really matters in this book is whether it is a humanly designed fact, an accidental coincidence, or a "mare's nest," that mounds, moats, beacons, and mark stones fall into straight lines throughout Britain, with fragmentary evidence of trackways on the alignments.'[17] Sir Norman Lockyer's work at Stonehenge, of which Watkins was previously unaware, formed the basis of new chapters on 'sun alignments' and 'orientation', for which he drew also upon the recent work of Admiral Somerville in Ireland. New categories of mark-point were added (beacons, 'notches' or clefts in distant hills), together with a new range of significant place-names: 'dod', derived from the 'dod-men', the stick-bearing surveyors; 'black', recalling the 'grimy face' of the 'beacon-lighter'; 'white' and 'wick', 'knap' and 'chip' recalling the salt and the flints that the early pedlars carried. There were also chapters on the folkloric survival of the ley, on the road-maintaining functions of the hermits, on the biblical injunction to keep to the straight path; and also a short chapter on the ley theory 'in other lands'.[18] *The Ley Hunters' Manual*, his 1927 field guide, adds more mark-points (for instance, cup-and-ring stones, zigzags in roads and – although he conceded that dating was problematic – 'ancient homesteads', with warnings to be wary of such 'mare's nests' as 'mining, quarry, pit, or pond-excavation heaps' that might well look like marker mounds; and some handy hints on excavation ('the aim should be rather to do a small bulk thoroughly, than to dig carelessly big holes').[19]

The Romance of the Road

These are the bare bones of the 'ley' hypothesis, as laid down by Alfred Watkins. It was a matter of fact and observation, not theory: 'I had no theory when, out of what appeared to be a tangle, I got hold of the one right end of this string of facts, and found to my amazement that it unwound in orderly fashion and complete logical sequence.'[20] However, whether Watkins was aware of it or not, his revelation was not without precedent. A variety of influences were clearly at work; the first of which was, as Jeremy Harte has perceptively pointed out, the ready availability of Ordnance Survey maps.[21] The first series of OS one-inch-to-the-mile maps was produced between 1805 and 1874; a second and fully revised version was available by the end of the century. The alignment that links Stonehenge to Old Sarum and Salisbury Cathedral was, rather significantly, first noted by an Ordnance Survey director-general, Colonel Duncan Johnston, in the 1890s, who pointed it out to Lockyer.[22] During the 1920s, the first 'popular' edition of the 1″ map was produced, explicitly aimed at the growing number of recreational users of the countryside. It seems that this was the map on which Watkins first detected the Blackwardine ley; certainly it was to the 'popular' edition that he was already referring readers in 1922.[23]

Nor was Watkins the first to find linear patterns in the landscape. Pennick and Devereux's thorough survey traces the history of alignment research in Britain back to 1778. They point out that, in 1870, the Assistant Keeper of the Public Records Office, W H Black, who postulated a massive – perhaps global – system of 'grand geometrical lines' linking monuments and mark-points, addressed a meeting of the British Archaeological Association in Hereford; and though the authors have not found any evidence to confirm that Watkins was aware of this talk, they suspect that he might have been. In addition to Lockyer's work, they cite no fewer than 11 other writers and antiquarians who, between the 1870s and the date of Watkins' revelation, had shared 'the sense of alignments in the landscape'.[24]

A third element, perhaps so obvious that it has been overlooked, is the contemporary rediscovery of the road. Marginalized by the railways, the main road network lay moribund for much of the nineteenth century, available for romantic rediscovery by cyclists, hikers and, eventually, by motorists. High antiquity was central to the romance of the road. R. Hippisley Cox's *The Green Roads of England* (1914) postulated a network of prehistoric tracks converging on Avebury, which he suggested constituted 'the seat of government'. To Hilaire Belloc in *The Old Road* (1904), 'The Road' was 'primal ... the humblest and the most subtle, but ... the greatest and most original of the spells which we inherit from the earliest of our race'. Its antiquity was central to its power: 'The sacredness which everywhere attaches to The Road has its sanction ... especially in that

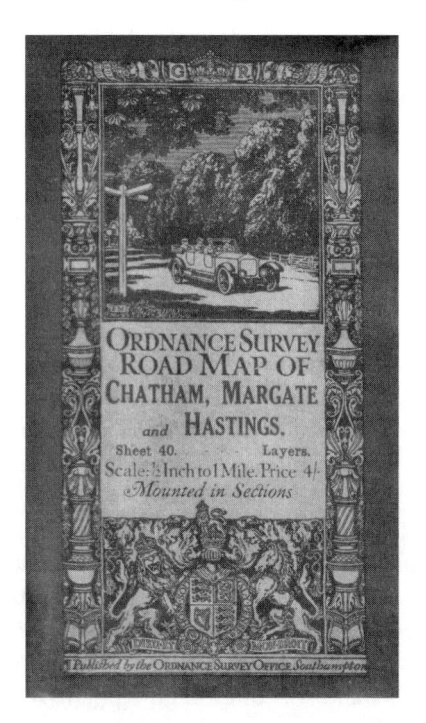

23 Ellis Martin's finely-designed map cover for the Ordnance Survey's ½" series invokes the romance of the road.

antiquity from which the quality of things sacred is drawn.' Following the course of an ancient road was 'to plunge right into the spirit of the oldest monument of the life men led on this island'.[25]

Watkins was to draw on Belloc's work in *Early British Trackways* and Cox's in *The Old Straight Track*, but even within the Woolhope Club the antiquity of local roads had already become a major interest. In January 1921, Hubert Reade read a paper in which he sought to apply Cox's findings to the 'Castles and Camps of South Herefordshire', and a week before Watkins' talk in September 1921, the Woolhope Central Committee had received an offer of £25 'towards a fund for the exploration of the old roads in the County'.[26]

Road history was thus in the air when Watkins had his revelation; and the ley theory unfolded during the 1920s against a backdrop of a rapid increase in road usage. Gradually, the ley fed into the mythology of road-lore; the *Hereford Times*, lavish in its praise of *The Old Straight Track*, drew an analogy between Watkins' view of medieval hermits and 'the grey liveried officials of the Royal Automobile Club'.[27] Donald Maxwell, in 1932, similarly likened Watkins' 'dod-men' to the familiar Automobile Association patrolmen,[28] and Matless has shown how the Old Straight Track became enshrined as the forerunner of all roads in various prosaic publications on the subject of roads throughout the 1920s and 1930s.[29]

Ruralism

The romance of the road was itself a part of the 'ruralist' phenomenon, the growing interest and enthusiasm for the countryside that is too easily and too often glossed simply as middle-class reaction to the accelerating pace of change. The sheer scale of the 'outdoor movement' puts the class-aspect in context. Walking for pleasure, now christened 'hiking', reached epidemic proportions by the early 1930s, with the railway companies running special 'excursion' trains most weekends that regularly carried 700–800 people and often many more: around 2,000 joined the Great Western Railway's 'Hikers' Mystery Express' of Easter 1932. The first youth hostel opened in 1930; six years later there were 260. The outdoor movement, as Harvey Taylor says, 'assumed the proportions and zeal of a "popular crusade" ', and was often highly politicized, as in the famous 'Mass Trespass' on Kinder Scout in 1932, or in the vocal opposition of the Clarion Cycling Club to the policies of the National Government in the 1930s.[30]

There was also a highly romantic aspect to the movement, one in which 'the Past' had a central place. Fourteen hundred people took part in the Southern Railway's Moonlight Ramble in July 1932, 'to witness the sunrise from Chanctonbury Ring', and Taylor has shown the importance that early rambling clubs placed on archaeology.[31] Indeed, influenced strongly (if unconsciously) by Edward Tylor's 'doctrine of survivals', the countryside in general was often perceived as belonging to the past. It was a spiritual home, a place to return to; inhabited by real people with real values. Thus 'Our Bill', an immensely popular 1930s radio character, invited listeners into the heart of rural England, where they could 'step aside into some small pool of history, to be lapped awhile in the healing peace of a rich, still-living past'.[32] It permeated the thinking of youth movement pioneers such as Leslie Paul, self-confessed Edward Carpenter socialist and founder of the Woodcraft Folk:

> I sought a deeper layer of English life, something about which I knew very little, but thought very often, the England which belonged to the green

roads which led to Stonehenge and Avebury, the primitive settlements of Glastonbury where I found the ruined monastery...'[33]

Reception

This sort of ruralism was clearly an attraction of the Old Straight Track itself. As Sandell points out, 'ley hunting... presented a countryside whose continuity and unchanging nature were emphasized. When churches, castles, manor houses, farm ponds or stretches of highway were found on ley lines it became proof that they represented continuities going right back to prehistoric times. History and nature became fused with each other.'[34]

It is perhaps not surprising to find that the ley hypothesis went down rather well with the general public. Watkins himself, very much aware of the importance of publicity, kept a scrapbook from 1924 to 1928 in which press notices of his work were pasted. Bad reviews were kept as well as good ones, so the scrapbook probably represents a reasonably comprehensive record of the ley's reception in the press.[35] Of 37 reviews of *The Old Straight Track* to express an opinion, eight were exuberant in their praise: to the *Oxford Times*, for instance, the book was 'one of the most interesting and conclusive works on the subject that has ever been written', while the *Hereford Times*, which might be forgiven a little bias, claimed that Watkins had found 'a Rosetta-Stone of topography'. A further 19 were complimentary, and, although national and regional newspapers were generally more cautious (*The Scotsman* pointed out that 'much more proof will be needed before it [the theory] meets with general acceptance'), only four out of 37 were unimpressed or sarcastic.[36]

The cuttings-book, however, contains no reviews from any archaeological journal, national or local. Watkins considered that he was writing from observation, not 'theory', and *The Old Straight Track* was explicitly presented for peer review;[37] yet right from the start, his peers were reticent in their enthusiasm. This was apparent from the first meeting of the Woolhope Club in September 1921. George Marshall, the Club's Hon. Sec., confided to his diary that Watkins' theory was 'received with... incredulity by most. He has overdone the whole thing.' Marshall's opinion was endorsed by the Club President, F R James, who thought that '[v]ery few of us, perhaps, will agree with his deductions'.[38]

The general lack of enthusiasm amongst Club members for the alignment theory did not deter Watkins from bringing it up at almost every conceivable Woolhope occasion, at field meetings and evening meetings, in articles on other topics and in the 'Archaeological Reports' that he annually produced.[39] Formal records are, as might be expected, sparing in their criticism, although on at least one occasion (February 1924) it seems that the Chairman tried to change the subject, and Watkins once alluded to his colleagues' lack of conviction by describing an alignment as 'significant to me (if not to others)'.[40] When the Woolhope Club held a joint meeting with the Straight Track Club in July 1933, Marshall noted in his diary that 'as far as I can gather from the members, a good many want something more definite about these "tracks" '. Marshall was later to write Watkins' 'Obituary Memoir' for the Club's *Transactions*, in which he stated frankly that 'the arguments he brought forward in support of them [i.e. "trackways"] did not always commend themselves to the more sceptical archaeologist'.[41]

In Crawford's Groove

Not all archaeological opinion was set against the ley theory. The Chairman of the Wolverhampton Archaeological Society recommended *The Old Straight Track* to his members, and the President of the Worthing Archaeological Society urged members to test the book's theories in the field.[42] The Beccles Archaeological Society, inspired by W A Dutt, who had been first joint secretary of the Prehistoric Society of East Anglia, was actively engaged in alignment-spotting;[43] and, as will be seen, many individual members of local societies, some quite influential, were 'ley-bitten'. As the *Western Daily Press* acknowledged on 7 April 1926, the theory had 'aroused a considerable amount of controversy'.[44]

Watkins was a central figure in the Woolhope Club. He played an indispensable role in its organization, and could be neither sidelined nor silenced. To Crawford and the 'scientific archaeologists', he must have epitomized everything that was wrong with the local archaeological societies. And yet there can be little doubt that Crawford was the archaeologist whom Watkins most respected, and whose good opinion he most wanted. Twice in *The Old Straight Track* Watkins referred readers to Crawford's monograph on *The Andover District*, which he described as 'invaluable to ley-hunters',[45] and he urged his supporters in the Straight Track Club to adopt the techniques of the new school:

> It is a commonplace saying amongst modern archaeologists that the spade is the all-important weapon, and that the older school who worked on

above-ground evidence, with the addition only of opinion of those who had written earlier on the subject, were on a very weak basis . . . I regard it as absolutely essential, if we as a body are to convince 'experts' of the reality of the Old Straight Track, that some of us at least employ the spade.[46]

Orthodox archaeology was not immune to the contemporary fascination for the origin of roads. Eliot Cecil Curwen and Aileen Fox were both inspired by Hilaire Belloc's work; Christopher Hawkes and Stuart Piggott by that of Hippisley Cox.[47] Crawford, writing to the 17-year-old Hawkes, called Cox's book 'very wild, but there is this to be said for it, that he rode about the country observing them [roads], and didn't merely grub them up from someone else's work'.[48] Cox was a friend of Crawford's mentor, Harold Peake, and Crawford was happy to acknowledge his own debt to Peake's training in the recognition of ' "Ancient British Trackways" ', which he placed at the heart of his own archaeological fieldwork: 'it gave me a grounding in the method which I was able to build upon and expand in many other directions'.[49] Tracing Roman roads was Crawford's 'own particular groove', as he put it, and he dedicated a whole chapter of *Man and his Past* (1921) to explaining how to do it in terms that may have contributed to the development of Watkins' theory.[50]

Watkins was therefore trespassing on territory which Crawford saw as very much his own. A surviving draft of 'subjects for the *Archaeological Review*' [i.e. *Antiquity*], dated 18 December 1925 and marked 'confidential', lists Watkins amongst '[s]ome master-minds of modern archaeology' whose follies were to be exposed, and there can be little doubt that Crawford had Watkins prominently in mind when he promised to warn readers of *Antiquity* of 'mare's nests' in his first *Antiquity* editorial: 'many bestsellers are written by quacks. The public is humbugged, but it is nobody's business to expose the fraud.' The same issue carried an article by Crawford's friend, the Wiltshire GP Dr Richard Clay, in which Watkins was described as 'ignorant of the first principles of the science of archaeology', and accused of 'attempting to startle the world with new theories'.[51]

Watkins claimed that Clay 'grossly mis-states what I say', and wrote to Crawford accordingly;[52] but Crawford simply refused to engage with him. Ignoring 'crankeries' was Crawford's avowed strategy for dealing with them. 'If you argue a case, you admit its existence, you give it publicity; and every publisher will tell you he would rather have an unfavourable review of a book than none at all.'[53] (These words were actually written to explain why 'the capitalist press' ignores the case for socialism, but it was clearly a transferable concept.) He notoriously refused to accept an advert for *The Old Straight Track* from Methuen, Watkins' publishers,[54] and not until 1951 did he allude directly to Watkins' theory in print, when he rejoiced in the success of his policy: 'how much confused nonsense have not we of the present generation seen faded out by silence? . . . Where today are the once-famous Children of the Sun, the Old Straight Trackers or the Phoenician tin-traders?' Two years later, he described *The Old Straight Track* as 'one of the craziest books ever written about British archaeology'.[55]

Unsurprisingly, Watkins became 'very bitter against Crawford', in the words of the Straight Track Club's Secretary.[56] He used his 1927 'Archaeological Report' in the Woolhope Club *Transactions* for a lengthy defence of his interpretation of the Symonds' Yat Queen Stone against criticisms that Crawford had made in that June's *Antiquity*,[57] and once noted with sarcasm that '[w]hat Mr Crawford lays down is not always to be accepted as final'[58] – a comment that nonetheless testifies to Crawford's reputation.

The Ley Hunter's Manual

It is in the context of orthodox rejection of ley theory that Watkins' next book, *The Ley Hunter's Manual*, needs to be considered. Again published by Watkins' own Watkins Meter Company, the preface is dated September 1927, six months after the appearance of Clay's *Antiquity* article. Where *The Old Straight Track* had invited readers to consider evidence for the ley theory and decide for themselves whether alignments were real or 'mare's nests', *The Ley Hunter's Manual* begins by saying 'I bain't a argying of yer, I'me a telling of yer.' Watkins, for the moment, had given up on archaeologists:

> while experts have been contemptuously denying (and referring to the 'best authorities' to prove it) that early man had ever organized his tracks over sighting points, a considerable body of healthy out-of-doors workers have been finding such tracks and alignments to be actual facts in their own districts.
>
> So I just go on 'a telling of yer' in this condensed manual, in the hopes that it may send forth many more out-of-doors folk over meadow, mountain, and moor, not only to view the ley of the land, but to find these old

24 *The Ley Hunter's Manual.* Alfred Watkins woos the walkers.

tracks on it, and perchance to spend a healthy, exhilarating, and profitable holiday in that way.'[59]

The Ley Hunter's Manual, a handy-sized, cloth-bound field-guide, was thus aimed quite consciously at the burgeoning outdoor movement. As the *Oxford Times* observed, 'this plentifully-illustrated little handbook is just the one to slip in the pocket, together with a good one-inch-to-the-mile map'. Propagating 'Purposeful Rambles' was its advertised intention,[60] and, to judge from the reviews preserved in Watkins' scrapbook, it succeeded. 'It is given to few people to create, even on a small scale, a new outdoor hobby', declared the *Birmingham Gazette*. In January 1928, *The Surveyor and Municipal and County Engineer* was able to report that ley-hunting was 'now being taken up by a considerable body of enthusiasts', and the new hobby's success might be gauged by such casual comments as those of Joyce Reason, whose article 'A Lone Woman's Hike from Glastonbury to Winchester' appeared in the first issue of *The Hiker and Camper* (February 1931): 'Because evenings in camp are sometimes long, I took with me *The Ley Hunter's Manual* and a good solid volume of archaeology, warranted to last a novice a long time.'[61] To many of this new wave of countryside explorers, the Old Straight Track was not just a reality, but a key component in the whole exhilarating experience.

Watkins had long seen the potential attraction of the ley theory to youth movements. As early as 1922, he had had 'a mental vision of a Scout Master of the future, out ley hunting with the elder boys of his troup [*sic*]', and had even sent a copy of *Early British Trackways* to Lord Baden-Powell, receiving 'a nice encouraging reply'.[62] Now the *Boys' Own Paper* (January 1928) found *The Ley Hunter's Manual* to be 'an intensely interesting little book' and recommended it to 'every boy who is interested in the history and topography of his own neighbourhood ... [it] may lead him to quite unexpected discoveries'.[63] Captain Wilkinson in *The Scouter*, while conceding that not all authorities were convinced, nonetheless thought that it would be useful for scouts: 'whether one believes it or not, there can be no doubt that it has the makings of a most fascinating hobby and has the power to turn any country walk into a thrilling adventure. It seems to open up many possibilities for Boy Scouts.'[64] The extent of Scout involvement in ley-hunting is hard to quantify; certainly Norman Woodhead, a botanist at the University College in Bangor and a member of the Straight Track Club, found the 1st City of Bangor Troop to be very helpful in his ley-hunting work.[65] The Kington scoutmaster brought selected members of his troop to the Hereford meeting of the Straight Track Club in 1933, and, in the same year, Watkins addressed about 250 members of the Woodcraft Folk (the Co-operative Movement's rival to the Scouts) at their camp on the Wye.[66]

In spite of its success amongst the outdoor movement, however, press reviews of *The Ley Hunters' Manual* were slightly less enthusiastic than they had been for *The Old Straight Track*. Although half of the 26 reviews were generally favourable, none were quite as exuberant as for the earlier book and two were positively scathing. The *Derbyshire Advertiser*, commenting on Watkins' idiosyncratic etymology, declared that '[s]uch puerilities show how dangerous a guide such a manual is for the unwary. It is worse than useless, being actually misleading.'[67] George Engleheart of the Wiltshire Archaeological & Natural History Society, scourge of the Universal Bond, was even more damning. He justified the length of his 12-inch review in the *Wiltshire Gazette* because of the need to rescue 'the unreasoning multitude who are so easily led further into the wilderness of ignorance', and, echoing Clay, accused Watkins of being 'absolutely ignorant' of the 'first rudiments' of archaeology. Watkins replied, claiming, somewhat disingenuously, that 'the very object of my book is to prevent the too enthusiastic beginner from . . . manufacturing "mares' nests" ', thereby permitting Engleheart to respond suggesting that Watkins himself should have set a better example: 'His advice to callow ley-hunters not to "manufacture mares' nests" is unlikely to be taken so long as he, an adult bird, can display for imitation the three-storeyed structure of that kind which he has built and occupies so suitably.'[68]

Watkins' final publication, *Archaic Tracks Round Cambridge*, published in 1932, met with further ridicule. Although his son Allen, then living in Cambridge, claims that the book was prompted by a visit that his father made,[69] it is possible that Watkins was aware of the new Department of Archaeology and hoped to make some converts. The tone is much more conciliatory, and he takes care to call Cyril Fox 'a brilliant expert', whose *Archaeology of the Cambridge Region* (1923) was 'absolutely necessary to the real investigator'. He gently criticizes Fox for assuming 'that straightness and alinement [*sic*] is an exclusive sign of Roman engineering', but otherwise found his book to be 'amazingly full, up-to-date, and open-minded'.[70]

Writing probably in April 1933, Allen Watkins claimed that the University Union Society's copy of *Archaic Tracks* 'has been taken out regularly every week since last October, also those dons whom I spoke to severally about the matter were all familiar with the thesis'.[71] However, this seems to have been the sum total of *Archaic Tracks*' influence on that august institution. An anonymous reviewer,

> [r]eflecting on the instinct of the unregenerate walker to make for the nearest pub . . . took the same one-inch map and, selecting inns as his sight-marks, obtained similar results to Mr Watkins. His first, and best, effort produced six inns in line; another, four inns and the significant place name Two Pots House. Four lines of four inns can be drawn, each terminating on one of the Noon Follies (associated with Watkins' midday sighting lines); and considering the original meaning of noon – about 3 o'clock – and the impossibility of obtaining a drink at that hour, the result is no doubt significant and our English road system is to be attributed to Mr Watkins' sight-walker, gradually developing into Mr Chesterton's reeling English drunkard.[72]

Nearly 30 years later, T C Lethbridge used the same analogy at a folklore meeting when 'a small man with an old Bill moustache got up suddenly and started talking about Straight Tracks'. He attributed it to Cyril Fox,[73] who may thus have been the original reviewer.

The willingness of orthodoxy to resort to ridicule was matched by a growing dislike for orthodoxy amongst Watkins' supporters. L Shepherd Munn, writing in December 1927, found that, in Northumberland, 'a pretty icy front has been presented' by over-cautious archaeologists '(for who should be a reactionary if not an archaeologist?)' who refused to look at the evidence for themselves: 'I can be sure, therefore, that any observations I have made may be regarded as pioneer efforts in this country and will be an excellent target for any one who can throw a missile of any kind.'[74]

The most outspoken opponent of orthodox attitudes to the ley theory was Donald Maxwell, artist, writer and novelist, who was apparently 'converted' after reading *The Ley Hunter's Manual*.[75] He took his enthusiasm for Watkins' 'most wonderful discovery' for approval to 'several "experts" ', who, however, 'all thought I had a touch of the sun'. He found a fellow-admirer in the flamboyant socialist Sidney Dark, editor of the *Church Times*, who had already lavished editorial praise on *The Old Straight Track*.[76] He 'alone dared to print my "fantastic conclusions" ',[77] in the form of a five-part series published in August and September 1932. His articles, illustrated by evocative line-drawings and maps of leys, were couched in the form of detective stories following topographical 'clues' around the mysteries of the home counties, and were developed into two full-length novels, *A Detective in Surrey* (1932) and *A Detective in Essex* (1933). Both carried prefaces in which Maxwell not only gave Watkins full and generous acknowledgement, but also defended him against his archaeological detractors:

> Mr Alfred Watkins has been treated by the archaeological world very much as Galileo was treated by the scientific world of his time . . . 'leys' or 'sighting lines', in spite of the ridicule of the 'experts', still exist . . . an archaeologist who is an expert or a professor must be considered to speak like the Pope, ex cathedra, and . . . all true believers will firmly shut their eyes to any new light from whatever direction it shall come.[78]

In spite of orthodox disapproval, the 'gospel' soon found plenty of converts in the wider world. Watkins believed that Maxwell's articles marked 'the turning point' in public acceptance, noting references in Ruth Anderson's *The Roads of England* (1932), an article in the *Times* on Peddars Way, and a ley-inspired 'playlet' by Lawrence du Garde Peach that was broadcast on BBC Children's Hour in February 1933. Another radio series, called *Explorations at Home*, included Watkins' *Early British Trackways* among its list of recommended books. 'I have seen the change coming', wrote Watkins prophetically. The essay was called 'The Ley Takes Hold'.[79]

Chapter 14

The Straight Track Postal Club

The Straight Track Club was set up by Watkins' admirers in order to investigate the ley phenomenon more fully. It was a remarkable organization, modelled on other 'postal contributory clubs' to which Watkins belonged: the English Mechanic Postal Photographic Club, established in the 1880s, was one of the first. Watkins described the STC to readers of *The Ley Hunter's Manual* (1927) as 'a strictly private club... regarding trackways', and likened it to 'the literary clubs... where members contribute their poems (or tales, or plays, as the case may be), and they are circulated, written or typed by preference, amongst members... each member sends on (by post usually) to the next member within a limit varying from 5 days to a week. It is found by experience that the number of members has to be strictly limited to about 30, otherwise the time taken to circulate becomes too long. In all cases, criticism by members is a feature.'[1]

Although Watkins was obviously the Club's leading light, credit for setting it up was later given to Barbara Carbonell, a thoughtful and erudite local historian and novelist from Devon, who wrote to Watkins in 1924/25 declaring herself 'keenly interested' in his 'track methods', as he gleefully told the dubious Woolhopians.[2]

Major Francis Tyler, also from Devon, was involved at an early stage; a letter of October 1925, the month that *The Old Straight Track* was published, quoted 22 years later by STC member Miss Woods, suggests that the Club was already in existence by then, and that Tyler had unsuccessfully tried to recruit Dr Arthur Hubbard, co-author of *Neolithic Dew*

Ponds and Cattle Ways (1905).[3] There is, however, some confusion about exactly when the Club began. Miss Woods claims that Hubbard had already 'seen our portfolio' by October 1925, although the first portfolio was not issued until April 1927. By that time, 21 members had been recruited, testimony to a fair amount of canvassing beforehand. Tyler was Honorary Secretary, a post he retained until 1932; effectively, he became Watkin's *aide-de-camp* until Watkins' death in 1935 and thereafter, in some measure, his successor.

Quite how members of the Club were gathered in the first place is unclear. It is possible that Carbonell and Tyler knew each other already, as they both came from Devon; Carbonell's husband also joined, and Mrs Knight from Burnham-on-Sea may also have been inspired by the Devon contingent. Some clearly knew Watkins already: in addition to his son Allen and his niece Joan Hatton, other Herefordshire figures included his friend and employee, Bill McKaig, Dr Clarke of Weobley and Walter Pritchard of the Woolhope Club, Miss Christine Crosland Taylor and Miss Chambers from Llandefalle, just over the Welsh border in Breconshire. Others seem to have been recruited by Watkins himself after they'd contacted him with leys that they had spotted. Frank Gossling, Alfred Pope, Boyle Somerville, and A B Watkins (apparently no relation) are all credited in *The Old Straight Track*; Mrs Cobbold was persuaded to join after contributing a lengthy article to the *Birmingham Post*. Arthur Mackmurdo's Essex ley was reported in the *Daily Express*, and subsequently in a letter to *The Times* from Mackmurdo himself:[4] this publicity may account for two more local founder members (A E Christy and Arthur Cross).

The drive for new people continued even after the Club was launched; in July 1929, Tyler urged his colleagues 'to try and recruit some more members, who are likely to prove active'.[5] Yet it is striking that many of those credited with ley-spotting in *The Old Straight Track* and *The Ley Hunter's Manual* did not become members, and even outspoken sympathizers such as W A Dutt and Donald Maxwell preferred to stay on the outside. The Straight Track Club was clearly not for every ley-hunter. It should be stressed that, although the Old Straight Track soon reached the national psyche, the STC itself had a very limited and indirect influence. It stayed a small and private club (in total, there were 67 members over its 20-year existence), and, apart from Watkins himself, the membership contained no prominent writers on heterodox archaeology. Several members regularly gave lectures; one (Fred Hando) published articles in local newspapers,[6] but not until 1939 did the Club itself venture into print. Nonetheless, the STC is a unique example of 'organized heterodoxy', and in demonstrating the ideas of some of the Straight Track's keenest followers, the Club's archive may be a good indicator of the sort of people who found Watkins' ideas most compelling.

Straight Track Sociology[7]

Straight Track Club members were generally well-heeled, as their postal addresses reveal. One member lived in Scotland and another in Ireland, but otherwise the geographical spread was fairly evenly distributed across the more prosperous parts of England and Wales. Of 106 addresses (several members moved, some several times, during the club's lifetime), only 10 were in the North; six were in Wales, 16 in the South-West, 15 in the West Midlands (including eight in Herefordshire), 12 in the East Midlands and East Anglia. The largest contingent (45) was in the South-East, including 18 within the London postal region: at 16 per cent of the total, this was a similar ratio to that between the total populations of London and the country as a whole. Over a third lived in towns with populations of less than 100,000. The list includes affluent stockbroker suburbs such as Pinner and Altrincham, Chorleywood and Cheam, seaside towns (Lymington, Bideford), and a whole range of more workaday rural towns such as Dorchester and Trowbridge, Leiston and, of course, Hereford. The truly surprising figure is that almost half of all addresses were in villages, settlements with fewer than 1,000 inhabitants. The STC can lay claim to having been largely a rural phenomenon, albeit a middle-class one, and quite a few members were clearly 'ruralists' of one kind or another. A H Mackmurdo founded the Rural Community Council of Essex in 1929, and both he and Harold Trew designed village halls; Mansfield Forbes was an active member of the Cambridge Preservation Society.[8]

Straight Track Club members belonged to a class that was relatively unaffected by the political and economic turmoil of the inter-war period. At a time when fewer than 2 per cent of the population owned a car, Watkins' observation that a 'very large proportion' of those attending the Hereford meeting in 1933 brought 'their own private cars' is revealing. As Barbara Carbonell wrote, 'the line of cars outside the Green Dragon, waiting for the signal from the "Green Flag" to start each morning was most imposing'.[9] Miss Woods, indeed, went ley-hunting with her chauffeur.[10]

It is equally striking, however, that none of them were titled: this was not the sort of club that sought legitimation of its activities through cultivating the landed gentry, as county archaeological societies had tended to do. It was also an unusually democratic one, in which a quarter of the membership was female. This was in marked contrast to the Woolhope Club which, despite the repeated efforts of Watkins and other modernizers, refused to allow women to join.[11]

Professionally, the membership of the Straight Track Club appears to have had a middle-class profile that was probably very similar to that of archaeology as a whole: Douglas Wintle was a neighbour of Flinders Petrie in Hampstead; Miss Williams lived in the same Cardiff suburb as Cyril and Aileen Fox. Like the 'professionals', many Straight Trackers were of more or less independent means, which makes it hard, and not necessarily all that helpful, to categorize this highly diverse range of people by occupation. There was a fair smattering of military titles, but that is not surprising in the first decade after the Great War and does not necessarily indicate that their holders were career servicemen: Colonel Powell, for instance, was headmaster of Nantwich Grammar School both before and after the war, in which he served and gained his rank.

The Straight Track Club membership included people from every part of the inter-war middle classes: seated southern squires (Colonel Phayre, of Bow in Devon) and small-town businessmen (Alfred Pope of Dorchester, a friend of Thomas Hardy, twice Mayor of Dorchester, was head of the Eldridge Pope brewery), northern businessmen (Edward Pilkington, Chairman of Pilkington Tiles; Harold Whitaker, Director of the Bradford Dyers' Association, map collector and historian). There were scientists, such as the botanist Norman Woodhead of University College Bangor, and the geologist Frank Gossling of the General Post Office; the Hampstead veteran Douglas Wintle as a youth had bandied words with Darwin about the aural capacity of the earthworm.[12] At least four members, including Culling Carr-Gomm, secretary from 1935, were engineers and another eight were surveyors and/or architects: occupations that are still well represented in alternative archaeology today. Amongst the architects were the famous Arts and Crafts veteran Arthur Heygate Mackmurdo, and John Hooper Harvey, who was to become a celebrated architectural historian; others with a keen interest in architecture included the Cambridge academic Mansfield Forbes, whose home, built in 1929, was a showpiece of the Modern movement and said to be 'the most visited house in England'. Three at least have an enduring reputation as visual artists: Sheila Hutchinson (calligrapher), Fred Hando (the 'Man of Gwent', writer and schoolmaster) and Harold Trew (architect). Not surprisingly, several members were actively interested in local history, with eight members at least publishing papers in local learned journals.

Club members' political predilections are hard to pin down. Most members lived in areas that generally voted Tory, and, no doubt, many of them did so too, but the Straight Track Club harboured at least one fascist sympathizer: John Hooper Harvey, who was married to the sister of an organizer for the Imperial Fascist League (IFL). In 1936 he ridiculed the likes of Mortimer Wheeler for 'waxing furious over the alleged *injustices* perpetrated on *science* and *scientists* by Hitler!'[13] In 1940 he published an unpleasant little book entitled *The Heritage of Britain*, which was advertised and sold through the IFL, in which he posited the existence of an 'ancient civilization' of 'Gothic Aryans' (ancestors, no doubt, of the cathedral-builders) who had 'introduced civilization and ruled the great empires and commonwealths of antiquity . . . This knowledge can yet save the British nation from the downfall which awaits those who lose race-consciousness and who mix their blood with that of lesser breeds.'[14]

The book was dedicated to Lawrence Waddell, 'who recovered for Britons the proof of their glorious past'. Waddell's *Phoenician Origins of Britons* (1925), which expounded the Aryan race theory, was cited with approval by several Straight Track Club members who might therefore be thought to have Aryan tendencies, but the evidence is not always that clear-cut. Miss Woods, for instance, described Waddell's work as 'a book to ponder over and re-read', a view that would surely place her over-against the fascists were it not that she also described Gordon Childe's Marxian *What Happened in History* as 'a wonderful book with a vague title'.[15] Watkins himself was a Liberal, actively agitating for the Cause in the 1906 election, and felt the need to reply 'rather fully' to a suggestion from Harvey's sister-in-law that the Imperial Fascist League might make 'the best and most reliable agents' for disseminating the ley theory.[16]

There were leftish members too. Arthur Mackmurdo advocated 'a Co-operative state upon terms that are the same for every citizen'; W W Tyrell considered that his 'progressive' views were unpopular with more 'conservative' members, and expressed his own support for Major Tyler, who might therefore have been politically 'progressive' himself. Beyond the Straight Track Club, ley theory was well received by socialists such as Sidney Dark, editor of the *Church Times*, and the left-wing *New Statesman* considered *The Old Straight Track* to be 'a first-rate piece of work'.[17]

The Straight Track Postal Club

How to aggregate such a herd of cats? Their eccentricity is about the only common denominator. Watkins himself drove a steam-powered car, and (like John Michell, who was to play the major role in the 1960s rediscovery of Watkins), he was such an ardent anti-decimalist that he went to print over it, publishing a pamphlet entitled *Must we Trade in Tenths?* G M Hayton described the Bedfordshire leys in Esperanto; John Simpson claimed that Bilberry Knoll in Derbyshire was 'the Mount of Baal of the ancient Sun Worshippers'; and it is clear from their contributions to the portfolios that many other members held unusual beliefs about the universe and its works. For all their affluence, Straight Trackers were definitely at odds with the orthodox world.[18]

How it Worked

Once in its stride, the STC held regular annual meetings in different parts of the country: Hereford (1933), Salisbury (1934), Exeter (1935), Cheltenham (1936) and Bangor (1937). Organized by local members, each lasted four or five days, and featured excursions to local sites of interest, with evening talks by local specialists.[19]

25 Members of the Straight Track Club gather around Alfred Watkins at Wellington, near Hereford, during their 1933 Annual Meeting. (*Hereford Library*)

Meetings apart, the STC functioned as a sort of ancestral form of the internet chatroom. Members submitted papers which were bound in numbered 'Portfolios'. The current portfolio was sent, together with another numbered volume called 'Remarks', by post to the next member on the list, who would comment accordingly. It was a very cumbersome process, and also necessarily restrained, since members signed their contributions and were generally more disposed to add observations than to criticize. In addition, submissions had to be made on special STC stationery, which, as it resembled school exam papers, must have seemed fairly intimidating to many members. It is not surprising to find that most people presented their ideas as 'notes' or 'remarks'. Only four members contributed five or more fully fledged papers to the portfolios. A further 14 contributed at least once, but the majority were content to add observations to the work of others, or simply to read what had been written and pass the volumes on.

On the face of it, this gives the impression that the work of the STC was effectively dominated by a very few people. It is certainly true that Watkins himself was the most prolific contributor, with a paper in every Portfolio until his death, but as we shall see, not even the originator of the Old Straight Track could control the direction of the membership's researches. Although usually very courteous (very formal, very 'English') with each other, the exchanges in the Portfolios early on betray an unwillingness to accept the yoke of academic discipline which Watkins endeavoured to impose: it seems that members were not accustomed to accepting authority of that kind, and furthermore, had no desire to find themselves so restricted. The relatively informal 'Remarks' could often become quite prolix, too: some members wrote much (and regularly) under this rubric who never contributed a formal paper. In all, perhaps a third of members took a regular part in STC exchanges during the 20 years in which portfolios were produced.

Work and Function

The intended remit of the STC was laid down for members by Alfred Watkins in the first paper of Portfolio 1. Entitled 'Pointers for Ley Hunters', he began by insisting on the importance of fieldwork. 'Two distinct branches of observation are essential – field-work and map work. One helps the other. Do not rest content with tracing leys on maps.' He went on to give a very detailed 'points system' for assessing the validity

26 The Straight Track Club in action. Climbing Pont Hendre castle mound, Longtown, Herefordshire in 1933. (*Hereford Library*).

of various features. A pioneer of archaeological photography himself, he was clearly inspired by Crawford's endeavours in aerial archaeology, arguing that 'An aeroplane is not only ideal for investigating leys from above, but also for taking air photographs from. It may come in time', he added optimistically.

Keenly aware of the need to convince orthodox archaeology, he tried to steer members away from the kind of speculation that he knew would induce incredulity.

> Ley investigation throws light on many different subjects which rightly tempts workers into fascinating special researches. Of these there are two which I find dangerous to follow if one's chief aim is to convince others of the reality of the sighted track.
>
> *Early Religion* is the first of these. The gain to knowledge may be considerable, but most people do not want new knowledge in this but only confirmation of their existing ideas or attitudes, and are at once prejudiced.[20]

The other, of which, it must be said, Watkins himself was extremely guilty, was speculation about place-name origins: 'When once we have said in public that a certain name has a certain derivation, it is like drawing a tooth to acknowledge some other derivation.' Finally, Watkins set out a list of possible research questions:

> The mystery of the union of way-marks and burial-places in one mound. The part played by beacons in marking out the track. Seasonal alignments at sunrise to sunset angles. To what races the ley-makers belonged. Whether straight sighted tracks are still in use in any country. In what countries are the mark-points to be found as in Britain. From whom did the Romans learn their alignment practice. Why such plain reference to straight tracks and mark points in the Old Testament and why in decay at that time.[21]

In time, most of these topics were covered in the portfolios. Other debate was prompted by new archaeological discoveries (the temple at Lydney, the tomb of Tutankhamun, the Gate of the Lion at Mycenae, the Avebury Sanctuary, Tintagel).[22] The STC's role as clearing-house for new information was cited by at least one member as the main reason for his membership: 'I so often read in its papers of new discoveries before they appear in the press.'[23] Other alignment work was duly noted and critiqued: W A Dutt's *Mark Stones of East Anglia*, Montague Sharpe's *Middlesex in Prehistoric, Roman and Saxon Times* and William Evans' *Sarns and Menhirs of Anglesey* (this last induced Colonel Powell to write to the Director-General of the Ordnance Survey for an opinion).[24]

The Atlantean Bun

Although members regularly contributed examples of new leys, sometimes with complex trigonometrical support, the detail of the ley system was early on subsumed beneath speculation about the people who had supposedly laid it out, and their motives for doing so.

In spite of his suggestion that members might investigate 'to what races the ley-makers belonged', it seems that, to begin with, Watkins himself seems to have considered his ley-makers to be locals. Although happy, Frazer-fashion, to bring in supporting evidence from anywhere in the world, the ley-men of his books were of indigenous evolution, first in a series of wise men: 'I feel that ley-man, astronomer-priest, druid, bard, wizard, witch, palmer, and hermit, were all more or less linked by one thread of ancient knowledge and power.'[25] The Druid link was an important one: after the publication of Kendrick's *The Druids* in 1927, Watkins wrote to *The Times* citing place-name evidence to support the existence of this 'specially skilled class of men' (and was roundly ridiculed for it by George Engleheart);[26] but it is clear that even now he was still not inclined to consider the ley-makers to have come from abroad.

Many club members, however, from the very beginning were inclined to think that ley-sighting involved skills way beyond the capacity of the Albion aboriginal, and sought links between the ley-makers and the exotic civilizations of the ancient world. Major Tyler summarized a whole set of members' speculations in his surmise that the 'people that they [the ley-makers] found here were the stone age folk, whom they organized and gradually civilized. They themselves would seem to have been the product of some early civilization, the origin of which is shrouded in mystery.'[27]

Solving that mystery became a central preoccupation to many club members, and it took them swiftly into hyperdiffusionist terrain. Some, like the Derbyshire architect John Simpson, accepted Waddell's unsavoury notion of an early influx of 'Phoenician Aryans'; to him, this race was 'the only ancient people of this country capable of laying down such tracks' – a supposition 'greatly strengthened' by the fact that they had been 'a sun-worshipping people'.[28] Others favoured Harold Bayley's theory of a Cretan origin for the British.[29] Egypt was another early candidate, prompted by the appearance of Massingham's *Downland Man* in 1926, which Mrs Carbonell found to be 'a most interesting book'. She noted his assertion that stone-work was 'purely religious in purpose, and that other building was not secularized until Roman times'.[30] The 'growing idea that the people who made our "megalithic monuments" were related to those who built the Great Pyramid' similarly allowed Tyler to speculate on an Egyptian source for the ley-makers: 'To make it possible to lay out a distant line, it would have been necessary to have geographical knowledge which we do not usually attribute to the ancients.'[31]

Watkins, although protesting that 'too much is being made of the technical difficulties' involved in ley-making, nonetheless deferred to the diffusionary expectations of the Club's members, while urging all due caution 'if we are to avoid condemnation by people who have good knowledge of facts . . . the more we can follow each link that connects British with Eastern usages, taking care to fully investigate each logical link, the more use our club will be'.[32]

His concession to members' oriental predilections was probably prompted by the realization that others were beginning to look very much further afield. Already in the second Portfolio (begun in July 1927), members had begun to speculate about the possibility of an Atlantean origin. Ignatius Donnelly, the American politician whose popularization of the Atlantean myth in his *Atlantis: The Antediluvian World* (1882) had a major influence on its later development, suggested that survivors from the drowned city had taken their sun-worship to both Egypt and Peru: a view most recently endorsed by Lewis Spence, whose three books on Atlantis appeared between 1924 and 1926. Many members sympathized with Tyler's 'sneaking affection for the idea that Atlantis was the original home of the civilizations of the world, the remains of which are being gradually recovered today'.[33] In January 1928, a paper by Douglas Wintle finally drove Watkins to respond, attacking neither the paper nor its contention, but rather the sources Wintle had used (chiefly Bayley and Waddell). These he described as 'simply deplorable in their logical weakness, and the way in which they "run a mock" [*sic*] and come to conclusions from the very beginnings of evidence'. He gently castigated Wintle, and declared that 'if this club is to be useful we shall attain it best by severe limitations in the scope of papers, and thus making them as complete as possible in their sequence of fact and argument, if we are to avoid condemnation by people who have good knowledge of facts'.[34]

But other members seemed to endorse Wintle's contention; and, thus fortified, he took on the 'Founder' more directly:

> Since I joined the Straight Track Club I have been searching for a Race, which could be said to have had, in pre-historic days, the supreme '*knowledge of the Egyptians* . . . *coupled* with the condition that their 'knowledge' had to be held by a skilled maritime Race, which I do not find would indicate the Egyptians . . . I regret that our Founder . . . alone, here in his Remarks, actively mistakes the intentions of my Paper, and I weary of his constant iteration of 'No proof, no proof' . . . my friends and I talked over the awful reception my Paper would get from our Founder, and we almost anticipated, word for word, the actual growl of 'Proof, Proof' with which the Atlantean bun thrown would be received.[35]

Revelation and Stern Logic

No one rallied to Watkins' position. Even such respected geometers as Admiral Somerville, it transpired, were sympathetic to the Atlantean theory;[36] and although he continued to do all he could to herd his motley flock along the straight track of archaeological righteousness, Watkins was in no position to insist. Indeed, faced with continued ridicule from orthodoxy, he began to concede ground to his fellow Club members. A major point of Atlantean theory was that culture had diffused to both sides of the Atlantic; in March 1931 Watkins drew members' attention to similar alignments in Egypt and Mexico.[37] Even more significantly, Watkins began to acknowledge that the ley theory required something more than a straightforwardly functional explanation. In November 1927, he had confessed to having 'some prejudices against the "mystic" groups of knowledge to battle against'.[38] In 1934 he claimed to have received an 'unusual gift' of something akin to second sight following a month or so of serious illness,[39] and told his son shortly before his death that 'I have been psychic all my life, but I have kept it under and never told anyone about it.'[40]

Was he 'psychic'? What does this word mean? The purpose of the Straight Track may have been mysterious, yet to Watkins it was blatantly and demonstrably There, apparent on any map. If orthodox folk saw Straight Trackers as dotty eccentrics for believing in a phenomenon which they felt to be evident to all, then Straight Trackers were quite literally 'occultists', able to perceive that which was apparently veiled to others. They were automatically rendered 'psychic' by the fact of mainstream disbelief.

Had he reflected on the matter, Watkins might have realized that his entire discovery owed much to a 'psychic' revelation that followed an earlier close shave with death. The diary of George Marshall, Hon. Secretary of the Woolhope Club, records that on 3 June 1921 he had been to visit Watkins: 'I saw him in bed with heart attack he seems to get worse and can do little.'[41] Seen in this light, Watkins' revelation at Blackwardine on 30 June takes on something of the quality of a near-death vision. It gave him a new lease of life, ready for 'the rush of revelations in the gorgeous year of sunshine just finished'. Behind it lay 'nearly fifty years' unusually intimate knowledge of our beautiful West Country border land, and I know now that my sub-conscious self had prepared the ground and worked at the problem I now see solved'.[42] Revelation was central not just to the nature of Watkins' discovery, but to its very name: 'The sighting line was called the ley or lay', he wrote simply, only subsequently finding place-name evidence that seemed to corroborate this knowledge,[43] and a chapter of *The Old Straight Track* was dedicated to the frequent 'vivid and strange bits of coincidence and verification' that brought 'confirmation' (the chapter title) to the ley theory.[44]

To Watkins, however, revelation had to be tempered by fieldwork:

> as an old investigator and inventor, I know that surmise and imagination are absolutely necessary in the first stages; and it is a mistake to sneer at these factors as being weak in themselves.
>
> But when a pioneer has to demonstrate the truth of his theories, surmise and imagination have to be relegated to the background, and stern logic, dealing (in our case) with topographical facts, must *alone* be employed.[45]

It was the need for 'stern logic', I suggest, that led him to explain his sightlines in terms of utilitarian trackways; but even before *The Old Straight Track* was published, Watkins was becoming aware that not all leys could be explained in this way. This was particularly true of the 'seasonal alignments' based on sunrise angles, which Watkins began to investigate in 1922 following the Malvern Geographical Society's Lockyer-inspired work into possible 'Sun Worship in the Malvern Hills'. Watkins, who had not previously read Lockyer's work, came to the conclusion not only that 'the sunrise alignments of Lockyer are identical with long-distance leys', but also, finding a close correlation between leys and beacon-hills, suggested that the beacons might originally have functioned as 'sun substitutes'. 'The sequence seems to suggest that the utilitarian trackways might have been the primary ones, that sun alignments followed, and then beacons evolved.'[46] In January 1928, responding to a request from Tyler for a tighter definition, Watkins replied that

> the word ley in my mind does not infer that a track *was* established exactly or at all along the line. It is a backbone which in most cases was used as a guide for a track, an optical line.
>
> But in both seasonal alignments (which are abundantly proved I think) and in some of the other camp alignments, I find less evidence of tracks than in other leys, and I regard it as quite possible that no track was ever established along them . . . but be it remembered that a ley was practical and not merely a theoretical line. The man walking on a ley had to walk for the next mark-point: he might make a departure to avoid a precipice, a marsh, the bend of a river, but when this was over *he had to get back* to a mark-point on the ley.[47]

In this way, Watkins safeguarded the primacy of his now-established trackway theory, but he can hardly be said to have closed the door to other interpretations.

Chapter 15

Straight Track to Beyond

Immaterial Evidence

Tyler's query was prompted by a sense of growing conviction that 'these alignments are not at all directly connected with tracks',[1] and he found himself increasingly drawn towards more occult explanations. In April 1929, Tyler cautiously recommended a book on occult teachings to fellow-members; whilst admitting that works of this kind 'may not appeal to all, it certainly seems that the chances of discovering (at any rate with any degree of certainty) the secrets of the past by ordinary scientific means, is very small, and it is worth while considering information given by writers of occult books'.[2] Three years later, he explained this more fully in a discussion of 'Aids to Natural Vision':

> It may be regarded as 'unscientific' (much-misused word, for 'Science' is merely 'Knowledge', and the word cannot be confined to academic knowledge only, or to deductions made by academic science) to suggest that there is any other power of vision, perfectly natural to man, but outside the range of what is commonly included in the natural – ie normal – faculties. Nevertheless I do venture to suggest that there is a 'super-normal' (though perfectly natural) power of vision, latent in man, which may perhaps have been made use of by the men of ancient times – or, at least, by certain of them – though it is only found sporadically today.[3]

In 1935 Alfred Watkins died; and Major Tyler, in a paper entitled 'Stock-taking', invited club members to consider taking the STC in a new direction. 'If the Club is satisfied that there is nothing more behind Mr Watkins' theory than the bare "Straight Track", then I submit, the work of the Club has been completed in marshalling all the evidence that we have collected. We have been finding "Straight Tracks" for years, and there seems little point in going on "ad infinitum".' Pointing out that members had been turning up lots of 'abnormalities', in particular the 'sun-worshipping line' that made it 'hard to see how worship can be directly connected with tracks, to the extent of being the cause of them', he proposed that the Club should 'abandon the original bare theory of the "Old Straight Track", and to cease talking of "straight tracks" at all, to clear our minds of the pre-conceived ideas; and to turn to and try to solve the real problem behind the original theory of Mr Watkins. This is not to kill Mr Watkins' brilliant discovery, but to carry on the work which he started.'[4]

Tyler's proposals were discussed at the Exeter meeting in July, and were subsequently sent to members, in which he asked them, amongst other things, how they felt about a possible name change. The replies, which fill a 'Special Portfolio', provide a fascinating insight into the range of reasons that members had for being members, including many who never otherwise contributed to the debates within the Portfolios. It transpired that many members held very different ideas from those of the Club's founder: as Herbert Hudson commented, 'nearly every member has his pet subject'.[5] Some suggested that the Club should divide into sub-sections; others were opposed to it. A range of alternative names were suggested, including 'The Orientation Club', the 'Prehistoric Research Club' and 'The Tangent Club'.[6] In the end, members opted merely to drop the word 'Postal' from the Straight Track Postal Club's title, and decided not to sub-divide their work: 'I should be very loathe to give up our joint investigation', as Captain Chudleigh put it.[7] Tyler's proposal to broaden the remit, however, was generally accepted;[8] indeed, the remit had been pretty broad from the start.

Tyler himself was keen to emphasize the Club's *difference* from conventional archaeology. He opposed a name-change for the Club that would incorporate the word 'archaeological' in the title 'because our quest is quite out of the running in what is generally held to be "archaeological". This "science" is based on material things, while ours rests on immaterial evidence; though I hold that it should be searched for in – as far as may be possible – a "scientific" manner".'[9] Summarizing the correspondence, Tyler strove to find a balance between the 'psychic' tendency and the rest. He rejected the suggestion of Herbert Hudson, one of the Club's more prosaic members, that members 'should not submit to the Portfolio any new evidence without having first obtained the opinion of an Accepted Authority': 'Where does one turn to as "authority" on a new idea?' Equally, Mr Hayton's desire to incorporate 'psychic knowledge' ('a remarkably large percentage of our members claim to have psychic powers or esoteric knowledge') was rejected as 'quite impossible in what is by way of being a "scientific" portfolio. For we must not put forward any evidence except that which may appeal to the ordinary senses', although he conceded that psychic information could be used as 'pointers'.[10]

Tyler's attempts to steer a middle course were not conspicuously successful. In the same year, Katharine Maltwood published her discovery of the Glastonbury Zodiac, which provoked some of the fiercest exchanges in the Club's history. Maltwood, artist, sculptor and Theosophist, had been commissioned to design a map for the 1929 Everyman edition of the *High History of the Holy Grail*, the events of which were presumed to have been set in the area around Glastonbury in Somerset. During this project, she discovered what she took to be the remains of a gigantic celestial zodiac, in which the outlines of the 12 constellations were to be found inscribed in a huge circle around the town, picked out in field-boundaries, streams, lanes and other features of the landscape. Her work was published as *A Guide to Glastonbury's Temple of the Stars* in 1935, and it instantly caught the imagination of many members of the Straight Track Club.[11]

Herbert Hudson, who had been ' "hammering" away at my object to persuade the Archaeologists and the Astronomers to join forces'[12] and thus, as Watkins had been, concerned for the Club's good reputation with the scientists, was dismayed to find that some members were inclined to take Maltwood's ideas seriously. Responding to a review by a Canadian Theosophist who suggested that 'Mother Earth first suggested the design', he expostulated: 'What the devil does he mean? Is he mad, or am I? Is he writing in plain prose, or is he speaking figuratively as in poetry? I submit that all members who are backing the author of this book are not conforming to the most elementary rules of "the laws of Evidence" which are universally accepted by the educated races of mankind.' This outburst provoked a catty response, which, unusually for the STC, was both typed and unsigned: 'How amusing that Mr Hudson should suspect that he may be mad; certainly a sane scientist would not express an opinion before examining the evidence! . . . And why, may we ask, does Mr Hudson belong to such an amateur society . . .?'[13]

Katharine Maltwood, though she never joined the STC, nonetheless took part in the 1936 Cheltenham Meeting,[14] and what differences there may have been between members seem to have been patched up. Six more portfolios were produced before the war, and in 1939 the Club arranged for the publication of Tyler's lecture, *The Geometrical Arrangement of Ancient Sites*, which had been delivered to the London Antiquarian Society in October 1938.

This was the only time that the STC ventured into print, although back in 1935 Culling Carr-Gomm (Tyler's successor as Hon. Secretary) had approached Methuen, Watkins' publishers, to see if they might be interested in publishing a selection of Portfolio articles in book form, as a 'continuation' of *The Old Straight Track*. His draft preface survives, emphasizing the wide range of views and also the geographic spread of members' research: 'To say the least of it, it is submitted that these papers and their illustrations and maps do furnish a very considerable quantity of evidence of an advanced state of culture in those remote epochs that are so vaguely spoken of as "prehistoric".'[15] The proposal was turned down in February 1936 because Methuen's reader believed that 'the book would stand little chance of sale outside the members of the Club'.[16]

Tyler himself was not in favour of bringing out a book just yet, probably because, as his supporter W W Tyrell told Carr-Gomm, 'some of our ideas are changing'. Tyrell recommended that Tyler, as 'the authority on the new investigations', should produce something himself 'at a later stage'.[17] This proved to be *The Geometrical Arrangement*, from which it was immediately apparent that the Club had come quite a long way off the Watkinsian straight-and-narrow. Described by Carr-Gomm (1939) as 'a very concise statement of what our members are studying',[18] Tyler's thesis was essentially Atlantean: 'we must, in all our investigations into the mysteries of antiquity, infer some wonderful (and possibly world-wide) civilization, as underlying all known history'. He cited with approval the work of Josef Heinsch, a German planner now living in Canada, who 'advances the thought that continued study of these alignments (believed by the ancients to be in harmony with "divine" laws of nature) will result in the discovery of laws of "siting" which would be beneficial to us moderns'.[19]

Tyler was once again at pains to stress the difference between the work of the STC and conventional archaeology: 'This idea is not, of course, at all in accordance with accepted ideas of the mental and practical capacity of our prehistoric forebears. So one who is a student of this theory must not be expected to follow the lines of "classical" archaeology.'[20] Carr-Gomm and Robert Rule, who had organized the publication of Tyler's work, accordingly decided against sending a review copy to *Antiquity* 'because they would only ridicule it'. They did send a copy to the *Proceedings of the Prehistoric Society*, but it was returned: the Society (presumably in the person of *Proceedings* editor Grahame Clark) declared itself 'unable to give a review'.[21]

Tyler's death in December 1939 ended mystical musings on the meaning of the ley for some time. *The Old Straight Track* was republished in 1946 and again in 1948, although copies were apparently still on sale in 1965.[22] This suggests a surge of interest immediately after the war, followed by a long period during which the ley theory was very much in the doldrums. There were new converts, notably the art student Tony Wedd, who first read *The Old Straight Track* while living in Hampstead in 1949 (it was his vision, fused with the 1950s flying saucer phenomenon, that led directly to the revival in the theory's fortunes in the 1960s).[23] Pennick and Devereux have likewise found evidence of a brief burst of interest in leys in Oxfordshire and Essex during the early 1950s, but otherwise there seems to be little reason to doubt Crawford's claim in 1951 that the 'Old Straight Trackers' typified a type of 'confused nonsense' that had now disappeared.[24] Orthodoxy had triumphed, for the moment.

A Bit Too Close to Home

To David Matless, 'Crawford's dismissal of leys as "crankeries" reflects the fact that Watkins is less his anti-rationalist opposite than an eccentric mirror-image of field archaeology.'[25] This is perhaps the most astute observation yet made about the ley phenomenon, and it is applicable not just to the main protagonists, but to their supporters in the 'heroic band' and the Straight Track Club. Both groups were not only products of the same narrow band of well-off middle-class society, but enjoyed (or endured) a similarly eccentric status (and arguably still do, of course!). It is the *similarities*, and not the differences, between 'Crawfordian' and 'Watkinsian' archaeology that made the latter so 'dangerous' to the former.

Watkins was no fuddy-duddy. He was an inventor and a pioneer, and in spite of his age he was also the Woolhope Club's most outspoken modernizer, on several occasions trying unsuccessfully to convince his

27 'Proof by spade'. Alfred Watkins' photograph of a 'stoned trackway' found in a Hereford sewer cutting (*The Old Straight Track*, figs. 54 and 55).

fellow-members to admit women. He was impressed by Crawford, and not only wanted to win Crawford's approval, but also to apply his methods ('fact' not 'theory', 'proof by spade', even aerial photography). Both were keen to recruit support from the growing outdoor movement; both were keen to assert the primacy of fieldwork. Here and there, the STC was even able to steal a march on orthodoxy: the 'environmental turn' pioneered by Cyril Fox and subsequently Grahame Clark's Fenland Research Committee was anticipated by STC botanist Norman Woodhead, who, as early as November 1927, was urging members to look out for 'striking features of relict vegetation'.[26] To cap it all, Watkins was every bit as good a publicist as Crawford. Not only were his books astutely tailored to specific markets, they were very well advertised. He monitored press response closely ('Eleven reviews . . . have averaged fifteen inches length in columns', he noted proudly in his scrapbook[27]), made a point of responding promptly to criticisms, and never missed an opportunity to plug the cause. When

Straight Track to Beyond 209

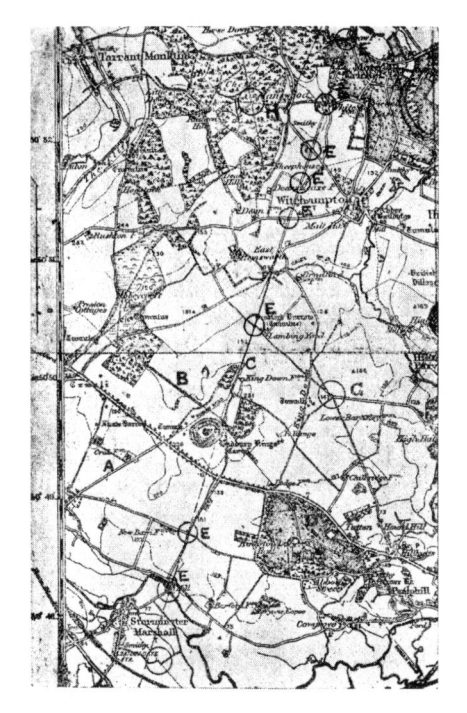

28 *Eccentric Mirror Images*: 'Tracks to Badbury Camp' (from Watkins, *The Ley Hunters Manual*, p. 27).

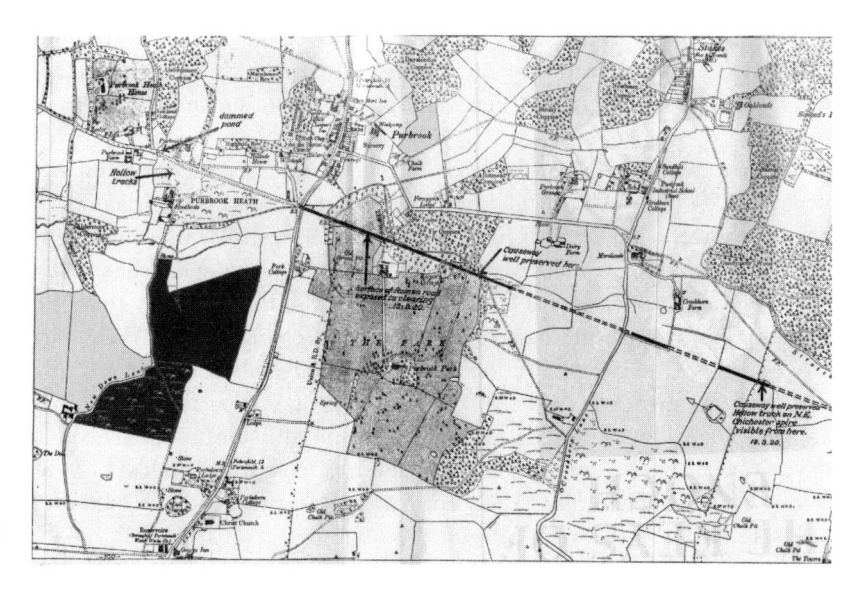

29 'A Typical Roman Road: The Road from Chichester to Bitterne, near Southampton' (from Crawford, *Man and his Past*, endpaper).

The Times described the Avebury Sanctuary as having been 'found by sighting', Watkins wrote in to say that 'I feel that topographical sighting on alignments is certain in the near future to become an important aspect – preceding the spade in antiquarian research, although neglected up to now.'[28]

In his official capacity as Archaeological Officer to the Ordnance Survey, inadvertently responsible for plotting and recording many of the sites that linked the leys, Crawford must have had a lot more to do with the Straight Track than he would have liked. He must surely have winced when he read, in the Quennells' popular *Everyday Life in the New Stone Age*, that 'long before the Romans there were men laying out roads by very much the same methods as the Royal Engineer Surveyors of the Ordnance Survey';[29] the offending suggestion certainly disappeared from later editions. Having initiated a policy in which enthusiastic would-be archaeologists such as Hawkes, Phillips and Piggott were encouraged to send him the fruits of their fieldwork for inclusion on the map,[30] Crawford would have been dismayed to discover that Major Tyler was in January 1928 urging Straight Track Club members to file their observations as well.[31] The Ordnance Survey was at that point largely the preserve of military personnel, who, as Crawford makes abundantly clear, had little respect for his activities.[32] Amongst the Club's surveyor members were some who had served as high-ranking officers in the forces: when Colonel Powell asked for an opinion from General Winterbotham, it was Second Lieutenant Crawford's boss he was addressing,[33] which must have been particularly galling. Another surveyor, Admiral Somerville, actually contributed versions of the same paper to the first issue of *Antiquity* and the STC – which, by curious coincidence, appeared within a month of each other.[34]

We have seen how Crawford chose to ignore the ley theory in public, while others (for instance George Engleheart) resorted to ridicule. In private, however, they took it much more seriously. Watkins' evident conviction, coupled with a style of writing and of reasoning that had much in common with those of contemporary orthodoxy, meant that the Straight Track constituted a considerable threat to mainstream meta-narratives. In 1937, Mr Tyrell of the STC told members that he had recently met 'a young man, still under 30, who had become a specialist in tumuli, and a valuable book under his name has recently been published'. I haven't been able to identify this enigmatic archaeologist, who had bought a copy of *The Old Straight Track*, but had apparently been ' "warned off" by the older school, as it was "dangerous" '.[35] A generation later W G Hoskins, pioneer landscape historian and admirer of Crawford, also described the book as 'dangerous', and one that 'should only be read by the most strong-minded reader'.[36]

Some archaeologists were certainly susceptible. Mr Tyrell's tumuli-man, for instance, agreed with him that *The Old Straight Track* contained 'much valuable information'.[37] In 1926, the President of the Worthing Archaeological Society was urging his members to investigate the ley theory. Eleven years later, STC member Melusine Wood visited the WAS excavation at Barrow Hill, and found that

> they were the most keenly interested group anyone could talk to . . . I told about Mr Watkins, and how unfortunately orthodoxy put up its back against him – and one of my listeners slapped his thigh and said it was good for orthodoxy to have its back put up, and the oftener the better. And in the end, my original kind guide got up slowly and said 'I would like to thank the lady for what she has been saying – it makes one think'.[38]

Club members considered themselves to be pioneers, promoting new ideas in the face of stuffy orthodoxy. Members were well aware that 'our knowledge of prehistory has been completely revolutionized in our generation', as Robert Rule put it. To Fred Hando, the attractions of ley-hunting included 'the sense of performing actual pioneer work – "putting something on the map" '; and 'contact with people who make the Romans seem Victorian . . . history, as traditionally taught in the schools, needs re-writing in Volume I'; he even suggested that the ley theory could help resolve other contemporary archaeological dilemmas, such as the vexed question of the 'Beaker Folk'.[39]

Mainstream rejection was thus seen as a symptom of its own shortcomings. 'The mental limitation of the expert is a psychological study in itself', as Allen Watkins told STC members.[40] John Hooper Harvey found Mortimer Wheeler to be 'impervious to "common sense". It is a fact (personally experienced) that very few of the "recognized" archaeologists are prepared, even in private, to admit that such a book as Alfred Watkins' Old Straight Track *would be worth their while to read*: in other words, the Old Straight Track (or any other new theory not evolved by the official archaeologists) is condemned absolutely unheard . . .'[41] Watkins' son, Allen, even claimed that his father had shocked the 'Old Guards of

30 A ley hunter's vision: 'Midwinter Sunrise on Grey Hill', by Fred Hando (Hando, *The Pleasant Lend of Gwent*, p. 60).

Archaeology . . . in exactly the same way as the Bishops were shocked by Charles Darwin'.[42]

Some members pinned their hopes on a more open younger generation: 'whilst the older generation of archaeologists presumably regards a new idea as a threat to some cherished theory, to the young it is a door opening on to fresh fields for exploration', suggested Wood. Tyrell agreed: 'the barriers raised by orthodox archaeologists will in time be thrown down, and . . . its members will look with tolerance and even interest on ideas at variance with their own'.[43]

His optimism came several decades too soon, however. Tyler's death in 1939 provoked a further crisis in the Club. 'I much fear we shall gradually peter out and die as a society,' wrote Mabel Woods in 1940, 'and just as the [Tyler] monograph is out, too . . . We mustn't expire, but live to preach the faith that is in us.' Carr-Gomm, the Secretary, could 'see no reason why we should peter out at all. We have still got some keen members...."[44] Not enough, however, to keep the Club functioning during the war years. The next portfolio appeared in June 1946, and included a paper by a new member, Eric Wills, on 'Egyptology and the STC' that resulted in a brief flurry of interest in Egyptian hyperdiffusion; but interest and enthusiasm were clearly waning. The last portfolio was circulated in July 1947; and when Carr-Gomm in 1951 was urged by his son to write about the Club's work, it was clear that even the Secretary had lost touch with some of the members: he had to write to Methuen to get the address of Allen Watkins, who at that time still had many of the early portfolios. He succeeded in tracking down most of them, which were deposited with the Club's Chairman, A T Morley Hewitt, who in turn presented the whole series to Hereford City Library in 1962, where it is still housed today.[45]

Why did the Club implode? The usual reason given is the age of the membership,[46] but in fact many were relatively youthful still. The deaths of the two most dynamic figures within five years of each other certainly undermined the Club's cohesion, but it seems clear that by the 1940s many members were becoming discouraged, or had simply ceased to believe in the ley theory. 'I don't seem to get much time myself for Straight Track pursuits now', wrote Harvey to Carr-Gomm in February 1944.[47] Even more striking is the lack of reference to leys in the work of former Club stalwarts. There are no leys at all in Barbara Carbonell's 1949 history of her own parish, *Thirteen Centuries in Bow*, and Watkins' name is absent from the bibliography. Morley Hewitt's local history, *The Story of Fordingbridge in fact and fancy* (1966), is similarly bereft of leys. Others revised their opinions over time. Fred Hando's *The Pleasant Land of Gwent*, published in 1944, has much to say about sunrise alignments and even old straight tracks, but all traces of the ley had disappeared by the time *Out and About in Monmouthshire* was published in 1958.

In these two latter examples it seems quite possible that the members were personally won over to orthodoxy. Hando's later book carried a preface by Lord Raglan, a close friend of Cyril Fox, who is cited several times in Hando's second volume, and it seems quite likely that the pair lured him off the straight track. Morley Hewitt tells us that Stuart Piggott 'resided for a time at Rockbourne', just outside his home-town. Again, it seems probable that Piggott may have similarly had a few discussions with the local antiquarian; certainly, from 1956 to 1974, Hewitt established himself as a thoroughly 'respectable' archaeologist with his excavation of a large Roman villa at Rockbourne.[48]

The Thrill of the Past

To most members, their investigation was essentially a fascinating pastime. Melusine Wood (a pioneer in the revival of the English folk-dance), responding to Tyler's 'stock-taking' exercise, saw the Club as faced with choosing either to pursue 'deep scientific work' or being

> a loose association of people with diverse interests only held together by a common (but not very deep) interest in Mr Watkins' theories. The last seems to be the true state of affairs and therefore not likely to accomplish anything of great importance. But much mental pleasure and interest is likely to result from the pooling of such varied ideas – provided individuals can be prevented from trying to stampede the rest of us in their own particular interest.[49]

On one level, the STC membership might be seen as indulging in a sort of protracted parlour-game. Like characters in the detective stories that typify that period, they were convinced that they were 'on to something': it is significant that Maxwell's popular ley-hunting novels took precisely this form (*A Detective in Essex*, *A Detective in Surrey*). Maxwell's books capture the thrill of ley-hunting very effectively: 'The excitement caused by their discovery of a ley within ten minutes of our becoming Watkinsians was intense. Every one of our party of intrepid explorers felt a spiritual kinship with Christopher Columbus.'[50]

Mystery, quest and adventure crop up regularly in writing on the leys. *The Old Straight Track* was advertised as 'a guide to a new quest',[51] and Watkins concluded his *Archaic Tracks Round Cambridge* by claiming that '[a]dventure lies lurking in these lines where I point the way for younger feet than mine. Detective work of sorts ... Who will strike the trail?'[52] The *Evening News* recommended *The Ley Hunter's Manual* to those who 'would read strange secrets in our homely countryside'.[53] It is clear that Straight Trackers believed that the ancient past was still a place of mystery, a place wherein the interested outsider could still make discoveries of mind-bending proportions. To Dutt, the ley-hunter was 'an adventurer on almost untrodden ground'; Hudson concluded his paper on 'Ancient Sun Alignments' with 'the satisfaction of knowing that the reader will not experience that flat feeling which the searcher experiences when there remains nothing further to be discovered'.[54] In short, Straight Trackers were epistemic *refuseniks*, incapable of accepting a limiting discipline that banished the scope for mystery and discovery to the fiction-writers.

Chapter 16

Visions of Civilization

In his lifetime, Alfred Watkins was known first and foremost as a photographer. 'No photographer can be unfamiliar with the name of Mr Alfred Watkins', began the *Western Morning News*' review of *The Ley Hunter's Manual*.[1] His photographic credentials ('Fellow and Progress Medallist, Royal Photographic Society') were proudly emblazoned on the title-pages of his books, and the quality of his photographs was regularly praised both by reviewers and his colleagues in the Woolhope Club. He knew himself to be an artist, and was clearly miffed when a pleased recipient of his photographs tactlessly praised the camera instead of the photographer.[2] He took great care in the presentation and design of his Watkins Meter Company books, designing his own title-font for *Early British Trackways* and using white-on-black woodcuts for the maps in *Archaic Tracks Around Cambridge*.

This aesthetic sensibility, this sensitivity to appearances, is significant: particularly considering the number of artists and architects who were drawn to the ley. As the *Brighton Gazette* observed in its review of *The Ley Hunter's Manual*, 'the first qualification' for the ley-hunter was 'simply an eye for country',[3] and Watkins certainly had that; his photographs remain as evocative and powerful today as they did when they were taken. Certain compositional formalities – for instance, the regular inclusion of the Scots Pine, which he once described as 'the Trees of the Ancient Track'[4] – serve to underscore a certain sense of order in the landscape: a straight track of purpose, perhaps, for a visionary who had come very close to death, or an artist's understanding of harmony and proportion, a 'golden mean' within the landscape. It seems relevant that to Arthur Mackmurdo, artist and architect, the ley theory satisfied 'our own sense of logical fitness'.[5]

David Matless makes the interesting suggestion that ley theory might be seen as 'emerging from the same discourse of landscape as much planning and preservationist thinking, particularly given Watkins' emphasis on geometry within topography, field survey, and the role of the expert planner-surveyor in either ancient or modern society'.[6]

There is much to be said for this view, particularly in the light of the attraction that the Straight Track clearly held for surveyors, architects and preservationists; but the theme of ancient order was hardly new to the heterodox. Since Stukeley at least, the ancients have regularly been ascribed a sense of spiritual geometry every bit as mystical as that which (literally) underpinned the cathedrals of the Gothic middle ages. The straight line of the ley, like the circle of the Glastonbury Zodiac, conforms to the same geometric rules: new-found signs of ancient order underlying troubled twentieth-century landscapes.

But 'straightness' was also the measure of civilization, a commodity traditionally deemed to be absent in prehistory. Crawford's one published outburst against Watkins stressed that 'the feature which distinguishes prehistoric from Roman and some modern roads is precisely the sinuosity of their course. Such an inversion of the facts [as the ley] reveals a complete failure to understand the nature of primitive culture.'[7] Orthodox archaeologists used a different sort of geometry to understand the past: an underlying order that determined the prehistory they examined, the way they set about examining it, and the role they felt that archaeology had to play in the present. This sense of order was no mere aesthetic abstraction. It played an important role not just in ensuring archaeology's disciplinary success, but in finding a role for the discipline as a source for the values that underpinned civilization at a time when civilization seemed very precarious.

Finding ever-earlier evidence for the start of national civilization was a widespread preoccupation of the inter-war years, perhaps in the hope of contextualizing the horror of 1914–18. It became common for writers and journalists to comment on how pre-Roman Britain, contrary to the beliefs of previous generations, was not inhabited by a bunch of woad-painted savages but by a people vested with the rudiments of civilization and the capacity to develop it at least as fast as anyone else. Thus, to take just one example, Arthur Weigall, writing in 1926:

We must rid our minds of the picture of barbarian ancient Britons, clad in skins, and using stone weapons, capering on the seashore when the Romans arrived; and we must understand that our civilization is at least two thousand years older than that.[8]

We've already seen how the Old Straight Track seemed to offer glimpses of an immensely ancient civilization, and 'contact with people who make the Romans seem Victorian'.[9] The challenge to scientists was to counter these claims; not only, as Mortimer Wheeler suggested, by revealing '[t]he various methods and the varying success with which our predecessors in this island have striven towards the common goal of civilization',[10] but by looking for 'scientific' evidence that would push back the origins of civilization in Britain.

The Meaning of Maiden Castle

Wheeler's excavation at Maiden Castle, between 1934 and 1937, was one of the most famous British archaeological investigations of the twentieth century. It was the classic 'Wheeler dig', both in terms of scale of operations and the publicity which it generated. Around a hundred people were involved in each of the four seasons, making up 'probably the largest force of the kind ever to be employed on a British dig before or since', in Jacquetta Hawkes' words.[11] There were in theory three directors: Wheeler and his wife Tessa, answerable to the Society of Antiquaries, and Colonel Charles Drew, who represented the Dorset Archaeological Society and took responsibility for the financial and logistical aspects; but no one was in any doubt that 'The Keeper' was in charge. 'I soon noticed that Mrs Wheeler and the staff which he had brought with him from London were trained almost like commandos to carry out the "Keeper's" instructions', recalled Bill Wedlake, the site foreman.[12] The final remodelling of Maiden Castle, wrote Wheeler, 'represents the work of a master-mind, wielding unquestioned authority and controlling vast resources of labour'.[13] It was a concept that his workforce certainly understood.

In his Report on Maiden Castle (1943), Wheeler claimed that the decision to dig at Maiden Castle had been initiated for three reasons: firstly, the 'complexity and magnitude' of its defences; secondly, its position 'in the midst of a region more prolific in major hill-forts than any other in the British Isles' in which archaeological work had barely begun (a 'large and important cultural province thus remained unsytematized'); and, thirdly, because his excavation at Verulamium was winding down due to 'an acute uncertainty as to the future of the site', thereby releasing '[a] considerable quantity of trained and semi-trained student-labour'.[14] Plans were well under way by November 1933, however, when the Maiden Castle Excavation Committee held its first meeting at the Society of Antiquaries; permission to dig had already been granted by the Office of Works and the site's owners.[15] In his autobiography, Wheeler claimed that 'the new objective was one which I had secretly meditated for several years before the moment came for action',[16] and this may indeed have been the case.

The excavation had an important educational function. A great many – possibly most – of the next generation of British archaeologists spent at least one season at Maiden Castle, in the process helping to change the public perception of archaeologists themselves. 'Too often too many think of them as absent-minded, bearded, crumbling fossils, more fossilized than the fossils they find . . . Just a foolish caricature that has printed itself in the minds of so many,' reported the *Southern Daily Echo*, contrasting this stereotype with the new-look Wheeler version, said to be 'adding colour to our background'.[17] To the *Evening Standard*, 'the working party has been unlike the cartoonist's conception of a cluster of archaeologists: it has consisted largely of undergraduates, with a sprinkling of young women'.[18] Wheeler took pains to publicize the youth – and the gender – of his workforce. '[A]rchaeology was now as much a science as physics,' he told an audience at Dorchester, 'and if a man was to be called a scientist he had to begin early.' His slides contrasted a nineteenth-century excavator in top hat, and 'the new order of things, youth in the scientific age – a young woman excavator at Maiden Castle clad in shirt and trousers'.[19]

The Wheeler approach was inculcated to members of local archaeological societies, who turned up on site regularly and in force to witness it, and perhaps to absorb its lessons.[20] In September 1936, 300 members of Wheeler's recently revamped Royal Archaeological Institute came by special train in 'one of the biggest archaeological outings ever staged in Great Britain'.[21] Anyone with an interest in the ancient past endeavoured to visit: even the Straight Track Club made it the object of their Sunday excursion from Salisbury in 1934.[22] (Two years later, STC member Herbert Hudson was one of a party of 120 members and friends from the Suffolk Institute of Archaeology and Natural History:

31 Mortimer Wheeler (left) welcoming O G S Crawford to Maiden Castle, 1934. (*Dorset County Museum, Archaeological Collections of the Dorset Natural History and Archaeological Society*).

his views on the orientation of stone circles were firmly quashed by Wheeler.[23])

The general public, too, was actively encouraged to visit the site. They did so in droves, 'hundreds of little folk from shops and factories and back-kitchens, who streamed on to the hill-top, day after day, and listened to the lecturettes which my students were carefully drilled to offer them'.[24] The *Evening News* claimed that 'as many as 50,000 of us' visited the site during 1936.[25] Around a third of the dig's expenses were met through small donations, the sale of interim reports (16,000 at a shilling each), postcards (64,000 at 2d each) and 'trivial oddments ... all marked in Indian ink with the name of the site'.[26] In short, Maiden Castle was a showpiece, a highly successful public-relations exercise for the new brand of archaeology.

Defeating the Führer

Wheeler made adroit use of the media. He actively encouraged their attentions, and the result was a gratifyingly vast amount of uncritical coverage, in both national and local newspapers. The London Museum employed a press-cuttings agency to scour the nation's press for references to their Director's activities, and the results were dutifully pasted in a series of surviving scrapbooks. From this valuable resource, it is apparent that, although Wheeler later claimed that '[w]e politely but cautiously steered the information which went out',[27] in fact he did much more than merely 'steer' it. Identical wording is to be found in the reports published by such geographically diverse publications as the *Dundee Evening Telegraph*, the *Nottingham Evening Post* and the *Leicester Mercury*,[28] implying that Wheeler was sending out press-releases which editors were usually happy to publish verbatim. It made their work that much easier, as Dorchester journalists acknowledged when, in 1936, they presented him with a silver cigarette-box 'for his assistance which had enabled them to give their readers "archaeology without tears" '.[29]

The scrapbook archive thus constitutes a valuable guide to how Wheeler's own interpretation was developing and how he chose to present his work. At the start of the first season, he outlined his expectations in a manner that hints at an ennui with matters Roman:

> Maiden Castle may be expected to illustrate, in the first place, that Celtic culture which is best represented for us by the famous lake village, in Glastonbury, Somerset, which is marked by the vigour of its decorative art. It shows Celtic civilization at its best in this country . . . The Belgic invaders, of whom we hope to find traces, were better equipped, in a material sense, than their predecessors . . . On the heels of Belgic invaders came the Romans with their mass-produced civilization . . .'[30]

Acknowledging that 'it seems certain that both the area covered and the height and width of the banks must have been greater than practical requirements', he attributed the construction to some 'prehistoric megalomaniac'.[31] By the end of the season, Wheeler felt able to claim that 'the prehistoric population of Maiden Castle was essentially peaceful in character and must have relied rather upon the strength of the town ramparts than its armoury for defence', a claim the press headlines made much of: 'Prehistoric Peace on Maiden Castle'.[32]

In March 1935, after a winter's reflection, Wheeler gave a lantern lecture to a capacity crowd in the Dorchester Corn Exchange, in which he elaborated his findings. Friction, he claimed, had begun to arise when iron ore was discovered, which induced a migration from the Continent, and 'land became mopped up'. 'There was a race for armaments: just like to-day when a country built submarines, and another followed suit.'[33] This appeal to the logic of *Lebensraum* was gleefully picked up by the press: 'RACE FOR ARMAMENTS 2500 YEARS AGO: Maiden Castle Built To Frighten Iron Age French', announced the *Dorset Daily Echo*. It even surfaced in Wheeler's formal report to the Society of Antiquaries in 1936: 'At this time [c. 300 BC], under conditions of increasing congestion and anxiety, began that prehistoric armaments-race which was to cover the downs with fortifications.'[34]

Wheeler's characterization of Maiden Castle's ruler grew grimmer by the year. The 'prehistoric megalomaniac' of 1934 had become a 'tyrannos' in 1935, who used 'hapless corvées or chain-gangs' to build it.[35] In 1936, the tyrannos became 'a prehistoric Führer . . . Maiden Castle shouts totalitarianism at you. There is nothing democratic about it';[36] and in 1937, he suggested that the last phase of work had been done 'by the enslaved population' who 'not infrequently died during the process and were buried as they fell. The picture is one of chain-gangs worked, in many cases literally, to death.'[37]

The net effect of this narrative was to pave the way for the advent of civilization, in the form of Vespasian, whose signal victory over the totalitarian Führer of Maiden Castle was effectively a metaphor of hope. In August 1936 'a girl student . . . conjured up a picture of enemy raiders tearing up the hillside, only to meet with a stout resistance from the occupants' for the benefit of journalists.[38] A year later, in the last of the four seasons of excavation, Wheeler conveniently discovered what he took to be the 'war-cemetery' of the defenders' last stand. His lurid account of the battle at the east gate, printed in *The Times*, won that paper's unequivocal support; his story, 'of the fall of this primitive fortress before the might of Rome', was 'supported in every detail by the evidence revealed by the spade . . . Its captor was undoubtedly VESPASIAN . . . No other interpretation of the evidence so impressively marshalled by Dr Wheeler is possible.'[39]

The triumph of Roman civilization – mass-produced though it may have been – was not lost on the 'little folk' who visited the site. In July 1939, the Dorset Federation of Women's Institutes staged a historical pageant in Lulworth Park. Entitled 'The Spirit of Dorset', the pageant

32 Digging for Victory: part of the 'war cemetery' at Maiden Castle. (*English Heritage*).

featured a tribe of 'Durotriges', who held out in vain against the Roman Army. The defeated tribespeople were offered 'the prosperity that only the Roman state can bring: "Submit yourselves, and live, free men" '.[40]

The Bungalow in Prehistory

How people became 'civilized' was Wheeler's particular interest. His definition was a literal one: 'it is perhaps as a citizen that man achieves the fullest scope for his various functions... Civilized man [is] a city-dweller.'[41] However, his experience at Maiden Castle now invited a broader, pre-Roman definition: 'One who has achieved, by agriculture and trade, and by increasing specialization, a sufficient stability and interdependence to "remain put", to develop a permanent neighbourliness, with the stimulus of all that constant adjustment of interests and values that neighbourliness involves.'[42]

The excavation was accordingly described in press-releases as a quest for a 'lost city';[43] archaeology was giving a history to the 'city without a history', extending a recognisable version of 'civilization' back into later prehistory. 'Each year the story of the British people finds its feet on firmer ground and the old romantic tradition of painted savages creeping in pre-Roman gloom gives place to the unfolding chronicle of an ordered and courageous civilization', rejoiced the *Western Mail*.[44] Public empathy was cajoled by the use of very contemporary metaphors to describe the features they discovered. Thus the pits, which Wheeler interpreted as habitations, were described as 'lower ground-floor flats' ('Things don't really change very much', commented the *Daily Express*. 'Large numbers of people live in basements nowadays.'[45]). Another, larger, pit was described by Tessa Wheeler as 'a semi-detached residence',[46] and a two-roomed building beside the Roman temple was termed a 'bungalow' by Colonel Drew.[47] Wherever possible, the site was described in 'city' terms. Maiden Castle stood 'in the middle of a great prehistoric urban zone',[48] and such 'fortified hills' were the lineal ancestors of the cities of today:

> [I]t is not too much to say that the continuous history of urban life in Great Britain begins with the great towns of which Maiden Castle is the most elaborate . . . the excavators are in fact investigating a primary factor in the history of modern England.
> Our modern cities – London, Birmingham, Liverpool and the rest, are, in a real sense, the direct heirs of Maiden Castle and its followers.[49]

Even the Neolithic settlement, which was inadvertently found in the first season's digging, could be claimed for civilization: 'the first cities of England appeared to date only [*sic*] from the end of the Stone Age', Wheeler told the Thoroton Society of Nottingham.[50] In the final report, he maintained that Maiden Castle provided sufficient evidence of 'civic discipline' to render it 'no longer possible to maintain, without qualifications, that the Romans were the first to furnish Britain with towns'.[51]

Educating our Masters

As a 'town', Maiden Castle fulfilled the first criteria of 'civilization': and Wheeler saw archaeology as having a crucial role to play in promoting – and defending – civilization in the modern world. He later claimed that at Maiden Castle 'the public for the first time became conscious of the Early Iron Age and the meaning of prehistory',[52] but the general effect of his accounts was to bring prehistory firmly within the purview of 1930s

England, thereby transforming it into an allegory of considerable contemporary relevance.

Wheeler told the people of Dorchester in 1937 that the three centuries of Iron Age occupation at Maiden Castle 'were vital in the formation of a civilization of which they were the ultimate heirs'.[53] This sense of inheritance he saw as having an important social function. In a 1931 speech to the Cambrian Archaeological Society, he had lauded the growth of amenity groups and public interest in the countryside as

> the first symptom of an awakening understanding . . . unquestionably tending to give the unpropertied population of the kingdom a new sense of what may be called vicarious ownership and responsibility . . . The urban population were too often the inhabitants of mean cities; if, at the same time, they dimly understood that they were citizens of no mean country all was not lost. There was still a hope of saving something from the wreckage of pre-industrial Britain.[54]

These sentiments help to explain Wheeler's enthusiastic desire to link an Iron Age hill-fort with a city such as Birmingham. Despite appearances, the two had much in common; if the people of modern Birmingham could learn to relate to the people of ancient Maiden Castle, they would feel a deeper awe for a civilization from which, in many ways, they might otherwise feel excluded. By civilizing prehistory, the present was being civilized too.

It is one of many ironies that the concept of 'civilization', which as other archaeologists, such as Grahame Clark,[55] were also at pains to point out, was synonymous with the concept of town-dwelling, was by the mid-twentieth century meaning almost the opposite. To Wheeler, modern cities were 'too often . . . mean cities'; to Clark, the drift from the land had created a proliferation of city-bound 'cultural orphans' whose lack of cultural connections and values meant that they constituted, 'like the infiltrating barbarians of antiquity, a fifth column of portentous dimensions'.[56] Civilization's real values were to be found in the countryside, where tradition and custom ensured some degree of cultural continuity. This was the discourse of 'ruralism', a recurrent phenomenon in English culture that has been much discussed in recent years. Some, such as John Lowerson (1992) or David Matless (1998), are inclined to see it as a more or less conscious exercise in obfuscation: a quasi-mystical retreat from post-war uncertainties, a form of political lullaby, as epitomized by the rustic utterances of Prime Minister Stanley Baldwin, crooned to a restless and troublesome nation. Others, such as Raphael Samuel (1994) and Harvey Taylor (1997), go to some lengths to emphasize the links between rural conservation movements and social progress. A distinction maybe needs to be made between the popular rediscovery of the countryside, the scale of which was hinted at in Chapter 13, and the uses to which opinion-formers put this new-found yearning for Merrie England. A sort of 'national ruralism' developed, the British (English) equivalent to more voracious nationalisms elsewhere. It was arguably the cultural dynamic of the National Government, fostering consensus around nostalgia; and archaeology had a clear role in this. Increasingly popular but politically 'safe', it was an activity that could both unite a divided population and, through engendering respect and even reverence for the monuments of the past, educate the population in the values of its rulers.

Village People

With varying degrees of subtlety, the archaeological past was harnessed for the cause of 'English civilization'. Archaeologists actively contributed to the inter-war quest for the roots of Englishness: at Cambridge, indeed, to judge from the Northern European emphasis in the Section B Archaeology Tripos (see p. 32 above), this was one of their main functions.

The traditional view of the English countryside was that it had been more or less empty when the Anglo-Saxon invaders arrived. This perception was not seriously challenged until the 1970s; so during the 1920s and 1930s orthodox archaeology shared in the general belief that the village was a quintessentially English creation. The English Place-Names Society (formed in 1923) was actively seeking to demonstrate the antiquity and the extent of the Anglo-Saxon settlement;[57] archaeologists supplemented its work by excavating early Anglo-Saxon villages (E T Leeds at Sutton Courtenay) and the earthworks that bounded their territories (Cyril Fox, T C Lethbridge in Cambridgeshire[58]).

There was some deep symbiosis between archaeologists, conservationists and planners. In *The English Village: The Origins and Decay of its Community: an anthropological interpretation* (1922), Harold Peake reiterated the Anglo-Saxon origin-myth while arguing the case for creating new, properly designed villages to help turn the tide of rural depopulation. Four years later, Patrick Abercrombie, later to become famous for his work in replanning post-war London, repeated the claim that England 'invented the village' in the document that served as manifesto for the Council for the Preservation of Rural England.[59] Beneath the disorder of the Industrial Revolution's destructive, sprawling cities, an older, truer order was to be found. Such notions had as big an influence on architects, planners and archaeologists as they had on Straight Trackers and terrestrial zodiackers.

Wheeler's reference to 'mean cities' was just such a restatement of the contemporary concern that the physical landscape of the modern world was, quite literally, out of balance. At the Museums Association National Conference in 1934, he and Cyril Fox spoke out strongly in favour of a National Folk Museum, which was to consist of a model village, with structures 'chosen to illustrate not so much the life of the landed gentry as the life of the yeoman'. Its function, according to Wheeler, would be 'to demonstrate the main phases in the development of English social life and customs prior to the Industrial Revolution'. It might feature '[a] village green where the stocks could be placed, houses or cottages of varying periods, a public-house, a windmill, water-mill and smithy, a weaver's cottage and bakery, a pottery glassworks and kiln, and a church'.[60] Wheeler emphasized the museum's social desirability:

> We are mechanizing our countryside today at an almost incredible speed, and not infrequently, I fear, at a speed that far outstrips our judgement. I am not one of those antiquarians who deplore machinery. We live in a streamline age, and streamlines are generally beautiful. But I do deplore the clumsiness with which we too often use our machinery – or it uses us.
>
> I conclude by pleading for our modest, reasonable sample of pre-Industrial England as a social, no less than an intellectual, necessity in the midst of our modern urban life and rapidly urbanizing countryside.[61]

Spoiling the Solstice

Cyril Fox thought that regional museums along similar lines might end the 'artistic chaos' prevalent amongst Western nations, and encourage people to adopt local techniques, thereby saving them 'from the worst vulgarization in construction and decoration of the present day'.[62] Concern at such 'vulgarization' was a defining trait of ruralist modernity; middle-class writers of all political persuasions sought to 'educate their masters' in style, aesthetics and values. H V Morton[63] even debated the need for a 'Ministry of Taste'.

In Chapter 12, we saw how the setting of Stonehenge was preserved from the vulgarization of suburbia; but there was little the authorities could do about the class of visitor the monument attracted – particularly at the summer solstice. Observing the solstice at Stonehenge was a well-established tradition, and in most years merited a paragraph in the local papers from which numbers and ambiance can be inferred; for some years, official accounts are kept of those who paid to go through the turnstile. From these records, it is clear that people had been going to Stonehenge for the solstice since at least 1875. During the 1890s, the monument became something of a focus for the new cycling craze, when estimates suggested that up to 2,000 would come. Numbers seem to have tailed off in the 1900s, probably because a fence had been erected and visitors were charged to enter. They picked up slowly after the Great War, to reach an inter-war peak of around 2,000 again in the early 1930s.

Perhaps unexpectedly, these all-night solstice-watchers were mainly from the lower orders. A posse of American tourists who visited the site in 1875 were surprised to find that the visitors were 'principally from the poorer classes'; the crowd of 1896 was of 'a mixed description', and, in 1932, the crowd was said to have 'a strong cockney accent'.[64]

From the press accounts it is clear that, then as now, a party atmosphere prevailed – and this the press increasingly viewed with distaste. The *Bath Evening Times* reporter chose to liken the 1930 solstice to proletarian Blackpool: 'An atmosphere reminiscent of Blackpool beach spread over the roadways leading to the ruin. Girls and boys danced by the lights of motor-cars which lined the roads to the music of gramophones and a complete jazz band.'[65] Two years later the *Salisbury Journal* declared that the solstice 'has become nothing more than a popular festival'; and 'John o'Wiltshire', in the *Wiltshire Times*, dismissed that year's throng as 'a twittering multitude ... They make it a joyous, laughing, almost ribald thing. They spoil it.'[66]

Nor could they could be trusted. A writer in the *Wiltshire Gazette* in 1932 deplored the suggestion that 'unrestricted access' could be restored 'in to-day's conditions ... Has he, or anyone else, tried to imagine what the Stones would be like to-day if the Toms, Dicks and Harrys swarmed round them by hundreds every day in the summer without some regulation?'[67]

Regulated, guided and controlled, however, the archaeological past could help to foster respect for middle-class values and social stability. To Wheeler, the growing public interest in archaeology was inculcating a new and, in our crowded land, much needed respect for the traditions which, in one form or another, make up so much of the fabric and beauty of our English landscape. Archaeology, in this applied sense, then becomes something more than a science or a cultural luxury; it takes upon itself incidentally a steadying social function which is not negligible in these days of easy destruction.[68]

The Power of the Underworld

Maiden Castle was a triumph for the forces of reason. Before the dig began, Sir George Hill, Director of the British Museum, 'slyly' suggested to Wheeler that 'It's a fine place to dig – and a fine place to leave undug.' Wheeler accused him of 'archaic sentiment', although he 'confessed also to a sneaking sympathy for his point of view; but by August [1934] we had resolutely dug ourselves in, and thereafter discovery after discovery issued upon us in unending stream'.[69] Gone was all mystery. 'Maiden Castle Capitulates. Yielding Up Secrets to excavators', reported the *Morning Post*.[70] Thomas Hardy, in a passage that Wheeler was fond of quoting, had likened Maiden Castle to 'the lifeless body of an antediluvian monster'. Wheeler concluded his final Report to the Antiquaries by claiming that four years of excavation had made the place 'come to life and sensibility'; Maiden Castle 'takes upon itself an organic vitality that is not of the imagination but is born of reason'.[71]

John Cowper Powys, whose novel, *Maiden Castle*, had been published a few months earlier, thought exactly the opposite. Powys (1872–1963) was a member of an influential literary family: his brothers Llewellyn and Theodore were almost as well known. All were prominent figures in the 'romantic' movement; all had strong connections with Dorset; all were proud of their Welsh ancestry. John Cowper saw himself as an 'Aboriginal Iberian',[72] and indeed was even described by Angus Wilson as 'the Druid of Wessex'.[73]

In January 1935, flushed with the success of his *A Glastonbury Romance* (1932), Powys moved to Dorchester, determined to write a major 'Dorchester Novel'. He was immediately smitten with Maiden Castle: 'Why does Maiden Castle thrill me so? Only because of the other horizons? Or is there another reason? A supernatural one?'[74] The earthwork became a major presence in his novel, which is much concerned with the relationship between scientific reason and a deeper, more primeval understanding of the world.

Visions of Civilization

The novel was written over the next 12 months, and Wheeler's excavations became something of a *Leitmotif*, a vain attempt to thwart the forces of nature. In March 1935, Powys attended Wheeler's capacity meeting at the Dorchester Corn Exchange, and discussed it with Llewellyn,[75] and though his diary has no details it is safe to say that he was not overly impressed. He once referred to the excavator as 'Dr Wheeling' in a letter to a relative,[76] and the novel has one sarcastic reference to a 'His Lordship' who can only be Wheeler.[77]

Powys has little enthusiasm for social evolution, or Romans. A character known as 'Claudius' collects subscriptions for the excavations because 'there's a great deal to be learnt about those early races, gaps – large gaps – in the history of Evolution that must be filled . . . Evolution means Scientific Excavation at one end and Scientific Experiment at the other. The more you know about what was, the faster you can create what will be. We must undermine all prejudices!'[78] Claudius is keen on Wheeler's new archaeology: 'it is important that we should realize how scientific, in the best sense, modern archaeology has become, getting rid of all the old romantic nonsense and studying instead the way our ancestors obtained their food-supply and their water-supply'.[79]

At the other extreme is a character called 'Uryen', whom Powys describes as 'a mysterious and rather sinister figure (of Welsh origin) who desires to get into touch with the old gods of Mai-Dun, or "Maiden Castle" '.[80] A strange bronze statuette of a bull with two human torsos had been excavated the previous summer, and this he sees as enduringly powerful: 'these things are like dark-finned fish embedded in ice. They have life in them that can be revived.'[81] Claudius agrees: 'things like that, brought into the air after being buried so long, have an evil effect! . . . They're full of the old self, full of the old subjective personal lie, that we must shake off if the world's to go on and get better . . . we must get rid of this perpetual "I, I, I", with all its cravings and hurt feelings! We must live in the race and in helping the race move forward.'[82]

To Uryen, however, the 'subjectivity' of prehistory is what makes it so important.

> [W]hat those fools can't see . . . is that the Power of the Underworld that our old Bards worshipped, though it was always defeated, is the Power of the Golden Age! Yes, it's the Power our race adored when they built Avebury and Maiden Castle and Stonehenge and Caer Drwyn, when there were no wars, no vivisection, no money, no ten-times-accursed nations! . . . this Hiraeth of my race, this baffled, this thwarted, this hopeless

230   *Order and Civilization*

33 The bronze bull with two human torsos, whose discovery at Maiden Castle unsettled John Cowper Powys: such things 'have life in them that can be revived'. (*Dorset County Museum, Archaeological Collections of the Dorset Natural History and Archaeological Society*).

> desire, that from the beginning of things has defied morality, custom, convention, usage, comfort, and all the wise and prudent of the world . . . will break through . . . And when it breaks through, these four thousand years wherein the world has been deceived, and has left the way will be redeemed, and what was intended to happen will be allowed to happen, and the superstition of science will be exploded forever![83]

The Triumph of Science?

His 'Hiraeth' did not break through in 1937, however. Even though Wheeler's dig was constantly in the news, Powys found it hard to find a British publisher (it was published first in America); when he succeeded, the book received mixed reviews, and Powys himself admitted that it was a 'fizzle'.[84] This is in striking contrast to the public enthusiasm for the dig itself, and can only be a measure of the scale of Wheeler's triumph. The 'superstition of science' was clearly in the ascendant. There are other measures in the form of those opinion-formers whose dangerously heterodox views were subverted by the dig. In May 1935 Edward Shanks, for instance, in the *Sunday Times* had declared that '[a]rchaeology is still far from being an exact science. It cannot but profit from the most luxurious proliferation of suggestions.' In August 1937, full of praise for Wheeler's work, he used the same newspaper to call for the creation of a fund for archaeology to be 'administered by a competent central authority' (which provided a cue for Woolley and Wheeler to suggest that their infant Institute of Archaeology might be just the thing[85]).

There are other indications that scientific archaeology was carrying the day. The immediate success of the reborn Prehistoric Society, for instance, which doubled its membership between 1934 and 1938;[86] and the number of students enrolled in Section A of the Cambridge Archaeology and Anthropology Tripos course, which rose from 41 in 1934 to 60 in 1939: Charles McBurney, who joined the course in 1935, recalled the intellectual climate there as 'one of new ideas characterized everywhere by an atmosphere of excitement and optimism'.[87]

This should be seen against a backdrop of unprecedented popular interest in science. 'Indeed', as John Stevenson points out, 'one of the most striking features of the period was the ready market for books of scientific exposition for the layman.' He contrasts the optimism of the scientists with 'the disillusion and fragmentation of much of the artistic and literary world', citing in evidence Lancelot Hogben's *Science for the Citizen* (1938): 'This is not the age of pamphleteers. It is the age of the engineers. The spark-gap is mightier than the pen. Democracy will not be salvaged by men who talk fluently, debate forcefully and quote aptly.' C P Snow, commenting on the optimism amongst the Cambridge scientists, wrote that 'it was difficult to find a scientist who did not believe that the scientific-technical-industrial revolution, accelerating under his eyes, was not doing incomparably more good than harm'.[88]

Conversely, there was a swift and tangible public move away from Romanticism. The 1920s had, for some at least, been a time of high idealism. Socialism was in the air: both the Labour Party and Soviet Communism were unknown quantities, offering believable alternatives to religious faith. The League of Nations was in its heyday, and no one dared to talk of rearmament or war. The years 1929–31 saw a spate of anti-war books (Graves' *Goodbye to All That*, Sherriff's *Journey's End*, Hemingway's *Farewell to Arms*, Remarque's *All Quiet on the Western Front*), and an optimistic assessment of human nature prevailed: on Armistice Day in 1928, President Coolidge of the USA had declared that 'peace is coming to be more and more realized as the natural state of mankind'.[89]

However, 1929 was also the year of the Wall Street Crash, and it may not be coincidence that thereafter enthusiasm for 'romantic' prehistory began to ebb. The number of people attending the Stonehenge solstice increased steadily throughout the 1920s and reached a peak in 1931, when as many as 3,000 may have taken part. Thereafter, however, estimated attendance figures never exceeded 1,000 until the 1950s;[90] and, although *The Old Straight Track* was republished in 1933, it seems significant that the Straight Track Club's proposal for a joint volume was turned down in 1936. James Webb's work confirmed a similar decline in occultism during the 1930s, suggesting that '[p]olitics and economics absorbed men's conscious minds and animated the anxieties of their unconscious'.[91]

Finding Comfort in Archaeology

From the excited environmental scientists around Clark to the high-profile 'Wheeler digs' with their precise and productive excavation, confident analyses and young workforce, scientific archaeology was palpably dynamic and sure of itself. In a time of social crisis and uncertainty, these were very appealing qualities. George Orwell in 1939, puzzling over the change in attitude since the Great War, suggested that people before 1914 'didn't think of the future as something to be terrified of'.[92] This was the sort of pessimism that drove Gordon Childe to write *Man Makes Himself* in 1936: to demonstrate that, 'from an impersonal scientific standpoint, history may still justify a belief in progress in days of depression'.[93]

In the same year, however, Sir John Squire, who had helped in Crawford's campaign to preserve the Stonehenge landscape, used his review of Wheeler's *Verulamium* to draw some despondent parallels between the fall of Rome and current geopolitics:

> We used to think that, at any rate, that sort of thing would not happen again; that wars of extermination, enslavement of populations, killings of prisoners, burnings of cities, relapses into barbarism, and 'dark ages', would never recur in a mapped and limited globe, full of petrol and printing presses. It doesn't seem so certain now.[94]

Visions of Civilization

He concluded with the telling observation that 'Perhaps in days like these more people might find comfort in archaeology – which only means old history... Security may come again.' Wheeler responded to sentiments of this kind by emphasizing the *rise* of Rome, rather than its fall, during the four-year archaeological soap-opera at Maiden Castle. Year by year his interpretations, as relayed to the press, mirrored current events. British rearmament began in 1934, but it was highly controversial: the Peace Ballot, whose results were announced in June 1935, found that well over 11 million people were still in favour of multilateral disarmament.[95] In March 1935, while the canvass was going on, Wheeler invoked the 'prehistoric armaments race', thereby lending ancient precedent for necessary government policy. Vespasian's victory, unearthed in 1937, suggested a positive outcome at the end of it.

The triumph of orthodox archaeology in the 1930s was a combination of apparent opposites: the dynamic optimism of science and the comforting reassurance of nostalgia. In a period of rapid and frightening change, the past at least appeared to be certain, and scientific archaeology, with its emphasis on 'fact', was as reassuring as penicillin. It was uncompromisingly functional, as dependable as the concrete underpinning the ancient stones of Avebury: modern technology literally propping up antiquity. Archaeology thus became a source of comfort, a 'steadying social influence' in troubled times – and an increasingly effective agent of the hegemony from which it derived its authority.

Conclusion: Archaeology and Social Transformation

Truth Production

In 1933, James Hilton's novel *Lost Horizon* was published, to instant acclaim. It tells of the discovery of Shangri La, a Tibetan Utopia: a place where 'the horizon lifted like a curtain; time expanded and space contracted'.[1]

There is a great deal of 'lost horizon' about many of the heterodox prehistories of the inter-war years; a nebulous yearning for a world outside and beyond the confines of the present. The lost horizon was at the end of the old straight track, and the same yearning's to be seen in the widespread credence given to the claims of the Stonehenge druids (and indeed Macgregor Reid claimed to have visited Tibet himself, and to be bringing Eastern wisdom and mystery to Clapham and to Salisbury Plain). Lost humanity, too. Wyndham-Lewis, reviewing Elliot Smith's *The Evolution of Man* for *Criterion* in 1924, found his arguments 'much more convincing than those of the ethnologists whose theories he combats', but the innate belligerence of proto-humanity in what he saw as Darwin's theory had already done the damage:

> Had Darwin been able to trace our descent as far as the pretty little squirrel, instead of only to a big, fierce, unprepossessing ape-like animal, the history of the last sixty years might have been very different. But the mischief has been done; and an ancestry involving us with a bird of Paradise would not help us now.[2]

To all this the scientific archaeologists offered a hopeful alternative; a sense of reassurance that humanity was on the right path after all. We no longer had to go 'away mopping and mowing with the lunatic fringe along Alfred Watkins' *Old Straight Track* in search of Massingham's *Downland Man*', in Piggott's words, for 'there were better things to come'.[3] 'Better' does not necessarily mean 'right', however. When, for instance, Niall Sharples came to re-examine Maiden Castle in the 1980s, he concluded that neither the 'war cemetery', nor the attack itself, could be taken as proven: 'the vivid description of the sack and slighting of the hillfort, followed by the hasty burial of the dead is not altogether consistent with the evidence on the ground'.[4] It seems that the archaeologists of the 'heroic band' were not immune to wishful thinking of their own. It was not because they'd succeeded in discovering some sure-fire method of establishing Truth that the radical generation managed to impose disciplinary authority upon archaeology, but because they had a common sense of purpose, a very keen understanding of how the social system functioned, and a huge amount of energy, determination, shrewdness and commitment.

Their success was due not only to systematic institutional 'infiltration', but also to the same sweet, if vulgar, oxygen of publicity that fanned the aspirations of their opponents. The theatricality of the Universal Bond ensured good press coverage for George Macgregor Reid's Druidry; Alfred Watkins astutely monitored newspaper reviews and never missed an opportunity to promote his ideas – and O G S Crawford told Wheeler proudly that 'I am a journalist. What I want is simple, clear-minded stuff that any intelligent fool can understand.'[5] The very independence of *Antiquity*, which played such an important role in establishing a sense of disciplinary community, rendered it much more dependent on sales than a subsidized institutional publication – and arguably, therefore, inscribed a journalistic zeal into the heart of orthodox archaeology. In the wider world, of course, the image of archaeology was transformed through the astute cultivation of the press by people such as Wheeler, creating a sizeable public constituency for their approach.

Their success was not, however, due simply to adroit manipulation of the *locales* of power. Both 'science' and 'archaeology' were very much part of the discourse of inter-war hegemony – and it is important to remember that 'hegemony', at least in Gramsci's usage, is a *recursive* affair, in which the ruled share happily in the epistemologies of the rulers.[6] The aspirations and approaches of the 'heroic band' were in harmony with those of wider society; this was why, as Clark said to Hawkes, 'we cannot help winning'.[7] Inter-war archaeology was a straightforward, no-nonsense, common-sense affair that seemed to produce very positive results; and in a period of high uncertainty, that was part of the attraction.

Very Simple Archaeology

In 1948 Stuart Piggott, replying to the critics of his outspoken *Archaeological News Letter* article about the place of amateurs in archaeology, claimed that 'there is no fear that unorthodox opinion will be suppressed or disregarded provided always that it fulfils the high standards of scholarship now demanded in our study'.[8] This 'scholarship', however, rested upon a series of very simplistic grand narratives, a framework of stadial and environmental determinism whose parameters had been decided within other disciplines.

Archaeological education was essentially about *training*. Charles Peers, probably paraphrasing Wheeler, claimed that students at the Institute of Archaeology needed access to an 'irreducible minimum' consisting of 'three things: namely, materials for study, instruction in the treatment of antiquities, and training in the archaeological method in research and the recording of research'.[9] This is a highly vocational 'irreducible minimum', and Grahame Clark of Cambridge suggested the emphasis on technical qualification was a particular shortcoming of the Institute, Cambridge's great rival.[10] Jacquetta Hawkes, however, an early Cambridge student, claimed that she could 'bear witness that the weaknesses of the London course were closely paralleled in the new Tripos at Cambridge'.[11]

The problem was that archaeology was lamentably under-theorized, even at Cambridge: as Clark noted, 'if British archaeology before the Second World War was long on fact it was miserably short on thought and narrow in perspective'.[12] Peers' checklist was closely matched by David Randall-MacIver's overview of the 'organization of archaeology' in 1931:

> First, there is the collection of the material in the field and the recording of it. Secondly there is the housing, conservation and exhibition of this material in museums. Thirdly there is the comparative study of all such material, and the digesting and dissemination of the results in books of synthesis and popularization.[13]

Not much sense here of epistemological complexity. Once again, archaeology was deemed to be a straightforward affair, essentially a set of skills and processes to be understood and techniques to be mastered.

Archaeology and Social Transformation

It could be argued that the determinism which archaeologists inherited from disciplines in the 'harder' sciences, such as geology, effectively submerged human agency in a sea of inevitability which left archaeologists with an a priori inability to perceive that their knowledge might be socially constructed. This is not anachronism: Scheler's *Problems of a Sociology of Knowledge* was published in 1924, and Mannheim's *Competition as a Cultural Phenomenon* in 1928, but the issues which they raised, to say the least of it, don't figure much in the literature.

There was one notable exception amongst the archaeologists of the 'heroic band': R G Collingwood, Oxford philosopher and probably the foremost authority on Roman archaeology of his day. Collingwood saw archaeology as 'a laboratory of knowledge', in which 'one found out nothing at all except in answer to a question; and not a vague question either, but a definite one'. From this he developed his own 'logic of question and answer': the doctrines of a philosopher, like the findings of an archaeologist, are his answers to his own questions – 'and no one who does not understand what the questions are can hope to understand the doctrines'.[14]

This awareness of the questioner's 'positionality' put Collingwood decades ahead of his contemporaries, and freed him up to ask some uncomfortable questions about the nature of the past itself. The 'first principle' of the philosophy of history was the idea that 'the past which an historian studies is not a dead past, but a past which in some sense is still living in the present'. It is called into being by 'disentangling it out of the present in which it actually exists'; and elsewhere, 'the past simply as past is wholly unknowable . . . it is the past as residually preserved in the present that is alone knowable'.[15]

The history of Collingwood's relationship with Crawford is instructive. He was invited to write on the cyclical theory of history for *Antiquity*, but Crawford then ignored his work when writing his own article on historical cycles in 1932 (see p. 68); and when Collingwood's *The Idea of History* was published posthumously after the war, Crawford chose not to review it but instead to publish a critique in which Collingwood's arguments were found to be 'unacceptable'.[16] This was in marked contrast to Crawford's admiration of Collingwood's contribution to archaeological technique. As well as commissioning or accepting several other pieces for *Antiquity* on more mundane topics, he penned an effusive review of Collingwood's *An Introduction to the Prehistory of Cumberland, Westmorland and Lancashire north of the Sands* (1934), which he described as being 'of great practical use' and praised for the methodological organization that it sought to impart to field-workers.[17]

By rejecting Collingwood's philosophy while praising his technical contribution, Crawford was more or less consciously defining the boundary of his discipline. What's surprising is that Collingwood seemed quite prepared to accept the role which Crawford allocated to him, and in his autobiography paid tribute to 'the bold initiative and unwearying toil of OGS Crawford – to whom future generations can never sufficiently realize their indebtedness'.[18] The most obvious explanation for this would seem to be that Collingwood recognized that archaeology, as a new discipline, needed tidy, well-defined boundaries. Complexity was simply not needed.

Relativism and its Discontents

This refusal to countenance complexity was underpinned by an optimistic and teleological faith in the truth of social evolution. It's a phenomenon common both to societies and to ideologies that see themselves as being as good as it gets, and might be called the 'End of History syndrome' after Francis Fukuyama's paean to American-style 'liberal democracy', written after the collapse of the Soviet Bloc. Thomas Arnold had said much the same thing when British power was still in the ascendant, in 1841 suggesting that modern history 'appears to bear marks of the fullness of time, as if there would be no future history beyond it'. A similar confidence underpins E H Carr's assertion that an emphasis on the role of chance or accident in history was an indication of a society 'riding in the trough, not on the crest, of historical events':[19] Carr shared Crawford's faith in a Communist destiny.

From the perspective of such epistemic machismo, doubt is the comforter of failure. To Carr, '[t]he view that examination results are all a lottery will always be popular among those who have been placed in the third class', a sentiment with which Fukuyama agrees.[20] Relativism flourishes in societies that are riding in the trough: the Sociology of Knowledge debate was first conducted in a Germany reeling from the defeat of 1918, and the discourses of post-modernity began in post-1968 France, in the context of major uncertainty about the future of French influence in the world.

Conversely, confident societies foster confident epistemologies. Does that help to explain why relativism is seen as *politically* threatening? To many modern archaeologists, 'fascism' still lurks implicitly in every heterodox discourse. It is the bogey that rules out relativism: the Lampeter Archaeology Workshop found nine examples of this caricature in the archaeological literature between 1989 and 1996 alone.[21] Only by a strict adherence to the values of enlightenment positivism can a scholar stay clean out of error.

My examination of approaches to the ancient past during the high tide of political fascism suggests a much more ambiguous relationship between fascism and archaeology, both orthodox and heterodox. It is true that at least one member of the Straight Track Club (the historian John Harvey) had fascist sympathies, but orthodoxy's claim to the moral high ground is unconvincing. In 1928, Crawford launched a project to map the whole Roman Empire. The project was to begin with Rome itself, partly to exploit 'nationalist enthusiasm', but also because he was impressed with the Italians' wholehearted approach to archaeology; in an *Antiquity* editorial the previous year, Crawford declared that 'Signor Mussolini deserves the gratitude of the whole civilized world for his magnificent schemes of excavation . . . nothing but good can come of public-spirited work like this.'[22]

The racial connotations of 'fascism' also were, if anything, more likely to surface amongst scientific social evolutionaries than the advocates of the Golden Age. Throughout the 1920s and 30s, Elliot Smith regularly countered the arguments of the racial supremacists, and in 1934 led the British Association's anthropological onslaught against 'the fallacy of attributing cultural achievements and inherent mental aptitudes to different races'.[23] Crawford, on the other hand, agreed with Flinders Petrie that the 'future progress of mankind' might depend upon applying the insights of eugenics to 'carefully segregate fine races and prohibit continual mixture', adding the suggestion that a society which had developed in isolation found it difficult to cross-breed: 'It gradually becomes a different species. It is a biological fact that the mating of individuals of different species is infertile'.[24] In this he was echoing George Pitt-Rivers (grandson of the excavation pioneer), whose recent work in Melanesia had convinced him that population decline was due to the mixing of incompatible races. Pitt-Rivers junior sought to combine anthropology and evolutionary theory into what he called 'the science of ethnogenetics, [the] interconnection of race, population and culture'. Virulently anti-Semitic, he became a prominent member of the British Union of Fascists and the Nordic League, and was interned during the Second World War,[25] yet in 1934 the flower of the 'heroic band' were happy to join Pitt-Rivers for his Easter field meeting in Dorset: Wheeler, Fox, Hemp, Hawkes, Piggott and Daniel, in the words of the latter 'all reading one another lectures and visiting sites around the county', including Maiden Castle.[26]

On the strength of these examples, most of the big names of inter-war archaeology could be seen as fellow-travellers or fascist sympathizers; Childe, too, could qualify, on grounds of anti-Semitism, since he once wrote flippantly to Christopher Hawkes about his dislike of Jews.[27] They weren't, of course; but these examples do more than merely highlight the dangers of anachronism and over-simplification inherent in retrospective witch-hunting. They also raise some profound questions about why so many scholars today are so ready to wave the fasces at those whose epistemologies run counter to their own. 'Fascism' has acquired a new meaning: it equates with 'unacceptable', and is thus brandished like a mop to hold back the insidious tides of relativism that threaten to flood the corridors of reason. Relativism is felt to be personally disempowering, while at the same time having the potential to empower the wrong sort of ideas: if the professionals relinquish claims to epistemic control, the vacuum will be filled by fascists eager to manipulate the facts of the past to support obnoxious regimes. The logical inference here is that fascism is the 'natural' default ideological position of humanity, only held in check by the civilized and civilizing construct of academic discipline. Without that disciplinary *imprimatur*, there are no logical, ethical or intellectual qualities in these academics' own work that would carry enough weight to combat this primal fascism. In fact, as Holtorf has demonstrated, fascism and relativism are uneasy bedfellows: totalitarian creeds are by definition intolerant; their truth-claims will not convince scholars who are not on their payroll, and in any case they are unlikely to pay much attention to dissentient archaeological voices.[28]

The assumption that unchecked fringe discourse will tend inexorably to intolerance suggests a degree of intolerance of different epistemologies, and consequent epistemic closure, which is itself pretty 'fascistic'. 'No discourse on the past is neutral', asserted Shanks and Tilley. 'The validity of a theory hinges on intention and interest: it is to be assessed in terms of the ends and goals of its archaeology, its politics and morality.'[29] Attempting to banish heterodox theorizing about the ancient past to the unacceptable margins of politics effectively reasserts the sole right of orthodoxy to legitimate critique: debate about the nature of the ancient past has to be held on its terrain, and by its rules. Orthodox archaeology, for instance, has seized upon the '*longue durée*' to search for laws: rules of culture change, immutable processes of evolutionary behaviour. In the process, it has sought to squeeze out other understandings by colonizing and annexing prehistory for its own world-view: an act of epistemological *Lebensraum*.

Boxed in

Archaeology is an art, theatre if you will;[30] a production whose performance changed enormously between the wars. The pastoral ruminations of Wyndham-Lewis's 'very aged sheep' made way for a new sort of dynamic drama with a cast of youthful scientists, and then it got stuck. Inter-war archaeology was inevitably a period piece, but this one runs and runs. For all its superficial changes, archaeology today is still set within an 'intellectual aesthetic' adopted in the 1920s.

This is partly because the process of discipline formation has had the effect of limiting the remit of orthodox archaeology rather than expanding it. Highly reductionist, (literally) materialist, hostile to speculation and suspicious of theory, the inter-war pioneers effectively established an epistemic benchmark: a common-sense, unproblematic understanding of archaeology as essentially a set of technical skills and techniques. It is a definition which has continued to haunt the understandings of public and professional alike. Even Michel Foucault, as Per Cornell perceptively points out, treated archaeology as a metaphor for a passive, manual 'skill', in which interpretation is the province of others: 'silent monuments, inert traces, objects without context, and things left by the past ... a metaphor for everything that is not interpretative, anything that is anti-hermeneutic'.[31]

Despite the challenges of the post-processualists, this definition of the discipline has not merely survived, but now looks set to be resurgent. Social theory came late to archaeology, and was greeted with a marked degree of hostility and incomprehension. 'Post-processualism' remains a rarified and academic creature, increasingly vulnerable as government funding priorities lay more and more emphasis on vocational skills. Now field-archaeologists such as Richard Hingley draw distinctions between 'professionals' (themselves) and 'academics'; theory is seen as self-indulgent and irrelevant, in Hingley's words 'something that postgraduates and certain university lecturers indulge in'.[32] Exponents are forced to justify their esoteric dalliance by endeavouring to 'ground' it in practical engagement with the material culture which in Britain at least, since the government-enforced Benchmarking Statement of January 2000, is enshrined as archaeology's First Principle: 'the study of the human past through material remains'.[33]

It is important to remember that this restrictive self-definition is itself an artefact of recent date. The *Oxford English Dictionary* defines archaeology as 'Ancient history generally; systematic description or study of antiquities'. The first definition is the original one (from Greek: *archaios* ('ancient') and *logos* ('word')), and was in use as late as 1869. There is, accordingly, nothing inherent in the word 'archaeology' to oblige its students to engage with 'material remains'. Here the legacy of the 'heroic band' becomes very apparent. For, through usage determined by the aims and objectives of those who made the discipline, the secondary meaning of the word has completely overshadowed the original. Although many archaeologists have sought to expand their horizons well beyond these limitations, venturing into philosophy, sociology and even art to try to help them understand 'what was going on in the past', always there is the necessary litmus of material culture to test their ideas upon; now reinforced by the Benchmarking Statement which for the first time has trussed up the discipline in formal definition. Archaeology is about Stuff.

The Need for Otherness

Some find this very reassuring. It's the academic equivalent of the 'steadying social function' supplied by the burgeoning television archaeology industry, in which interpretation is often shorn of ambiguity, and archaeologists make confident pronouncements that tend to demonstrate that the past – unlike the present – *is* straightforward. For as David Lowenthal said, acknowledging the malleability of the past 'understandably arouses anxiety. A past seen as open to manipulation not only undermines supposed historical verities but implies a fragile present and portends a shaky future.' His way out of the bind is to draw an analogy with psychoanalytical re-examination of personal pasts, which can

> free us from myths that constrained previous perceptions ... Once aware that relics, history, and memory are continually refashioned, we are less inhibited by the past, less frustrated by a fruitless search for sacrosanct originals ... We can use the past fruitfully only when we realize that to inherit is also to transform ... the past is best used by being domesticated – and by our accepting and rejoicing that we do so.[34]

Archaeology and Social Transformation

Yet this process of 'domestication' was already a central plank of the interwar archaeology project: remember that 'bungalow' at Maiden Castle. Prehistory was explained in terms of recognizable historic civilization, rendered tame and comprehensible, the differences between past and present minimized.

Ideas such as 'mystery' and 'otherness' are quite deliberately excluded from this discourse of domestication. Otherness is scary, profoundly destabilizing. As Johan Hegardt observes,

> our desire as archaeologists is our will or wish to reach the otherness of the Other. But we turn away from this desire because we understand it as metaphysics. Every time we get a brief glimpse of the Other we look away because we know that the presence of the Other will problematize our self-sufficient understanding of history. We want archaeology to be 'Our Archaeology': an archaeology that must not be disturbed by the presence of a metaphysical Other. We want the other to be exactly as we are, making archaeology unproblematic...[35]

Where does 'Otherness' begin? At the point, surely, where rational definition starts to fail, where material knowledge starts to tail off into metaphysics. This is the 'legitimate place' beyond the social construction of knowledge at which, according to Mannheim, 'the mystery' is there for those unafraid to face it.[36] It is the point at which reason stops and rhyme begins: here, according to Heidegger, poetry takes over from the description of mere things 'to express the inexhaustibility of that which cannot be spoken... a way of existing in humility before the things which we cannot understand'. These are the words of Julian Thomas, one of the few contemporary archaeologists to speculate about the metaphysical limits of the discipline, who suggests that

> this conception of the poetic is one which has some relevance for archaeologists. After all, we spend much of our time talking about things which are in the full sense unknowable. We write about the past in the present, and in the process attempt to understand the lives of people who are now dead. Being historically and culturally distant from ourselves, there is much about these lives that lies beyond our experience. Perhaps an archaeological poetics which attempts to 'take the measure' of this difference would allow us to open up a relationship with the past which involves a proper degree of reverence?[37]

This is diametrically the opposite position to that of Lowenthal, or for that matter Wheeler. Thomas seems to be suggesting that a different form of narrative ('poetics') might serve to *emphasize* distance and difference instead of constantly endeavouring to collapse them. Thereby, who knows?, perhaps finally freeing the ancient past from our desperate attempts to naturalize modernity.

Back to the Future

Acknowledging the mysteriousness of the past means acknowledging that archaeologists are mystics. To some extent they know that already. They know that the process of truth-making is an intense, subtle and subjective process, often defiant of received wisdom. Mysticism is subversive too: Michel Foucault describes Christian mysticism as 'one of the first great forms of revolt in the West' because it resisted the authority of written scripture.[38]

Utopianism belongs in the category of mystical resistance. It is also an active force for change. In the words of peace activist Andrew Rigby, 'To be "utopian" is to be out of step with taken for granted views of the world, to be utopian is to believe in the human power to transform the given in the direction of a potential reality – a "heaven on earth", a true commonwealth.'[39] To Karl Mannheim, without Utopia 'man would lose his will to shape history and therewith his ability to understand it'.[40] Compare this with Gordon Childe's flow-chart analysis of human history:

> Progress is real if discontinuous. The upward curve resolves itself into a series of troughs and crests. But in those domains that archaeology as well as written history can survey, no trough ever declines to the low level of the preceding one; each crest out-tops its last precursor.[41]

To Childe, ineluctable historical forces will propel humanity ever upwards, and the scope for individual agency to affect the course of history is, to say the least, limited. Utopia was a redundant distraction, outlawed by Engels from the canons of progressive socialism, its absence now reiterated by progressive archaeology. There was no need to dream, or to try to make the dream come true, since humanity was borne on the wings of destiny.

Today, the idea of progress itself has become the stuff of nostalgia: not just the possibility of social change, but faith in the possibility of a future, seems to some like hopeless idealism. No surprise, then, to find that nostalgia is starting to lose its stigma as people look back for signs of hope. Svetlana Boym's *The Future of Nostalgia*, published in 2001, suggests that 'reflective nostalgia' can be positive, fostering resistance to 'the uncritical acceptance of the present'. Janelle Wilson similarly believes that nostalgia for a more fluid past is unsurprising, 'in the face of a present that seems overly static and monolithic'. Peter Glazer calls for a 'radical nostalgia', claiming that nostalgia has the power to 'unsettle' the status quo 'by creating emotional bridges to times when the possibility for social change was a commonly held assumption'.[42]

What is there here for archaeology, a discipline developed almost as an antidote to nostalgia, by people who looked forward with confidence and back with distaste? What might a radical 'archaeology of nostalgia' comprise? We could try to break the complacency that lies implicit within the idea of progress, and the negative imagery that surrounds 'the past' as something that we've been lucky enough to escape from, from which there's nothing to learn except how wrong they were and how right we are. We could attempt to find hope in the past, perhaps furnishing evidence that an unsustainable consumption of stuff is not a prerequisite for human well-being; that people are capable of working together and living joyfully, simply, harmoniously. It all depends on where we choose to shine the spotlight. In the words of the historian and social activist Howard Zinn,

> human history is a history not only of cruelty but also of compassion, sacrifice, courage, kindness. What we choose to emphasize in this complex history will determine our lives. If we see only the worst, it destroys our capacity to do something. If we remember those times and places – and there are so many – where people have behaved magnificently, this gives us the energy to act, and at least the possibility of sending this spinning top of a world in a different direction.[43]

There are echoes of Geertz' contention that 'there is no such thing as a human nature independent of culture' in this: we are making human nature up as we go along. Developing an archaeology that did not have the effect of naturalizing and normalizing greed, selfishness, competition and violence could be a very empowering project for the twenty-first century, in this postscript to the End of History. However, I agree with Julian Thomas that '[i]t is in its *difference* that the past reveals truly radical possibilities, rather than as precedent' (my italics).[44] The challenge of 'otherness' must be accepted, and the essence of otherness is unattainability.

Further, deeper, beyond, always out of reach: the past is always unattainable. We are chasing rainbows. But why not? 'The ethical task of archaeology is thus *to bear witness to the past other*', says Thomas (his italics).[45] To which I would only add that we can best do this by honouring the 'present other'. We could be encouraging new ideas about antiquity, from whatever quarter and however outrageous. Accepting that the past is fluid, we need to be as inventive with it as we need to be with the future.

Notes

Short references (author, date) are to published books and articles, listed in the Bibliography. References to manuscript material are given in full, and uncredited newspaper extracts are treated as manuscripts, with details of scrapbook references and other finding information. I've used the following abbreviations:

AWS	Alfred Watkins' Scrapbook, in the Herefordshire Records Office (ref. HRO M90/2)
Cambridge	University of Cambridge Library
Crawford MSS	Papers of O G S Crawford, at the Bodleian Library, Oxford (Department of Western Manuscripts)
Daniel MSS	Papers of Glyn Daniel, in the Library of St John's College, Cambridge
DC	London Museum Scrapbooks, at the Museum of London
DCM	Dorset County Museum, Dorchester
Fox MSS	Papers of Cyril Fox, at the Cambridge University Museum of Archaeology and Anthropology
Hawkes MSS	Papers of C F C Hawkes, at the Bodleian Library, Oxford (Department of Western Manuscripts)
HRO	Herefordshire Records Office
LMA	London Metropolitan Archives
Manley	V S Manley Cuttings Book, in the Library of the Wiltshire Archaeological & Natural History Society, Devizes Museum, Box 80, MSS 935
Massingham MSS	Massingham Papers, University of Reading, Rural History Centre

Myres MS	Papers of J L Myres, at the Bodleian Library, Oxford (Department of Western Manuscripts)
Perry MSS	University College London Archives, Add. MS 279, Papers of W J Perry
Philip Carr-Gomm	may be contacted through his website, philipcarrgomm.druidry.org/
Smith Letters I and II	Letters of G E Smith, mostly transcribed by W R Dawson, British Library Add. Ms 56303 (I) and 56304 (II)
STC	papers and portfolios of the Straight Track Club, at Hereford Reference Library
UCL MSS	University College, London Special Collections Library
WANHSS	Scrapbooks in the Library of the Wiltshire Archaeological and Natural History Society, Devizes Museum
WORK 14/2135	Office of Works file marked 'Correspondence with Druids, 1919–39' (14/2136 is a continuation), in the National Archives, Kew
WRO	Wiltshire Records Office
Yorke Collection	in the Library of the Warburg Institute, University of London

Introduction

1. Figures and quotation from www.archaeology.org, July 2007
2. Fagan 2003; LeBlanc 2003; Young 2003
3. anon 2003
4. quoted in Engel 1983:239–40
5. Tilley 1993:11, 17
6. Hodder 1992:170
7. Gramsci 1971:12
8. Thompson 1993:108–9
9. Stout 2004
10. O G S Crawford, letter to Christopher Hawkes 18 December 1940, *Hawkes MSS* 8; Piggott 1963:5

Chapter 1

1. Parr 1801:112; cf Ward 1965, Engel 1983:22 for later quotations
2. Gay 1969; Eyerman 1994

Notes to pp. 10–17

3. Ward 1965:276 and 406n69; Engel 1983:268–9
4. anon 1820:446–7
5. Eyerman 1994:47, 97; Debray 1981:43
6. Engel 1983:11–12
7. Ward 1965:64
8. anon 1873
9. Levine 1986:80–6; cf Slee 1986:90
10. Creasy 1840:30–1
11. Levine 1986:37; cf Slee 1986:61
12. Slee 1986:99–101; cf Engel 1983:135–8
13. Goldstein 1983:14; Slee 1986:62
14. Goldstein 1983:16–17
15. Levine 1986:146–9
16. 'A Sinecure Fellow':302–3
17. Engel 1983:191
18. Engel 1983:255, 265n; Levine 1986:145, 157 and n107
19. Levine 1986:9, 55; 178
20. Haverfield 1924:82
21. Levine 1986:39
22. quoted in Levine 1986:75
23. Levine 1986:168, 173–4, cf 38–9
24. quoted in Daniel 1962:70–1
25. Petrie 1883:xiii
26. Levine 1986:36, 39, 89, 141–2; Engel 1983:215
27. Levine 1986:29, 71, 91, 165, 168; Hodgkin 1891:265, 267
28. Clark 1989:8, 34
29. quoted in Daniel 1986:209
30. Janssen 1992; E A Gardner, manuscript notes on the history of Classical Archaeology at the University of London, in *UCL MSS* Mem. II A/1, *Materials for the History of the University*
31. Daniel 1959; Clark 1989:10
32. Clark 1989:10
33. anon 1896
34. Hawkes 1982:41
35. Clark 1989:15, 19
36. Ridgeway 1909:11
37. Clark 1989:11
38. Marett 1908:5

Chapter 2

1. Freidson 1983:19; cf Freidson 1970
2. Johnson 1972; Turner 1987

3. O G S Crawford, letter to Christopher Hawkes 18 December 1940, *Hawkes MSS* 8; Goldstein 1983:15
4. Piggott 1989:24; Wheeler 1927:247
5. Evans 1956; Crawford 1956:230
6. Goldstein 1983:23
7. See my doctoral thesis, Stout 2004, for the full survey and a more detailed analysis
8. Becher 1989:66–7
9. Crawford 1927a:1
10. Crawford 1950:2
11. Tylor 1871 2:410; Crawford 1936a
12. Daniel 1986:232; Hawkes 1982:6, 374; Fagan 2001:96
13. Becher 1989:66–7; Piggott 1963:5
14. Phillips 1987:15
15. Bowden 2001:35
16. Myres 1951; E. Minns, letter to O G S Crawford 12 December 1946, *Crawford MSS* 18/99; Scott-Fox 2002:44; Piggott 1989:22; Clark 1958:296
17. Crawford 1921:37; Piggott 1935:94; Childe 1935:10
18. O G S Crawford, 'Papers Concerning *Antiquity*' *Crawford MSS* 104 [cf Stoddart and Malone 2002]; Crawford 1936a
19. Ashbee 1960; Mercer 1998:417, 420; Scott-Fox 2002:53; Hawkes 1951:173
20. see correspondence in *Crawford MSS*, file 67
21. Stout 2004:53–4 and Appendix I
22. Crawford 1955:172, 312
23. Crawford 1936a
24. Crawford 1955:180
25. Hauser 2003:120–1, 272; Grigson 1984:115–9; Mellor 1987:38
26. Wheeler 1958a; V G Childe, letter to O G S Crawford 8 March 1942, *Crawford MSS* 67/40
27. Goldstein 1983:23
28. J G D Clark, letter to Christopher Hawkes 26 November 1936, *Hawkes MSS* 7
29. Piggott 1989:24; Fox 2000:58
30. Crawford 1956:232
31. O G S Crawford, letter to J Bellows 18 January 1926, *Crawford MSS* 104/3
32. Crawford 1955:168, 201
33. Fox 2000:60
34. Chippindale 1983:179
35. Society of Antiquaries of London Annual *List of the Society of Antiquaries of London as at 30 June* (unpublished, in the Society's Library)

Notes to pp. 26–35

36. Piggott 1989:23–4
37. Read 1921; Evans 1956:387–93
38. Hawley *et al* 1921
39. See for instance *Congress of Archaeological Societies, Annual Report* 1922, back cover
40. Hawkes 1982:125; Wheeler 1971
41. Hawkes 1982:105; Society of Antiquaries, Annual Lists (see note 35, above)
42. Wheeler 1958b:72
43. Wheeler 1958a:3
44. Hawkes 1982:125–6; cf Piggott 1963:6
45. Wheeler 1958b:75
46. Varley 1943
47. Piggott 1958; cf Daniel 1977
48. Wheeler 1958b:76
49. Wheeler 1958b:83; Crawford 1955:183; R E M Wheeler, letter to O G S Crawford, 30 December 1954, *Crawford MSS* 107/112
50. Wheeler 1958b:65, cf 73, 72
51. *The Guardian*, *The Observer* and *The Times*, all on 12 January: *DC11/6*
52. Hawkes 1982:127
53. Wheeler 1958b:77–8; Hawkes 1982:129–30; University of London Senate, Approval of the Memorandum of the Principal, 16 May 1934, *UCL MSS* A611/5, Box 1, folder marked 'Scheme to set up Institute of Archaeology'
54. Hawkes 1982:131–2, Ormsby-Gore 1935
55. Hawkes 1982:131, 140; Wheeler 1958b:80
56. Clark 1989:25–9, 34, 37
57. Daniel 1986:82, 83–4
58. Clark 1989:34–6; Daniel 1986:65; Burkitt 1970
59. Clark 1989:34–7, 91; Burkitt 1970; Burkitt 1921:322–32
60. University of Edinburgh *Calendar* (1927) pp 146–7
61. Smith 1998; Daniel 1986:67–8
62. Daniel 1986:216, 337
63. Smith 1997:14 and *passim*
64. Phillips 1987:48; Smith 1997:12
65. See note 52, above
66. Daniel 1986:407–8
67. M. Burkitt, letter to Tessa Wheeler, nd [January 1933] *UCL MSS* A611/5 Box 1, 'Scheme to set up Institute of Archaeology' folder
68. C Hawkes, notes on 'Future of Archaeology' Conference, *Hawkes MSS* 58A, folder marked ' Council for British Archaeology'; W F Grimes, letter to O G S Crawford nd [December 1943], *Crawford MSS* 68/118; cf Smith 1997
69. Smith 1998

Chapter 3

1. Crawford 1940
2. Clark 1989:26, 41; Thompson 1990; Crawford 1955:58
3. Crawford 1931b
4. Levine 1986:173–4, cf 38–9
5. Fox 2000:113
6. Clark 1985; Smith 1999; Matless *in press*; Clark 1989:34–5
7. Chapman 1985:255
8. Piggott 1989; Phillips 1987:51–65
9. Smith 1997:25; her paraphrase
10. Clark 1985:1, 2
11. Smith 1999; Fagan 2001:62–3
12. anon 1936:147
13. anon 1936:260
14. J G D Clark, letter to Christopher Hawkes 26 November 1936, *Hawkes MSS* 7
15. anon 1937
16. Piggott 1963:6; Smith 1997, 1999; Clark 1989:56
17. O'Neil 1946:66
18. O'Neil 1946:61, 64, 65–6
19. O'Neil 1946, and see also eponymous pamphlet in *Hawkes MSS* 58A Council for British Archaeology Folder, probably an earlier version; Congress of Archaeological Societies, *Annual Reports* 1922–34
20. Clark 1989:5
21. Webster 1991:186–90
22. Smith 1997:25n4
23. Hawkes 1932, Hawkes and Hawkes 1933, 1934; Evans 1949; Hawkes 1982:123–4
24. Hawkes and Hawkes 1958:162–3
25. O'Neill 1946
26. C Hawkes, letter to O G S Crawford 1 December 1940, *Crawford MSS* 79/2
27. C Hawkes, letter to Henry Cleere 5 July 1984, *Hawkes MSS* 58A folder marked 'Council for British Archaeology; papers concerning 40th Anniversary'
28. C Hawkes *et al* letter to President of Society of Antiquaries 21 December 1942, in Hawkes' handwriting, *Hawkes MSS* 58A Council for British Archaeology Folder; cf Evans 1956:427
29. Hawkes to Cleere, note 27 above; O'Neil 1946:66, cf 79
30. C Hawkes, notes on 'Future of Archaeology' Conference, *Hawkes MSS* 58A, folder marked 'Council for British Archaeology'; W F Grimes, letter to O G S Crawford nd [December 1943], *Crawford MSS* 68/118

Notes to pp. 42–51

31. Hawkes, Conference notes
32. W F Grimes, letter to O G S Crawford 2 March 1943, *Crawford MSS* 68/116
33. C Hawkes, letter to O G S Crawford 14 August 1941, *Crawford MSS* 79/10
34. Hawkes Conference notes; Grimes to Crawford, both at note 30, above
35. K Kenyon, letter to O G S Crawford, 14 November 1944, *Crawford MSS* 12/183
36. J G D Clark, letter to C Hawkes 4 January 1944, *Hawkes MSS* 58A, folder marked 'Council for British Archaeology'
37. K Kenyon, letter to O G S Crawford 10 July 1943, *Crawford MSS* 14/103
38. Council for British Archaeology, Minutes of First Meeting 8 March 1944, in *Crawford MSS* 11/78
39. Hencken 1945; Myres 1943; Clark 1943b
40. Fox 1943
41. anon 1943
42. K Kenyon, letter to O G S Crawford 6 April 1944, *Crawford MSS* 11/66
43. Fox 1943
44. Fox 2000:100–1
45. 'Memorandum' from the Principal of the University of London, sent with Institute of Archaeology funding applications (almost certainly drafted by R E M Wheeler) in *UCL MSS* A 611/5, Institute of Archaeology Senate House Files, Box 1, folder marked 'Appeals for Funds to establish Institute of Archaeology 1932-2'
46. G F Hill, letter in support of Institute of Archaeology, 22 November 1932, in same folder
47. Woolley 1937; cf anon 1934a
48. Council for British Archaeology, Minutes of First Meeting 8 March 1944, in *Crawford MSS* 11/78
49. O'Neil 1946:66
50. Piggott 1948a
51. Reed 1948
52. Crawford 1949
53. Wainwright 1949
54. Clark 1976a
55. Gramsci 1971:453

Chapter 4

1. Crawford 1955:178
2. Geertz 1993:49

3. Dawkins 1880:3
4. Buckle 1869:231–2
5. Buckle 1891 I:192–3 and note
6. Bowler 1989:134–5, cf 158
7. Crook 1994:202–3
8. Darwin 1874:178
9. Bowler 1989:76–7
10. Bowler 1989:30, 36–7, 80–1, cf 87–8
11. Lubbock 1870:323
12. McLennan 1896:78–9
13. Dawkins 1880, quoted in Bowler 1989:115
14. Abercromby 1912:64
15. Hobbes 1651, chapter XIII
16. Bowler 1989:195–7
17. Kropotkin 1902
18. Sollas 1924:599–600
19. Myres 1916:80 [expanded version of his Presidential Address to British Association for the Advancement of Science 1909]
20. Petrie 1911:125–6
21. Pearson 1909:34
22. Crook 1994:76–7
23. McLennan 1896:51–2
24. Stocking 1987:62–3
25. Chapman 1978, 1992
26. Smiles 1994:118–9, 124–5
27. Wright 1861:4
28. Arnold 1841; Stubbs 1926:1:2; Curtis 1968:138n13
29. Curtis 1968:79; cf Hingley 2000:46, 64, 131
30. Knox 1862:26; Smiles 1994: 122–3, 231; cf Bowler 1989:107
31. Smiles 1994:117
32. Tylor 1871:1:44
33. Bowler 1989:115, 122; Bowler 1987:82; Curtis 1968:133
34. Dawkins 1880:283n
35. Bowden 1991:10
36. Beddoe 1971:297–8
37. Korg 1963; Smiles 1994:146
38. Smiles 1994:142–6
39. Hingley 2000:147
40. Frazer 1908
41. Underdown 1985:126–7; Thompson 1991; Snauwaert and Theobald 1994
42. Thompson 1993:xv
43. Gosden 1973:39–40

44. Gosden 1973:3
45. Ancient Order of Druids 1850:7, 9. See Hutton 2007 for a comprehensive study of druidry ancient and modern
46. quoted in Mee 2005:179
47. Williams 1982:252; Morgan 1983:64–5, 96
48. Jenkins 2005 is a new and definitive study of Iolo; Morgan 1983; Miles 1968:60–3

Chapter 5

1. Carpenter 1889:10–11, 35
2. quoted in Thompson 1977:718
3. Engels 1972:236–7
4. Engels 1972:237
5. Engels 1972:160
6. Engels 1972:160
7. Engels 1972:215–6
8. quoted in Thompson 1977:655–6, 614
9. quoted in Thompson 1977:235
10. Engels 1892:26–7, 40–2
11. Walker 1987:61
12. Blatchford 1977:48
13. Penty 1906:94, vii
14. Martin 1967:214–6
15. Martin 1967:20–21
16. Orage 1926
17. Lowenthal 1985:379–81
18. Crawford 1921:32–3
19. Wheeler 1958a:3–4
20. Hodgkin 1891:265, 170–1
21. Carr 1977:38–43
22. Crawford 1921:37
23. Collingwood 1927a and b
24. Crawford 1930:369
25. Petrie 1928a
26. Crawford 1931a:17,18
27. Childe 1960:282
28. Crawford 1932
29. O G S Crawford, letter to Neil Hunter 7 August 1933, *Crawford MSS* 1/5B
30. O G S Crawford, 'A Museum of Human Evolution', rough notes dated (f.7) 14 May 1932; *Crawford MSS* 102/155, 156

31. O G S Crawford, *Bunk of England*, unpublished manuscript, *Crawford MSS* 108–9, f 141
32. Childe 1936:261, 266–7
33. University of Edinburgh *Calendar* (1927):146–7
34. Childe 1936:1, 5
35. Crawford 1936b:404
36. R E M Wheeler, letter to O G S Crawford 7 January 1948, *Crawford MSS* 87/219
37. W J Wedlake, *Reminiscences and Stories*, unpublished typescript, *DCME* 1174.16
38. O G S Crawford, letter to H G Wells 12 November 1940, *Crawford MSS* 3/124
39. Daniel 1975:244–7; Trigger 1989:163–7
40. Fox 1932:82
41. Clark 1989:37; Daniel 1986:81–4
42. Crawford 1921:27
43. Marett 1908:5
44. Clark 1976b
45. Clark 1961:113
46. Bowden 2001:39
47. Crawford 1955:174
48. Childe 1936:57, 74, 114; Childe 1933
49. Childe 1944:114
50. Piggott 1935:35–8
51. Petrie 1928b
52. Clark 1952:171

Chapter 6

1. Smith 1926a:xiii
2. Stocking 1996:210
3. Smith 1912
4. Smith 1912
5. Bowler 1987:215
6. Kuklick 1991:126
7. Smith 1915:167–8
8. Spencer 1990:56–8
9. Keith 1915a:500, 506
10. Keith 1915a:viii; cf Landau 1991 and Stepan 1987
11. Spencer 1990:220 n33
12. Keith 1915b; Keith 1916:32
13. G E Smith, letter to W J Perry, 3 April 1916, *Smith Letters* I f 392; Costall 2001

Notes to pp. 78–85

14. Harris 1938
15. Head 1924:xlv–xlvi; anon 1918–19:18
16. Kuklick 1991:165
17. Pear 1960:230–1
18. G E Smith, letter to W J Perry, 29 July 1915, *Smith Letters* I f 344
19. Smith 1915
20. Smith 1916a; Smith and Pear 1917a, preface
21. Smith and Pear 1917a:88
22. Armstrong–Jones 1917; Smith and Pear 1917b
23. Shephard 1996:446
24. Shephard 2000:83
25. Pear 1960:231; Smith 1926a:xvii
26. Kuklick 1991:144
27. Rivers 1917
28. Pear 1960
29. Rivers 1924:3–5
30. Rivers 1924:210; Rivers 1922a
31. Wallace 1983:37–8; cf Bernfeld 1951
32. quoted in Wallace 1983:243. See Thomas 2004:161–9 for a recent consideration of 'Freudian archaeology'.
33. Smith 1925a:317
34. Freud 1949:295, 308–9, 316; Freud 1952:790–2; Freud 1918:258–65
35. Smith 1924a:7
36. Rieff 1960:225
37. Rivers 1924:239–40 and *passim*
38. Freud 1949:295
39. Stocking 1996:214–5
40. Langham 1981:153; Stocking 1996:216
41. anon 1912; Crook 1994:103–5; W J Perry, *'The Problem of Civilisation'*, unpublished manuscript, *Perry MSS* B1/1, fol.2–3
42. anon 1913
43. Rivers 1917
44. anon 1916
45. G E Smith, letter to W J Perry, 27 February 1916, *Smith Letters* I f 383; W H R Rivers, letter to W J Perry, March 2 [1916] in *Perry MSS*, A1/1
46. G E Smith, letter to W H R Rivers, 4 October 1916, *Smith Letters* I f 493–4
47. Bryce 1918:65–91
48. Dawson 1938:83
49. Smith 1916b
50. Taylor 1975:95
51. G E Smith, letter to W J Perry, 14 December 1916, *Smith Letters* I f 437
52. Perry 1917a

53. Perry 1917b
54. G E Smith, letter to W J Perry, 21 February 1917, *Smith Letters* I f 440; cf Smith to Dr Guppy (Rylands Librarian), sent the same day, in which Guppy is told that Perry will be speaking on War... 21 February 1917, *Smith Letters* I f 168
55. Perry 1918, original emphasis
56. Shephard 1996:442
57. Pear 1960:232; Smith 1926a:xvii
58. *Regeneration* (1991), *The Eye in the Door* (1993) and *The Ghost Road* (1995), which won the Booker Prize in 1995
59. 'Early Chronology', in Sassoon 1919:15
60. Langham 1981:141
61. Smith 1916b:502
62. Rivers 1924:260–73
63. Smith 1919:233–4
64. Smith 1919:xiii
65. Smith 1919:76
66. see for instance G E Smith, letter to D Mackenzie, 16 February 1930 *Smith Letters* I, f 281
67. Smith 1919:vii, xiii
68. W J Perry, 'A Course of Ten Lectures on Comparative Religion', programme, in *Perry MSS* A1/2
69. Perry 1937:15
70. G E Smith, letters to D Mackenzie, 16 February and 2 March 1930 *Smith Letters* I, f 281, 282; cf Dawson 1938:95–6
71. Pohl 1926a,b; Sandon 1928
72. Perry 1931

Chapter 7

1. Dawson 1938:49
2. Costall 2001; Goldstein 1983:20
3. Stopford 1938:164; cf anon 1918–19:83–4
4. Dawson 1938:71–2
5. Stopford 1938:163–4
6. Daniel 1973:425; Stopford 1938:163; Goldstein 1983:20
7. 'Professor G. Elliot Smith: An Appreciation' *Manchester Guardian* 30 May 1919:9
8. Daniel 1973:425
9. G E Smith, letter to W J Perry, 21 March 1916, *Smith Letters* I f 390
10. G E Smith, letters to W J Perry, 28 February and 3 April 1916, *Smith Letters* I f 384 and 392

Notes to pp. 92–6

11. G E Smith, letter to W J Perry, 8 March 1915, *Smith Letters* I f 309
12. Perry 1927:viii
13. G E Smith, letter to W J Perry, 13 May 1916, *Smith Letters* I f 399; correspondence with Mackenzie from 15 June 1922, *Smith Letters* I f 272
14. Rivers 1922b
15. Perry 1923:vii; Perry 1937:viii; cf Corley 2001
16. Harrison 1923
17. Harris 1938:172–3; Fisher 1978:21, 28–30; Fosdick 1952:114, 127; Smith and Pear 1917a:110–11; Langham 1981:185; Dawson 1938:108
18. Dawson 1938:76
19. Smith 1924b:17, 19; G E Smith, letter to Dr C M Hinks, 29 January 1926, *Smith Letters* II f 30 (reprinted in Dawson 1938:89–95)
20. Dart 1974:36; Harris 1938:178
21. Perry 1937:viii; Trigger 1980:9
22. G E Smith, letter to D Mackenzie, 8 March 1930, *Smith Letters* I, f 283
23. Massingham 1942:56; H J Massingham, 'Does Man Delight to Bark and Bite?', undated and unprovenanced review of Perry, 'The Growth of Civilisation', in *Massingham MSS* MASM E3
24. Massingham 1926:13
25. Smith 1923a and b
26. Harris 1938:176
27. Dawson 1938:54; Champion 2003
28. G E Smith, letter to W J Perry, 3 April 1916, *Smith Letters* I f 392; 'autobiographical fragments in the handwriting of GES', *Smith Letters* II, f 63
29. Langham 1981:161
30. G E Smith, letter to Myres, quoted in Langham 1981:161; G E Smith, letter to W H R Rivers, 4 November 1916, *Smith Letters* I f 495
31. G E Smith, letter to L Munn, 16 April 1917 in *Perry MSS* A4–A11; O G S Crawford, letter to J Bellows 18 January 1926, *Crawford MSS* 104/3
32. Langham 1981:147, 160, 161–2
33. Smith 1922:148
34. Dawson 1938:77–8
35. Smith 1925b
36. Langham 1981:166
37. quoted in Langham 1981:179
38. Kendrick 1925:88
39. Langham 1981:179–80; cf Stocking 1996:303
40. G E Smith, letter to Dr C M Hinks, 29 January 1926, *Smith Letters* II f 30 (reprinted in Dawson 1938:89–95)
41. Smith 1926a:xviii
42. Perry 1921–2; Rivers 1919; Smith 1926b
43. Rivers 1922c
44. Stocking 1996:393

45. G E Smith, letter to Sir Walter Fletcher, undated (?1926), *Smith Letters* I f 130
46. Langham 1981:185
47. G E Smith, letter to C G Seligman, 5 December 1931, *Smith Letters* I:f 507–8
48. Stocking 1996:394–5, 398; Stocking 1992:178–211
49. G E Smith, letter to C G Seligman, 5 December 1931, *Smith Letters* I:f 507–8; Langham 1981:185
50. Stocking 1996:397–8; Kuklick 1991:208, 211
51. Kuklick 1991:186n6
52. Langham 1981:184–5
53. quoted in Stocking 1996:275
54. Malinowski 1924
55. Stocking 1996:275–6
56. G E Smith: 'autobiographical fragments in the handwriting of GES', *Smith Letters* II, f 60
57. Smith 1926b
58. Smith 1928
59. Smith 1925a:299, 1927:v–vi
60. Langham 1981:196–7
61. Langham 1981:192
62. Langham 1981:196; G E Smith, letter to C G Seligman, 5 December 1931, *Smith Letters* I:f 507–8
63. G E Smith, letter to C G Seligman 9 June 1932 *Smith Letters* I f 516
64. Stocking 1996:220; Joel 1950
65. Perry 1935:v; cf Malinowski 1924
66. Smith 1938:259
67. G E Smith, letter to C G Seligman, 13 August 1934, *Smith Letters* I f 530; Keith 1934
68. Perry 1938:212
69. Radcliffe-Brown 1931:148
70. G E Smith, letter to Donald Mackenzie, 15 April 1922, *Smith Letters* I f 272
71. Langham 1981:159
72. R E M Wheeler, letter to Prof. Launder Jones, Rockefeller Foundation, 13 January 1933, *UCL MSS* A 611/5 Institute of Archaeology Senate House Files, Box 1, folder marked 'Appeals for Funds to Establish Institute of Archaeology 1932–3' (letter mis-filed under 'Carnegie')

Chapter 8

1. Gosden 1999:xi
2. Stocking 1996:289, 291

Notes to pp. 103–9   261

3. Radcliffe-Brown 1931:167–8
4. Crawford 1955:77–8; Crawford 1921:59
5. Crawford 1921:60–1
6. Daniel 1986:77
7. Clark 1974:38, 1944:1
8. Stocking 1996:292
9. Malinowski 1922
10. Childe 1936:51–3
11. Crawford 1924a:101
12. O G S Crawford, letter to J Bellows, 18 January 1926, *Crawford MSS* 104/3
13. Kendrick 1925:98
14. Peake 1922
15. Childe 1926:101
16. Hooke 1927
17. V G Childe, letters to J L Myres, 8 Dec 1923 (*Myres MSS* 8/14), 17 Mar 1924 (8/22), 17 June 1925 (8/29), 26 June [1926] (8/31)
18. G E Smith, letters to D Mackenzie, 3 March and 8 March 1930, *Smith Letters* I, f 282, 283
19. Childe 1941:126
20. Childe 1936:150
21. Childe 1941
22. Clark 1946:1, 103–4
23. Keith 1931:54; Clark 1976a:242–3
24. Clay 1927b; Landau 1991:95
25. Crawford 1921:10–13, 29n
26. Crawford 1931a:15
27. Keith 1931:49
28. Daniel 1944
29. Hawkes 1982:198
30. Wheeler 1958b:117
31. Peet 1924:64
32. Massingham 1926:141
33. Smith 1934a:11
34. Bowler 1987:217–22
35. Kuklick 1991:265, 165–74
36. Elkin 1974:12–13
37. Stocking 1996:217–8
38. Landau 1991:139–40
39. Champion 2003:133, 144–5
40. Myres 1911:9–10
41. Smith 1916c
42. e.g. Smith 1924a, 1931

43. Smith 1916b:502
44. Childe 1951:12
45. Daniel 1962:117
46. Trigger 1989:153
47. Richards 2004
48. Landau 1991:118n4; Bowler 1987:170, 216–7
49. Wheeler 1958b:117

Chapter 9

1. Eyerman 1994:85–6
2. Stocking 1996:56 and *passim*; Hutton 1999:112–7
3. Piggott 1935:40–1
4. G Daniel, '*The People Articles – Two*' unpublished autobiographical typescript, *Daniel MSS*, in red box file labelled 'Photos – Glyn Daniel'; S Casson, letter to O G S Crawford, 17 December [1936?], *Crawford MSS* 1/101; Scott-Fox 2002:79; Hawkes 1982:228–9
5. O G S Crawford 'Religion staging a "come-back" ', unpublished notes, undated [probably 1932], *Crawford MSS* 102/162, 163
6. Crawford 1954
7. Curwen 1929:2–3
8. Fagan 2001:254; Scott-Fox 2002:12; Webster 1991:101–3
9. Childe 1936:261, 266–8
10. Childe 1960:269
11. Fox 1945:52
12. Childe 1936:12–3
13. Stevens 1924:59–62
14. Chapman 1947:6–7, 15
15. Tylor 1871:1:100–1
16. Hutton 1999:112–31; cf Stocking 1996:148–51
17. Dorson 1968a:202
18. Stocking 1996:50–63
19. Stocking 1996:57–8
20. Hutton 1999:123; cf Dorson 1968a
21. Oates and Wood 1998; Hutton 1999:194–201; Janssen 1992:10, 28
22. Hutton 1999:129
23. Wheeler 1925:120–1; Cambridge Antiquarian Society, 'The Cerne Abbas Giant: report of CAS trip April–May 1931', unpublished MSS, *Cambridge* Add. 9258/4–7
24. Gellner 1988
25. Stocking 1996:148; Hutton 1999:116

26. see for instance Huxley (1873), Greenwell (1877), Allen (1881), Beddoe (1885) and Taylor (1889)
27. Arnold 1867:15, 84, 96, 169
28. Arnold 1867:vii–viii
29. Arnold 1867:158–9
30. Chapman 1978:99
31. Knox 1862:322
32. Arnold 1867, esp. 12–13
33. Rhys 1904:69
34. Dorson 1968a:419, 1968b:688
35. Grayson 1992:26–7; Dorson 1968a:230, 409; Curtis 1968:110–13
36. Chapman 1978:81, 91–103
37. Yeats 1961:175–6

Chapter 10

1. Barrow 1986:96–105 and *passim*
2. Penty 1906:62–4
3. Barrow 1986:161–193
4. Taylor 1997:2, 11
5. Blatchford 1977:51; Pye 1995
6. Carpenter 1889:45
7. Stout 2005 is a fuller attempt at a biography of Macgregor Reid and the source of all uncredited assertions in this chapter
8. *Salisbury Journal* 1 July 1932, in Manley, Scrapbook, ff 36–40; 'Labour Movement Pioneer. Dr MacGregor Reid dead' *Clapham Observer* 16 August 1946
9. R B Aubry *George Watson Macgregor Reid* unpublished notes, 1986 lent by Andrew Hill
10. Seaburg 2004
11. Reid 1893:2, 10, 12, 16
12. Stout 2005
13. anon 1907–8:xiii
14. Reid 1907:11
15. 'Subhadra' 1910:143, 156
16. 'A Rational View of Life and Thought', *The New Life* 1913:335. Hutton 2007 is now the first port-of-call for information about the Druidic revival
17. *The Morning Leader* in *Wiltshire Gazette* 30 August 1905, copy in *WANHSS* 16:24; Chippindale 1983:172–3
18. Bradley 1907:268
19. 'Sun-Worship at Stonehenge' *Salisbury Journal* 29 June 1912:7
20. Walker 1987:71–3; Chippindale 1978
21. Chippindale 1983:172–3

Notes to pp. 130–4

22. Editorial commentary (by Reid), *The New Life* 1913:272, 275, 335–8
23. 'Sun-Worshippers at Stonehenge' *Wiltshire Gazette* 25 June 1914:3
24. *ibid*; 'Annual Pilgrimage to Stonehenge. Scenes with Sun Worshippers. Serious Accident to motor cyclist' *Salisbury Journal* 27 June 1914:7; 'Sunrise at Stonehenge. Exciting Incidents on the 21st. 'Thousands' of spectators' *Salisbury Times* 26 June 1914:7
25. 'Sunrise at Stonehenge. The Altar Stone illumined. Latter Day Druids' protest' *Salisbury Journal* 26 June 1915:2; 'Sunrise at Stonehenge. A Rare Sight, Perfectly Clear' *Salisbury Times* 25 June 1915:2
26. 'Londoner' column in *London Evening News* 22 June 1915
27. 'Midsummer Sunrise at Stonehenge: Druids' Ritual Within the Enclosure' *Salisbury Journal* 24 June 1916:5
28. 'Druids at Stonehenge. A unique ceremony' *Salisbury Times* 26 June 1918:5
29. Ap Llywellyn 1924
30. Nichols 1990:108
31. 'Druids on Salisbury Plain. Summer Solstice Festival. Chief Druid's Extraordinary Address' *Salisbury Journal* 29 June 1923:4; V Haig, letter to Office of Works, 13 July 1925, in *WORK 14/2135*
32. 'The Druids' Camp at Springbottom' *The New Life* 337–8; Ap Llywellyn 1924
33. Peacock 1945; Seaburg 2004
34. Soul 1927
35. Underwood 1962; F H Smith, letter to A Heaseman 8 July 1922, in *WORK 14/2135*
36. Seaburg 2004
37. Custodian's Reports, 30 June 1928 and 26 June 1929, in *WORK 14/2135*; 'Midsummer Solstice at Stonehenge: A Perfect Sunrise' *Salisbury Journal* 23 June 1929:10
38. Grey 1923:115–7
39. 'Sunrise at Stonehenge. The Altar Stone illumined. Latter Day Druids' protest' *Salisbury Journal* 26 June 1915:2
40. 'The Druids' Camp at Springbottom' *The New Life* 337–8; 'Midsummer Ceremony at Stonehenge: Druids celebrate "Rites of Caevron"' *Salisbury Journal* 25 June 1943:7
41. [G W M Reid] *Book of Concealed Mystery (Sephra DT3nioutha) [sic] Yorke Collection*, New Series 55 f.70
42. G W M Reid, letter to Lord Crawford, President of the Society of Antiquaries, September 1924; *The Druids and Stonehenge* ms dated 21 June 1925, both in *WORK 14/2135*; 'The summer solstice of the Druid Order. From whence came the Foundation of the Order' typescript, WRO 2860/22; 'Druids on Salisbury Plain. Summer Solstice Festival. Chief Druid's Extraordinary Address' *Salisbury Journal* 29 June 1923:4

Notes to pp. 135–9

43. unsigned editorial comment (? by G W M Reid) in *The Druid Journal* 1929:13
44. 'John Barry O'Callaghan' *The Nature Cure* 2, no. 11, April 1909:1, 96–7, 228–32
45. Reid 1913
46. 'A Rational View of Life and Thought' *The New Life*:334–5
47. 'A Pioneer of Socialism. Dr MacGregor-Reid Dies, Aged 95' *South Western Star* 16 August 1946
48. papers re conduct of Clapham Labour Party and resignation of Reid, *LMA* 4284/01/012; Peacock 1945:16–17
49. 'Ancient Druid Bond. Services at Stonehenge. Chief Druid Predicts troublesome future' *Salisbury Journal* 2 July 1926:9
50. 'Druid Pilgrimage to Stonehenge. Picturesque Ritual at the Altar-Stone. Chief Druid on "Where and Whither"' *Salisbury Journal* 29 June 1928:5; 'Midsummer Solstice at Stonehenge: A Perfect Sunrise' *Salisbury Journal* 23 June 1929:10; 'Midsummer Sunrise at Stonehenge: Viewers Disappointed on Longest Day' *Salisbury Journal* 27 June 1930:9

Chapter 11

1. Manley 1932
2. 'Thomas Ireland', letter to D. Lloyd George, 7 June 1919, in *WORK 14*/2135
3. C Peers, notes dated 6 June 1919, 28 June 1919, in *WORK 14*/2135
4. quoted in Emerick 1998:183
5. C Peers, endorsements to letters from 'Thomas Ireland' 27 May 1920, 5 June 1920, in *WORK 14*/2135
6. 'The Sunrising: This year's scene at Stonehenge' *Salisbury Times* 25 June 1920:8; 'Thomas Ireland', letter to First Commissioner 7 June 1921, in *WORK 14*/2135
7. 'Thomas Ireland', letter to First Commissioner 16 June 1921, in *WORK 14*/2135
8. 'The Druids and Religious Toleration' handbill in *WORK 14*/2135; cf *Salisbury Journal* 30 June 1922
9. Eversley 1910
10. Chippindale 1983:179–83
11. W Hawley, letter to A Heaseman, Office of Works, 16 July 1922, in *WORK 14*/2135
12. Ap Llywellyn 1924
13. 'The Sunrising: This year's scene at Stonehenge' *Salisbury Times* 25 June 1920:8

14. G W M Reid, letter to Lord Crawford September 1924, in *WORK 14/2135*
15. And may have done so: a burial container of the right sort of date was found in 1956. Chippindale 1983:204
16. 'Thomas Ireland', letter to First Commissioner 14 June 1924, in *WORK 14/2135*; cf Jowett 1925
17. Murray 1999:33–4
18. WANHS Report of Annual Meeting, in *WANHSS* c/11/34
19. A J Bonwick, letter to First Commissioner of Works 20 August 1924, in *WORK 14/2135*
20. Crawford and Balcarres 1925:224–5
21. Lord Crawford and Balcarres, letter to First Commissioner 26 August 1924, in *WORK 14/2135*
22. Crawford and Balcarres 1924
23. anon 1925
24. Lewis 1924
25. 'Londoner', 'The Druids' Petition' *London Evening News* 29 August 1924. This and other press cuttings relating to the Burials controversy are to be found in *WORK 14/2135*
26. F W Jowett, letter to G W M Reid 5 September 1924, in *WORK 14/2135*
27. *Manchester Guardian* 13 September 1924
28. 'Thomas Ireland', letter to First Commissioner 10 September 1924, in *WORK 14/2135*
29. G W M Reid, letter to Ramsay Macdonald 23 September 1924, in *WORK 14/2135*
30. F H Smith, letter to P Anderson 21 June 1925, in *WORK 14/2135*
31. 'Druid Pilgrimage to Stonehenge. Picturesque Ritual at the Altar-Stone. Chief Druid on "Where and Whither"' *Salisbury Journal* 29 June 1928:5
32. 'DMH', Memo to Mr Connolly dated 28 July 1925; R M Reid, letter to Office of Works dated 4 June 1928, in *WORK 14/2135*
33. 'Druid Pilgrimage to Stonehenge. Picturesque Ritual at the Altar-Stone. Chief Druid on "Where and Whither"' *Salisbury Journal* 29 June 1928:5
34. Lansdown 1925:26–7; AOD, letter to Office of Works 16 March 1925, in *WORK 14/2135*
35. 'Ancient Order of Druids Pilgrimage to Stonehenge' *Salisbury Journal* 19 June 1925:9
36. 'Midsummer Solstice at Stonehenge. Record Attendance Disappointed. Druids and the Officials' *Salisbury Journal* 26 June 1925:9
37. Lockyer 1906
38. Slade 1936; Engleheart 1930
39. Wheeler 1925:68, 106; Kendrick 1927:190
40. Crawford 1924b

Notes to pp. 145–151

41. W Boyd Dawkins, letters to *The Times* 28 August 1924, *Manchester Guardian* 16 September 1924
42. Kendrick 1927:1–2
43. Kendrick 1927:153, 155–6
44. Kendrick 1927:210; Cunnington 1935:135
45. Spence 1928:36, 40–1
46. Major M Wheatley, letter to Office of Works 23 June 1930, in *WORK 14/2135*
47. R C Burgess, Stonehenge custodian, report dated 22 June 1930, in *WORK 14/2135*
48. A Peacock, letter to Office of Works 28 June 1932, in *WORK 14/2135*; cf C R Peers, letter to Edward Goddard 12 September 1923, in *WORK 14/2463*; *Salisbury Journal* 1 July 1932, in *Manley, Scrapbook*, ff 36–40
49. *Salisbury Journal* 1 July 1932, in *Manley, Scrapbook*, ff 36–40
50. 'Hob Nob' 1939
51. Peacock 1945:108–9; 'Labour Movement Pioneer. Dr MacGregor Reid dead' *Clapham Observer* 16 August 1946
52. Seaburg 2004:552, 555–7
53. 'A Pioneer of Socialism. Dr MacGregor-Reid Dies, Aged 95' *South Western Star* 16 August 1946
54. Smith 1945
55. G W Smith, letters to Office of Works 13 June 1938 and 22 May 1939, in *WORK 14/2135*
56. Hooper 1935:9, 37; 1941:17–20
57. 'Midsummer Ceremony at Stonehenge: Druids celebrate "Rites of Caevron"' *Salisbury Journal* 25 June 1943:7
58. 'Festival of the Summer Solstice: Druid Hermetists at Stonehenge' *Salisbury Journal* 28 June 1946:8; G W Smith, letters to Office of Works, 20 May 1946, 7 May 1947 in *WORK 14/2136*
59. 'Looking Round: a running commentary' *Salisbury Journal* 25 June 1948:6
60. G W Smith, letter to Office of Works 11 January 1951, in *WORK 14/2136*
61. Nichols 1990:109
62. G W Smith, letter to Office of Works 31 May 1952, in *WORK 14/2136*
63. 'The summer solstice of the Druid Order. From whence came the Foundation of the Order', typescript *WRO 2860/22*
64. G W Smith, letters to Office of Works 11 January 1951 and 31 May 1952; R S Pith, letter to Office of Works 4 April 1953; miscellaneous memos and notes concerning legitimacy of various Druidic groups, Jan–Feb 1953, all in *WORK 14/2136*
65. See Stout 2003, Stout 2006 and above all Worthington 2004 for later developments at Stonehenge around the summer solstice

66. Chippindale *et al* 1990; Bender *et al* 1998
67. Chippindale 1983:143–7, 160, 282n10
68. Chippindale 1978
69. Piper 1949
70. Long 1930:141n
71. unsigned editorial comment (? by G W M Reid) in *The Druid Journal* 1929:11–12; 'Ancient Druid Bond. Services at Stonehenge. Chief Druid Predicts Troublesome Future' *Salisbury Journal* 2 July 1926:9; *Salisbury Journal* 1 July 1932

Chapter 12

1. Thomas 2004:63
2. editorial comment in *The New Life*, Summer Solstitial Number
3. Stocking 1996:292
4. Crawford 1929, 1939; Fox 1944:156
5. Clark 1939:2–3
6. Jones 2002; Childe 1960:43; Crawford 1921:223
7. Piggott 1937:38
8. Crawford 1955:166
9. 'The Summer Spade', leading article, *The Times* 21 August 1936, p 11
10. Emerick 1998
11. Wheeler 1971
12. 'Londoner' column in *London Evening News* 22 June 1915
13. advert in Soul [1927]: p. 1
14. quoted in Chippindale 1983:195
15. Crawford 1928
16. Crawford 1955:182; Murray 1999:47
17. Stonehenge Protection Committee: 'Stonehenge: An Appeal to Save It', 1929, copy in *WORK 14/488*
18. 'Save Stonehenge! The "Frontispiece to English History" in peril' *Illustrated London News* March 23 1929:481
19. Bennett *et al* 1929
20. as above, note 18
21. Chippindale 1983:192–5
22. Hawkes 1967:174
23. Murray 1999:23–5
24. Piggott 1989:26
25. Murray 1999:72, 78, 86, 175
26. Edwards 2000:70–1
27. Ormsby-Gore 1935:8–9
28. Matless 1998:78–9
29. Ormsby-Gore 1935:8

Notes to pp. 165–173

30. e.g. Wheeler 1925:68, Piggott 1937:38
31. Wheeler 1956:141
32. Piggott 1940
33. quoted in Hingley 2000:37, 46
34. Wheeler 1958b:90; Hawkes 1982:305–6
35. Hawkes 1982:273–6
36. Wheeler 1958b:87, 90, 94–6
37. Haverfield 1905:6
38. Haverfield 1908/9:174
39. Wheeler 1958b:60, 62
40. Wheeler 1958b:60
41. Wheeler 1925:221
42. Wheeler 1925:267
43. Wheeler 1925:232–3
44. Wheeler 1925:291–2
45. Wheeler 1925:6–7, 283–8
46. Wheeler 1925:5; 1929:23
47. Watts-Dunton 1906:xi, xiv
48. Wheeler 1958b:57
49. Wheeler 1958b:58; *Observer*, 28? February 1926 (in *AWS*, f.117)
50. Haverfield 1908–9:54
51. Wheeler 1929:5–6
52. Wheeler 1929:12
53. Wheeler 1929:5–6, 13
54. Wheeler 1929:3, 13
55. Wheeler 1929:5–6
56. Wheeler 1927
57. Wheeler 1927; cf Mercer 1998:417–8; Daniel 1986:342
58. G W M Reid, letter to Lord Crawford, President of the Society of Antiquaries, September 1924, in *WORK 14/2135*
59. quoted in Hutton 1999:161
60. Massingham 1942:93
61. Massingham 1935:xi, 178–80, 242–9, 266–7, 276–290
62. Smiles 2004:84
63. Smiles 2004:88
64. quoted in Smiles 2004:91
65. Smiles 2005:148–50

Chapter 13

1. Crawford 1953:269
2. Shoesmith 1990:64 and *passim*

3. anon 1935
4. Marshall 1938
5. anon 1935
6. Watkins 1922:9
7. Minutes of Central Committee Meetings of the Woolhope Club, 25 July 1921, 21 November 1921, *HRO* BH 70/10; Diaries of George Marshall, 9 August 1921, *HRO* K38/CC/1-53
8. anon 1921
9. Watkins 1925a:v
10. Watkins 1922:34
11. Watkins 1922:10, 11
12. Watkins 1922:16-18
13. Watkins 1922:9, 30-1
14. Watkins 1925a:192-6
15. Watkins 1923; Watkins 1925a:38-9, 191-2
16. Watkins 1925a:40, 48, 199-200, 201, 203
17. Watkins 1925a:vi
18. Watkins 1925a:11, 107, 78, 79-81, 92-5, 95-6
19. Watkins 1927a:23, 74-5, 72
20. Watkins 1922:7
21. Harte 1997
22. Pennick and Devereux 1989:37
23. Watkins 1922:9, 32
24. Pennick and Devereux 1989:30-41
25. Cox 1944:vii; Belloc 1911:4, 8
26. Reade 1921; Minutes of Central Committee Meetings of the Woolhope Club, 25 July 1921, 21 November 1921, *HRO* BH 70/10
27. 'A Rosetta-stone of topography' Pathfinder column, *Hereford Times* 28 November 1925
28. Maxwell 1932b
29. Matless 1998:58
30. Taylor 1997:229-52
31. Walker 1987:315; Taylor 1997:83, 240
32. quoted in Lowenthal 1985:9
33. Paul 1951:115
34. Sandell 1988
35. For an analysis, see Stout 2004, Appendix III
36. *Oxford Times*, 6 November 1925; *AWS*, f 6; *Hereford Times*, 28 November 1925; *AWS*, f 11; *The Scotsman*, 30 November 1925, *AWS* f 8
37. Watkins 1925a:vi
38. Diaries of George Marshall, 29 September 1921, *HRO* K38/CC/1-53; James 1922
39. anon 1924a,b,c; 1927; 1928a,b; 1930; 1931a,b; 1933a,b; 1934b; Watkins 1928a:145; 1928b; 1929; 1930a; 1931a,b; 1932b; 1933a

Notes to pp. 182–7

40. anon 1924a; Watkins 1929
41. Diaries of George Marshall, entries 13, 15, 16 July 1933, *HRO* K38/CC/1–53; Marshall 1938
42. Wolverhampton: *Staffordshire Advertiser* 28 November 1925, *AWS*, f 15; Worthing: *Sussex Daily News* 16 March 1926, *AWS*, f 31
43. A Watkins, in *STC* 31/ f 114; Matless, in press
44. *AWS*, f 34
45. Watkins 1925a:96, 123
46. A Watkins, 'Proof by Spade', *STC* 11/1 f 1
47. Curwen: J Middleton, *Encyclopaedia of Hove & Portslade* Vol.3, C 2002 (unpublished manuscript in Brighton & Hove History Centre); Fox 2000:3; O G S Crawford, letter to C F C Hawkes 29 May 1922, in *Hawkes MSS* 8; Piggott 1989:21
48. O G S Crawford, letter to C F C Hawkes 29 May 1922, in *Hawkes MSS* 8
49. Crawford 1955:40; cf Piggott 1989:21
50. Crawford 1921:163–207, esp 163, 189
51. O G S Crawford, 'Papers Concerning *Antiquity*' *Crawford MSS* 104, f10; Crawford 1927a:2; Clay 1927a
52. A Watkins 'Outside Criticism of the Old Straight Track' 1927 *STC* 2/1–15, f 1
53. O G S Crawford, 'Bunk of England', *Crawford MSS* 108–9, f 141
54. Grinsell 1988:77
55. Crawford 1951:9; Crawford 1953:269
56. M C Carr-Gomm, letters to Robert Rule, 3 and 11 December 1939 *STC* 55/2/1/50
57. Watkins 1927c
58. A Watkins, in *STC* 16/3 (1929) ff 11, 11v
59. Watkins 1927a:3
60. *Oxford Times* 18 September 1927, *AWS*, f 61; advert *AWS*, f 113
61. *Birmingham Gazette*, 23 September 1927, *AWS*, f 61; *Surveyor and Municipal and County Engineer*, *AWS*, f 72; Reason 1931
62. Watkins 1922:33; *STC* 6/12 f 1 (Baden-Powell)
63. *AWS*, f 68
64. Wilkinson 1927
65. N Woodhead, in *STC* 2/9 (1927) ff 1, 2
66. 'Straight Tracks. Interesting Field Day Explorations. Hereford Gathering' *Hereford Times* 21 July 1933 (copy in *STC* 38/1); Watkins 1933b
67. *Derbyshire Advertiser*, 14 January 1928, *AWS*, f 70
68. *Wiltshire Gazette* 1 December, 7 December nd; *AWS*, ff 63–4
69. Watkins 1972:37
70. Watkins 1932a:47–8
71. Allen Watkins, letter to C Carr-Gomm, 25 April 1933, loose in *STC* 37/ –, 1933

Notes to pp. 187–194

72. quoted in Shoesmith 1990:134–5
73. T C Lethbridge, letter to Cyril Fox 8 July 1961, *Fox MSS*, Box 42, WO5/3/1, 2
74. L S Munn, 'Leys in Northumberland', unprovenanced cutting dated 3 December 1927, in *AWS* ff 65–6
75. Maxwell 1932a; Maxwell 1932c:87
76. Dark 1926
77. Maxwell 1932c:vi–vii
78. Maxwell 1933:i–viii
79. A Watkins, 'The Ley Takes Hold' *STC* 37/2 (1933)

Chapter 14

1. Watkins 1927a:83.
2. Watkins 1925b; M K Woods, 'Some Impressions of our Summer Meeting' *STC* 51/3
3. M K Woods, 'Some Reflections on a Paper "Mysteries of Ancient Man" by Arthur Lawton' *STC* 58/61947, f 7
4. '4000 year old road. Celtic worship of its mark stones.' *Daily Express* 11 October 1926, *AWS*, f 42; Mackmurdo 1926 (in *AWS* f.37)
5. F C Tyler, in *STC* 3/preface (1929)
5. H Hudson 'Short Guide for finding Ancient Sun Alignments', *STC* 36/24–7 (1933)
6. Hando 1934a, b, c
7. For a more detailed analysis, together with background biographical notes on individual members, see Stout 2004, Appendix IV
8. Mackmurdo: www.essexinfo.net/test-community/files/view/history/The_History_of_the_Rural_Community_Council_of_Essex.doc; Trew: 'Death of Noted Local Architect', *Gloucester Citizen* 22 June 1968
9. B Carbonell, 'The Summer Field Meeting at Hereford' *STC* 38/4 (1933); A Watkins 'Some Organising Notes for Summer Meetings' *STC* 38/3 (1933)
10. M K Woods, 'The Severn River and Estuary', *STC* 28/8 f 8, Pt II (1931) f 1
11. Shoesmith 1990:120–1; cf Minutes of Central Committee Meetings of the Woolhope Club, 25 April 1918, *HRO* BH 70/10; anon 1931c
12. D Wintle, in *STC* 14/11 f 2 (1929)
13. J H Harvey 'Dr Wheeler and Orientation' *STC* 49/10/1–3 (1936); cf A Watkins, Correspondence with Myra Story, September 1934 in *STC* 41/15–16
14. Harvey 1940; cf Thurlow 1987:73

Notes to pp. 194–9

15. M K Woods, 'Some Thoughts on sun worship in Britain' *STC* 44/6 (1935) f 8; 'Some Reflections on a Paper "Mysteries of Ancient Man" by Arthur Lawton' *STC* 58/6 (1947) f 17
16. Watkins 1972:2–3; Watkins, endorsement to correspondence with Myra Story, September 1934 in *STC* 41/15–16
17. Mackmurdo 1933; W W Tyrell, letter to M C Carr-Gomm 20 December 1935, Philip Carr-Gomm collection; 'Travel and Country. The Old Straight Track' *New Statesman* 12 December 1925, *AWS* f 18; cf Dark 1926
18. Watkins: Shoesmith 1990. For Hayton, see 'Prehistoric Trackways in Bedfordshire: Some Curious Observations' *Bedfordshire Times* 12 April 1929, in *STC* 17 n13; for Simpson, see 'Druids' "Mount of Baal" ' *Salisbury Journal* 27 June 1913
19. Reports by Barbara Carbonell: 'The Summer Field Meeting at Hereford' *STC* 38/4; 'Account of the Second Annual Meeting, held at Salisbury' *STC* 42/2; 'Report on the Meeting in Exeter' *STC* 46/1; 'Cheltenham Summer Meeting' *STC* 49/1/1–2; by M K Woods: 'Some Impressions of our Summer Meeting' *STC* 51/3; cf 'Straight Tracks. Interesting Field Day Explorations. Hereford Gathering' *Hereford Times* 21 July 1933 (copy in *STC* 38/1); 'Straight Track Club. Archaeologists in Salisbury District. Visits to Historical Sites' *Western Gazette* 27 July 1934 (copy in *STC* 42/3)
20. A Watkins, 'Pointers for Ley Hunters' *STC* 1/1 (1927)
21. *ibid*
22. 'Straight Tracks. Interesting Field Day Explorations. Hereford Gathering' *Hereford Times* 21 July 1933 (copy in *STC* 38/1); D Wintle, 'The Pillar Worshippers: were they the ancestors of the pioneers of the Old Straight Track?' *STC* 7/12 (1928); A Watkins, *STC* 28/Note 1 (1931); C A E Chudleigh, contribution to discussion on 'Arthur and the Cromlechs' *STC* 49/10/1–3 (1935)
23. H Hudson *STC* 46/3 (loose), 1935
24. A T Powell 'Menhirs in Anglesey' *STC* 4/1, Notes (1927); A T Powell 'Ordnance Survey Maps. Correspondence between Colonel A T Powell and the Director-General of the Ordnance Survey' *STC* 36/5 (1932); A Watkins *STC* 3/Notes 1 (1927), *STC* 4/Note 1, Remarks (1928)
25. Watkins 1925a:83
26. Watkins 1927b; Engleheart 1927
27. F C Tyler, *STC* 14/3 f 1 (1929)
28. J Simpson, *STC* 4/Note 1, Remarks, f 1 (1928)
29. Wintle *et al*, *STC* 3/ 4, ff 2–4 (1927)
30. B Carbonell, 'Some Notes on Waymarks', *STC* 9/2 f 1 (1928)
31. F C Tyler, 'A Camp Alignment, and the church on Gare Hill' *STC* 9/11 f 2 (1928)
32. A Watkins, *STC* 8/12 ff 1–2 (1928)

33. F C Tyler, *STC* 6/10 f 1 (1927)
34. A Watkins, *STC* 8/12 ff 1–2 (1928)
35. D Wintle, *STC* 8/12 ff 5–7 (1928)
36. B Somerville, *STC* 21/Note 7, f 2 (1929)
37. A Watkins, *STC* 28/Note 1 (1931)
38. A Watkins, *STC* 6/10 f 1 (1927)
39. A Watkins, correspondence with Myra Story, September 1934 in *STC* 41/15–16 (1934)
40. Watkins 1972:44
41. Diaries of George Marshall, 3 June 1921, *HRO* K38/CC/1–53
42. Watkins 1922:34
43. Watkins 1922:12; Watkins 1925a:158–61
44. Watkins 1925a:189–196
45. A Watkins, *STC* 6/5 f 1 (1927)
46. Watkins 1925a:101–7
47. A Watkins, *STC* 10/4 f 2 (1928)

Chapter 15

1. F C Tyler, 'A Camp Alignment, and the church on Gare Hill' *STC* 9/11 f 2 (1928)
2. F C Tyler, 'on Atlantean Origin of Roads', *STC* 15/ note 15 (1929)
3. F C Tyler, 'A Criticism and a Reply' *STC* 32/9 (1932)
4. F C Tyler, 'Stock-taking' *STC* 44/4 (1935)
5. H Hudson, *STC* 46/3 (loose) (1935)
6. Hudson, as above; W Pritchard, *STC* 46/2/22; G Liddell, *STC* 46/2/7
7. C A E Chudleigh, *STC* 46/2/22
8. F C Tyler, *STC* 46/3 (loose) (1935)
9. F C Tyler, *STC* 46/2/13 (1935)
10. F C Tyler, *STC* 46/3 (loose) (1935); H Hudson, *STC* 46/3 (loose) (1935); G M Hayton, *STC* 46/2/5 (1935)
11. Maltwood 1935; cf Brown 1981
12. H Hudson, *STC* 46/3 (loose) (1935)
13. H Hudson, *STC* 49/13/1–2 (1938); anonymous comment on same page
14. B Carbonell, 'Cheltenham Summer Meeting' *STC* 49/1/1–2 (1936)
15. M C Carr-Gomm, 'Ancient Trackways and Alignments', preface for unpublished book (*Philip Carr-Gomm*)
16. J H White, letter to M C Carr-Gomm dated 4 February 1936 (*Philip Carr-Gomm*)
17. W W Tyrell 1935, letter to M C Carr-Gomm 20 December 1935 (*Philip Carr-Gomm*)

Notes to pp. 206–14

18. M C Carr-Gomm, letter to Robert Rule, 11 December 1939, *STC* 55/2/1/50
19. Tyler 1939. For Heinsch and inter-war German 'alignment research', see Pennick and Devereux 1989:42–5. By 1939, he was thought to be living in Victoria, British Columbia: M C Carr-Gomm, letter to R Rule, 21 November 1939, in *STC* 55/2/1/50
20. Tyler 1939
21. M C Carr-Gomm, letter to Robert Rule, 3 December 1939; Simpkin, Marshall to Rule, 18 December 1939, both *STC* 55/2/1/50
22. Screeton 1993:33
23. Heselton 1986:76 and *passim*
24. Pennick and Devereux 1989:206–8; Crawford 1951:9
25. Matless 1998:82
26. N Woodhead, 'The Extent of Primitive Forest' *STC* 5/12 (1927); cf Smith 1997, Fox 1932
27. *AWS*, f 20
28. Watkins 1930b
29. Quennell and Quennell 1922:109
30. Webster 1991:84; Piggott 1989:21–2
31. F C Tyler, *STC* 8/5 f 1 (1928)
32. Crawford 1955:154–167, 214–31
33. A T Powell, 'Ordnance Survey Maps. Correspondence between Colonel A T Powell and the Director-General of the Ordnance Survey' *STC* 36/5 (1932)
34. B Somerville, 'Orientation' *STC* 3/6; Somerville 1927
35. W W Tyrell, *STC* 50/4/1–2 (1937)
36. Hoskins 1983:137
37. Tyrell, *ibid*.
38. M Wood, 'A Friendly Encounter with Orthodoxy' *STC* 50/4/1–2 (1937)
39. R Rule, *STC* 46/2/11 (1935); F Hando, *STC* 46/2/3 (1935)
40. A Watkins, *STC* 50/4/1–2 (1937)
41. J H Harvey, 'Dr Wheeler and Orientation' *STC* 49/10/1–3 (1936)
42. Watkins 1972:27–8
43. as notes 35 and 38 above
44. M K Woods, letter to Robert Rule 3 January 1940, *STC* 55/2/1; M C Carr-Gomm, letter to Robert Rule, 7 January 1940, in *STC* 55/2/1
45. Harper 1979; M C Carr-Gomm, correspondence concerning whereabouts of STC Portfolios, 1951 (*Philip Carr-Gomm*)
46. e.g. Screeton 1993:15
47. J H Harvey, letter to M C Carr-Gomm 10 February 1944 (*Philip Carr-Gomm*)
48. Hewitt 1966:72; Hewitt 1971
49. M Wood, *STC* 46/2/16 (1935)

50. Maxwell 1932c:107
51. *Country Life* 14 November 1925, in *AWS*, f 4
52. Watkins 1932a:50
53. 'London Ghost Tracks. Secrets that Ley-Hunting Reveals' *London Evening News* 4 January 1928, in *AWS* f70
54. Dutt 1926, 'prefatory note'; Hudson 1932:135

Chapter 16

1. 6 February 1928, in *AWS*, f 72
2. Watkins 1972:41. Daniels 2006 is an exploration of the relationship between Watkins' photography and the development of ley theory
3. 23 November 1927, in *AWS*, f 61
4. anon 1931b
5. A H Mackmurdo, 'The "Straight Track" from the scientific point of view' *STC* 5/5, f 3
6. Matless 1993, 178n65
7. Crawford 1953:269
8. Weigall 1926:331
9. F Hando, *STC* 46/2/3 (1935)
10. *Bristol Evening World*, 26 May 1931, *DC11/6*
11. Hawkes 1982:163
12. W J Wedlake, 'Reminiscences and Stories', unpublished typescript, *DCM* 1174.16
13. Wheeler 1943:45
14. Wheeler 1943:xxi
15. Maiden Castle Excavation Committee 1933–38, Minute Book, *DCM* Box 64, doc. 5
16. Wheeler 1958b:91
17. August 1924: *DC11/7*
18. 8 September 1936: *DC11/8*
19. *Southern Times* 30 March 1935, *DC11/7*
20. *Dorset Echo* 24 August 1934, in *DCM* 64/3
21. *Sunday Times* 27 September 1936, *DC11/8*
22. R Rule, 'Dorsetshire Jottings. Maiden Castle' *STC* 42/15 (1934)
23. anon 1936c; 'Archaeologists' Enjoyable Excursion' *East Anglian Daily Times* 25 August 1936
24. Wheeler 1958b:92
25. 1 March 1937, *DC11/8*
26. Wheeler 1943:3
27. Wheeler 1958b:92

Notes to pp. 220–7 277

28. 11 August 1934, all pasted alongside each other in the London Museum Scrapbook (*DC11/7*)
29. *Dorset Daily Echo* 15 September 1936, *DC11/8*
30. *Morning Post* 21 May 1934, *DC11/7*; Wheeler 1958b:90–1
31. *Morning Post* 21 May 1934
32. *Dorset Daily Echo*, 12 September 1934, *DC11/7*
33. *Southern Times*, 30 March 1935, *DC11/7*;
34. *Dorset Daily Echo* 23 March 1935, *DC11/8*; R E M Wheeler, ms Report to the Society of Antiquaries 1936, *DCM 63/1*
35. R E M Wheeler, ms Report to the Society of Antiquaries 1935, *DCM 63/1*
36. *Observer* 30 August 1936; *DC11/8*
37. *Daily Telegraph* 24 September 1937, *DC11/8*
38. *Evening News* 13 August 1936, *DC11/8*
39. 'Maiden Castle', leader in *The Times* 25 February 1938
40. Ramsden 1939
41. R E M Wheeler, manuscript of untitled lecture, [no date, but between May and September 1936], in *DCM 63/1*
42. *ibid*
43. *Hackney Gazette* 12 September 1934, *DC11/7*
44. 8 September 1935, *DC11/8*
45. August 1934, *DC11/7*
46. *Western Gazette* 30 August 1935, *DC11/8*
47. *Bournemouth Daily Echo* 8 December 1936, *DCM 64/3*
48. *Cambridge Independent* 28 May 1936, *DC11/8*
49. *Observer* 30 August 1936, *DC11/8*
50. *Nottingham Guardian* 8 January 1937, *DC11/8*
51. Wheeler 1943:69
52. Wheeler 1958b:92
53. *Pulman's Weekly News* 7 April 1937, *DC11/8*
54. *Manchester Guardian*, *Western Mail*, both 2 September 1931, *DC11/6*
55. Clark 1946:88
56. Clark 1943a:121
57. Coates 1999
58. Leeds 1947; Fox 1930; Lethbridge 1930
59. Matless 1998:43
60. *Liverpool Post* 4 July 1934, *DC11/7*
61. 'Who will start a Folk Museum? Pioneering hint at Bristol Conference' *Western Daily Press* 4 July 1934, in LMS, *DC11/7*
62. *ibid*
63. Morton 1942:173
64. Stout 2003; for statistics, see Stout 2004, Appendix V
65. *Bath Evening Times* 21 June 1930, in *Manley, Scrapbook* f 54
66. *Wiltshire Times* 25 June 1932, in *Manley, Scrapbook* f 32

67. 28 August 1932, copy in *WANHSS* 17:f 172
68. R E M Wheeler, manuscript of untitled lecture, no date [but between May and September 1936], *DCM* 63/1
69. Wheeler 1958b:91–2
70. 17 October 1934, *DC11/7*
71. R E M Wheeler, ms of Report to the Society of Antiquaries, 1937 *DCM* 63/1
72. Krissdottir and Peers 1998:190
73. Wilson 1973
74. Krissdottir and Peers 1998:152
75. Krissdottir and Peers 1998:209
76. Head 1996:93
77. Powys 1966:386
78. Powys 1966:125–6
79. Powys 1966:164
80. Powys 1966:13
81. Powys 1966:167
82. Powys 1966:382
83. Powys 1966:467–8
84. Elwin 1975:262
85. Shanks 1935; Woolley 1937 and *Sunday Times* 29 August 1937 (letter from Wheeler), both in *DC11/8*
86. Chapman 1985:19
87. Smith 1997:27
88. Stevenson 1984:430–2
89. Smith 1929
90. Stout 2004, Appendix V; Stout 2003
91. Webb 1976:25
92. Orwell 1984:106
93. Childe 1936:1, 5
94. Squire 1936
95. Mowat 1968:539–40

Conclusion

1. Online at gutenberg.net.au/ebooks05/0500141h.html.
2. Lewis 1924–5
3. Piggott 1963:3
4. Sharples 1991:125
5. Wheeler 1958a:4
6. Gramsci 1971:12
7. J G D Clark, letter to Christopher Hawkes 26 November 1936, *Hawkes MSS* 7

Notes to pp. 236–46

8. Piggott 1948b
9. quoted in Wheeler 1958b:80
10. Clark 1989:13–14
11. Hawkes 1982:128
12. Clark 1989:52
13. Randall-MacIver 1933:8
14. Collingwood 1939:21–2, 41
15. Collingwood 1939:67; Collingwood 1928:220–1; 1926:150
16. Slotkin 1948
17. Crawford 1934
18. Collingwood 1939:91–2
19. Fukuyama 1992; Carr 1977:101 and 114 (citing Arnold)
20. Carr 1977:101; Fukuyama 1992:306–7
21. LAW 1997:164–6
22. Crawford 1927b:131; Crawford 1955:29, 162–5, 201–2
23. Smith 1924c:11; Smith 1934b; Smith 1938
24. Crawford 1931a:9
25. Stocking 1996:394; Griffiths 1980:323–4
26. Scott-Fox 2002:135
27. V G Childe, nd [1934], letter to Christopher Hawkes, *Hawkes MSS 7*
28. Holtorf 1996; LAW 1997:174
29. Shanks and Tilley 1987:213
30. Shanks 1991; Pearson and Shanks 2001
31. Cornell 2000:176
32. Hingley 2001:89
33. Barker *et al* 2001:55
34. Lowenthal 1985:411–2
35. Hegardt 2000:88
36. Mannheim 1990:84
37. Thomas 2000:167
38. Foucault 1997:74
39. Rigby 1984:192
40. Mannheim 1936:262–3
41. Childe 1960:282
42. Wilson 2005:46; Glazer 2005:7
43. Zinn 2004
44. Thomas 2004:233
45. Thomas 2004:238

Bibliography

'A Sinecure Fellow' 1872 'Strike, but Hear' *Macmillan's Magazine* 25 (1872):300–6
Abercromby, J 1912 *A Study of the Bronze Age Pottery of Great Britain and Ireland and its Assorted Grave-goods* Vol. I Oxford: Clarendon Press
Allen, G 1881 *Early Britain: Anglo-Saxon Britain* London: Society for Promoting Christian Knowledge
Ancient Order of Druids 1850 *Introductory Book* London: Thomas Brettell
Angell, N 1909 *The Great Illusion: A Study of the relation of Military Power to National Advantage* London: William Heinemann
anon 1820 'State of Society, &c, in Germany', *Quarterly Review* 23:434–54
anon 1873 Leader, *The Times* 21 August 1873:9
anon 1896 'Reginald Stuart Poole (1832–1895)' entry in S. Lee (ed), *Dictionary of National Biography* Vol. 46:101–3 London: Smith, Elder
anon 1907–8 Prefatory notes *Nature Cure Annual & Health and Pleasure Guide* London: Macgregor Reid & Shaw
anon 1912 'Debating Society' *The Pocklingtonian* Midsummer 1912:31–3
anon 1913 'Debating Society' *The Pocklingtonian* Lent 1913:21
anon 1916 'Science Club' *The Pocklingtonian* Lent 1916:17
anon 1918–19 Untitled notes *Victoria University of Manchester Almanac, Staff Lists etc 1918–19* Manchester: Victoria University of Manchester
anon 1921 'Autumn Meeting' *Transactions of the Woolhope Naturalists' Field Club* 1921-2-3:xxxii–xxxiv
anon 1924a 'Proceedings' *Transactions of the Woolhope Naturalists' Field Club* 1924-5-6:i–iii
anon 1924b 'First Field Meeting' *Transactions of the Woolhope Naturalists' Field Club* 1924-5-6:xiv–xv

anon 1924c 'Fourth Field Meeting', in *Transactions of the Woolhope Naturalists' Field Club* 1924-5-6:xxi
anon 1925 'Stonehenge as a Cemetery', leading article, *The Times* 28 August 1924
anon 1927 'Fourth Field Meeting' *Transactions of the Woolhope Naturalists' Field Club* 1927-8-9:xxiii
anon 1928a 'Second Winter Meeting' *Transactions of the Woolhope Naturalists' Field Club* 1927-8-9:xxxviii
anon 1928b 'First Field Meeting' *Transactions of the Woolhope Naturalists' Field Club* 1927-8-9:lx-lxi
anon 1930 'Third Field Meeting' *Transactions of the Woolhope Naturalists' Field Club* 1930-1-2:xxiv
anon 1931a 'Second Field Meeting' *Transactions of the Woolhope Naturalists' Field Club* 1930-1-2:liv
anon 1931b 'Third Winter Meeting' *Transactions of the Woolhope Naturalists' Field Club* 1930-1-2:lxvi-lxviii
anon 1931c 'Special General Meeting' *Transactions of the Woolhope Naturalists' Field Club* 1930-1-2:xliii, xlv-xlvi
anon 1933a 'First Field Meeting' *Transactions of the Woolhope Naturalists' Field Club* 1933-4-5:xvii
anon 1933b 'Evening Meeting' *Transactions of the Woolhope Naturalists' Field Club* 1933-4-5:xxi
anon 1934a 'The Institute of Archaeology' *Antiquity* 8 (1934):455-6
anon 1934b 'Fifth Winter Meeting' *Transactions of the Woolhope Naturalists' Field Club* 1933-4-5:l
anon 1935 'Spring Annual Meeting' *Transactions of the Woolhope Naturalists' Field Club* 1933-4-5:lxxxi
anon 1936 'Summary of Proceedings' *Proceedings of the Prehistoric Society* 2 (1936):147, 260
anon 1937 'Summary of Proceedings' *Proceedings of the Prehistoric Society* 3 (1937):489-92
anon 1943 (ed) 'Foreword' and 'Societies, Museums and Universities Officially Represented at the Conference', in University of London, Institute of Archaeology *Conference on the Future of Archaeology* London: University of London:4, 100
anon 2003 'A Baghdad bounce', leader, *The Guardian* 21 April 2003
Ap Llywellyn, A T 1924 'Druids and Stonehenge', letter, *Salisbury and Winchester Journal* 23 August 1924
Armstrong-Jones, R 1917 'The Psychopathy of the barbed wire', *Nature* 6 September 1917:1-3
Arnold, M 1867 *On the Study of Celtic Literature* London: Smith, Elder & Co
Arnold, T 1841 *An Inaugural Lecture on the Study of Modern History* Oxford: J H Parker

Ashbee, P 1960 *The Bronze Age Round Barrow in Britain: an Introduction to the Study of the Funerary Practice and Culture of the British and Irish Single-grave People of the Second Millennium B.C.* London: Phoenix House

Barker, G et al 2001 'Benchmarking Statement for Archaeology – January 2000' in Rainbird, P and Hamilakis, Y *Interrogating Pedagogies: Archaeology in Higher Education* Oxford: Archaeopress: 55–61

Barrow, L 1986 *Independent Spirits: Spiritualism and English Plebeians 1850–1910* London: Routledge & Kegan Paul

Becher, T 1989 *Academic Tribes and Territories: Intellectual Enquiry and the Cultures of Disciplines* Buckingham: Open University Press

Beddoe, J 1971 *The Races of Men: a Contribution to the Anthropology of Western Europe* London: Hutchinson [first edition 1885]

Belloc, H 1911 *The Old Road* London: A. Constable & Co. [first published 1904]

Bender, B et al 1998 *Stonehenge: Making Space* Oxford: Berg

Bennett, A et al 1929 'Stonehenge', letter in *The Times* 23 March 1929, signed by nine prominent figures

Bernfeld, S C 1951 'Freud and Archaeology' *America Imago* 8 (1951):107–28

Blatchford, R ('Nunquam') 1977 *Merrie England* London: The Journeyman Press [first published 1893]

Bowden, M 1991 *Pitt Rivers: The Life and Archaeological Work of Lieutenant-General Augustus Henry Lane Fox Pitt Rivers, DCL, FRS, FSA* Cambridge: Cambridge University Press

Bowden, M 2001 'Mapping the Past: O G S Crawford and the Development of Landscape Studies' *Landscapes* 2:29–45

Bowler, P J 1987 *Theories of Human Evolution: a Century of Debate, 1844–1944* Oxford: Basil Blackwell [first published 1986]

Bowler, P J 1989 *The Invention of Progress: the Victorians and the Past* Oxford: Basil Blackwell

Boym, Svetlana 2001 *The Future of Nostalgia* New York: Basic Books

Bradley, A G 1907 *Round About Wiltshire* London: Methuen

Brown, R A 1981 *Katharine Emma Maltwood, Artist 1878–1961* Victoria, BC: Sono Nis Press

Bryce, J 1918 'War and Human Progress', in Bryce, J *Essays and Addresses in War Time* London: Macmillan & Co 1918:65–91

Buckle, H T 1869, 1891 *History of Civilization in England* London: Longman, Green & Co [first published 1857 (Vol. 1) and 1861 (Vol. 2)]

Burkitt, M 1921 *Prehistory: A Study of Early Cultures in Europe and the Mediterranean Basin* Cambridge: Cambridge University Press

Burkitt, M 1970 'Reminiscences' *Antiquity* 44 (1970):254–7

Carbonell, B and Wauton, M 1949 *Thirteen Centuries in Bow alias Nymet Tracy with Broadnymet, Devon* Exeter: James Townsend & Sons

Bibliography

Carpenter, E **1889** *Civilisation: Its Cause and Cure and Other Essays* London: Swan Sonnenschein

Carr, E H **1977** *What is History?* Harmondsworth: Penguin [first published 1961]

Champion, T **2003** 'Egypt and the Diffusion of Culture' in D Jeffreys (ed), *Views of Ancient Egypt Since Napoleon Bonaparte: Imperialism, Colonialism and Modern Appropriation* London: UCL Press:127–46

Chapman, D E **1947** *Is This Your First Visit to Avebury?* London: HMSO [first published 1939]

Chapman, M **1978** *The Gaelic Vision in Scottish Culture* London: Croom Helm

Chapman, M **1992** *The Celts: The Construction of a Myth* Basingstoke: Macmillan

Chapman, R **1985** 'The Prehistoric Society, Prehistory and Society' *Proceedings of the Prehistoric Society* 51 (1985):15–29

Childe, V G **1926** *The Dawn of European Civilisation* London: Kegan Paul

Childe, V G **1933** 'Is Prehistory Practical?' *Antiquity* 7 (1933):410–18

Childe, V G **1935** 'Changing Methods and Aims in Prehistory: Presidential Address for 1935' *Proceedings of the Prehistoric Society* 1 (1935):1–15

Childe, V G **1936** *Man Makes Himself* London: Watts & Co

Childe, V G **1941** 'War in Prehistoric Societies' *Sociological Review* 32 (1941):127–38

Childe, V G **1944** *Progress and Archaeology* London: Watts & Co

Childe, V G **1951** *Social Evolution* London: Watts and Co

Childe, V G **1960** *What Happened in History* Harmondsworth: Penguin [first published 1942]

Chippindale, C **1978** 'The enclosure of Stonehenge' *Wiltshire Archaeological Magazine* 70-1 (1978):109–23

Chippindale, C **1983** *Stonehenge Complete* London: Thames & Hudson

Chippindale, C et al **1990** *Who Owns Stonehenge?* London: Batsford

Clark, J G D **1932** *The Mesolithic Age in Britain* Cambridge: Cambridge University Press

Clark, J G D **1939** *Archaeology and Society* London: Methuen

Clark, J G D **1943a** 'Education and the Study of Man' *Antiquity* 17 (1943):113–121

Clark, J G D **1943b** Discussion, on 'The Need for Planning', in University of London, Institute of Archaeology *Conference on the Future of Archaeology* London: University of London:62–3

Clark, J G D **1944** 'Water in Antiquity' *Antiquity* 18 (1944):1–15

Clark, J G D **1946** *From Savagery to Civilisation* London: Cobbett Press

Clark, J G D **1952** *Prehistoric Europe: The Economic Basis* London: Methuen

Clark, J G D **1958** 'O G S Crawford 1884–1957' *Proceedings of the British Academy* 44 (1958):281–96

Clark, J G D 1961 *World Prehistory: An Outline* Cambridge: Cambridge University Press

Clark, J G D 1974 'Prehistoric Europe' in G R Willy (ed), *Archaeological Researches in Retrospect* Cambridge (Mass): Winthrop:33–57

Clark, J G D 1976a 'New Perspectives in Canadian Archaeology: A Summation' in Mackay, A G (ed), *New Perspectives in Canadian Archaeology* Toronto: Royal Society of Canada

Clark, J G D 1976b 'Prehistory since Childe' *Bulletin of the London Institute of Archaeology* 13 (1976):1–21

Clark, J G D 1985 'The Prehistoric Society: From East Anglia to the World' *Proceedings of the Prehistoric Society* 51 (1985):1–13

Clark, J G D 1989 *Prehistory at Cambridge and Beyond* Cambridge: Cambridge University Press

Clay, R C C 1927a 'Some Prehistoric Ways', *Antiquity* 1 (1927):54–65

Clay, R C C 1927b 'Review of H J Massingham, *Downland Man*' *Antiquity* I (1927):12–2

Coates, R 1999 'The Survey of English Place-Names' *British Academy Review* July–December 1999. Online at www.britac.ac.uk/pubs/review/02-99b/15-coates.html

Collingwood, R G 1926 'Some perplexities about time, with an attempted solution' *Proceedings of the Aristotelian Society* ns 26 (1926):135–50

Collingwood, R G 1927a 'Oswald Spengler and the Theory of Historical Cycles' *Antiquity* 1 (1927):311–25

Collingwood, R G 1927b 'The Theory of Historical Cycles II. Cycles and Progress' *Antiquity* 1 (1927):435–46

Collingwood, R G 1928 'The Limits of Historical Knowledge' *Journal of Philosophical Studies* 3 (1928):213–22

Collingwood, R G 1939 *An Autobiography* Oxford: Oxford University Press

Corley, T A B 2001 'George Unwin: A Manchester Economic Historian Extraordinary', online at www.rdg.ac.uk/Econ/Econ/workingpapers/emdp435.pdf

Cornell, P 2000 'Post-structuralism and 'Archaeology': Michel Foucault and Jacques Derrida' in C Holtorf and H Karlsson (eds), *Philosophy and Archaeological Practice: Perspectives for the 21st Century* Goteborg: Bricoleur: 173–184

Costall, A 2001 'Pear and His Peers: The Beginnings of Psychology at Manchester' in G C Bunn, A D Lovie, and G D Richards (eds) *Psychology in Britain. Historical Essays and Personal Reflections*, Leicester: BPS Books:188–204

Cox, R H 1944 *The Green Roads of England* London: Methuen [first published 1914]

Crawford and Balcarres, Earl of 1924 'Druid Burial at Stonehenge. Lord Crawford's protest. Archaeology and Sentiment', Letter to *The Times* 28 August 1924

Bibliography

Crawford and Balcarres, Earl of 1925 'Presidential Anniversary Address' 27 June 1925 *Antiquaries Journal* 5 (1925):221–36
Crawford, O G S 1921 *Man and His Past* London: Humphrey Milford
Crawford, O G S 1924a 'The Origins of Civilisation' *Edinburgh Review* 239 (January–April 1924):101–16
Crawford, O G S 1924b 'Stonehenge', Letter to *The Times* 5 September 1924
Crawford, O G S 1927a Editorial Notes *Antiquity* 1(1927):1–4
Crawford, O G S 1927b Editorial Notes *Antiquity* 1 (1927):129–132
Crawford, O G S 1928 Editorial Notes *Antiquity* 2 (1928):385–6
Crawford, O G S 1929 Foreword to E C Curwen 1929 (unpaginated)
Crawford, O G S 1930 Notes and News *Antiquity* 4 (1930):352–78
Crawford, O G S 1931a 'Historical Cycles' *Antiquity* 5 (1931):5–20
Crawford, O G S 1931b Editorial Notes *Antiquity* 7 (1931):1–4
Crawford, O G S 1932 'Putting *The Past* in Its *Place*' *Russia To-day*, September 1932
Crawford, O G S 1934 review of R G Collingwood, *An Introduction to the Prehistory of Cumberland, Westmorland and Lancashire North of the Sands* in *Antiquity* 8 (1934):361–2
Crawford, O G S 1936a Editorial Notes in *Antiquity* 10 (1936):385–90
Crawford, O G S 1936b 'Human Progress: A Review' *Antiquity* 10 (1936):391–404
Crawford, O G S 1939 review of S Casson, 'The Discovery of Man' *Antiquity* 12 (1939):379–80
Crawford, O G S 1940 Editorial Notes *Antiquity* 14 (1940):113–6
Crawford, O G S 1949 Editorial Notes *Antiquity* 23 (1949):1–4
Crawford, O G S 1950 Editorial Notes *Antiquity* 24 (1950):1–2
Crawford, O G S 1951 'Archaeological History: A Review' *Antiquity* 25 (1951): 9–12
Crawford, O G S 1953 *Archaeology in the Field* London: Phoenix House 1953
Crawford, O G S 1954 letter to *The Listener* 27 January 1954
Crawford, O G S 1955 *Said and Done* London: Phoenix House
Crawford, O G S 1956 review of Joan Evans, 'A History of the Society of Antiquaries' *Antiquity* 30 (1956):230–2
Creasy, E S 1840 *The Spirit of Historical Study* London: Taylor and Walton
Crook, P 1994 *Darwinism, War and History: The Debate over the Biology of War from the 'Origin of Species' to the First World War* Cambridge: Cambridge University Press
Cunnington, R H 1935 *Stonehenge and Its Date* London: Methuen
Curtis, L P 1968 *Anglo-Saxons and Celts: A Study of Anti-Irish Prejudice in Victorian England* Bridgeport, CT: Conference on British Studies, University of Bridgeport

Curwen, E C 1929 *Prehistoric Sussex* London: The Homeland Association
Daniel, G 1944 'Anti-christ and my cat Toby' *Exposure* (Christmas Miscellany):20–2 (copy in Daniel MSS, Daniel/7/1/2)
Daniel, G 1959 Editorial Notes *Antiquity* 33 (1959):1–3
Daniel, G 1962 *The Idea of Prehistory* London: C A Watts
Daniel, G 1973 'Grafton Elliot Smith: Egypt and Diffusionism' in S Zuckerman et al 1973 *The Concepts of Human Evolution* London: Academic Press: 405–47
Daniel, G 1975 *A Hundred and Fifty Years of Archaeology* London: Duckworth
Daniel, G 1977 Editorial *Antiquity* 51 (1977):1–7
Daniel, G 1986 *Some Small Harvest* London: Thames & Hudson
Daniels, S 2006 'Lines of Sight: Alfred Watkins, Photography and Topography in Early Twentieth-Century Britain', *Tate Research*, Autumn 2006, online at www.tate.org.uk/research/tateresearch/tatepapers/06autumn/daniels.htm
Dark, S 1926 'The Editor's Table: Straight and Narrow Ways' *Church Times* 20 November 1926
Dart, R A 1974 'Sir Grafton Elliot Smith and the Evolution of Man', in A P Elkin and N W G Macintosh (eds) *Grafton Elliot Smith: The Man and His Work* Sydney: Sydney University Press: 25–38
Darwin, C 1874 *The Descent of Man* New York: A L Burt Co [first edition 1871]
Dawkins, W Boyd 1880 *Early Man in Britain and His Place in the Tertiary Period* London: MacMillan
Dawson, W R 1938 'A General Biography', in W R Dawson (ed) *Sir Grafton Elliot Smith. A Biographical Record by His Colleagues* London: Jonathan Cape: 17–120
Debray, R 1981 *Teachers, Writers, Celebrities* London: New Left Books
Dorson, R M 1968a *The British Folklorists: A History* Chicago: University of Chicago Press
Dorson, R M 1968b *Peasant Customs and Savage Myths: Selections from the British Folklorists* Vol. 2, London: Routledge & Kegan Paul
Dutt, W A 1926 *The Ancient Mark-Stones of East Anglia: Their Origin and Folklore* Lowestoft: Flood & Son
Edwards, B 2000 'Avebury and other not-so-ancient places: the making of the English heritage landscape' in H Kean, P Martin and S J Morgan (eds) *Seeing History: Public History in Britain Now* London: Francis Boutle: 65–79
Elkin, A P 1974 'Sir Grafton Elliot Smith: The Man and his Work – A personal testimony' in A P Elkin and N W G Macintosh (eds) *Grafton Elliot Smith: The Man and His Work* Sydney: Sydney University Press:8–15
Elwin, M (ed) 1975 *Letters of John Cowper Powys to his Brother Llewelyn* Vol. 2: 1925–1939 London: Village Press

Emerick, K 1998 'Sir Charles Peers and After: From Frozen Monuments to Fluid Landscapes' in J Arnold, K Davis and S Ditchfield (eds) *History and Heritage: Consuming the Past in Contemporary Culture* Shaftesbury: Donhead 1998:183–95

Engel, A J 1983 *From Clergyman to Don: The Rise of the Academic Profession in Nineteenth-century Oxford* Oxford: Clarendon Press

Engels, F 1892 *Socialism: Utopian and Scientific* London: Swan Sonnenschein

Engels, F 1972 *The Origin of the Family, Private Property and the State: In the Light of the Researches of Lewis H. Morgan* London: Lawrence & Wishart [first published 1884]

Engleheart, G 1927 'Druids in Britain', letters in *The Times* 2 and 12 November 1927

Engleheart, G 1930 'Concerning Orientation' *Antiquity* 4 (1930):340–6

Evans, J 1949 'The Royal Archaeological Institute: A Retrospect' *Archaeological Journal* 106 (1943):1–11

Evans, J 1956 *A History of the Society of Antiquaries* Oxford: Oxford University Press

Eversley, G 1910 *Commons, Forests and Footpaths: The Story of the Battle during the Last Forty-five Years for Public Rights over the Commons, Forests and Footpaths of England and Wales* London: Cassell

Eyerman, R 1994 *Between Culture and Politics: Intellectuals in Modern Society* Cambridge: Polity

Fagan, B 2001 *Grahame Clark: An Intellectual Life of an Archaeologist* Boulder, CO: Westview Press

Fagan, G T 2003 'Seductions of Pseudoarchaeology' *Archaeology* 56, 3 (2003):44–53

Fisher, D 1978 'The Rockefeller Foundation and the Development of Scientific Medicine in Great Britain' *Minerva* 16 (1978):20–41

Fosdick, R B 1952 *The Story of the Rockefeller Foundation* London: Odhams

Foucault, M 1997 *The Politics of Truth* (ed. Sylvere Lotringer and Lysa Hochroth) New York: Semiotext(e)

Fox, A 1944 'The place of archaeology in British education' *Antiquity* 18 (1944):153–7

Fox, A 2000 *Aileen – A Pioneering Archaeologist* Leominster: Gracewing

Fox, C 1930 'Excavations in the Cambridgeshire Dykes' in C Lucas *et al* (eds) *The Fenman's world. Memories of a Fenland Physician* Norwich: Jarrold & Sons

Fox, C 1932 *The Personality of Britain: Its Influence on Inhabitant and Invader in Prehistoric and Early Historic Times* Cardiff: National Museum of Wales

Fox, C 1943 'Summing up', in University of London, Institute of Archaeology *Conference on the Future of Archaeology* London: University of London: 96–9

Fox, C 1945 *A Find of the Early Iron Age from Llyn Cerrig Bach, Anglesey: Interim Report* Cardiff: National Museum of Wales

Frazer, Sir J G 1908 *The Scope of Social Anthropology. A Lecture [Inaugural] Delivered before the University of Liverpool* London: Macmillan

Freidson, E 1970 *Profession of Medicine: A Study of the Sociology of Applied Knowledge* New York: Dodd, Mead & Company

Freidson, E 1983 'The Theory of Professions: State of the Art' in R Dingwall and P Lewis (eds) *The Sociology of the Professions: Lawyers, Doctors and Others* London: Macmillan

Freud, S 1918 *Totem and Taboo: Resemblances between the Psychic Lives of Savages and Neurotics* New York: Moffat, Yard and Co [first published 1912–13]

Freud, S 1949 'Thoughts for the Times on War and Death', *Collected Papers IV* (1949):288–317 [written in 1915]

Freud, S 1952 'Civilisation and its Discontents', *Britannica Great Books of the Western World 54 (Sigmund Freud)* 1952:767–802 [written in 1929]

Fukuyama, F 1992 *The End of History and the Last Man* Harmondsworth: Penguin

Gay, P 1969 *The Enlightenment: An Interpretation* New York: Vintage Books [first published 1966]

Geertz, C 1993 *The Interpretation of Cultures: Selected Essays* London: Fontana

Gellner, E 1988 'Leaves from the Golden Bough' *Times Higher Education Supplement* 15 January 1988:18

Glazer, Peter 2005 *Radical Nostalgia: Spanish Civil War Commemoration in America* Rochester, NY: University of Rochester Press

Goldstein, D 1983 'The Professionalisation of History in the Late Nineteenth and Early Twentieth Centuries' *Storia della Storiografia* 3 (1983):3–26

Gosden, C 1999 *Anthropology and Archaeology: A Changing Relationship* London: Routledge

Gosden, P H J H 1973 *Self-Help: Voluntary Associations in Nineteenth-Century Britain* London: Batsford

Gramsci, A 1971 *Selections from the 'Prison Notebooks'* (ed Q Hoare and G N Smith) London: Lawrence & Wishart

Grayson, J 1992 *In Quest of Jessie Weston* in R. Barber (ed) *Arthurian Studies* XI (1992):1–80

Greenwell, W 1877 *British Barrows: A Record of the Examination of Sepulchral Barrows in Various Parts of England*. Oxford: Clarendon Press

Grey, P 1923 *Shepherd's Crown: A Volume of Essays* Oxford: Basil Blackwell

Griffiths, R 1980 *Fellow-Travellers of the Right: British Enthusiasts for Nazi Germany 1933–9* London: Constable

Grigson, G 1984 *Recollections, Mainly of Writers and Artists* London: Chatto & Windus

Grinsell, L 1988 'Alfred Watkins and *The Old Straight Track*' *Transactions of the Woolhope Naturalists' Field Club* 1988:76–9

Hando, F 1934a ' "Ley Spotting" as you ramble in Gwent. Prehistoric Pointers of the Countryside. Sighting points on the old-time track-ways' *South Wales Argus* 17 April 1934

Hando, F 1934b 'Ley spotting in Gwent' *South Wales Argus* 18 April 1934

Hando, F 1934c 'Straight Tracks in the Heart of England. Enthusiasts' Examinations near Salisbury' *South Wales Argus* 9 August 1934

Hando, F 1944 *The Pleasant Land of Gwent* Newport: R H Johns

Hando, F 1958 *Out and About in Monmouthshire* Newport: R H Johns

Harper, H C 1979 'Straight Track Portfolios: A Guide to their Contents' Hereford: Hereford Philosophical and Antiquarian Society

Harris, H A 1938 'At University College', in W R Dawson (ed) *Sir Grafton Elliot Smith. A Biographical Record by his Colleagues* London: Jonathan Cape: 169–82

Harrison, J E 1923 review of 'Evolution and the Dragon', *Folk-Lore* 34 (1923):177–81

Harte, J 1997 'Taking leave of Dod' *The Ley Hunter* 126 (1997):21–5

Harvey, J H 1940 *The Heritage of Britain: Our Historic Past through 53 Centuries* London: The Right Review

Hauser, K 2003 *Photography and the Archaeological Imagination: Britain c1927–1951* Unpublished DPhil dissertation, University of Oxford

Haverfield, F J 1905 *The Romanization of Roman Britain* London: H. Frowde

Haverfield, F J 1908/9 'Military Aspects of Roman Wales' *Transactions of the Honourable Society of Cymmrodorion*: 53–187

Haverfield, F J 1924 *Roman Occupation of Britain* revised by George Macdonald Oxford: Clarendon Press

Hawkes, C and Hawkes, J 1933 'Prehistoric Britain in 1933: a review of periodical publications' *Archaeological Journal* 90 (1933):315–38

Hawkes, C and Hawkes, J 1934 'Prehistoric Britain in 1934: a review of periodical publications' *Archaeological Journal* 91 (1934):301–29

Hawkes, C and Hawkes, J 1958 *Prehistoric Britain* Harmondsworth: Penguin [first published 1944]

Hawkes, C 1932 'Prehistoric Britain in 1931 and 1932: a review of periodical publications' *Archaeological Journal* 89 (1932):275–97

Hawkes, J 1951 'A Quarter Century of Antiquity', *Antiquity* 25 (1951): 171–3. Online at antiquity.ac.uk/Listing/hawkesed.html)

Hawkes, J 1967 'God in the Machine' *Antiquity* 41 (1967):174–180

Hawkes, J 1982 *Mortimer Wheeler: Adventurer in Archaeology* London: Weidenfeld & Nicolson

Hawley, W *et al* 1921 'The Excavations at Stonehenge' *Antiquaries' Journal* 1 (1921):19–41

Head, A (ed) 1996 *The Letters of John Cowper Powys to Philippa Powys* London: Cecil Woolf

Head, H 1924 'William Halse Rivers Rivers' Obituary Notices of Fellows Deceased, *Proceedings of the Royal Society of London. Series B, Containing Papers of a Biological Character*, 95 (1924):xliii–lxvii

Hegardt, J 2000 'Kwame Gyeke, Emmanuel Levinas, and the Emergence of the Other' in C Holtorf and H Karlsson *Philosophy and Archaeological Practice: Perspectives for the 21st Century* Goteborg: Bricoleur:87–106

Hencken, H 1945 'The London Conferences on Archaeology 1943 and 1944' *Archaeological Journal* 102 (1945):1–11

Heselton, P 1986 *Tony Wedd: New Age Pioneer* Hull: Northern Earth Mysteries

Hewitt, A T M 1966 *The story of Fordingbridge in fact and fancy* Fordingbridge: A T M Hewitt

Hewitt, A T M 1971 *Roman villa, West Park, Rockbourne, near Fordingbridge, Hants: a fully illustrated report* Fordingbridge: A T M Hewitt

Hingley, R 2000 *Roman Officers and English Gentlemen: The imperial origins of Roman archaeology* London: Routledge

Hingley, R 2001 'Profession and academic: the teaching of heritage management' in Rainbird, P and Hamilakis, Y *Interrogating Pedagogies: Archaeology in higher education* Oxford: Archaeopress: 89–92

'Hob Nob' 1939 'Looking Round: The Trek to Stonehenge' *Salisbury Journal* 23 June 1939:8

Hobbes, T 1651 *Leviathan* Online at http://oregonstate.edu/instruct/phl302/texts/hobbes/leviathan-c.html#

Hodder, I 1992 *Theory and Practice in Archaeology* London: Routledge

Hodgkin, T 1891 'Opening Address of the Historical Section at the Meeting of the Institute at Edinburgh' *Archaeological Journal* 48 (1891):263–73

Holtorf, C 1996 'Why fascists don't like "post-processualism" ', in *Assemblage* 1. Online at www.assemblage.group.shef.ac.uk/1/holtorf.html

Hooke, S H 1927 'Diffusionism with a Difference' *American Anthropologist* 29 (1927) p 621

Hooper, W G 1935 *Ether and the Living Universe* London: C W Daniel

Hooper, W G 1941 *The Beloved* Bournemouth: The Author

Hoskins, W G 1983 *Fieldwork in Local History* London: Book Club Associates [first published 1967]

Hudson, H 1932 'Ancient Sun Alignments: The Meaning of Artificial Mounds and Mark Stones' *Proceedings of the Suffolk Institute of Archaeology and Natural History* 21 (1932):120–138

Hutton, R 1999 *The Triumph of the Moon: A History of Modern Pagan Witchcraft* Oxford: Oxford University Press

Hutton, R 2007 *The Druids: A History* London: Hambledon Continuum

Huxley, T H 1873 'On Some Fixed Points in British Ethnology' in Huxley, *Critiques and Addresses* London: Macmillan, pp 167–80 [first published 1871]

James, F R 1922 'Presidential Address' *Transactions of the Woolhope Naturalists' Field Club* 1921-2-3:xlviii

Janssen, R M 1992 *The First Hundred Years: Egyptology at University College London 1892–1992* London: UCL
Jenkins, G H 2005 (ed) *A Rattleskull Genius: The Many Faces of Iolo Morganwg* Cardiff: University of Wales Press
Joel, C 1950 'William James Perry, 1887–1949' *Man* 50 (1950):6–7
Johnson, T J 1972 *Professions and Power* London: Macmillan
Jones, J 2002 '30,000 years of modern art' *Guardian Weekend* 15 June 2002:18–19
Jowett, F W 1925 *What Made Me a Socialist* London: Independent Labour Party Publications Department
Keith, A 1915a *The Antiquity of Man*, London: Williams and Norgate
Keith, A 1915b 'War as a Factor in Racial Evolution', *St Thomas's Hospital Gazette* 25 (December 1915):153–162
Keith, A 1916 'On Certain Factors Concerned in the Evolution of Human Races', Presidential Address, *Journal of the Royal Anthropological Institute* 46 (1916):10–24
Keith, A 1931 *The Place of Prejudice in Modern Civilization (Prejudice and Politics)* London: Williams and Norgate
Keith, A 1934 'Aryans and Semites: A Race without a Homeland', Letter, *The Times*, 13 August 1934, p. 6
Kendrick, T D 1925 *The Axe Age: A Study in British Prehistory* London: Methuen
Kendrick, T D 1927 *The Druids: A Study in Keltic Prehistory* London: Methuen
Knox, R 1862 *The Races of Men: A Philosophical Enquiry into the Influence of Race over the Destinies of Nations* London: Henry Renshaw [first edition 1850]
Korg, J 1963 *George Gissing: A Critical Biography* Seattle: University of Washington Press
Krissdottir, M and Peers, R (eds) 1998 *The Dorset Year: The Diary of John Cowper Powys, June 1934–July 1935* Kilmersdon: The Powys Press
Kropotkin, P 1902 *Mutual Aid: A Factor of Evolution* London: William Heinemann. Online at www.spunk.org/library/writers/kropotki/sp001503/conclu.html
Kuklick, H 1991 *The Savage Within: The Social History of British Anthropology, 1885–1945* Cambridge: Cambridge University Press
Landau, M 1991 *Narratives of Human Evolution* Yale UP: New Haven and London
Langham, I 1981 *The Building of British Social Anthropology: W H R Rivers and his Cambridge Disciples in the Development of Kinship Studies 1898–1931* Dordrecht, London: Reidel
Lansdown, G 1925 *Stonehenge* Trowbridge: B Lansdown
LAW 1997 (Lampeter Archaeology Workshop) 'Relativism, objectivity and the politics of the past' *Archaeological Dialogues* 4:164–98

LeBlanc, S A 2003 'Prehistory of War', *Archaeology* 56, 3 (2003):18–25

Leeds, E T 1947 *A Saxon Village near Sutton Courtenay, Berkshire* Oxford: Frederick Hall

Lethbridge, T C 1930 'The Anglo-Saxon cemetery, Burwell, Cambs' in C. Lucas *et al* 1930 *The Fenman's World: Memories of a Fenland Physician* Norwich: Jarrold & Sons

Levine, P 1986 *The Amateur and the Professional: Antiquarians, Historians and Archaeologists in Victorian England, 1838–1886* Cambridge: Cambridge University Press

Lewis, D W 1924 'The English Humorist [*sic*]. At the sign of the Blue Moon' *Daily Mail* 3 September 1924

Lewis, D W 1924–5 Review of G E Smith, 'Essays on the Evolution of Man', *Criterion* 3 (1924–5):311–15

Lockyer, Sir N 1906 *Stonehenge and Other British Stone Monuments, Astronomically Considered* London: Macmillan

Long, G 1930 *The Folklore Calendar* London: P. Allan

Lowenthal, D 1985 *The Past is a Foreign Country* Cambridge: Cambridge University Press

Lowerson, J 1992 'The Mystical Geography of the English' in B Short (ed) *The English Rural Community* Cambridge: Cambridge University Press:152–74

Lubbock, Sir J 1870 *The Origin of Civilisation and the Primitive Condition of Man: Mental and Social Conditions of Savages* London: Longman, Green & Co

Mackmurdo, A H 1926 'The Cobbled Way at York', letter to *The Times*, 3 September 1926

Mackmurdo, A H 1933 *A People's Charter, or, The Terms of Prosperity and Freedom within a Community* London: Williams & Norgate

Malinowski, B 1922 'Ethnology and the Study of Society' *Economica* 2 (1922):208–19

Malinowski, B 1924 'New and Old Anthropology' *Nature* 113 (1 March 1924): 299–301

Maltwood, K 1935 *A Guide to Glastonbury's Temple of the Stars* London: John Watkins

Manley, V S 1932 'First Wonder of the Land. Druid Lament at Stonehenge.' *Wiltshire Times* 2 July 1932 in WANHS Box 80 Mss 935 (Manley, f 19)

Mannheim, K 1936 *Ideology and Utopia: An Introduction to the Sociology of Knowledge* (trans. by L. Wirth and E. Shils) London: Kegan Paul & Co

Mannheim, K 1990 'Competition as a Cultural Phenomenon', in V Meja and N Stehr (eds) *Knowledge and Politics: the Sociology of Knowledge Dispute* London: Routledge 1990: 53–85; first published 1928

Marett, R R 1908 Preface to *Anthropology and the Classics* (ed R R Marett), Oxford: Clarendon Press

Marshall, G 1938 'Obituary Memoir: Alfred Watkins FRPS, JP' *Transactions of the Woolhope Naturalists' Field Club 1933–35*:165–7

Martin, W 1967 *The New Age under Orage: Chapters in English Cultural History* Manchester: Manchester University Press

Marx, K and Engels, F 1888 *Manifesto of the Communist Party* London

Massingham, H J 1926 *Downland Man* London: Jonathan Cape

Massingham, H J 1927 *The Golden Age: The Story of Human Nature* London: Gerald Howe

Massingham, H J 1935 *Through the Wilderness* London: Cobden & Sanderson

Massingham, H J 1942 *Remembrance. An Autobiography* London: B T Batsford

Matless, D 1993 'Appropriate Geography: Patrick Abercrombie and the Energy of the World' *Journal of Design History* 6:3:167–178

Matless, D 1998 *Landscape and Englishness* London: Reaktion Books

Matless, D *in press* 'East Anglian Stones: erratic prehistories from the early twentieth century'

Maxwell, D 1932a 'Travels with a Sketch-Book: 1. The Clue of the Grey Snail' *Church Times* August 19 1932

Maxwell, D 1932b 'Travels with a Sketch-Book: 5. The Clue of the Invisible Lines' *Church Times* September 16 1932

Maxwell, D 1932c *A Detective in Surrey: Landscape Clues to Invisible Roads* London: John Lane

Maxwell, D 1933 *A Detective in Essex: Landscape Clues to an Essex of the Past* London: John Lane

McLennan, J 1896 *Studies in Ancient History: The Second Series: Comprising an Inquiry into the Origin of Exogamy* (eds E McLennan, A Platt) London: Macmillan

Mee, J 2005 ' "Images of Truth New Born": Iolo, William Blake and the Literary Radicalism of the 1790s', in Geraint H Jenkins (ed), *A Rattleskull Genius: The Many Faces of Iolo Morganwg* Cardiff: University of Wales Press: 173–93

Mellor, D (ed) 1987 *A Paradise Lost: The Neo-Romantic Imagination in Britain 1935–55* London: Lund Humphries

Mercer, R 1998 'Stuart Piggott 1910–1996' *Proceedings of the British Academy* 97 (1998):413–42

Miles, D 1968 *The Royal National Eisteddfod of Wales* Swansea: Christopher Davies

Morgan, L H 1877 *Ancient Society, or, Researches in the Lines of Human Progress from Savagery, through Barbarism to Civilization* Chicago: C H Kerr

Morgan, P 1983 'From a death to a view: the hunt for the Welsh past in the Romantic period' in E Hobsbawm and T Ranger (eds) *The Invention of Tradition* Cambridge: Cambridge University Press:43–100

Morton, H V 1942 *I Saw Two Englands: The Record of a Journey before the War, and after the Outbreak of War, in the Year 1939* London: Methuen

Mowat, C L 1968 *Britain between the Wars 1918–1940* London: Methuen [first edition 1955]

Murray, L J 1999 *A Zest for Life: The Story of Alexander Keiller* Wootton Bassett: Morven Books

Myres, J L 1911 *The Dawn of History* London: Williams and Norgate

Myres, J L 1916 *The Influence of Anthropology on the Course of Political Science* Berkeley: University of California Press

Myres, J L 1943 'The Need for Planning' in University of London, Institute of Archaeology *Conference on the Future of Archaeology* London: University of London: 54–6

Myres, J L 1951 Foreword in W F Grimes (ed), *Aspects of Archaeology in Britain and beyond: Essays Presented to O.G.S. Crawford* London: H W Edwards

Nichols, R 1990 *The Book of Druidry* (John Matthews and Philip Carr-Gomm, eds) Wellingborough: Aquarian

O'Neil, B H St J 1946 'The Congress of Archaeological Societies' *Antiquaries Journal* 26 (1946):61–6

Oates, C and Wood, J 1998 *A Coven of Scholars: Margaret Murray and her Working Methods* London: Folklore Society

Orage, A R 1926 'Socialism', *The New Age* 38, 20 (18 March 1926):235

Ormsby-Gore, W G 1935 'Address' *Report of the 43rd Annual Congress of Archaeological Societies* 1936:7–12

Orwell, G 1984 *Coming Up For Air* Harmondsworth: Penguin [first published 1939]

Parr, S 1801 *A Spital Sermon, Preached at Christ Church, upon Easter Tuesday, April 15, 1800* London: J Mawman

Paul, L 1951 *Angry Young Man* London: Faber & Faber

Peacock, A 1945 *Yours Fraternally* London: Pendulum Publications

Peake, H 1922 *The Bronze Age and the Celtic World* London: Benn Brothers

Pear, T H 1960 'Some Early Relations between English Ethnologists and Psychologists', *Journal of the Royal Anthropological Institute* 90 (1960):227–37

Pearson, K 1909 *The Problem of Practical Eugenics* London: Dulau and Co

Pearson, M and Shanks, M 2001 *Theatre/Archaeology: Disciplinary Dialogues* London: Routledge

Peet, T E 1924 Review of W J Perry, 'The Origin of Magic and Religion', *Journal of Egyptian Archaeology* 10 (1924):63–9

Pennick, N and Devereux, P 1989 *Lines on the Landscape: Leys and Other Linear Enigmas* London: Hale

Penty, A J 1906 *The Restoration of the Gild System* London: Swan Sonnenschein & Co

Perry, W J 1917a 'An Ethnological Study of Warfare', *Manchester Memoirs* 61(1917) no. 6

Perry, W J 1917b 'The Peaceable Habits of Primitive Communities: An Anthropological Study of the Golden Age' *Hibbert Journal* 16 (October 1917–July 1918):28–46

Perry, W J 1918 'War and Civilization: A Lecture' *Bulletin of the John Rylands Library* 4 (February–July 1918)

Perry, W J 1921-2 'The relation of class division to social conduct' *Hibbert Journal* 20 (1921-2):507–23

Perry, W J 1923 *The Children of the Sun: A Study in the Early History of Civilisation* London: Methuen

Perry, W J 1927 *The Children of the Sun: A Study in the Early History of Civilisation* (2nd edn) London: Methuen

Perry, W J 1931 'Anthropology and the Social Sciences' *The Highway* November 1931:23–5

Perry, W J 1935 *The Primordial Ocean: An Introductory Contribution to Social Psychology* London: Methuen

Perry, W J 1937 *The Growth of Civilisation* Harmondsworth: Penguin [first published in 1926]

Perry, W J 1938 'Anthropologist and Ethnologist', W R Dawson (ed) *Sir Grafton Elliot Smith. A Biographical Record by His Colleagues* London: Jonathan Cape:205–15

Petrie, W M F 1883 *The Pyramids and Temples of Gizeh* London: Field and Tuer

Petrie, W M F 1911 *The Revolutions of Civilisation* London: Harper & Brothers

Petrie, W M F 1928a 'Historical Cycles' *Antiquity* 2 (1928):207–8

Petrie, W M F 1928b Review of *The Beginnings of Things* series *Antiquity* 2 (1928):113–4

Phillips, C W 1987 *My Life in Archaeology* Gloucester: Sutton

Piggott, S 1935 *The Progress of Early Man* London: A & C Black

Piggott, S 1937 'Prehistory and the Romantic Movement' *Antiquity* 11 (1937):31–8

Piggott, S 1940 Review of J G D Clark, *Archaeology & Society* in *Antiquaries Journal* 20 (1940):399–400

Piggott, S 1948a 'Archaeology and the Amateur' *Archaeological News Letter* 1 (April 1948):1–2

Piggott, S 1948b letter in *Archaeological News Letter* 4 (July 1948):10

Piggott, S 1958 'Vere Gordon Childe 1892–1957' *Proceedings of the British Academy* 44:305–12

Piggott, S 1963 'Archaeology and Prehistory: Presidential Address' *Proceedings of the Prehistoric Society* 29 (1963–4):1–16

Piggott, S 1989 'Archaeological Retrospect', in G Daniel and C Chippindale, *The Pastmasters* London: Thames & Hudson 1989 (originally in *Antiquity* 57 (1983):28–37

Piper, J 1949 'Stonehenge' *Architectural Review* 106 (1949):177–82

Pohl, W 1926a 'War and Human Nature' *Youth* I (March 1926):12–13

Pohl, W 1926b 'The Origins of War' *Youth* II (April 1926):28–9

Powys, J C 1966 *Maiden Castle* London: Macdonald [first published 1937]

Pye, D 1995 *Fellowship is Life: The National Clarion Cycling Club, 1895–1995* Bolton: Clarion

Quennell, M and Quennell, C H B 1922 *Everyday Life in the New Stone, Bronze & Early Iron Ages* London: B T Batsford

Radcliffe-Brown, A R 1931 'The Present Position of Anthropological Studies' *Report of the British Association for the Advancement of Science* 1931:141–71

Ramsden, E A 1939 *The Spirit of Dorset* Dorchester (?): Dorset Federation of Women's Institutes

Randall-MacIver, D 1933 'Archaeology as a Science' *Antiquity* 7 (1933):5–20

Read, C H 1921 Foreword to *Antiquaries' Journal* 1 (1921):1–2

Reade, H 1921 'Castles and Camps of South Herefordshire' *Transactions of the Woolhope Naturalists' Field Club* 1921:1–17

Reason, J 1931 'A Lone Woman's Hike from Glastonbury to Winchester' *The Hiker and Camper* 1 (February 1931):36–8

Reed, T D 1948 letter in *Archaeological News Letter* 2 (May 1948):7

Reid, G W 1893 *The Natural Basis of Civilization* London: Proletarian Publishing Company

Reid, G W 1907 editorial, *The Nature Cure*, 2 no. 13, September 1907

Reid, G W 1913 review of A H Mackmurdo, 'Pressing Questions', *The New Life* 1913:281–3

Rhys, J 1904 *Celtic Britain* London: Society for Promoting Christian Knowledge [first published 1882]

Richards, G 2004 'Smith, Sir Grafton Elliot (1871–1937)' *Oxford Dictionary of National Biography* Oxford: Oxford University Press

Ridgeway, W 1909 'Presidential Address: The Relation of Anthropology to Classical Studies' *Journal of the Royal Anthropological Institute* 39 (1909):10–25

Rieff, P 1960 *Freud: The Mind of the Moralist* London: Victor Gollancz

Rigby, A 1984 *Initiation and Initiative: An Exploration of the Life and Ideas of Dimitrije Mitrinovic* Boulder, CO: East European Monograph Press

Rivers, W H R 1917 'Freud's Psychology of the Unconscious', *The Lancet* 16 June 1917:912–14

Rivers, W H R 1919 'Inaugural Address as Chairman of the British Psychological Society' *The Lancet* 24 May 1919:889–92

Rivers, W H R 1922a Witness statement, *Report of the War Office Committee of Enquiry into 'Shell-Shock'* London: HMSO: 55–7

Rivers, W H R 1922b *History and Ethnology* London: Society for Promoting Christian Knowledge

Bibliography

Rivers, W H R 1922c 'Presidential Address: The Unity of Anthropology' *Journal of the Royal Anthropological Institute* 52 (1922):12–25

Rivers, W H R 1924 *Instinct and the Unconscious: A Contribution to a Biological Theory of the Psycho-neuroses* Cambridge: Cambridge University Press [first edition 1920]

Samuel, R 1994 *Theatres of Memory* Vol. 1: *Past and Present in Contemporary Culture* London and New York: Verso

Sandell, R 1988 'Notes Towards a Social History of Ley-Hunting' *Magonia* 29 April

Sandon, H 1928 'The Recapitulation Myth', *Youth* 2 (12) Feb 1928:244–7

Sassoon, S 1919 *Picture Show* Cambridge: Cambridge University Press

Scott-Fox C 2002 *Cyril Fox, Archaeologist Extraordinary* Oxford: Oxbow

Screeton, P 1993 *Seekers of the Linear Vision* Santa Barbara, California: Stonehenge Viewpoint

Seaburg, Alan 2004 'The Last Two Universalist Parsons in the United Kingdom: George Watson Macgregor Reid and Arthur Peacock' *Transactions of the Unitarian Historical Society* 23:2, April 2004:530–62

Shanks, E 1935 'The Old King Cole legend: When Theorist Meets Theorist' *Sunday Times* 5 May 1935

Shanks, M and Tilley, C 1987 *Social Theory and Archaeology* Cambridge: Polity

Shanks, M 1991 *Experiencing the Past: On the Character of Archaeology* London: Routledge

Sharples, N 1991 *The English Heritage Book of Maiden Castle* London: Batsford and English Heritage

Shephard, B 1996 ' "The early treatment of Mental Disorders": R G Rows and Maghull 1914–1918' in H Freeman and G E Berrios (eds) *150 Years of British Psychiatry Volume II: the Aftermath* London: Athlone 1996:434–64

Shephard, B 2000 *A War of Nerves* London: Jonathan Cape

Shoesmith, R 1990 *Alfred Watkins: A Herefordshire Man* Little Logaston: Logaston Press

Slade, J J 1936 'George Engleheart' *Wiltshire Gazette* 26 March 1936:10

Slee, P R H 1986 *Learning and a Liberal Education: The Study of Modern History in the Universities of Oxford, Cambridge and Manchester, 1800–1914* Manchester: Manchester University Press

Slotkin, J S 1948 'Reflections on Collingwood's Idea of History' *Antiquity* 22 (1948):98–102

Smiles, S 1994 *The Image of Antiquity: Ancient Britain and the Romantic Imagination* New Haven and London: Yale University Press

Smiles, S 2004 'Antiquity and Modern Art in Britain, c.1930–1959' *Archaeological Review from Cambridge* 19.1 (2004):81–98

Smiles, S 2005 'Thomas Guest and Paul Nash in Wiltshire: Two Episodes in the Artistic Approach to British Antiquity' in S Smiles and S Moser (eds), *Envisioning the Past: Archaeology and the Image* Oxford: Blackwell:133–57

Smith, G E 1912 'Presidential Address', in British Association of the Advancement of Science, *Report of Dundee Meeting: Address, Reports and Abstracts of Papers* London: BAAS: 575–98

Smith, G E 1915 'The Influence of Racial Admixture in Egypt' *Eugenics Review* 7 (1915):163–83

Smith, G E 1916a 'Shock and the Soldier' *The Lancet* 15 April 1916:813–16

Smith, G E 1916b 'Primitive Man' *Proceedings of the British Academy* 7 (1915–16):455–504

Smith, G E 1916c 'Men of the Old Stone Age' *American Museum Journal* 16 (1916):319–25

Smith, G E 1919 *The Evolution of the Dragon* Manchester: University Press

Smith, G E 1922 'Anthropology' *Encyclopaedia Britannica* 12th edition, I:143–154

Smith, G E 1923a *University College London: New Building for the Department of Anatomy and Extension of the Physiological Institute, opened by His Majesty the King May 31 1923* London: University College

Smith, G E 1923b 'The Scope and Equipment of an Anatomical Institute' *British Medical Journal* 17 July 1923:67–8

Smith, G E 1924a 'The Galton Lecture' *Eugenics Review* 16 (1924):1–8

Smith, G E 1924b 'University College (London), Department of Anatomy' in Rockefeller Foundation, Division of Medical Education *Methods and Problems of Medical Science,* first series New York: Rockefeller Foundation:11–24

Smith, G E 1924c *The Evolution of Man: Essays* London: H Milford, Oxford University Press

Smith, G E 1925a 'Anthropology' in *Evolution in the Light of Modern Knowledge: A Collective Work* London: Blackie

Smith, G E 1925b 'Races of the Empire. Anthropology and Policy. Need of Trained Advisers', letter in *The Times* 17 January 1925

Smith, G E 1926a 'Dr Rivers and the New Vision in Ethnology', introduction to W H R Rivers *Psychology and Ethnology,* London: Kegan Paul, Trench, Trubner & Co 1926:ix–xxviii

Smith, G E 1926b 'India and Egypt', letter in *The Times,* 27 September 1926

Smith, G E 1927 *The Evolution of Man* (2nd edn) Oxford: Oxford University Press

Smith, G E 1928 *Conversion in Science* London: Macmillan

Smith, G E 1929 'Natural Man. Living at Peace' letter in *The Times* 18 November 1929

Smith, G E 1931 'The Origin of Civilisation' *The Highway: Journal of the Workers Educational Association* October 1931:4–8

Smith, G E 1934a *Human History,* 2nd edn London: Jonathan Cape

Smith, G E 1934b 'Marriage with Jewess', letter to *The Times* 22 May 1934

Bibliography

Smith, G E 1938 'Nordic Race Claims', in W R Dawson (ed) *Sir Grafton Elliot Smith. A Biographical Record by his Colleagues* London: Jonathan Cape: 257–61

Smith, G E and Pear, T H 1917a *Shell Shock and its Lessons* Manchester: University Press

Smith, G E and Pear, T H 1917b 'Response' *Nature* 27 September 1917:64–6

Smith, G W 1945 Letter to *Clapham Observer*, 10 August 1945:5

Smith, P J 1997 'Grahame Clark's New Archaeology: The Fenland Research Committee and Cambridge Prehistory in the 1930s' *Antiquity* 71 (1997):11–30

Smith, P J 1998 *From 'Small, Dark and Alive' to 'Crippingly Shy': Dorothy Garrod as the First Woman Professor at Cambridge University.* Online at www.geocities.com/Athens/Aegean/8481/

Smith, P J 1999 ' "The Coup": How did the Prehistoric Society of East Anglia become the Prehistoric Society?' *Proceedings of the Prehistoric Society* 65 (1999):465–70

Snauwaert, D and Theobald, P 1994 'Two Liberal Trajectories of Civic Education: The Political and Educational Thought of Hobbes and Winstanley' *Journal of Educational Thought/Revue de la Pensée Educative* 28 (1994):179–97

Sollas, W J 1924 *Ancient Hunters and their Modern Representatives* London: Methuen [first edition 1911]

Somerville, B 1927 'Orientation' *Antiquity* 1 (1927):31–41

Soul, J [1927] *Stonehenge and the Ancient Mysteries* Amesbury, privately printed, nd [1927]

Spence, J L 1928 *The Mysteries of Britain; or, the Secret Rites and Traditions of Ancient Britain restored* London: Rider & Co

Spencer, F 1990 *Piltdown: A Scientific Forgery* London: Natural History Museum

Squire, Sir J 1936 'The Past of St Albans' *Daily Telegraph* 8 September 1936

Stepan, N L 1987 ' "Nature's Pruning Hook": War, Race and Evolution, 1914–18' in J M W Bean (ed) *The Political Culture of Modern Britain: Studies in memory of Stephen Koss* London: Hamish Hamilton: 129–48

Stevens, F 1924 *Stonehenge Today and Yesterday* London: HMSO [first published 1916]

Stevenson, J 1984 *British Society 1914–45* Harmondsworth: Penguin

Stocking, G 1992 *The Ethnographer's Magic and Other Essays in the History of Anthropology* Madison, WI: University of Wisconsin Press

Stocking, G W 1987 *Victorian Anthropology* New York: Free Press

Stocking, G W 1996 *After Tylor: British Social Anthropology 1888–1951* London: Athlone

Stoddart, S and Malone, C 2002 *Antiquity* Editorial 76 (2002):1063–5
Stopford, J 1938 'The Manchester Years' in W R Dawson (ed) *Sir Grafton Elliot Smith. A Biographical Record by His Colleagues* London: Jonathan Cape: 151–65
Stout, A 2003 'The World Turned Upside Down: Stonehenge Summer Solstice Before the Hippies' *3rd Stone* 46 (2003):38–42
Stout, A 2004 *Choosing a Past: The Politics of Prehistory in Pre-war Britain* unpublished PhD thesis, University of Wales Lampeter
Stout, A 2005 'Universal Majesty, Verity & Love Infinite: A Life of George Watson Macgregor Reid' Lewes: OBOD, online at druidry.org/pdfs/fifth_mt_haemus_lecture.pdf
Stout, A 2006 *What's Real and What is Not: Reflections Upon Archaeology and Earth Mysteries in Britain* Bath: Runetree
Stubbs, W 1926 *The Constitutional History of England* Oxford: Clarendon Press [first edition 1875]
'Subhadra, Ayu' (G W Reid) 1910 *The Path that is Light* London: Tribune Publishing Company
Taylor, A J P 1975 *English History 1914–1945* Harmondsworth: Penguin
Taylor, H 1997 *A Claim on the Countryside: A History of the British Outdoor Movement* Keele: Keele University Press
Taylor, I 1889 *The Origin of the Aryans: An Account of the Prehistoric Ethnology and Civilisation of Europe* London: Walter Scott
Thomas, J 2000 Comment: Poetics and Politics in Holtorf, Cornelius and Karlsson, Hakan (eds) *Philosophy and Archaeological Practice: Perspectives for the 21st Century* Goteborg: Bricoleur:153–73
Thomas, Julian 2004 *Archaeology and Modernity* London: Routledge
Thompson, E P 1977 *William Morris: Romantic to Revolutionary* London: Merlin Press
Thompson, E P 1991 *Customs in Common* London: Merlin Press
Thompson, E P 1993 *Witness Against the Beast: William Blake and the Moral Law* Cambridge: Cambridge University Press
Thompson, M W 1990 *The Cambridge Antiquarian Society 1840–1990* Cambridge: Cambridge Antiquarian Society
Thurlow, R 1987 *Fascism in Britain: A History, 1918–85* Oxford: Basil Blackwell
Tilley, C 1993 'Introduction: Interpretation and a Poetics of the Past' in C Tilley (ed) *Interpretative Archaeology* Oxford: Berg:1–27
Trigger, B 1980 *Gordon Childe: Revolutions in Archaeology* London: Thames & Hudson
Trigger, B 1989 *A History of Archaeological Thought* Cambridge: Cambridge University Press
Turner, B S 1987 *Medical Power and Social Knowledge* London: Sage
Tyler, F C 1939 *The Geometrical Arrangement of Ancient Sites: A Development of the 'Straight Track' Theory* London: Simpkin Marshall

Tylor, E 1871 *Primitive Culture: Researches into the Development of Mythology, Philosophy, Religion, Art, and Custom* London: John Murray
Underdown, D 1985 *Revel, Riot and Rebellion* Oxford: Oxford University Press
Underwood, A 1962 'Stonehenge, Druids: What of the future? *Southern Evening Echo* June 15: p. 9
Varley, W J 1943 'Universities: (c) Other Universities' in University of London, Institute of Archaeology *Conference on the Future of Archaeology* London: University of London: 91–2
Wainwright, F T 1949 'Problems and Policies' *Antiquity* 23 (1949):73–82
Walker, H J 1987 *The Outdoor Movement in England and Wales 1900–1939* unpublished DPhil, University of Sussex
Wallace, E R 1983 *Freud and Anthropology: A History and Reappraisal* New York: International Universities Press
Ward, W R 1965 *Victorian Oxford* London: Frank Cass
Watkins, A 1922 *Early British Trackways: Moats, Mounds, Camps and Sites* Hereford: Watkins Meter Company
Watkins, A 1923 'Two Hereford Trackways' *Transactions of the Woolhope Naturalists' Field Club* 1921-2-3:174–5
Watkins, A 1925a *The Old Straight Track* London: Methuen
Watkins, A 1925b 'Archaeological Report' *Transactions of the Woolhope Naturalists' Field Club* 1924–5–6:150–1
Watkins, A 1927a *The Ley Hunter's Manual* Hereford: Watkins Meter Co
Watkins, A 1927b 'Druids in Britain', letter in *The Times* 29 October 1927
Watkins, A 1927c 'Archaeological Report' *Transactions of the Woolhope Naturalists' Field Club* 1927–8–9:109–13
Watkins, A 1928a 'A "Cottage Pottery" near Kempley' *Transactions of the Woolhope Naturalists' Field Club* 1927–8–9:144–6
Watkins, A 1928b 'Archaeological Report' *Transactions of the Woolhope Naturalists' Field Club* 1927–8–9:177–81
Watkins, A 1929 'Archaeological Report' *Transactions of the Woolhope Naturalists' Field Club* 1927–8–9:228–231
Watkins, A 1930a 'Archaeological Report' *Transactions of the Woolhope Naturalists' Field Club* 1930–1–2:52
Watkins, A 1930b 'Sighting in Excavation', letter to *The Times* 13 August 1930
Watkins, A 1931a 'A Romano-British Pottery in Herefordshire' *Transactions of the Woolhope Naturalists' Field Club* 1930–1–2:110–12
Watkins, A 1931b 'Archaeological Report' *Transactions of the Woolhope Naturalists' Field Club* 1930–1–2:130
Watkins, A 1932a *Archaic Tracks around Cambridge* London: Simpkin Marshall

Watkins, A 1932b 'Archaeological Report' *Transactions of the Woolhope Naturalists' Field Club* 1930-1-2:184

Watkins, A 1933a 'Poston Camp-Group Alinement' *Transactions of the Woolhope Naturalists' Field Club* 1933-4-5:xxvi-xxviii

Watkins, A 1933b 'Archaeological Report' *Transactions of the Woolhope Naturalists' Field Club* 1933-4-5:41-3

Watkins, A 1972 *Alfred Watkins of Hereford: His Life and Pioneer Work in the Three Worlds of Archaeology, Photography and Flour Milling, 1855-1935: A First-hand Account* London: Garnstone

Watts-Dunton, T nd [1906] Introduction to George Borrow, *Wild Wales*, Everyman Edition London: J M Dent

Webb, J 1976 *The Occult Establishment* La Salle, Illinois: Open Court

Webster, D B 1991 *Hawkeseye: The Early Life of Christopher Hawkes* Stroud: Sutton

Weigall, A 1926 *Wanderings in Roman Britain* London: Thornton Butterworth

Wheeler, R E M 1925 *Prehistoric and Roman Wales* Oxford: Clarendon Press

Wheeler, R E M 1927 'Royal Commission of Ancient and Historical Monuments and Constructions in Wales and Monmouthshire: VII, County of Pembroke' *Antiquity* 1 (1927):245-7

Wheeler, R E M 1929 *Wales and Archaeology:* The Sir John Rhys Memorial Lecture, London: British Academy

Wheeler, R E M 1943 *Maiden Castle, Dorset* Reports of the Research Committee of the Society of Antiquaries of London, No XII: London, Oxford: Oxford University Press and Society of Antiquaries

Wheeler, R E M 1956 *Archaeology from the Earth* Harmondsworth: Penguin (first published 1954)

Wheeler, R E M 1958a 'Crawford and *Antiquity*' *Antiquity* 32 (1958): 3-4

Wheeler, R E M 1958b *Still Digging: Adventures in Archaeology* London: Pan Books (first published 1955)

Wheeler, R E M 1971 'Sir Charles Reed Peers' in H M Palmer and E T Williams (eds), *Dictionary of National Biography 1951-1960* Oxford: Oxford University Press:800-801

Wilkinson, R J 1927 'A New Game for Pathfinders: The Old Straight Track' *The Scouter* June 1927:197

Williams, G A 1982 'Druids and Democrats: Organic Intellectuals and the First Welsh Radicalism' in R Samuel and G S Jones (eds) *Culture, Ideology and Politics: Essays for Eric Hobsbawm* London: Routledge & Kegan Paul: 246-76

Wilson, A 1973 'The Druid of Wessex' *Observer* 2 December 1973

Wilson, Janelle 2005 *Nostalgia: Sanctuary of Meaning* Lewisburg: Bucknell University Press

Woolley, L 1937 'Endowing British Archaeology' letter in *Sunday Times* 22 August 1937

Worthington, A 2004 *Stonehenge: Celebration & Subversion* Leicester: Heart of Albion

Wright, T 1861 *The Celt, the Roman and the Saxon: A history of the Early Inhabitants of Britain, down to the Conversion of the Anglo-Saxons to Christianity* London: Arthur Hall, Victor & Co

Yeats, W B 1961 'The Celtic Element in Literature' in Yeats, *Essays and Introductions* London: Macmillan & Co: 173–188 [first published 1902]

Young, Peter A 2003 ' "Alternative" Archaeology: Why is Bad Science so Popular?' *Archaeology* 56, 3 (2003):2

Zinn, Howard 2004 'The Optimism of Uncertainty' *The Nation* 2 September 2004

Index

Page entries in italic refer to illustrations

Abercrombie, Patrick 225–6
Abercromby, Lord 54
alinements, alignments *see* ley theory
An Druidh Uileach Braithreachas see
    Universal Bond, the
Anatomy, and Anthropology *see*
    Diffusionism
Ancient Monuments Acts: (1913) 27,
    (1931) 164
Ancoats Brotherhood 86
Anderson, Ruth Mary Clementi 188
Angell, Norman 83
Anglo-Saxon
    institutions 11, 57
    vs Celt 56, 120, 169
    national origins 56–7, 225
anthropology
    archaeology and 15–16, 102–4
    Diffusionism and 90, 93–101, 102–4
        and *qv*
    Functionalism 97, 99, 100, 103–4, 158
    Great War and 103–4
    social evolution and 103
Antiquarianism 13–16
Antiquaries, Society of *see* Society of
    Antiquaries

Antiquity 22, *24*, 25, 48, 70–1, 95, 183, 207
    contributors, analysis of 18–19
    role 23–4
    see also Crawford and individual
        contributors
Antrobus, Sir Edmund (fourth
    baronet) 127–8, 130–1, 139, 152
Antrobus, Sir Edmund (third
    baronet) 127, 152
Archaeological Institute of America 1
archaeology
    aerial 20, 25, 197
    amateurs and 36–8, 46–7, 158
    anthropology and 15–16, 102–04
    antiquarianism and 14–16, 37
    authority and 3–5, 47–8, 101, 233, 235, 240–2
    British Schools 15, 44
    civilization and 222–6
    classical world and 14–16, 71
    cultures, archaeological 71
    Diffusionism, *qv* and 104–11
    education and training 218–9, 231, 236–7 *see also* individual institutions
    'eolithic' 38

archaeology (cont'd)
  fascism and 239–41
  functionalism 72, 158–160
  Great War and 67, 111
  hegemony see authority
  'heroic band', the 5, 18–20, 27, 28, 47, 118, 166, 235, 237, 239–40, 242
  history and 14–15, 37, 66–7, 158–9
  in Wales 167–70
  internationalist 71–2
  local societies 13, 24, 26, 41–2, 218
    see also individual societies
  longue durée, the 67, 68, 70, 72–3, 111, 240–1
  Marxism and 69–70
  missionary zeal 19–20
  nationalist 71–2
  nostalgia and 245
  otherness and 242–5
  Palaeolithic 15, 22, 32, 71, 72, 106, 158–9
  poetics 243–4
  post-processualism 3–4, 241
  processualism 157
  professionalisation of, chs 2 and 3
  proto-human 75–6
  psychology and 81
  public perception of 142, 218, 219, 241
  publicity and see media
  relativism and 3–4, 238–41
  religion and 115–18
  simple 235–8, 241–2
  social function of 219, 228, 232–3, 242
arms race 221, 233
Armstrong, Albert Leslie 39
Arnold, Edwin 134
Arnold, Matthew 120–1
Arnold, Thomas 56, 238
Aryans, Aryanism 71, 121, 194, 199
  see also social Darwinism
Ashbee, Paul 22
astro-archaeology see orientation theories
Atlantis 200–1, 206
Aubrey, John 134
Aubry, Robert Bruce 123
Austin, Roland 22, 29

Avebury 117–18, 198, 210
  as hub of ancient road network 178, 181
  restoration 163–65, 171–2, 233
'Ayu Subhadra' see Reid, G W M

Baden-Powell, Robert 186
Bain, James Macbeth 149
Baldwin, Stanley 162, 224
Barker, Pat 87
Barrow Hill, Sussex, excavation at 211
Barrow, Logie 59, 122
Bayley, Harold 199, 200
Beccles Archaeological Society 182
Becher, Tony 19, 20
Beddoe, John 58
Belloc, Hilaire 178–9, 183
Bellows, John 104
Bennett, Arnold 163
Bilberry Knoll, Derbs 195
Billett, Margaret 160
Birley, Eric 166
Black, William Henry 178
Blackwardine (Herefs) 174, 201
Blake, William 134
Blatchford, Robert 65, 123, 140
Bonwick, Alfred James 141
Bowden, Mark 20, 58, 72
Bowler, Peter 52, 53, 54, 75, 108, 110
Boym, Svetlana 245
Brailsford, John 32
Breuil, Abbé Henri 32
British Academy 84, 169
British Archaeological Association 178
British Association for the Advancement of Science 83, 94, 102, 110
British Federation of Youth 89
British Museum 26, 29, 33, 45, 145, 146, 228
British Nature Cure Association 125
British Union of Fascists 239
Brotherhood Movement 149
Brown, Ford Maddox 59
Browne, Henry 152
Bryce, James 84
Buckland, B E 144
Buckle, Henry 52

Burkitt, Miles 15, 32, 33, 34, 42, 71
Burrows, Montague 13–14
Buxton, Leonard Halford Dudley 95

Caerleon (Mon), excavation at 167
Cambrian Archaeological Society 168, 224
Cambridge Antiquarian Society 36, 119
Cambridge Preservation Society 192
Cambridge, University of
  anthropology at 16, 95–6
  archaeology in the nineteenth century 14
  Disney Chair 15, 16, 33, 35: Archaeology and Anthropology tripos 31–2, 71, 225, 231, 236; Archaeology and Anthropology, faculty of 32–5, 187; Institute of Archaeology and 33–4; Prehistoric Society and 40
  science at 231
Canney, Maurice 91–2
Carbonell, Barbara 190, 191, 192, 199, 213
Carbonell, John R 191
Carlyle, Thomas 57
Carpenter, Edward 62, 123, 124, 125, 140, 180
Carr, Edward Hallett 67, 238
Carr-Gomm, Mark Culling 184, 193, 206, 207, 212–13
Casson, Stanley 68, 116
Catchlove, George 130, 132–3
cave paintings 32, 63, 158–9
Celts
  Arnold and 120–1
  Arthur and 121
  Celtic renascence 120–1
  English and 55–7, 120, 169: 'primitives' 55, 56–8, 121
  Rhys and 121, 169–70
  Romans and 59, 166–171, 220–2
  slavery and 56, 117, 221
  Stonehenge and 137, 146
  Wheeler and 168, 220–2
  see also Wales

Cerne Abbas Giant (Dorset) 119
Chadwick, Harry 151
Chadwick, Hector Munro 32, 71
Chambers, M H 191
Champion, Tim 108–9
Chanctonbury Ring, Sussex 180
Chapman, Doris 117–8
Chapman, Malcolm 56, 120, 121
Childe, Vere Gordon 22, 24, 29, *30*, 32, 45, 72, 104, 105, 106, 111, 116, 117, 159, 240
  Abercromby Professor at Edinburgh 29, 46, 69, 93
  anthropology 104
  archaeological cultures 71
  Dawn of European Civilization 71, 105
  Diffusionism 93, 105–6, 109
  Man Makes Himself 69–70, 105–6, 232
  Marxism 69–70
  progress and 68, 69–70, 244
  Social Evolution 109
  What Happened in History 68, 194
Chippindale, Chris 139, 152
Christianity *see* religion
Christy, Archibald Ernest 191
Chubb, Cecil 131, 137
Chudleigh, C O E 204
civilization
  archaeology and 222–6
  Carpenter and 62, 123
  cities and 223
  Engels and 62–4
  Freud and 81–2
  Morris and 62–4
  order and 216
  Perry on 83
  pre-Roman 216, 222–3
  Reid and 124
  Romans and 216–17, 223
  ruralism and 224–6
  Wheeler and 166–7, 217, 222–6
clairvoyance 118–19
Clapham, Sir Alfred 42, 45
Clarion Cycle Clubs 123, 180
Clarion, The 123, 133

Clark, John Grahame Douglas 20, 21, 22, 25, 33, 34, *34*, 41, 42, 43, 44, 45, 48, 71–2, 72, 103, 106, 116, 158, 207, 224, 232, 236
  Fenland Research Committee 33, 208
  Prehistoric Society of East Anglia and 38–40, 235
  University of Cambridge and 33–5, 236
Clarke, J S 191
Clay, Richard Challoner Cobbe 22, 107, 183, 184, 187
Cobbold, H M 191
Collingwood, Robin George 22, 67, 166, 237–8
  archaeological complexity and 237–8
  historical cycles and 67–8
Commonwealth and Free State League 135
communism 62–3, 64, 69, 231, 238
Conference on the Future of British Archaeology (1943) 43–4, 45
Congress of Archaeological Societies 40–1, 42, 46
Coolidge, Calvin 232
Cornell, Per 241
Council for British Archaeology 40, 41, 42–5, 47
Council for the Preservation of Rural England 226
countryside *see* outdoors movement, ruralism
Cox, R Hippisley 178, 179, 183
Crane, Walter 134
Crawford, Lord 26, 139, 141, 152
Crawford, Osbert Guy Stanhope 19, 20, 21, *21*, 23, 24, 25, 27, 30, 36, 37, 42, 43, 45, 48, 72, 107, 111, 116, 119, 145, 158, 159, 160, 162, 163–4, 182, 183, 197, 210, 216, *219*, 232, 235, 237, 238, 239
  amateurs and professionals 18, 36–7, 47
  anthropology and 103
  Diffusionism and 104, 184
  internationalism 71
  ley theory and 173, 182–4, 207–10, *209*, 216

Man and his Past 21–2, 103, 183, *209*
  Marxism and 69–70
  Ordnance Survey and 21, 159, 210
  progress and 51, 66–8
  Society of Antiquaries and 18, 25, 26, 28
  Stonehenge and 26, 162–3
  see also Antiquity
Creasy, Edward Shepherd 11
Croft Ambury (Herefs) 174
Crook, Paul 53
Cross, Arthur 191
Cunnington family 140, 146
Cunnington, Robert Henry 146
Curwen, Eliot Cecil 29, 116, 183

Daniel, Glyn Edmund 20, 32, 33, 71, 103, 107, 109–10, 116, 240
Dark, Sidney 188, 194
Dart, Raymond 93
Darwin, Charles 19, 52, 53, 74, 77, 98, 193, 212, 234
Darwinism, social *see* social Darwinism
Dawkins, William Boyd 14, 15, 52, 54, 58, 141, 145
Dawson, Warren 91
Debray, Régis 10
Devereux, Paul 178, 207
Devon Archaeological Exploration Society 38
Dickens, Charles 54, 134
diffusion of culture, from
  Atlantis 200–1, 206
  Crete 171, 199
  Egypt 199, 200, 201, 213 *see also* Diffusionism
  Phoenicia 184, 194, 199
  Sumeria 105
Diffusionism 74–111
  archaeology and 104–11
  dream symbolism and 86–7
  Egypt and 74–5, 83, 88, 99–100, 109, 171
  'Manchester School' 91–2
  myth and 87–8

Index

palaeoanatomy and 75–7
'Prospectors' 104–5
psychology and 77–82, 96
'doctrine of survivals' see Tylor, Edward
Donnelly, Ignatius Loyola 200
Dorchester, Dorset 193, 218, 221, 229
Dorset Federation of Women's
 Institutes 221
Dorset Natural History and Archaeological
 Society 217
Dorson, Richard 118
'Double Circle, the' see Stonehenge
Drew, Charles 28, 217, 223
Druids:
 Ancient Order of 60, 126–7, 128,
  144
 Ancient Order of Druid Hermetists 148,
  149–51, *150*
 Stonehenge and 115, 126–7, 128,
  144–6, 152, 153, 154
 Wales and 60–1, 117, 169
 Watkins and 176, 199
 see also Universal Bond, the
Dutt, W A 176, 182, 191, 198, 214

Edinburgh, University of (Abercromby
 professorship) 29, 46, 69, 105
Edwards, Brian 164
Egypt and Egyptology 74–5, 91–2, 109,
 119, 198 see also diffusion,
 Diffusionism
Elkin, Adolphus Peter 108
Elliot Smith see Smith, G Elliot
Embree, Edwin 96–7
Emerick, Keith 138, 159–60
End of History, The (Fukuyama) 238
Engels, Friedrich 62–4, 244
Engleheart, George 137, 140, 141,
 144–5, 153, 186–7, 199, 210
English Historical Review 13, 14
English Place-Names Society 225
Essex, Rural Community Council 192
eugenics 77 see also social Darwinism
Evans, Sir Arthur 15, 94, 139, 144
Evans, Joan 18
Evans, William 198
Eversley, Lord 139

Everyday Life in the New Stone Age (M and
 C H B Quennell) 210
Eyerman, Ron 10, 12

Fagan, Garrett 1, 2
fascism 194, 239–41
Fisher, Herbert Albert Laurens 67
Fleure, Herbert John 119, 168
Flexner, Abraham 93, 97
Folk-Lore Society 118, 121
Forbes, Mansfield 192, 193
Foucault, Michel 241, 244
Fox, Aileen 25, 38, 44, 158, 183, 193
Fox, Sir Cyril 21, 29, 43, 44, 71, 107,
 116, 117, 187–8, 193, 208, 213,
 225, 226, 240
France 32, 77, 149, 238
Frazer, Sir James 59, 97, 115, 116
 The Golden Bough 88, 118, 119–20
Freeman, Edward Augustus 3, 12, 15, 56,
 57
Freud, Sigmund 79–82, 88
Friedson, Eliot 17
Friendly Societies 60 see also Druids,
 Ancient Order of
Froude, James Anthony 12
Fukuyama, Francis 238
Functionalism 72, 100, 103, 158–60
 as an aesthetic of science 158–65
Future, the 11, 70, 232, 245
 see also progress

Gaer, excavation at 167
Galton, Francis 77
Gardiner, Alan 92
Gardner, Ernest 15, 16, 27, 30
Gardner, Percy 15
Garrod, Dorothy 33, 35
Geertz, Clifford 51, 245
Gellner, Ernest 119
General Strike, the 135–6
Germany, Germans 71, 77, 83
 innate aggression 84
 innate vitality 63
 Sociology of Knowledge debate 238
 universities and 9, 10, 11
 see also Anglo-Saxons

Gissing, George 58
Gladstone, William Ewart 11
Glastonbury, Somerset 181, 185, 205, 216, 220, 228
Glazer, Peter 245
Gleaves (educational psychologist) 92
Glenconner *see* Tennant, Pamela
Golden Age, the 72, 84, 85, *86*, 89, 157, 229–30, 239
Golden Dawn, Order of the 125
Goldstein, Doris 12, 18, 24, 91
Gomme, Sir George Lawrence 22, 119
Gosden, Chris 102
Gosden, Peter Henry John Heather 60
Gossling, Frank 191, 193
Gramsci, Antonio 4, 6, 17, 48, 235
Graves, Robert 8*7*, 231
Great War 66, 69–70, 77, 78, 79, 81, 82, 83, 84, 86, 103, 110, 111, 131, 135, 139, 149, 153, 160, 166, 193, 216, 231–2
see also shell-shock
Green, John Richard 12
Grey, Lady *see* Tennant, Pamela
Grigson, Geoffrey 23
Grimes, William Francis 35, 42–3
Groom, Tom 123
Guppy, Henry 91

Haddon, Alfred Cort 83, 95–6, 103
Haig, Valentine 133
Hando, Fred 191, 193, 211, *212*, 213
Hardy, Thomas 193, 228
Harris, Henry Albert 93
Harris, James Rendell 92
Harrison, Jane Ellen 92
Harte, Jeremy 178
Harvey, John Hooper 193, 194, 211, 213, 239
Hatton, Joan 191
Haverfield, Francis 13, 166, 167
Hawkes, Christopher 23, 27, 28, 38, 39, 41, 41–2, 42–3, 47, 116, 145, 183, 210, 240
Hawkes, Jacquetta 28, 41, 41–2, 107, 163, 166, 217, 236

Hawley, William 26–7, 139–40, 142, 144, 145
Hayton, George Markham 195, 205
Hegardt, Johan 243
hegemony, social 4–5, 6, 47–8
Heidegger, Martin 243
Heinsch, Josef 206
Hemp, Wilfrid James 33, 116, 170, 240
Herbert, Alan Patrick 163
Hereford, Herefs 173, 176, 178, 192
Hewitt, Albert Tenyson Morley 213
Higgins, Godfrey 134
Highcliffe on Sea, Dorset 149
hiking 180, 185–6
Hill, Sir George 45, 228
Hilton, James 234
Hingley, Richard 59, 166, 241
history
  antiquarianism and 13, 37
  archaeology and 14–15, 37, 102–3, 158–9
  discipline of, professionalization 11–15
  end of, the 238, 245
  Great War and 66–7
  politics and 3, 11
  University of Manchester 91
Hoare, Richard Colt 140, 158
Hobbes, Thomas 59, 72
Hodder, Ian 4
Hodgkin, Thomas 14–15, 37, 66–7
Hogben, Lancelot 231
Holtorf, Cornelius 240
Hooke, Samuel 105
Hooper, William George 149
Hoskins, William George 211
Howorth, Sir Henry 14
Hubbard, Arthur 190–1
Hudson, Herbert 204, 205, 214, 218
Hughes, Thomas McKenny 15
'Human Biology' 96, 99, 101, 102
  see also anthropology, Diffusionism
human nature:
  civilization and 62–5, 67
  innately peaceful 59–61, 62, 65, 78–9, 81–2, 82–6, 89, 108–10, 124, 231–2
  see Maghull, Golden Age, Diffusionism

innately warlike 1–2, 52, 53, 54, 55, 63, 67, 72–3, 76–7, 105–8, 234 *see* social Darwinism, natural selection
'primitives' and 51–9; Celts as 55, 56, 57–8; working class as 58–9
progress and 52–5 *see* progress, social evolution
Hutchinson, Sheila 193
Hutton, Ronald 118, 119
Huxley, Thomas Henry 54
Hyperdiffusion *see* diffusion of culture, Diffusionism

Imperial Fascist League 194
Institute of Archaeology, London 29–31, 33, 34, 43–5, 101, 231, 236
  University of Cambridge and 33–4
International Congress of Anthropological and Ethnological Sciences 99–100
International Congress of Pre- and Proto-historic Sciences 41
International Geographical Congress 25
Iolo Morganwg *see* Williams, Edward
'Ireland, Thomas' 133
Irish, as Celts 57, 58

Jackson, John Wilfrid 92
James, Francis Reginald 181
Johnson, Terence 17
Johnston, Duncan 178
journals, journalism *see* media
Jowett, Benjamin 13
Jowett, Fred 140–2

Keiller, Alexander 22, 25, 140, 162, 171,
  Avebury restoration 163–5, 171–2, 233
Keiller, Doris *see* Chapman, Doris
Keith, Arthur 75, 76, *76*, 77, 85, 100, 106, 107
Kendrick, Thomas Downing 29, 41, 95, 104–5, 145, 146, 153, 199
Kenyon, Kathleen 29, 31, 43
Kerr, John Graham 90
Kinder Scout (Derbs) Mass Trespass 180
Kingsley, Charles 12
Kington (Herefs) 186
Knight, Mrs F A 191

knowledge, construction of
  institutions and associations, importance of 24–5, 101 *see also* individual institutions
  authority and 3–4, 9, 17, 47–8, 151–5 *see also* hegemony
  'enlightenment agenda' 9, 19–20
  intellectuals as missionaries 10–11, 12, 18, 19, 20, 115
  Smith on 98
  Maxwell on 188
  Straight Track Club on 211–2 *see also* media, relativism
Knowledge, lost 144, 145, 157, 215–16, 228–31
  see also Atlantis, Golden Age
Knox, Robert 56, 57, 120
Kossinna, Gustaf 71
Kropotkin, Peter 54
Kuklick, Henrika 75–6, 79, 103, 108

Labour Party 66, 135, 140, 149, 231
Lampeter Archaeology Workshop 239
Landau, Misia 107, 108, 110
Lang, Andrew 118–121
Langham, Ian 90, 95, 98–9, 101
Lawrence, D H 171
LeBlanc, Steven A 2
Leeds, Edward Thurlow 225
Lethbridge, Thomas Charles 187–8, 225
Levi, Eliphas 134
Levine, Philippa 11, 13, 14
ley theory (leys, ley-lines) 172, 174, *176*, 178, 186, 187, 198, 204, 210, 211, 213, 214, 217
  archaeologists and 173, 177, 181, 182–4, 187, 188, 197, 201–2, 204, 205, 206, 207–10, *208, 209*, 210, 211, 212, 216
  artists and 193, 215–16
  defended 188
  defined 175, 177, 202
  'ley' 173, 175, 201
  makers 176, 177, 178, 198–200
  order and 215–16
  popularity of 181, 185–6, 188–9
  purpose 175, 177, 178, 202

ley theory (leys, ley-lines) (*cont'd*)
  ruralism and 181, 184–6
  see also Watkins, Straight Track Club
Liberal Party 134, 141, 194
Lilburne, John 134
Liverpool, University of 29, 59
Lloyd, John Edward 168
Llyn Cerrig Bach, Anglesey, find from 117
Llywellyn, Thomas ap 132
Lockyer, Sir Norman 144, 145, 177, 178, 202
London Antiquarian Society 206
London Museum 27, 41, 220
London, University of 11, 13
  archaeology at 15, 16, 27, 30, 31, 119
  see also Institute of Archaeology
  London School of Economics 96
  University College, Department of Anatomy: anthropology at 93–5; 'Department of Human Biology', proposed 96, 101; 'Institute of Ethnology' proposed 93; Rockefeller grant 92–3, 96
Long, George 153
Lost Horizon (Hilton) 234
Lowenthal, David 242, 243
Lowerson, John 224
Lubbock, Sir John 53
Lulworth Park (Dorset) 221
Lydney (Glos) temple at 198

Macaulay, Thomas Babington 12
Macgregor Reid, G W *see* Reid, G W M
Macgregor-Reid, Robert 125, 132, 135, 142–3, 151
Mackenzie, Donald 92
Mackmurdo, Arthur Heygate 191, 192, 193, 194, 216
Maghull War Hospital (Lancs) 78–81, 82, 84, 87, 96
Maiden Castle (Dorset), excavation at 70, 166, 217–224, *219*, 228–31, *230*, 240
  educational function of 218–19, 231
  J C Powys and 228–31
  storyline 220–2, 233
  'war-cemetery' 221, *222*, 235

Malinowski, Bronislaw 16, 94, 96, 97, 99, 100, 101, 102, 103–4
Maltwood, Katherine 205, 206
Malvern Geographical Society 202
Manchester
  Egyptian Association 91
  Literary & Philosophical Society 84, 91, 94
  Museum 91
  Oriental Society 91
  University of 15, 75, 77, 83, 84, 85–6, 88, 90–1, 92, 93
Mann, James Gow 45
Mannheim, Karl 237, 244
Marett, Robert Ranulph 71, 103
Marr, John Edward 15
Marshall, George 174, 175, 181, 182, 201
Martin, Ellis *24, 179*
Marx, Karl 64, 85, 66, 67, 69, 70
  see also communism, socialism
Massey, Gerald 134
Massingham, H J 72, 93–4, 108, 171
  Downland Man 89, 94, 199, 235
Matless, David 165, 180, 207, 216, 224
Maxwell, Donald 180, 188, 191, 214
Maynard, Guy 39
McBurney, Charles 231
McDougall, William 77, 85
McKaig, William H 191
McLennan, John 53, 55
media and publicity
  academic journals, importance of 18, 91, 94–5 *see also Antiquity*
  newspapers: Wheeler and 220–2, 233, 235; Stonehenge solstice and 153; 154, 235; Watkins and 208–9, 235
  radio 150, 180, 188–9
  television 242
Mellor, David 24
Mercer, Roger 22
Michell, John 195
Minns, Ellis 21, 33
Moir, James Reid 32, 38–9, 40
Morgan, Lewis 63
Morris, William 62–5, 66, 124, 134, 140

Morton, Henry Vollam 226
motoring 179–80, *179*, 192
Moulton, John Fletcher 141
Munn, L Shepherd 188
Murray, Margaret 119
Museums Association 226
museums, proposed
  'Museum of Human Evolution' 69
  'National Folk Museum' 226
  'World Museum' 159
Museums, *see* British, London, Newbury, Salisbury, Wales
Mycenae, Gate of the Lion 198
Myres, John Linton 15, 20, 44, 55, 94, 103, 109
Myres, John Nowell Linton 29, 42
mysticism, subversive 244
mythology and symbolism 87–8, 92, 116

Nash, Paul 171–2
National Amalgamated Union of Sailors and Firemen 123
National Government 180, 225
National Trade Union Club 133
National Trust 26, 148, 162–3
Natural Selection 55
  see also social Darwinism
Nature Cure 125, 148
Navarro, José Maria de 29
newspapers *see* media
nostalgia 3, 225, 233, 244–5
Nutt, Alfred 121

O'Callaghan, John Barry 135
occultism 201, 202, 203, 204–5, 232
Office of Works 26, 164–5, 218
  heritage management policy 138, 159–60, 164–5
  Stonehenge 137–144, 146–8, 149, 150, 151, 152, 154, 160–1, 162
Olcott, Henry 134
Old Sarum, Wilts 178
Old Straight Track, The see Watkins, Alfred
Oldham, Joseph 97
Orage, Alfred Richard 65–6

order
  archaeologists and 157–8, 165, 241
  society and 226, 227–8
  Straight Track Club and 157, 215–16
Ordnance Survey 21, 159, 178, *179*, 198, 210
orientation theories 140, 141, 144–5, 177, 178, 202, 204, 205, 206, *212*, 216, 219, 202
Ormsby-Gore, William George 31, 164, 165
Orwell, George 232
otherness 242–4, 245–6
outdoors movement 122–3, 133, 180
  see also ruralism, hiking, Simple Life
Owen, Robert 134
Oxford, University of 12, 13, 14, 15, 16, 19, 21, 121

Paine, Tom 134
Parr, Samuel 9
past, the
  Celts and 120–1, 169
  countryside and 180
  fluidity of 242, 246
  future, and 242, 245
  Great War and 66
  modernizing 165
  Nash and the vitality of 172
  ordering 157
  personal past 242
  politics and 3, 11
  proletarian views on 59–61
  R G Collingwood on 237–8
  Reid and 126, 131, 144
  thrill of 214
  Wales and 60–1, 169
  why it matters 2–3
Paul, Leslie 180–1
Peace Ballot 233
Peach, Lawrence du Garde 188–9
Peacock, Arthur 133, 147, 148–9, 151
Peake, Harold 21, 22, 105, 183, 225
Pear, Thomas Hatherley 77, 78–9, 80, 87, 92, 93
Pearson, Karl 55, 76, 100

Peers, Charles 27, 152, 160, 164, 236
  and Stonehenge 137–8
  heritage policy 138, 159–60, 165
Peet, Thomas Eric 92, 108
Pennick, Nigel 178, 207
Penty, Arthur 65, 122
Perry, William James 82–89, *88*, 92, 93, 94, 95, 96, 97, 99, 100, 101, 104, 105, 108, 109, 110
  Children of the Sun 88–9, 92, 97, 104–5
  Growth of Civilisation, The 88–9, 92, 93, 105
  University of London and 92–4, 95
  University of Manchester and 85–7, 88
Petrie, William Matthew Flinders 14, 15, 22, 30–1, 33, 55, 68, 72, 119, 239
Phayre, R B 193
Phillips, Charles 20, 33, 34, 38, 210
Phoenicians *see* hyperdiffusion
phrenology 54, 58
Piggott, Stuart Ernest 21, 23, 25, *30*, 42, 68, 72, 116, 119, 159, 164, 171, 183, 210, 213, 235, 240
  and amateurs in archaeology 46, 47, 165, 236
  and professionalizing of archaeology 18, 20, 40, 236
Pilkington, Edward 193
Piper, John 24, 152–3, 171
Pitt-Rivers, Augustus Henry 14, 58
Pitt-Rivers, George Henry Lane 239–40
place-names 198, 225
Pocklington School (Yorks) 83
Pohl, Wilfred 89
Poole, Reginald 15–16
Pope, Alfred 191, 193
Powell, Alfred T 193, 198, 210
Powys, John Cowper 228–31
Prehistoric Society 40, 207, 231
  see also Prehistoric Society of East Anglia
Prehistoric Society of East Anglia 29, 32, 38–40, 182
Pritchard, Walter 191
professionalization 10, 17
  of archaeology *see* archaeology

progress
  Celts and 56
  Childe and 68, 69–70, 244
  Crawford and 51, 66–8
  cycles and 67, 68
  Darwin and 52, 53
  English and 52
  nostalgia and 244
  poor and 59
  'progressionism' 52
  socialism and 54, 62–6
  spiral of 68
  teleology and 51, 52, 75–6
  updated 72–3
  see also social evolution
Proudhon, Pierre-Joseph 134
psychology 77, 79, 81–2, 87–9, 96 *see also* shell-shock
publicity *see* media

Radcliffe-Brown, Alfred Reginald 16, 101, 102–3
radio *see* media
Raglan, Lord 213
Randall-McIver, David 236
Rational Reform League 135
Read, Sir Charles Hercules 26
Reade, Hubert 179
Reason, Joyce 185–6
Reed, Trelawney Dayrell 46–7
Reid Moir J *see* Moir
Reid, George Watson Macgregor 123–8, *128–30*, 130–1, 130–40, 142, 146, 148, 149, 150, 151, 157, 170–1, 234
  and Stonehenge 127–8, 130–40, 142, 146, 148, 150, 153–4
  see also Universal Bond, the
Reid, Robert M *see* Macgregor-Reid, Robert
relativism 3–4, 236–7, 238–241 *see also* knowledge, construction of religion
  Christianity and archaeology 13, 116–18
  dream symbolism and 86–7, 116
  'Early Religion', Watkins and 197
  esoteric revival 118–19
  Frazer and 115, 118, 119–20

humanism, and archaeology 9, 115, 116
natural religion 118–19, 123
nature religion 123, 157
pagan survivals 119
paganism and archaeology 117–18, 138
spiritualism and 60, 122–3
Tylor and 115
universal religion 118–120
Universalism 124, 133, 134, 148
Zoroastrianism 130
see also druids, Universal Bond, occultism, Otherness, spiritualism, Stonehenge, mythology
Relly, James 124, 134
Rhys, John 121, 169–70
Richards, Graham 110
Ridgeway, William 16, 32
Rieff, Philip 82
Rigby, Andrew 244
Rivers, William Halse Rivers *80* 74, 77, 79–80, 80–1, *80*, 82, 83, 87, 94, 95, 96, 100, 101, 110
psychology and 79–82, 87, 96
roads 178–80, 183, 216
see also ley theory, motoring
Rockbourne, Hants, Roman villa at 213
Rockefeller Foundation 92–3, 96–7, 101
Rodway, Walter 132, 133
Romans and *romanitas* 25, 59, 68, 69, 146, 166–71, 198, *209*, 210, 211, 213, 216, 216–17, 220, 222–3, 229, 232–3, 239
Rossetti, Dante Gabriel 134
Royal Anthropological Institute 16, 77, 94–5, 98–100
Royal Archaeological Institute 40, 41, 56, 141, 218
Royal Commission on the Ancient and Historical Monuments of Wales 22, 168, 170
Royal Commission on the Historical Monuments of England 27
Royal Geographical Society 25
Royal Photographic Society 215
Royal Society 40
Rule, Robert 207, 211

ruralism 178, 180–1, 192, 214, 224–6
Ruskin, John 65, 125, 134

Sainty, James Edward 39–40
Salisbury, Blackmore Museum 159
Samuel, Raphael 225
Sandell, Roger 181
Sassoon, Siegfried 87
Scott, William Bell 59
scouting 186
Seaburg, Alan 124, 125
Seeley, John Robert 12, 37
Segontium (Caernarfon), excavation at 167
Seligman, Charles Gabriel 99, 100, 102
Shanks, Edward 231
Shanks, Michael 240
Sharpe, Montague 198
Sharples, Niall 235
Shaw, George Bernard 65
shell-shock 77–81, 84, 87, 93
Shephard, Ben 79
sighting-lines *see* ley theory
Simple Life, Simplicitarians 72, 125–6, 135
Simpson, John 195, 199
Slee, Peter 11, 12
Smiles, Sam 56, 57, 58–9, 171–2
Smith, George William 149–51
Smith, Grafton Elliot 74–9, *80*, 81, 82, 83–102, *88*, 104–10
Childe and 93, 105, 109
Evolution of Man, The 98, 110, 234
Evolution of the Dragon 87–8
Human History 89, 108
institutional ambitions 93, 95, 96, 101
London, University College 93, 95, 96–7, 99
Manchester, University of 75, 90–3
palaeoanatomy 75–6, 98
Perry and 83–6, 88, *88*, 93, 94, 95, 99, 100, 110
refutes Nazi race claims 99–100, 239
shell-shock work 77–9, 93
Smith, Reginald Allender 29
Snow, Charles Percy 231

social Darwinism 54–5, 76, 106–8
Social Democratic Federation 123
social evolution 51–9, 68, 71–3, 103–4, 229, 235, 238
    see also progress, human nature
socialism
    archaeology and 69–70
    aspiration 65–6
    Engels and 62–4
    Fabian 65, 66
    fear of 54
    Guild 65–6, 122, 133
    Marxist 62–4, 65–6, 69–70
    Merrie England 65, 123
    Morris and 62–6, 74
    spiritualism and 60, 122–3
    utopian 64
    see also Carpenter, communism, Labour Party, Morris, Marx, Reid, Shaw
Society of Antiquaries 18, 24–29, 36, 41, 42, 47, 48, 94, 115, 139, 141, 152, 171, 218, 221
Society for Psychical Research 118
Sollas, William Johnson 15, 55, 76
solstice, at Stonehenge *see* Stonehenge
Somerville, Henry Boyle Townsend 177, 191, 200, 210
Soul, John 133
Soviet Union 69, 231, 238
Spence, Lewis 146, 200
Spengler, Oswald 67
Squire, Sir John 162, 232–3
Stanwick, Yorks, excavation at 166–7
Steer, Julia 133
Stevens, Frank 117, 141, 147–8, 152, 160
Stevenson, John 231
Stocking, George 55–6, 96, 103, 108, 118, 158
Stonehenge 145–6, 152, 178, 181
    buildings at 160–2, *161*
    campaign to buy hinterland 26, 148, *161–2*, 162–3
    'Double Circle', near 134, 136, 138, 143–4, 148, 150
    druids and 115, 126–7, 128, 144, 145–6, 148: Ancient Order of Druid Hermetists 149–51, *150*
    enclosure of 127–8, 139, *143*, 227, 153
    iconic, in Great War 131, 160
    interpretation and control 115, 117, 152, 153
    Office of Works and 133, 137–44, 146–8, 149, 150, 151, 152, 154, 160–1, 162
    'orientation theory' 140–1, 144
    replica proposed at 'Double Circle' 148
    Royal Archaeological Institute, on burials 141
    Society of Antiquaries and 26, 139, 141: Hawley's excavations 26, 139–40, 141, 142, 144, 145
    solstice, midsummer 127–32, *128–30*, 133, 136, 137–9, 142–4, 146–8, 149–51, 153–4, 227, 232
    Stonehenge Today and Yesterday (Stevens/Sumner) 117, 147–8, 152, 160, *161*
    Universal Bond 127–32, *128–30*, *132*, 133, 136, 137, 138, 144, 146, *147*, 148, 152, 153–4: burial dispute 132, 140–2, 145
Straight Track Club (Straight Track Postal Club) 182, 186, 190–214 *195, 197*, 218, 232, 239
    academic discipline and 196, 200, 205
    aims and objectives 196–8
    archaeology and 197, 198, 204–5, 210–12, 213
    Atlantis 200–1
    how it worked 195–6
    hyperdiffusion 199, 213
    membership 191–5
    occultism 201, 202, 204–5
    ruralism 192, 214
Straight Track *see* ley theory
Stretton Grandison (Herefs) 174
Stubbs, William 12, 56
Stukeley, William 60, 134, 152, 216
Suffolk Institute of Archaeology and Natural History 218–19
Sumner, Heywood 160, *161*

Index

Sutton Courtenay, Oxon, excavation at 225
Symonds Yat (Herefs) Queen Stone 184

Taylor, Alan John Percivale 84
Taylor, Christine Crosland 191
Taylor, Harvey 122, 180, 225
Taylor, Marjorie Venables 42
Tennant, Pamela 134
Thomas, Julian 157, 243, 245–6
Thompson, Edward Palmer 4, 59
Thorndike, Sybil 163
Thoroton Society 223
Tibet 123, 127, 234
Tilley, Christopher 240
Tintagel, Cornwall excavation at 198
Toland, John 134
Tout, Thomas Frederick 91
Trew, Harold Fletcher 192, 194
Trigger, Bruce 110
Turnbull, J 127
Turner, Bryan S 17
Tyler, Francis Cameron 190, 191, 194, 199, 200, 202, 203–7, 212, 214
Tylor, E 19–20, 53, 95, 103, 115, 118
  'doctrine of survivals' 53, 57–8, 118–20, 121, 180
Tyrell, W W 194, 206, 210–11, 212

Underdown, David 59
Underwood, Austin 133
Universal Bond, the 125–6, 127–48, *128–30, 132, 147,* 151, 170, 235
  see also Stonehenge, G W M Reid
universities
  archaeology in the 1920s 29
  nineteenth-century 9–13
  see also under individual universities
Unwin, George 92
utopia and utopianism 62–5, 108, 234, 244

Verulamium (St Albans, Herts), excavation at 218, 232
Victoria University of Manchester *see* Manchester, University of

Waddell, Lawrence Austine 194, 199, 200
Wainwright, Frederick Threlfall 47
Wales
  archaeology in 167–70
  Celts and 58, 121, 167, 168, 169–70, 228, 229–30
  druids and 60–1, 169
  folklore and 121
  National Museum of 27, 29, 168
  Roman conquest of 167–8
  Royal Commission on the Ancient and Historical Monuments of 22, 168, 170
  scholarship in, Wheeler on 169
  University of 44, 168, 169, 186
walking *see* hiking
Wall Street Crash 232
War, First World *see* Great War
Watkins, A B 191
Watkins, Alfred 37, 173, 174, *174,* 175, 176, 177, 178, 183, 184, 186–7, 195, *195,* 197, 198, 199, 200–1, 202, 203, 207–8, 215
  archaeology 173, 174, 177, 181, 182–3, 184, 187, 188, 197, 201–2, 207–10, *208, 209,* 211, 216
  Archaic Tracks Around Cambridge 187–8, 214, 215
  Early British Trackways 175–6, *176,* 179, 186, 189, 215
  Ley Hunters' Manual, The 177, 184–7, *185,* 186–7, 188, 190, 191, *209,* 214, 215
  Old Straight Track, The 173, 177, 179, 181, 182, 184, 188, 190, 191, 201, 202, 206, 207, 211, 214, 215, 232, 235
  outdoors movement 180, 184–6, 208
  publicity 181, 184, 188, 208–9, 235
  Straight Track Club 190, 196–8, 199–200, 201, 204, 213
  Woolhope Club and 37, 173–5, 176, 181–2, 184, 207–8
  see also ley theory, Straight Track Club
Watkins, Allen 187, 191, 211, 213
Watts-Dunton, Theodore 169

Webb, James 232
Wedd, Tony 207
Wedlake, William James 70, 217
Weigall, Arthur 216–17
Wellington (Herefs) *195*
Wells, Herbert Gorge 54, 70–1
Welsh National Eisteddfod 61
West, Rebecca 163
Weston, Jessie Laidlay 119
Wheathampstead (Herts) excavation at 166
Wheeler, Robert Eric Mortimer 16, 18, 20, 24, 27–8, *28*, 33, 43, 45, 66, 101, 116, 119, 121, 160, 194, 218, *219*, 221, 226, 229, 232, 240
  Celts and 168
  civilization and 217, 222–4, 226
  Institute of Archaeology and 29–31, 33, 43, 45, 48, 101, 231
  London Museum and 27, 41, 217, 220
  Maiden Castle and, 217–24, 228, 229, 230–1
  orientation of stone circles 145, 219
  publicity, flair for 220–2, 230, 233, 235
  purpose of archaeology 70, 227–8, 231
  Romans and 166–8
  Royal Archaeological Institute and 41, 218
  Society of Antiquaries and 27–9
  Wales 27, 121, 167–70
  warfare and 'human nature' 107–8, 111
Wheeler, Tessa 28, 31, 34, 217, 223
Whitaker, Harold 193
Whitman, Walt 125
Wilkinson, R J 186
Williams, D P 193
Williams, Edward (Iolo Morganwg) 60–1

Wills, Eric Foulger 213
Wilson, Janelle 245
Wiltshire Archaeological and Natural History Society 37, 137, 140–1, 142, 144, 147, 152, 162, 186
Windmill Hill (Wilts) 140, 163–4
Winstanley, Gerard 126, 134
Winterbotham, Harold St J L 198, 210
Wintle, Douglas 193, 200
Wolverhampton Archaeological Society 182
women, involvement in
  Antiquity 19
  Society of Antiquaries 25
  Straight Track Club 193, 207–8
  Woolhope Club 193
  Maiden Castle dig 218
Wood, Melusine 211, 212, 214
Woodcraft Folk 180, 186
Woodhead, Norman 186, 193, 208
Woods, Mabel 190–1, 192, 194, 212
Woolhope Naturalists' Field Club 37, 173–4, 175, 176, 179, 181–2, 184, 190, 191, 193, 201, 207–8
Woolley, Charles Leonard 33, 45, 231
Workers' Education Association 89
Worthing Archaeological Society 182, 211
Wright, Thomas 56
Wyndham-Lewis, Dominic Bevan 141–2, 234, 241

Yeats, William Butler 121
youth movements *see* British Federation of Youth, Woodcraft Folk, scouts

Zinn, Howard 245
zodiac, Glastonbury 205, 216